The Blue Guides

D1091520

Please write in with your comments, suggestions and corrections for the next edition of the Blue Guide. Writers of the most helpful letters will be awarded a free Blue Guide of their choice.

City Guide
Athens

Robin Barber

A&C Black • London
WW Norton • New York

Fifth edition May 2002
Published by A&C Black Publishers Limited
37 Soho Square, London W1D 3QZ

www.acblack.com

© Robin Barber, 2002

Maps by RJS Associates, Hen Blas Consultants and John Flower © A&C Black Publishers Ltd
Drawings © Colin Ross
Illustrations on pages 73, 127, 167, 255, 282 courtesy of Robin Barber.

ISBN 0–7136–6129–1

Published in the United States of America by
W W Norton & Company, Incorporated
500 Fifth Avenue, New York, NY 10110

Published simultaneously in Canada by
Penguin Books Canada Limited
10 Alcorn Avenue, Toronto
Ontario M4V 3BE

ISBN 0–393–32342–0 USA

Cover picture: Battle over the body of Patroklos, black-figure krater, c 530 BC, in the
Manner of Exekias, from Pharsalus, Greece (Volos Museum) © The Art Archive/
Archaeological Museum of Athens.

Title page illustration: The Roman Market: the Gate of Athena Archegetes.

Robin Barber has travelled in Greece since 1963. Formerly Assistant Director of the
British School at Athens and later Head of the Department of Classical Archaeology at
Edinburgh University, he has excavated in Crete and the Cyclades and published numerous
articles on Greek art and archaeology, including *The Cyclades in the Bronze Age* (1987; Greek
translation, 1994). His more recent interests are 19C and 20C Greek art and architecture,
and the Greek experiences of Giorgio de Chirico. Also the author of *Blue Guide Greece* and
Blue Guide Rhodes and the Dodecanese, his particular Greek enthusiasms are the poems of
G. Seferis, the rebétika songs of Sotiría Béllou, the films of Thódhoros Angelopoúlos—and
the Greek countryside.

Printed and bound in Great Britain by Butler & Tanner Ltd, Frome and London.

A&C Black uses paper produced with elemental chlorine-free pulp, harvested from managed
sustainable forests.

Contents

Practical information

Background information

The Guide

Athens

Days out of the city

Maps and plans

Introduction

'No schoolbooks ever prepared us for this sock in the jaw...'. So Kevin Andrews, the most evocative writer on Athens, forecast the impact of the modern city on visitors primed with sober expectations of her Classical past. He was right. Athens confounds virtually all expectations, but not only those of seekers after the past.

The city (population just over 3 million) has had a bad press in recent years, with bouts of atmospheric pollution highlighted by damage to the Parthenon, and preparations for the next Olympic Games (2004) disrupting daily life. But her many attractions are less well advertised. The centre can indeed be noisy, frenzied and sometimes gimcrack, but its restless energy is endlessly exciting; and at the end of the street so often shines the Acropolis, marble columns reaching for the boundless blue of the sky. Raise your head above pavement level and fine neoclassical buildings have been generously refurbished—and there are plenty of them, reviving the stateliness of life in the not-so-distant past. Spacious archaeological sites, tree-lined streets and squares, and shady cafés all offer oases in the busy life of the city.

The famous purity of the Attic light, never long concealed, lets you pick out sharp and clear the lines of buildings miles away. Mt Hymettos (modern Imittós) glows rosy in the sunset; Mt Parnes (Párnitha) reflects the dawn. From Lykabettos (Likavittós) you can get a panoramic view of the city, reaching to the sea where the coast of Phaleron (Fáliro) Bay curls up to the hill of Kastélla, hiding Piraeus, itself a bustling and exciting modern port, with a long ancient history.

Watch the splendour of a Mediterranean dawn over the bay or mountains; see and smell the vivid scents and colours of fruit and flowers and vegetables in neighbourhood street markets; relax in pavement cafés, each with its tables grasping the last inch of shade; search out some of the innumerable eating places in back streets, in suburbs, on the mountainsides and in the country. Dine in crowded parlours, at street-side tables, in jasmine-scented courtyards or convivial basements, on the harbourside or with the sea lapping at your feet. Try simple local fare or the sophisticated cuisine of chefs who hold to the Greek traditions of Póli ('The City'—that is, Constantinople).

Not much about antiquity so far, but it's all there, even if not always in mint condition—the ancient Agora (town centre), a large excavated area with the public buildings of Classical Athens, the surprising Pnyx (seat of the Assembly), the tall columns of the never-completed Temple of Olympian Zeus, the depleted remains of 'Plato's Academy', the arch erected by the Roman emperor Hadrian to mark his affection for and patronage of Athens, the walls of the ancient city and burial monuments in its cemetery, the Kerameikos, not to mention the contents of several outstanding museums and towering above them all—the Acropolis.

Nor should you make the mistake of thinking that the Classical period is all there is. Both Athens herself and the surrounding countryside are rich in Byzantine churches and monasteries, from little crooked chapels with rustic art to the dazzling mosaics of Dhafní. Searching for them will lead you into unexpected and, as often as not, delightful corners. Nearer the present are the tiny houses and winding alleys of Anafiótika huddled on the slopes of the Acropolis, settled by island immigrants and offering a striking contrast to the elegant mansions of the wealthy and ostentatious public buildings of the new Bavarian dynasty of early 19C Athens.

If sightseeing and generous refreshment (remember too that Attica is known for its wines) are not enough, the city has a rich intellectual and artistic life reflected in numerous theatres, cinemas, art galleries and summer festivals. There is a grand new concert hall and the different strands of the country's rich musical tradition can be widely enjoyed in clubs and concerts. Cosmopolitan club and café society is there as well and, if you need a dose of sport, Athens has three football teams of international class, thriving basketball and a racecourse.

Days in the country are easy to arrange. Take a boat across to the island of Aíyina, or ramble on the deserted mountainsides of Párnitha, both less than an hour away, and explore some of the villages, churches, antiquities or beaches of central, rural and coastal Attica.

Acknowledgements

As always I am indebted to a host of people for comments, suggestions and various items of useful information. Since this edition follows quite rapidly on the heels of its predecessor, the contributions of those named in the introduction to the 4th edition have in many cases remained fundamental. Ann Thomas has once again put at my disposal her time, energy and patience, especially in the tedious task of checking details of practical information; Bill Phelps responded graciously on several occasions to importunate demands for information. Particularly helpful comments and suggestions concerning the text, plans and illustrations have been offered by Judith Binder, Hector Catling, Dick Elliott, Eleanor Loughlin and Michael Stanley. I thank also Gemma Davies and Kim Teo of A&C Black, and Penny Butler, for their work on the planning, editing and production of the volume.

Illustrations

The author would like to thank the American School of Classical Studies at Athens (Agora Excavations) for permission to reproduce the line drawings of the Agora on p 153 and the reconstruction of the Monument to the Eponymous Heroes on p 155; and the German Archaeological Institute in Athens for permission to reproduce the plan of Kerameikós on pp 176–77 and the line drawing of a funeral plot on p 180.

About this Guide

The chapters describing the city of Athens are presented as walks, mostly 1.5–2km in length. Instructions are also given for following the routes—or reaching various points in them—by public transport. It is thus possible to cover a whole route by either means, or to head for a specific point of interest within it. The layout of the city can be best appreciated by surveying the view from the top of Mt Likavittós, as described on p 217.

If your timetable is at all flexible, a few precautionary measures will help you see the sights as comfortably as possible. The main streets of central Athens can be very crowded, and the traffic slow-moving, during much of the working day. For that reason the city centre is best walked at weekends (especially Sundays and public holidays) or in the late afternoon on days when shops do not open in the evening. Major sites and museums (especially the Acropolis and National Archaeological Museum) can also get very busy, especially in the tourist season. Here the solution is to make sure that you arrive at opening time and get ahead of tour groups. The city itself is quietest in July and August (until the 15th, the major church festival of the Assumption of the Panayía).

The remainder of the Guide is organised as a series of excursions of varying length, some of which can be combined. Although the routes described can be most thoroughly investigated with a car, the majority are followed easily by bus; one or two by train. Where signposting is poor, detailed directions are given.

The longer excursions normally contain one or two major focuses of interest which can be approached directly by public transport. If you want to look more closely at an area, the author strongly recommends staying locally for a night or two. This avoids the need to travel continually in and out of Athens and gives you more time on the spot. From a local centre of any size, taxis (sometimes buses) will get you to out-of-the way places, unless the roads are very poor.

The main text includes biographical information about important personalities, as well as some technical terms not covered by the Glossary. These can be located through the index.

The population figures given in the text are taken from the 1991 census statistics. The results of the 2001 census, which have so far been published only in provisional form, show an increase of c 3 per cent in the populations of Greater Athens and Piraeus, but a much larger growth (c 29 per cent overall) in those of East and West Attica.

Names in the Guide

These are written principally in two ways, according to the context. One represents the modern spoken form (Aíyina); the other is that traditionally used by historians and scholars of Classical antiquity (*Aegina*). The first will help in asking directions or discussing matters with local people (few people would recognise Euripides, when the modern pronounciation is Evripídhis)—and the accent indicates the stress. The second enables easier reference to other books. See also p 43f.

Modern terms used in text

dhimarkhíon town hall
kafeneíon café
limenarkhíon port authority
nomós county, region
plateía square or open space in a town or village
yimnásion (gymnasium) secondary school

Abbreviations

AJA	American Journal of Archaeology
Anc.	Ancient
Ay. (Ayy.)	Ayios / Ayía (Ayioi)—Saint, Saints
BCH	Bulletin de Correspondance Hellénique
BSA	Annual of the British School at Athens
Byz.	Byzantine
c	circa

C	century
€	Euro
EOT (NTOG)	Ελληνικός Οργανισμός Τουρισμού (Ellinikós Organismós Tourismoú). National Tourist Organisation of Greece
f. / ff.	following page / following pages
fl.	*floruit* (flourished)
Hdt.	Herodotos
JHS	Journal of Hellenic Studies
ΚΤΕΛ (KTEL)	Κοινόν Ταμείον Εισπράξεων Λεωφορείων, Joint Pool of Bus Owners
Lit.	Literally
Mod.	Modern
Od. / Odhós	(Street)
OTE (ό, té)	Οργανισμός Τηλεπικοινωνιών Ελλάδος, Telecommunications Organisation of Greece
Thuc.	Thucydides

Changing telephone codes

Until 30 September 2002

Athens area code, which must be used even when dialling Athens from within the city itself, is 010.

From 1 October 2002

Athens area code will change from 010 to 210.

Other Greek area codes will begin with 2 instead of 0 (thus the code for Lávrio before 1 Oct 2002 is 02920, after 1 Oct it will be 22920).

Mobile telephone numbers will begin with 6.

Telephone codes in this guide

The codes throughout this guide have been writen as they will be *from 1 October 2002*. If you are consulting the book before that date, please remember that the codes will differ as described above. See p 42 for further details regarding making telephone calls.

Map symbols

▬▬▬	Road or major pathway	▬▬▬	Ancient wall
⋯⋯⋯	Line of ancient road	▣	Ancient site
▬▬▬	Railway track	○	Ancient or historical monument, or site of interest
---Ⓜ---	Metro line and station	310m ▲	Height above sea level
▒▒▒	Park, square or other open space	●	Modern settlement
✠ or ✝	Church		

Highlights of Athens

Prehistoric and Classical Antiquity

Museums

The National Archaeological Museum has objects of all kinds and every period of Prehistoric and Classical antiquity, and deserves several visits. Wonderfully well-preserved frescoes from the island of Thera (16C BC) will be on show here, and the stunning collection of finds from Mycenae represents the glories of Mycenaean Greece. The main sculpture collection extends from Archaic kouroi to the excellent new galleries of Roman material. The large and fascinating collection of reliefs is often neglected by visitors. A huge range of vases is on display, as well as bronzes and terracottas. Note that some rooms remain closed because of earthquake damage in 1999.

The Acropolis Museum is one of the most exciting. Lively and colourful pediments and freestanding korai are the highlights of the Archaic period. Some of the Parthenon sculptures are here, and exquisite late 5C panels from the balustrade of the Temple of Athena Nike.

The Goulandris Museum of Ancient and Cycladic Art is particularly rich in Early Bronze Age marble figurines. The Kerameikos Museum is strong on the beginnings of post-Mycenaean Greece (Sub-Mycenaean and Geometric periods). These and other smaller museums (the Agora) illustrate the span of antiquity in a more digestible way. There are outstanding bronze statues in the excellent Piraeus Museum.

Sites and buildings

The Acropolis must be the focus of any visit to Athens. Its major temples—the Parthenon, Erechtheion and Athena Nike—and the Propylaia, are supreme achievements of Classical architecture. The Agora is remarkable for another temple, the Hephaisteion, and the impressively restored Hellenistic Stoa of Attalos, but is ultimately more important for putting us in touch, through finds and buildings, with the processes of ancient Athenian democracy. The Kerameikos site has important public buildings (the Pompeion), also a fine section of the city wall with gates, but is best known for the funerary monuments of the principal cemetery area of ancient Athens.

The Pnyx was the meeting-place of the Assembly, and there are good views from the site. On the south side of the Acropolis are a charming Sanctuary of Asklepios, the Theatre of Dionysos (much altered in later antiquity but a key venue in the history of ancient Greek drama) and the Odeion of Herodes Atticus, the best preserved Roman building in Athens. The Roman Market is another reminder of the city's continued importance after the Classical period.

Sites in the Attic countryside include several fascinating sanctuaries. Quiet Brauron (dedicated to Artemis) has a good restored 4C BC stoa and an excellent museum. The Amphiaraion, near Kálamos, has a theatre and spa complex in a lovely wooded setting. The Eleusis sanctuary (of Demeter), with traces of the past ranging from Prehistoric to Roman and another interesting museum, has substantial remains whose elusive character suit its mystery cult. The Sanctuary of Poseidon at Sounion boasts an unrivalled seaside setting and a temple made famous by Lord Byron; Rhamnous is as appealing for its situation as its antiquities; the Marathon tomb is an essential place of pilgrimage.

In northern Attica, on the border with Boeotia, are some fine fortifications. The fort at Aigósthena, by the sea, has much of its towers and circuit wall intact. Eleutherai too good walls and a commanding situation.

Ancient towns are not so well preserved but, apart from the Athenian agora and houses round about, Thorikos has an excavated suburb, interesting remains related to ancient mining, an unusual theatre and Mycenaean tholos tombs.

Byzantine and Medieval

Museums
The Byzantine and Benáki Museums have the best collections of antiquities of the period. Note also the Kanellópoulos Museum.

Churches and sites
Important Byzantine churches in Athens include Ayy. Apóstoli in the Agora, the Kapnikaréa in Ermoú, the Little Mitrópolis next to the main cathedral, Ayy. Asómati on the way to Kerameikos, the Sotíra Likodhímou (Russian Orthodox) in Fillellínon and, in the suburb of Galátsi, the Omorfi Ekklisía.

The monasteries on Imittós are lovely: Kaisarianí is the most popular, but Astéri, Ay. Ioánnis Karéas and Ay. Ioánnis Kinigós are all attractively situated. Dhafní Monastery is a must—especially for its mosaics.

In the countryside of Attica tiny chapels abound. The island of Aíyina has the intriguing Byzantine town of Palaiokhóra.

Representative of Frankish towers is a well-preserved example between Markópoulo and Brauron. From the Ottoman period is the Mosque of Tsistarákis in Monastiráki and the Medresse gateway by the Tower of the Winds, both in Athens itself. Near the Medresse is the splendidly restored hammam of Abid Efendi (Loutró Aéridhon): don't miss this, if it is open.

Post-Byzantine and Modern
Dominant among the 19C neoclassical buildings which served the capital of newly independent Greece is the triad in Od. Panepistimíou—the National Library, University and Academy. Amongst others to be seen are Schliemann's House (also in Panepistimíou), the Old Parliament (Stadhíou), tombs in the (First) Cemetery (A´ Nekrotafío), the Villa Ilissia (now the Byzantine Museum), the Palace of Rhodhodháfnis at Pendéli, and houses and early public buildings on Aíyina.

The Museum of Greek Folk Art has the best collection of its kind, with very fine embroideries. The permanent collection of the National Gallery, recently rehung, shows the astonishing wealth of Greek painting of the 19C and 20C. Other collections include the Tsaroúkhis Museum in Maroússi and the City Art Gallery in Piraiós. Don't neglect the private galleries. The Railway Museum does not only appeal to enthusiasts.

The Benáki Museum deserves a special mention here because its collections range over virtually all periods and fill in many gaps, especially in the 19C and 20C. Among its riches are outstanding icons, embroideries and prints.

Town and country

In town, Athenian shops and markets (p 56) are colourful. In Od. Athinás are the meat and fish markets, and the streets to either side are crammed with a plethora of small traditional traders, busy, informal and cheap. Flowers are in Aiólou, near the church of Ayía Iríni. If you don't mind crowds, visit the flea market in Monastiráki on Sunday mornings. Pláka is full of tourist goods, while Kolonáki has more cosmopolitan shops.

Piraeus is easy to reach. Its most appealing aspects are the smaller harbours of Zéa and Tourkolímano but the main harbour is always busy and exciting. The Nautical Museum at Zéa is unique and the Archaeological Museum has excellent displays and some astonishing ancient bronzes. The massive Eëtioneía gate in the ancient fortifications has been cleaned and restored.

There are good views of Athens from a number of vantage points. Likavittós is best and most accessible, but the Acropolis and Pnyx, and the hillsides outside the city all give different panoramas.

The countryside is not so remote as it sometimes seems from the centre of the city. You can take a bus to Varibóbi, near the Tatóï estate in the foothills of Párnitha, and continue (no bus) over the mountain on the lovely road towards Malakása. In the north, Pórto Yermenó (*Aigósthena*), which can be reached from the Thebes road, is on an attractive bay, and Vília is an old-fashioned hill village with a nice atmosphere. A boat trip to Aíyina is quick (only 35 minutes by hydrofoil) and pleasant and there are interesting things to see (amongst them the alluring Temple of Aphaia, Byzantine Palaiokhóra and Aíyina town, which was the first capital of Greece).

If you are short of time . . .

The Acropolis and the National Archaeological Museum (especially the finds from Mycenae) are paramount, the ascent of Mt Likavittós provides a fine panorama of the city, and a coach trip to Sounion would give you a view of the Attic coastline as well as a sight of the temple made famous by Byron and its sunsets. For a taste of Byzantium, go to the Kapnikaréa church in central Athens (Od. Ermoú), or Kaisarianí monastery on the slopes of Imittós. For something a little different, visit the Pnyx. If you only have a few hours, the Acropolis, with its splendid museum, is the place to head for.

PRACTICAL INFORMATION

 Planning your trip

When to go

Greece is most pleasant in April to mid-June and September to October, when temperatures are comfortable and the main sites quieter. In spring the flowers are stunning.

July and August can be very hot (22–32°C average), and temperatures in the shade may top 38°C in Athens in a heatwave. Nevertheless, if you take care to start early and avoid the hottest times of day, high summer is an excellent time to see the city, with many people on holiday and traffic levels drastically reduced. Make the most of Sundays, when the city is much quieter.

In early spring and late autumn the weather is less predictable, with surprisingly warm days and long hours of sunshine in late autumn, or rainy periods with chilly evenings until well into April. Winter weather in Athens is very changeable, bitter winds and squally rain alternating with dazzling sunny intervals and fresh, clear days. Snow is often visible on the surrounding hills but rarely settles in the city.

Holiday periods (e.g. between Christmas and New Year) are also quieter for walking and sightseeing, but you need to check carefully the opening days and hours of museums, sites, galleries, etc. Public-holiday closures are relatively few, but some smaller institutions shut completely for a few weeks during the summer.

Pedestrianisation

An ambitious project is under way to link all the major archaeological sites with pedestrianised streets, some of which will eventually be served by trams. Much of this should be completed by the Olympic Games in 2004; meanwhile it inevitably involves some disruption of traffic and temporary relocation of bus stops, site entrances, etc. An extensive programme of building restoration and refurbishment is also in progress.

Passports and formalities

Passports are the only travel documents necessary for British (and other EU) nationals to travel in Greece. Application forms are available from any post office in the UK: allow several weeks for processing. If you want to stay in Greece for longer than three months you must apply (at the end of that period and not before), for a *permis de séjour* (άδεια παραμονής; adhia paramonís). You may need to submit proof of financial self-sufficiency. In Athens this is done at the **Aliens' Bureau** (Κέντρον Αλλοδαπών; Kéntron Allodhapón), Leofóros Alexándras 173, ☎ 210 770 5711; elsewhere at local police stations.

Citizens of the USA, Canada, Australia, New Zealand etc also require a valid passport for a visit to Greece of up to three months. For visits exceeding three months you must obtain authorisation by applying in person to the Aliens' Bureau (see previous page) at least ten days before the three-month expiry date.

Sources of information

See also tourist information, p 20. You can get information on any topic connected with visiting Greece from the **National Tourist Organisation of Greece** (NTOG, GNTO or EOT). Leaflets about Athens, Attica and other parts of Greece, and the regularly revised booklet, *General information about Greece*, are available. The Athens and Attica material includes useful maps and street plans. Its offices abroad include:

UK 4 Conduit St, London W1R 0DJ, ☎ 0207 499 8161, fax 0207 287 1369, www.touristoffices.org.uk, email eot-greektouristoffice@btinternet.com.
Eire There is no office in Eire at present.
Netherlands 61 Kerkstraat, 1017 GC Amsterdam, ☎ 202 5905, 625 4212/4, fax 620 7031, email gnot@planet.nl.
USA 645 Fifth Avenue, Olympic Tower, New York, NY 10022, ☎ 212 421 5777, fax 212 826 6940, email gnto@greektourism.com.
Canada 1300 Bay St, Toronto, Ontario M5R 3K8, ☎ 416 968 2220, fax 416 968 6533, email gnto.tor@sympatico.ca; 1170 Place du Frère André, Suite 300, Montreal, Quebec H3B 3C6, ☎ 514 871 1535, fax 514 871 1498.
Australia 51–57 Pitt Street, Sydney, NSW 2000, ☎ 9241 1663-5, fax 9235 2174; email hto@pg.com.au.

Web sites

Greek National Tourist Organisation: www.gnto.gr
Ministry of Culture (carries details of archaeological sites and museums with opening times): www.culture.gr
Information about Greek history and culture: www.ime.gr
Travel information from the journal *Hellenic Travelling* (see below): www.travelling@travelling.gr

Travel journals

Two English-language travel monthlies, published in Athens, are invaluable for planning travel both to and within Greece. They are *Greek Travel Pages* (price in Athens c €16, ☎ 210 324 7511, fax 210 323 3384; can be sent abroad) and *Hellenic Travelling* (c €20, ☎ 210 994 0109). These publications give details of air, rail and bus travel, hotel information (not below C category) and much other useful matter (customs, shop hours, etc).

Tour operators

Several firms offer 'City Breaks' to Athens from the UK. A good way of seeing both Athens and something of Attica would be to arrange a package providing one week in Athens with booked accommodation and one week's car hire, with or without accommodation elsewhere. It is possible to visit places in Attica quite easily while based in Athens, but travelling in and out of the city can be both time-consuming and wearing, especially in a car. A firm which offers holidays of this kind is **Sunvil**, Sunvil House, Upper Square, Old Isleworth, Middlesex, TW7 7BJ, ☎ 020 8568 4499, 020 8232 9797, fax 020 8568 8330, www.sunvil.co.uk/sires/sunvil/greece/, email greece@sunvil.co.uk. Other companies include **Cresta**, ☎ 0870 161 0979, www.crestaholidays.co.uk; and **Thomas Cook Holidays**, ☎ 0870 443 4449, www.tcholidays.com, email signature@tcholidays.com.

Maps and plans

Stanfords (12 Long Acre, Covent Garden, London, WC2E 9EP, ☎ 020 7836 1321, fax 020 7836 0189; www.stanfords.co.uk, email customer.services @stanfords.co.uk) have a good selection of Greek maps, although it is difficult to find thoroughly reliable sheets, and the range of Athens/Attica publications is limited.

A good, if somewhat lurid, 1:150,000 map of Attica and Boeotia (Viotía) is published by Loukópoulos, Panepistimíou 39 (Stoá Pesmazóglou 18), ☎ 210 323 2729, 210 322 7942, fax 210 322 0991. More conventional, and based on army survey maps is the Attica/Αττική sheet of **Road Editions** (Ippokrátous 39, ☎ 210 361 3242, fax 210 362 4681, www.road.gr, email road@enet.gr), also from many booksellers; it does not however show anything like the whole of the modern nomós, for which you need the Central Greece (Stereá Ellás/Στερεά Ελλάς) sheet of the same publisher's 1: 250,000 series. The most up-to-date, though much smaller in scale, are the Athens/Attica pages of ΕΛΛΑΣ, οδικοί–τουριστικοί χάρτες (GREECE, route-tourist maps), a road atlas, published by S. Kapranídhis. This is widely available in Athens but be sure to get the most recent edition since it is regularly revised. It contains plenty of other useful information, about hotels, museums, etc.

Official maps compiled by the **Army Geographical Service** are the most detailed but are only available in Athens, from the AGS (Γεωγραφική Υπηρεσία Στρατού, ☎ 210 884 2811-5), Evelpídhon 4 (Pedhíon tou Areos); open Mon, Wed and Fri mornings, 11.30–13.30. Passport required.

The best **street plans** of Athens (Vol A) and suburbs (Vol B) are those published in book form by N. & I. Fótis (A) and S. Kapranídhis (B). These are widely available in Athens (as above), or see Booksellers, pp 49, 89. Again note that the books are updated two or three times a year.

Disabled travellers

Greece, especially Athens, has promising plans to make life easier for the disabled traveller. Although some progress has been made since the previous edition of this guide, there are still many difficulties to be overcome. Narrow pavements are often crowded and further obstructed by parked cars; special toilet facilities are rare and provisions for wheelchair access limited, except in recently pedestrianised areas or newly built or refurbished museums (the Benáki, the Lalaoúnis Museum of Jewellery). *The museums of Athens* (see Bibliography, p 86) has useful information (p 329) on museums where there are special facilities.

In the UK consult **RADAR** (Royal Association for Disability and Rehabilitation), 12 City Forum, 250 City Rd, London, EC1V 8AF, ☎ 020 7250 3222, fax 020 7250 0212, minicom 020 7250 4119, www.radar.org.uk, email radar@radar.org.uk.

In the USA there are a number of tours geared for the disabled:
Society for Accessible Travel & Hospitality, 347 Fifth Avenue, Suite 610, New York, NY 10016, ☎ 212 447 7284, fax 212 725 8253, www.sath.org, email sathtravel@aol.com.

Catholic Travel Office, 10081 Cedar Ln, Kensington, MD 20895, ☎ 301 530 8963.

New Directions, 5276 Hollister Avenue, Suite 207, Santa Barbara, CA 93111 ☎ 805 967 2841, fax 805 964 7344.

In Greece, the **Panhellenic Association for the Blind** is situated at Veranzérou 31, Athens 104 32, ☎ 210 522 8333, fax 210 522 2112.

Getting there

By air

There are **scheduled air services** to Athens from London (by *British Airways*, ☎ 0345 222 111, fax 01667 462840, www.britishairways.com; *Olympic Airways*, ☎ 0870 606 0460, fax 0207 629 9891, www.olympicairways.com, email info@olympicairways.com; *Virgin Atlantic*, flight information ☎ 01293 511 581, reservations ☎ 01293 747747, fax 01293 561721, www.virgin-atlantic.com; also from Manchester, by *Olympic*; or via Amsterdam, Brussels, Frankfurt, etc., using a combination of British and foreign carriers). The latter are often both convenient and good value for travellers from British regional centres.

Easyjet operates a twice-daily service to Athens from Luton, ☎ 0870 6000 000, fax 01582 443355; in Athens 210 967 0000; but most seats are booked over the internet on www.easyjet.com.

Monarch is a budget airline offering generally cheaper fares but a less sophisticated service and less convenient timings, from London Gatwick to Athens, ☎ 01582 400000, fax 01582 411000, www.monarch-airlines.com, email general.enquiries@monarch-airlines.com.

There are direct flights from New York to Athens through *Olympic Airways*, New York ☎ 718 269 2200, fax 718 269 2207; Boston ☎ 617 451 0500, fax 617 451 2081. *Olympic Airways* also operates a service to Athens from Canada (Montreal via Toronto). Toronto, ☎ 416 964 7137, fax 416 920 3686; Montreal, ☎ 514 878 3891, fax 514 878 4783. Several tour operators run charter flights to Greece from the US and Canada. Contact the NTOG for further information (p 16). For flights from Australia, ☎ 008 221663, fax 0292 522262 (Sydney).

Scheduled flights can be cheaper out of season and are best booked through a good travel agent. The cheapest scheduled fares usually apply to tickets booked well in advance and with no change at all permitted to the dates or times. As there are frequent changes in fare structures, current information should be sought from the airlines.

If seats are available on **charter flights**, which are mainly geared to package holidays, they may be sold on a flight-only basis. You are, however, restricted as to season (May–early Oct) and dates.

Airport information ☎ 210 353 0000.

The only **airport hotel** at Athens is the luxury-class, *Sofitel*, ☎ 210 354 4000.

Transport to central Athens and Piraeus

Express buses as follows: **E 95** Airport–central Athens (Síntagma Square) every 25 mins from 06.30 to 21.20, every 25–35 mins at other times; **E 94** Airport–Ethnikí Amina, the nearest Métró station (Line 3), every 10 mins from 06.30 to 21.00, every 13 mins from 21.00 to 00.30, every 30–35 mins at other times; **E 96** Airport–Piraeus harbour, via Vári, Glifádha and the west coast of Attica, every 20 mins from 07.00 to 20.45, every 25 mins from 20.45 to 22.05, every 40 mins from 22.05 to 06.00, every 30 mins from 06.00 to 07.00. Times in the opposite directions are similar but not identical. For enquiries, ☎ 185.

The **taxi** fare to central Athens is about €11 in daytime and €19 at night, plus any supplements for luggage.

By train

Except with an InterRail or other discount pass (limited period), rail travel is no longer cheap or, unless the cost is further inflated by the purchase of sleepers or couchettes, particularly comfortable.

Routes are from Northern European ports either via France and Italy, or via Belgium/Netherlands, Germany and Austria, and former Yugoslavia (not operational at present). Couchettes or sleepers should be booked well in advance.

You might consider taking the train to an Italian port (Venice, Ancona or Brindisi are the most used), then a boat crossing to Greece, arriving at either Igoumenítsa (on the coast opposite Corfú), or Pátras (followed by a three-hour bus journey to Athens).

Timetable and other information about rail travel is available in the UK from *British Rail Travel Centres* (best at the larger stations), or *Rail Europe and French Travel Service*, 179 Piccadilly, London W1, ☎ 08705 300 003, www.raileurope.co.uk. For sea crossings consult one of the larger travel agents (e.g. *Thomas Cook*).

In Athens the international Lárissa **railway station** (Map 2,2; about 1km from Omónia) has a **Métró station** (Stathmós Laríssis) on Line 2; it is also connected by **bus 405** with Leofóros Alexándras and by **trolley bus 1** with Leofóros Amalías or Panepistimíou (passing close to Omónia and Síntagma).

There are in-town booking offices at Karólou 1, Sína 6 (Panepistimíou; **Map 3,6**), Filellínon 17, ☎ 210 362 7947 (info), 362 4402-6. No telephone bookings.

By car

For travellers by car, the shortest overland route of c 3150km, via southern Germany, Austria, Slovenia, Croatia, Bosnia-Herzegovina, Yugoslavia and Macedonia, is not practicable at present because of the political situation in former Yugoslavia. It takes an absolute minimum of four days. Alternatively, car ferries may be used from one of the Italian ports mentioned above (the Brindisi route is the fastest, but not necessarily the most pleasant). Motorail services from a Channel port or Paris to southern France or Italy (preferably Milan) reduce the strain of driving (information and booking through *Rail Europe* (above) or the *French Railways* web site www.sncf.com. The services (including route and customs information, and bookings) provided in the UK by the *AA* (☎ 08705 500 600, www.theaa.com, email customer.services@theAA.com) and *RAC* (☎ 0800 550 550, www.rac.co.uk) are essential. For the *Greek Motoring Organisation* (*ELPA*), see p 31.

By coach

Coach travel is the least comfortable method of getting to Greece from the UK, and not necessarily the cheapest when the cost of lost time, plus food and accommodation en route, is taken into account. Vehicles travel either direct (not at present, see above) from a Channel port, or via one of the Adriatic ferries. There may or may not be night stops. Choose a reliable operator. Information from **National Express** (☎ 08705 808080, www.goby.coach.com), **Eurolines** (☎ 01582 404511, Mon–Fri 09.00–17.00, www.eurolines.co.uk), student travel agencies, or newspaper advertisements (see Sources of information, p16). The journey take between three and four days.

By boat

There are no scheduled services between the UK and Greece but cargo ships sometimes carry passengers. Priority is given to clients wanting a full Mediterranean circuit, but passages to Greece (only) are sometimes available. Contact **The Cruise People**, ☎ 020 7723 2450, 0800 526 313 (freephone), email freighters@cruisepeople.co.uk. For sea routes from Italy, see rail travel, p 19.

Tourist information

There are **National Tourist Organisation of Greece** (**NTOG/GNTO/EOT**) offices at Amerikís 2 (**Map 6,3**), near Síntagma Square; at Stadhíou 4; and at the Airport. All kinds of information are provided. The **NTOG** publishes (weekly, free) *Athens Today*, in English and French; also (every two months) *Now in Athens* (information on culture and entertainment).

   Telephone information (any topic) is provided by the tourist police (☎ 171) and *ELPA*, the Greek Motoring Organisation (☎ 104). English is spoken. The former is excellent.

Travel agents

American Express, Ermoú 2, ☎ 210 324 4975/9, fax 210 322 7893, email domestic@amxco.gr.

Hermes en Grèce and **CHAT**, Stadhíou 4, ☎ (CHAT) 210 322 3137, 322 2886, fax 210 323 1200; (Hermes) 210 323 7431, fax 210 323 5370.

Galaxy, Voulis 35, ☎ 210 322 5960, 210 322 2091, 210 322 9761, fax 210 322 9538, email info@galaxytravel.gr, www.galaxytravel.gr.

Pacific Travel, Níkis 26 (Síntagma), ☎ 210 324 1007, 210 322 3213, 210 960 0767, fax 210 323 3685, email pacific@hol.gr; also at airport (open 24hrs), ☎ 210 353 0160 (taxis can be arranged).

Astória, Stadhíou 48 (in arcade), ☎ 210 325 0780, 210 325 0380, 210 321 0598, 210 321 5383, fax 210 321 5520, email astoriatvl@hotmail.com.

Where to stay

The detailed and comprehensive *Guide to the Greek hotels*, published annually in mid-March by the Hellenic Chamber of Hotels (Address: XENEPEL, Stadhíou 24, Athens 105 64, ☎ 210 331 0022-6, fax 210 323 6962, 210 322 5449, www.users.otenet.gr/grhotels, email grhotels@otenet.gr) and available through EOT (price c €18) gives information about hotels of all categories, with prices. In Greece, most hotels have copies which they will allow you to consult. Other publications tend not to list hotels in categories below C.

There are six official categories of hotel (Ξενοδοχεία, Xenodhokhía): L and A–E. The de luxe (L) hotels are comparable with those elsewhere. In hotels above Class D (and even in some of those) almost all rooms have a private bath or shower. Class C is the most common and the most variable. Greek hotels do not usually have restaurants, unless they are primarily geared to the tourist trade, although many serve a continental breakfast. D and E hotels can often be adequate, but it is best either to inspect the accommodation or to have a recommendation. (Note that F/A = furnished apartments.)

Charges for hotels and rooms are fixed annually by the Government and local authorities. The legal charge for each room, quoted with service and taxes included, should be advertised at the reception desk, and on a notice in each room, usually on the back of the door. Substantial reductions are often given in the off-season (November–March).

Despite the official categorisation, hotels can vary widely. Many hotels are geared to package tours and coach groups rather than the casual overnight guest; some can legally insist on half-board terms, thus tying you to their usually unimaginative restaurants. It is difficult to get single rooms; single occupation of a double room is often charged at the full price, especially in high season. It is advisable to inspect the accommodation on offer; hoteliers are always willing to show rooms and respect an adverse decision.

Charges also vary considerably within each category, so that a cheap B-class hotel can be less expensive than a dearer C. It is thus worth investigating establishments which seem at first sight likely to be too expensive.

Athens has numerous hotels in all classes. Several in the higher categories are in or near Síntagma Square or in Leofóros Singroú, with more modest ones round Omónia. Pláka (streets near Síntagma), Thisío and the area south of the Acropolis (Od. Mitséon, etc.) are also worth trying.

Booking

XENEPEL (see above for details) offers a postal service. You can book on the spot at their desk in the National Bank of Greece in Síntagma (Karayeóryi Servías 2, ☎ 210 322 9912, 210 323 7193).

Bookings can also sometimes be made by travel agents at home (but choose one with experience of Greece).

Hotels in Athens

De Luxe

Grande Bretagne (Megáli Vretannía), Vasiléos Yeoryíou 1, Plateía Sintágmatos, Athens 105 63, ☎ 210 333 0000, fax 210 322 8034, www.hotelgrandbretagneath.gr, email gbhotel@otenet.gr. One of the great hotels of Athens and a city landmark, built in 1842 as a private mansion. Old-world grandeur and elegance, with a fine marble lobby. Extensively refurbished in 1992. Double glazing.

Hilton, Vasilíssis Sofías 46, Athens 106 76, ☎ 210 728 1000, fax 210 728 1111, www.fomathens@hilton.com, email info.Athens@hilton.com. The first 'international' hotel in Athens, central and with extensive facilities. Unfortunately an architectural eyesore. Will be closed for refurbishment for most or all of 2002.

Intercontinental, Singroú 89–93, Athens 117 45, ☎ 210 920 6000, fax 210 920 6500, www.interconti.com, email athens@interconti.com. One of a group of large, modern but rather anonymous luxury hotels on Leofóros Singroú, a little out of the centre. Could be anywhere in the world.

Ledra Marriott, Singroú 115, Athens 117 45, ☎ 210 930 0000, fax 210 935 8603, www.marriott.com, email marriott@otenet.gr. A huge 'international' hotel with facilities to match, also on Leofóros Singroú.

St George, Lycabettus, Kleoménous 2, Plateía Dhexamenís, Kolonáki, Athens 106 75, ☎ 210 729 0711/8, fax 210 724 7610, 210 729 0439, www.sglycabettus.gr, email info@sglycabettus.gr. Pleasant situation on the side of Likavittós, with good views over the city and the floodlit Acropolis. The roof garden surrounds a swimming pool.

Sofitel, at airport, ☎ 210 354 4000. The only airport hotel.

Class A

Aléxandros, Timoléontos Vássou 8, Ambelókipi, Athens 115 21, ☎ 210 643 0464, fax 210 644 1084, email airotel@otenet.gr. Well-appointed tourist hotel at the better end of the package range, a little out of the centre and fairly quiet.

Electra Palace, Nikodhímou 18, Pláka, Athens 106 58, ☎ 210 337 0000, fax 210 324 1875, www.herodion.gr, email electrahotels@ath.forthnet.gr. Roof garden with spectacular view; swimming-pool; own parking. Highly recommended.

Herodion, Rovértou Gálli 4, Athens 117 42, ☎ 210 923 6832/6, email herodion@otenet.gr. Very pleasant atrium surrounded by greenery, plus a rooftop solarium with view of the Acropolis. Recommended.

Class B

Phílippos, Mitséon 3, Athens 117 42, ☎ 210 922 3611/5, fax 210 922 2412, www.herodion.gr/philippos, email philippos@herodion.gr. South of the Acropolis (views from the roof), near the Odeion of Herodes Atticus. A well-run and comfortable establishment, under same management as the *Herodion*.

Pláka, Kapnikaréas 7, Pláka, Athens 105 36, ☎ 210 322 2096/8, fax 210 322 2412, www.plakahotel.gr, email plaka@tourhotel.gr. Roof garden with panoramic view. Pleasant atmosphere. Recommended.

Class C

Akhilléas, Lékka 21, Omónia, ☎ 210 322 5826, 210 323 3197, fax 210 322 2412; www.achilleashotel.gr, email achilleas@tourhotel.gr. Smallish, comfortable and very central. Run by the same family as the Pláka.

Acropolis House, Kódhrou 6–8, Pláka, Athens 105 58, ☎ 210 322 2344, 210 322 6241, fax 210 324 4143. Family-run pension in a well-preserved neo-classical house.

Acropolis View, Webster 10, Filopáppou, Athens 117 42, ☎ 210 921 7303/5. In a quiet street opposite the Odeion of Herodes Atticus. Roof garden restaurant. Recommended.

Athenian Inn, Kháritos 22, Kolonáki, Athens 106 75, ☎ 210 721 8756, 210 723 8097, 210 723 9552, fax 210 724 2268. A small, attractive, recently renovated hotel in a quiet pedestrianised street in Kolonáki. Has one or two single rooms.

Erechtheíon, Flamaríou 8, Thisío, Athens 118 51, ☎ 210 345 9606, fax 210 346 2756. Close to the Pnyx, Hephaisteion temple and the Agora. A lively area with many cafés and ouzeris.

Exarkhíon, Themistokléous 55, Plateía Exarkhíon, Athens 106 83, ☎ 210 380 0731, 210 360 1256, fax 210 360 3296. Near a square with busy café life. Hotel is a good standard but the area can be noisy.

Lycabette, Valaorítou 6, Athens 106 71, ☎ 210 363 3514/8, fax 210 363 3518. Pleasant small hotel on a central pedestrian street, full of cafés, between Panepistimíou and Akadhimías.

Marína, Voúlgari 13, Omónia, Athens 104 37, ☎ 210 523 7832/3, fax 210 522 9107. On the corner of Omónia though also faces on to a pedestrian way. Large and utilitarian, often catering for package tours.

Mouseíon (Museum), Bouboulínas 16/Tosítsa, Athens 106 82, ☎ 210 380 5611/3, fax 210 380 0507. Well-run and situated hotel close to the National Archaeological Museum. Closed for renovation at time of writing.

Myrtó, Níkis 40, Athens 105 58, ☎ 210 322 7237, 210 322 7311, fax 210 323 4560. Small (12 rooms), close to Síntagma and Pláka.

Class D

Marble House Pension, off Zínni 35, Koukáki, ☎ 210 923 4058, fax 210 922 6461. In a cul-de-sac a little out of the centre but not too far from the Acropolis. Most rooms en suite; two self-catering studios. Very popular and essential to book in advance.

Orion and Driádhes, Emmanuel Benáki 105/Anexartissías, Athens 114 73, ☎ 210 382 7362, 210 382 0191, fax 210 380 5193, 330 2388. 15 mins' walk from Omónia, on the upper slopes of the Lófos tou Stréfi. Two hotels side by side under the same management. Clean and well-kept. The Orion has a self-service kitchen. Communal area on the roof with splendid view of central Athens.

Témbi, Aiólou 29, Athens 105 51, ☎ 210 321 3175, fax 210 325 4179. On a central but pedestrianised street, opposite the church of Ayía Irini and the flower market. Good value simple accommodation.

Hotels in Piraeus

Class B

Mistral, Vasiléos Pávlou 105, Kastélla, Piraeus 185 34, ☎ 210 411 7150, fax 210 412 2096. Nicely situated overlooking Fáliro Bay. A trolley bus or taxi ride to the main harbour.

Park, Kolokotróni 103, Piraeus 185 35, ☎ 210 452 4611/4, fax 210 452 4615, www.bestwestern.com/gr/thepark. In central Piraeus.

Class C
Dhelfíni, Leokhárous 7, Piraeus 185 31, ☎ 210 412 3512, 210 412 3579. Close to the Metró (Line 1) and main harbour.

Hotels in Attica

Saronic Gulf

De Luxe
Astir Palace, Vouliagméni, Athens 166 71, ☎ 210 890 2000, fax 210 896 2582, www.astir.gr. On the beach. Swimming-pool and extensive gardens.

Class A
Aigaíon, Soúnio, Athens 195 00, ☎ 22920 39200, fax 22920 39234. A pleasant, slightly old-fashioned hotel, on the sea, close to Temple of Poseidon. Outdoor restaurant on the terrace.
The Margi, Litoús 11, Vouliagméni, Athens 166 71, ☎ 210 896 2061/5, fax 210 896 0229, www.themargi.gr. Just 100m from the beach.

Eastern Attica

Class A
Artemis, Pórto Ráfti 190 07, ☎ 22990 72000, 2290 72400/2, fax 22990 74403. Standard, modern seaside apartments, also functions as a year-round hotel.
Golden Coast, Marathónas 190 07, ☎ 22940 57100, 210 362 0662, fax 22940 57300. A large tourist hotel complex on the Néa Mákri side of Marathon.

Class B
Leon Akti Village Inn (bungalows), Skhiniá Beach, ☎ 22940 56910/1, 22940 55908, fax 22940 55857. Beach hotel with both rooms and chalets.

Class C
Marathon, Tímvos, Marathónas 190 07, ☎ 22940 55122, 22940 55222. Near Marathon coast, between the Sorós and the sea. Convenient position for visiting Marathon, but indifferent facilities.

Northern Attica

Class B
Aktaíon, Ath. Vápa 3, Vília 190 12, ☎ 22630 22560, 22630 22226. A basic but quite adequate hotel in the centre of a pleasant inland village and summer resort. (Closed Jan–Mar.)

Class C
Aigosthénion, Pórto Yermenó 190 12, ☎ 22630 41226, (Athens) 210 821 9013, fax 210 823 5569. A large secluded hotel in a beautiful situation overlooking the ancient fort and bay of Aigósthena. Used by Athenian weekenders.
Néon Veróri, Vília 190 12; ☎ 22630 22291/4, fax 22630 23661. Modern, rather featureless but comfortable hotel, on the edge of the village.

Northeastern Attica

Class C
The Despo, near Markópoulo Oropoú, ☎ 22950 32324/5. Small (17 rooms), close to the sea.
Flísvos, Skála Oropoú, ☎ 22950 32480/3. Standard, modern, middle-of-the-road facilities.

Southern Attica

Class C
Pántheon, near Markópoulo 190 03, ☎ 22990 40664. Basic, in a convenient position outside Markópoulo, but on the very busy main road to Lávrio/Soúnio (ask for a room at the back).
Belle Epoque, Lávrio 195 00, ☎ 22920 27130. Modest. In an interesting old house. The only hotel in the place.

Hotels in Aíyina

Aíyina town

Class A
Aiyinítiko Arkhontikó, Aíyina 180 10, ☎ 22970 24968, fax 22970 26716. Old house converted into hotel, in the town but well situated back from the noise of the harbour.

Class C
Aretí, Aíyina 180 10, ☎ 22970 23593. Simple hotel close to the sea on the way to Kolónna promontory.
Pávlou, Aíyina 180 10, ☎ 22970 22795.

Ayía Marína

Class B
Apollo, Aíyina 180 10, ☎ 22970 32271/4, 32281, fax 22970 32688; email apolo@otenet.gr, www.saronic.com.

Pérdhika

Class B
Moondy Bay (bungalows), Profítis Ilías, Pérdhika, Aíyina 180 10, ☎ 22970 61622, 22970 61146, fax 22970 61147, email moondy@netplay.gr.

Youth hostels
Only the first-named hostel below is affiliated to the International Youth Hostels Federation. There are other so-called Youth Hostels which do not belong to the organisation and must be investigated on the spot.
Athens International Youth Hostel, Víktoros Ougo 16 (close to the Lárissa railway station), ☎ 210 523 4170. 138 beds. Excellent—and in a fine neoclassical building. The only IYHA hostel in Greece.
Greek Youth Hostel, Dhamáreos 75, Pankráti, ☎ 210 751 9530. Clean, with 70 beds and a friendly atmosphere.
The *YWCA* (Greek XEN), Amerikís 11 (Síntagma), ☎ 210 362 4291, has rooms

for women only. The hostel of the **YMCA** (Greek **XAN**), Omírou 28, does not provide accommodation (Greek and English lessons are offered).

Camping

A leaflet on sites is available from the NTOG. The main **Athens** campsite is on the Corinth road (Leofóros Athinón 198–200) near the Dhafní monastery, ☎ 210 581 4114, winter ☎ 210 581 4101, fax 210 582 0353. Other sites are *Dhionissiótis* 17km out of Athens near the highway to Lamía and the north, ☎ 210 807 1494, and *Dokórou Akriví* at Kókkino Limanáki near Rafína, ☎ 22940 31603/4, fax 22940 31603. There are also sites at Alepokhóri, Kinéta (Corinthian Gulf), Marathon, Néa Kifissiá, Néa Mákri, Soúnio and Várkiza.

 # Getting around

Information about individual tickets is given below, but note that there are **day tickets** (covering Metró, train, bus and trolley bus) and weekly and monthly tickets of various kinds. These can be good value.

Athens is best seen by a judicious combination of walking and public transport. The most comfortable times for **walking** are early morning and late afternoon and at weekends (especially Sundays). Some of the streets are long and tiring, and pavements can be narrow and uneven. Most routes can be covered by bus or trolley bus.

Walking in parts of Attica can be a great pleasure though it is virtually impossible to plan walks in the Greek countryside in any detail, since large-scale maps showing footpaths are not generally available. When asking directions locally you may want to make use of some of the words and phrases given on pp 46–47.

The best parts of Attica for walking are to the north of Athens, on the slopes of Mt Párnitha, and in the area of Grammatikó–Varnáva–Kapandríti, although some places have been severely affected by forest fires in recent years.

By Metró and train

In Athens the Metró (see plan on p 1 of street atlas at the back of the book) is usually the fastest way of moving about. Line 1 (ΗΣΑΠ/ESAP = Ilektrikós Sidhiródhromos Athinón-Piraiás), the original Athens–Piraeus Electric Railway, opened in 1869 and subsequently extended, is operated by a different company from the other two lines (Attikó Metró) and the station signs carry different symbols. Apart from this the only difference of interest to passengers is in fare structure (see below). The system operates from c 05.00 to c midnight, though it is advisable to check, if times are critical. The recently opened stations have displays of photographs and of archaeological finds made during their construction, and some fine works of sculpture by contemporary artists.

Line 1 (ΗΣΑΠ) carries frequent services **from Kifissiá** via Omónia **to Piraeus** in c 40 mins.

Line 2 runs from **Sepólia** (west of the railway stations), through **central**

Athens, to **Dháfni**, a suburb to the east (not to be confused with the monastery of Dhafní which is elsewhere).

Line 3 runs from **Monastiráki** (this station is not open at the time of writing) to **Ethnikí Amina** (the Defence Ministry, usually known as the Pentágono) near the eastern suburb of Papágos.

Tickets These are different from bus/trolley bus tickets, are bought at stations and must be cancelled at machines on the platform before boarding. If you are caught without a cancelled ticket for the journey, you will have to pay an on-the-spot fine of 40 times the standard fare. It is a good idea to keep a supply of tickets to avoid queuing.

There are two types of ticket: €0.60 tickets for journeys on Line 1 not entering more than two of its three zones (Kifissiá–Perissós; Ano Patísia–Omónia; Monastiráki–Piraeus) and €0.70 tickets that can be used on any line or lines and for any length of journey.

Mainline trains

Mainline railways are of limited use in Attica but might be considered for trips to Elefsína and/or Mégara on the Peloponnesian line, or places in northern Attica (Afídhnes, etc) on the line to the north, mostly served by trains for Khalkís in Evvia. These journeys are good for seeing parts of the suburbs and countryside which you would otherwise miss.

Lárissa Station (Stathmós Laríssis; **Map 2,2**), c 1km from Omónia, serves the standard-gauge line to the north and the Khalkídha line. Access to Stathmós Laríssis is by Metró (Line 2), bus 405 from Leofóros Alexándras, trolley bus 1 from Leofóros Amalías or Panepistimíou.

Peloponnese Station (Stathmós Peloponnísou; **Map 2,3**) adjoins the Lárissa station, to the southwest, but is on the further side of the complex and is reached by a bridge over the lines at the Omónia end. For trains to Elefsína, Mégara, Corinth and the Peloponnese. Access by bus 057 (Skouzé) from Panepistimíou.

Booking offices at stations or, in town, as for international services (p 19).

By bus and trolley bus

The network is extensive, cheap and efficient, though vehicles can be very crowded, and slow at busy times of day. Because of one-way traffic systems, outward routes through the city seldom coincide with the return journeys. Between the Omónia area and Síntagma Square, traffic goes north by Panepistimíou (Venizélou), south by either Stadhíou or Akadhimías.

As an approximate guide, the first digit of the bus number indicates its general destination, as follows:

0 central Athens
1 coastal suburbs south towards Vouliagméni
2 southern suburbs on slopes of Imittós
3 and **4** southeastern and eastern to central and eastern Attica
5 Kifissiá and north suburbs
6 and **7** northwest
8 west towards Dhafní
9 southwest to Piraeus.

For other suburban services, see p 29.

Trolley buses

Within Athens, among the most useful are:

3 Patísia • Patisíon • Akadhimías • Vasilíssis Sofías • Ambelókipi • Erithrós Stavrós (Leofóros Kifissías)

4/11 Patisíon • Stadhíou • Síntagma • Filellínon • Vasilíssis Olgas (for Olimpieion, etc) • Stádhion • Pankráti

7 (clockwise) and **8** (anticlockwise) Ambelókipi • Vasilíssis Sofías • Síntagma • Panepistimíou • Patisíon • Leofóros Alexándras • Ambelókipi

All Patisíon trolley buses stop at the Polytechnic (Politekhnío), for the National Archaeological Museum.

Town buses

Useful routes include:

022 Kipséli • Plat. Kánningos • Kolonáki • Maráslio • Gennádhion Library

023 Ippokrátous • Síntagma • Monastiráki • Asomáton • Votanikós

040 Síntagma (Od. Filellínon) • Piraeus (Aktí Xaveríou), via Singroú, Kallithéa and Tsitsifiés and entering Piraeus by Odd. Gr. Lamvráki, Vasiléos Yioryíou and Iróön Politekhníou

049 Omónia (Od. Athinás) • Piraeus (Dhimotikó Théatro, then Aktí Xaveríou), via Od. Piraiós, entering Piraeus by Odd. Sint. Pezikoú and Iróön Politekhníou

051 Od. Veranzérou • Akadhimía Plátonos (Plato's Academy) · Long-distance bus station at Kavállas/Kifissoú

060 (minibus, circular) National Archaeological Museum (Od. Vasiléos Iraklíou) • Exárkhia • Kánningos • Akadhimías • Kanári • Plat. Kolonakíou • Patriárkhou Ioakeím • Alopekís • Likavittós

100 (minibus, circular) Od. Zínonos (near Omónia) • Márnis • Akadhimías • Síntagma • Sofokléous • Zínonos

200 (minibus, circular) National Archaeological Museum (Od. Vasiléos Iraklíou) • Exárkhia • Menándrou • Kolokotróni • Kolonáki • Vas. Sofías • Perikléous • Athinás • 3 Septemvríou

230 Goudhí • Od. Ippokrátous • Akadhimías • Acrópolis • Thisío • Plat. Koumoundoúrou (note that this route may change with the future pedestrianisation of Apostólou Pávlou).

Tickets must be bought in advance, from certain kiosks, shops and street vendors (look for the sign ΠΩΛΟΥΝΤΑΙ ΕΙΣΙΤΗΡΙΑ). It is best to keep a stock as they can be irritatingly unavailable when you need them most. Tickets must be cancelled in machines immediately you board the bus. Failure to do so incurs an on-the-spot fine of 40 times the standard fare. The current fare is €0.45—for any journey within the network of town buses, trolley buses and suburban buses.

Suburban bus services

A series of mainline buses (routes A, B, Γ, nos 1–18) serve suburban terminals on which are based a further set of localised services. Thus, to reach the Tatóï area, you take the A7 from central Athens to Kifissiá and there change to the local 503. The same ticket is valid for the whole trip but must be cancelled twice.

The main A routes are listed below with some more important destinations highlighted. The B and Γ routes are variants on the A, reaching the same or a neighbouring destination by a different route. Connecting services are mentioned, as appropriate, in the main text.

A1	Piraeus (Aktí Xaveríou) • Voúla (Dhimarkhío), via coast
A2	Athens (Panepistimíou) • Voúla (Dhimarkhío), via Leof. Amfithéas
A3	Panepistimíou • **Glifádha** (Plateía Glifádhas), via inland route and Vouliagméni
A4	Akadhimías • Aryiroúpolis · Terpsithéa
A5	Akadhimías • **Ay. Paraskeví** (Trikálon, via Plateía Ayías Paraskevís and EPT) (B5 for Ay. Paraskeví from Stathmós Laríssis, via Leofóros Alexándras; Γ5 for Kholargós)
A6	Vasiléos Iraklíou, National Archaeological Museum • **Khalándri** (Ethnikís Antistáseos)
A7	Kánningos • **Kifissiá** (Plateía), some continuing to Néa Erithraía (B7 is for Kifissiá via Maroússi)
A8	Stournári • Néa Ionía and Maroússi (OTE)
A9	Khalkokondíli • Néa Filadhélfia and Metamórfosi (Likovrísiss) (Γ9 for **Kókkinos Mílos** and Akharnés)
A10	Akharnón • Akharnés (Mesoníkhi) (Γ10 to Ay. Anáryiri, circular)
A11	Faviérou • Petroúpoli (Théatro Pétras)
A12	Márnis • Ano Lióssia · **Filí**
A13	Zínonos • Kipoúpoli/Peristéri (Meteóron)
A14	Agesiláou • Nea Zoí
A15	Dheliyióryi • Dhásos
A16	Plateía Koumoundoúrou • **Elefsína** (Paralía), via the Ierá Odhós (B16 goes via Leofóros Athinón)
A17	Zínonos • Koridhallós (Skhistó)
A18	**Pérama**, via Pétrou Rálli (Γ18 via Gr. Lamvráki)

For **enquiries** (in Greek), ☎ 185 (07.30–21.00, Mon–Fri). Leaflets showing the main routes can be obtained from the Athens Transport Office (OASA) at Metsóvou 15 (**Map 3,2**), near the National Archaeological Museum, www.oasa.gr.

For **rural Attica**, details of transport are given with the descriptions of excursions. **To eastern Attica**, including Soúnio (via coast or inland), Lávrio, Pórto Ráfti, Markópoulo/Vravróna (Brauron), Kálamos/Amphiáraio, Oropós, etc, buses from 14 Od. Mavrommatéon (**Map 3,1**), at the junction of Leofóros Alexándras and Patisíon. **Enquiries** (Greek) ☎ 210 821 3203.

To Marathon, Rafína, Ayía Marína/Rhamnoúnda (Rhamnous), buses from 29 Mavrommatéon / Leof. Alexándras (**Map 3,1**). **Enquiries** (Greek) ☎ 210 821 3203.

To northwestern Attica, including Mégara, Alepokhóri, Vília (and Erithrai), Pórto Yermenó (Aigósthena), buses from Thisío (**Map 4,2**). **Enquiries** (Greek) ☎ 210 346 4731.

Long-distance bus stations

Services to the Peloponnese, Macedonia, Epirus and the Ionian Islands leave from Kifissoú 100 (reached in 15 mins by bus 051 from Menándrou, near Plateía Ayíou Konstandínou, below Omónia). Services to Evvia, Central Greece, and Thessaly from Liosíon 260 (reached by bus 024 from Leofóros Amalías or Panepistimíou). Telephone numbers for the booking offices can be got by dialling 142.

Bus tours

Several companies run tours to places of interest in Attica, such as Sounion, as well as further afield (e.g. Delphi, Mycenae, Metéora). Also boat trips to Aíyina and the islands of the Saronic Gulf. These can be booked either direct with the firms concerned or at most travel agents.

Leading operators include: *CHAT* and *Hermes en Grèce*, both at Stadhíou 4 (**Map 6,5**), *CHAT* ☎ 210 322 3137, 322 2886, fax 323 1200, (*Hermes*) ☎ 210 323 7431, fax 323 5370, and *Key Tours*, Kallirόïs 4, ☎ 210 923 3166, 923 3266, 923 2008.

The Greek Touring Club (*Periiyitikí Léskhi*, Mesoyíon 395, ☎ 210 606 8800) is mainly used by local members, but has an excellent programme of excursions in which non-members can participate.

By taxi

A notice of taxi rates and list of radio taxi firms is available from EOT (for the latter, see also daily papers).

Metered taxis are numerous and cheap in Athens, reasonably easy to find in small towns, chancy elsewhere. In towns there is a minimum fare of €1.47, then €0.24 per km (or by time if you get stuck in a traffic jam); or €0.44 between midnight and 05.00. Supplements are payable for journeys originating at the airport (€1.18) and other major public transport terminals (€0.59). Outside the city boundary, a higher tariff applies (see below). There is a charge of €0.30 per item for luggage weighing over 10kg.

At busy times and with (or sometimes without) the permission of the original hirer, the driver may pick up other passengers going in roughly the same direction. You enquire by shouting your destination through the window. A deduction should be made for such passengers when they reach their destination, since the fare shown on the meter will be that from the original point of hire. This may not always be easy to negotiate but, at peak hours, it is probably worth ignoring the relatively small mark-up.

In country areas, meters are usually (but not always) fitted. The higher tarrif applies. If there is no meter, there will still be a standard tariff which may or may not be publicly displayed or adhered to. In these rare cases the fare should always be agreed in advance. If in doubt, enquire about the price from several drivers. Tip by rounding up to the nearest €0.50 (more if it has been a long journey).

Taxis are well worth using for excursions, even quite long ones, and especially if there are several people sharing. For example, a trip from Athens to Rafína (30km) costs about €17.50, depending on traffic. The charge for taking you to your destination, waiting a reasonable time and then bringing you back is less than for two quite separate trips. Drivers will sometimes negotiate a fixed price, but will normally go by the meter, having given you an accurate idea in advance of the likely cost.

Radio taxis (supplements for call to private house or hotel are about €2) are mostly reliable but their telephone lines can be very busy. Amongst a number of firms are: *Astéras*, ☎ 210 614 4000; *Enótita*, ☎ 210 645 9000/5; *Ikaros*, ☎ 210 515 2800; and *Protoporía*, ☎ 210 213 0400.

By bicycle

Cycling is not a realistic option in Athens or most of Attica, though some resorts (e.g. Marathon) may have bicycles for hire locally.

By car

Driving (on the right) is conducted in a competitive spirit which can be alarming to the inexperienced and gives Greece the dubious distinction of one of the highest accident rates in Europe. Traffic in Athens and suburbs, and on the major roads in Attica, is heavy, but can be avoided to some extent if you choose your travel times carefully. Try to enter and leave the city early in the morning or late at night and avoid arriving on Sundays after about 15.00, when returning weekenders can stretch a half-hour journey by four or five times.

The Athens headquarters of the *Greek Motoring Organisation* (ELPA) is at Mesoyíon 395 (Ayía Paraskeví), ☎ 210 606 8800, fax 210 606 8981, www.elpa.gr. There is also an office at the Pírgos Athinón (**Map 7,2**): Vasilíssis Sofías / Mesoyíon 2–4, ☎ 210 779 1615, fax 778 6642. There are reciprocal arrangements with the organisations of other countries; otherwise the subscription is c £70.00 per year. An alternative and equally efficient rescue service is *Express*, Leofóros Singroú 234, ☎ 154 (office enquiries ☎ 210 952 4950) c £45.00 for six months, £85.00 for one year.

Car hire (self-drive). There are numerous car hire companies in Greece (list from the National Tourist Organisation). In Athens these include:

Autos Abroad, UK number only, ☎ 0870 066 7788.
Avis, Amalías 48, ☎ 210 322 4951/5, fax 210 322 0216
Budget, Singroú 90, ☎ 210 342 6226, fax 210 342 5098
Hellascars, Stadhíou 7, ☎ 210 323 7734
Hertz, Singroú 12, ☎ 210 942 0102, fax 210 922 7921
Holiday Autos, Singroú 8, ☎ 210 922 3088, fax 210 922 5989
Just, Singroú 43, ☎ 210 924 7331/2, 210 923 9104, 210 923 8566, fax 210 924 7248

The larger firms have desks at the airport.

Rental charges vary a great deal and are often open to negotiation (roughly £120 per week for a small car, with unlimited mileage, in the high season). Three-day unlimited mileage rates are also available. Otherwise the cost is calculated by adding a charge per kilometre to a modest daily rate: this may be the cheapest option if you want the car more for convenience than for covering long distances. When calculating rates from hire company leaflets, be sure to include taxes (about 20 per cent) and any charges for additional insurance cover which is required. The **insurance** cover included in the price may be third party only and quite restrictive.

Some travel firms offer inclusive fly drive packages with a car on arrival; others provide the option of car hire at a reduced rate. Large firms have Europe-wide booking services. Booking in advance saves time and may save money. There are sometimes special offers.

Food and drink

Traditional Greek cuisine is Middle Eastern rather than European in character. Contrary to popular opinion, influenced by the regrettably large number of indifferent tourist-orientated restaurants, Greek food can be both varied and excellent, with a wide range of fresh ingredients of high quality. The availability of such ingredients makes Greece a potential paradise for vegetarians. Some Greek dishes can be too oily for western Europeans. Frozen (*katapsigméno*) food must be indicated on the menu by the letters 'KAT'.

A full **Greek meal** can begin with a **foundation course** consisting of rice with a sauce (*piláfi sáltsa*), or of pasta (*makarónia*), perhaps baked with minced meat (*pastítsio*), or *tirópita* (cheese pie). Alternatives are soup or **hors-d'oeuvre** (*mezédhes*). The latter are particularly enticing and include *taramosaláta*, a paste made from the roe of grey mullet and olive oil, and *tzatzíki*, chopped cucumber in yoghurt heavily flavoured with garlic.

The **main course** may be meat (*kréas*), or fish (*psári*) or a dish on a vegetable base, baked (*tou foúrnou*), boiled (*vrastó*), fried (*tiganitó*), roast (*psitó*), or grilled (*skháras*). The chef's suggestions will be found under *piáta tis iméras*, dishes of the day. *Moussaká* consists of layers of aubergines, minced beef and cheese, with butter and spices, baked in the oven.

Souvlákia, known too by the Turkish name 'shish kebab', are pieces of meat grilled on a skewer. Also cooked in this fashion is *kokorétsi* (banned under EU legislation as a health risk, but still widely available), which consists of alternate pieces of lamb's liver, kidney, sweetbreads and heart, wrapped in intestines. When not grilled, meat is often stewed with oil in pieces, frequently with tomato added (*kokkinistó*).

Several foreign dishes appear on menus, e.g. *Schnitzel Holstein, Bintok à la Russe, crème caramel, salade de fruits*.

Of Greek **cheeses**, *féta* is best eaten peasant fashion, with black pepper, oil and *rígani* (oregano). The smoked cheese of Métsovo is distinctive and excellent, and there are many local Gruyère-type cheeses (*graviéra*), or the slightly more salty and interesting *kéfalograviéras*.

Sweets are elaborate and varied, though more often eaten separately at a *zakharoplasteíon* (p 40) than as a course of a meal. Among the most popular are *baklavás*, consisting of layered wafer-thin pastry (*fílo*) filled with honey and nuts; *kataïfi*, wheat shredded and filled with sweetened nuts; and *galaktoboúreko*, pastry filled with vanilla custard.

Greeks rarely lunch before 13.00 and often as late as 15.00–16.00 (earlier on Sunday). Dinner times are roughly 20.00–23.00 (in summer 21.00–01.00, or even later), though hotels catering mainly for foreigners have a more western timetable.

Wine (*krasí*) in Greece is generally good, and stronger than French wine. The range and quality have improved dramatically in the last 20 years, though you need to be selective. *Retsína*, the traditional resinated white wine, flavoured with resin from pine trees and particularly characteristic of Attica and the Peloponnese, is ubiquitous and can be excellent, though for some an acquired taste. It is always obtainable bottled, but the can or jug filled from the barrel is to be preferred. There are also rosé varieties, called *kokinélli*. Good unresinated **table wines** (*arretsínoto*), both red and white, are obtainable in bottle form everywhere: white (*aspro*), red (*mávro*, literally 'black'), or rosé (*kókkino*, literally 'red').

There are good draught red wines from Nemea, Rhodes and Corfu. It is invidious to recommend bottled wines from the vast range available but you could try some of the following: Hymettos (red and white), Sánta Elena (white), Pallíni (white), Vílitsa (white), Zítsa (white, semi-sparkling), Makedhonikó (red and white), Sámaina (white), Oreinó (white) and other wines by Spirópoulos (many available in the UK), Montenéro (red), Castel Daniélis (red), Katóï Avéroff (red and white), Tsántali (white, rosé), Náoussa (red), Robólla (white). The latter four are rather more expensive but no Greek wine is costly by British standards. The wines of the Carrás estate are also of high quality. Rhodes produces good wines, including a pleasant champagne-type; Chevalier de Rhodes is an excellent red.

Wines are widely available in both specialist shops (look for the sign Káva/ΚΑΒΑ) and supermarkets. An interesting **wine emporium** in Athens, representing a union of wine-producing co-operatives from different areas, is at L. Riankoúr 73, off Od. Panórmou which connects Leofóros Alexándras with Leofóros Kifissías.

There is a **wine festival** in the woods near Dhafní monastery (p 262) in September at which many varieties can be tasted.

Beer (Bavarian type) is brewed in Greece, and other lagers are brewed under licence or imported. Some cafés now have a much wider range of beers, imported from western Europe.

The favourite Greek **aperitif** is *oúzo*, a strong, colourless drink made from grape-stems and flavoured with aniseed; it is served with *mezédhes*, snacks consisting of anything from a simple slice of cheese or tomato or an olive to pieces of smoked eel or fried octopus. An alternative is *rakí* (arak), in various forms.

Tap water is almost always safe, but still mineral waters from spas such as Loutráki are ubiquitous and may be preferable in some places.

Restaurants and tavernas

Traditionally restaurants (*estiatória*) are for lunch and tavernas (*tavérnes*) for evening meals, although some serve both. The taverna may be less formal and, partly at least, out of doors. A table, once occupied, is often kept for the evening.

The **exokhikó kéntro** (literally 'rural centre') combines the functions of café and taverna in a country or seaside setting.

Eating places of all classes display a menu, showing their category (Luxury, A–D) and the prices of each dish, both basic and with tax and service included. There are usually translations into English, frequently an entertainment in themselves. Restaurant and taverna meals are relatively inexpensive. A service charge is added by law but it is usual also to leave a modest tip of not more than 10 per cent.

The pattern of meals is less stereotyped than in the west, with portions often being shared. It is a good idea to order each course separately if you don't want all the dishes to arrive together. It is usual to visit the kitchens to choose food; in waterside tavernas, fish can be selected from the ice and then weighed, the price appearing on the menu per kilo.

In larger centres a few restaurants and de luxe hotels provide an international cuisine, and Athens has now acquired a substantial number of foreign restaurants. Well-prepared Greek food, however, is far preferable to imitations of foreign dishes. All Greeks eat out frequently, and it is best always to choose establishments crowded with locals. The food will be better (and cheaper) and the atmosphere livelier than in tourist-orientated restaurants which are, on the whole, best avoided. There are plenty of good restaurants which provide an astonishing range of excellent and interesting dishes, and a host of small neighbourhood eating places where the range may be limited and the surroundings informal, but the quality of the food is excellent. Generally speaking good food and a high standard of service go together.

Restaurants in Athens and Piraeus

Every neighbourhood has a range of tavernas and searching them out is a recreation in itself. While Pláka has an obvious attraction in terms of setting, the standard of restaurants there is not very high. The fish tavernas of Mikró Limáni (Tourkolímano) in Piraeus are famous and the setting again attractive but, since they can be very expensive and the service obtrusive, you may be better advised to seek out less fashionable parts of the port.

Most of the establishments contained in this list are of traditional Greek type. Even those marked '☆', as being more expensive than the average, are modestly priced, at least by UK standards. Luxury hotels and restaurants serving non-Greek food are listed in the various sources of information (see below). Some are best for lunch and may not be open in the evenings (marked 'Lunch'); the reverse is true of the remainder, though many tavernas now open at lunchtime, especially in the tourist season. Places which do not close on Sundays usually do so on another day early in the week. Since arrangements vary with the season, it is a good idea to check by telephone.

For further guidance consult current periodicals, e.g. *Athinórama* (see Newspapers, p 55).

Alexándreia, Metsóvou 13 /Rethímnou (Museum), ☎ 210 821 0004. An excellent Greek-Egyptian restaurant with good food, beautifully served. A small courtyard for summer.
Anna, Grigoríou 10 (Néa Filothéi suburb), ☎ 210 692 8435. Good food, quiet atmosphere, attentive service. Garden for the summer.
Arkhaíon Yévseis ☆ (Tastes of the Ancient Greeks) Kodhrátou 22, near Plateía

Karaïskáki, below Omónia, ☎ 210 523 9661. Ancient cuisine re-created. Good, but quite expensive (c €30) by Greek standards.

Arkhontikó, Evrou 49 (near the Hilton), ☎ 210 777 7742. Attractive interior. Extensive menu and well-prepared Greek food. Both lunch and evening.

Bakalariákia, Kidhathenaíon 41 (Pláka), ☎ 210 322 5084. A colourful traditional basement restaurant specialising in cod.

Bárba Yiánnis, Emmanouíl Benáki 94 (Exárkhia), ☎ 210 330 0185. A bustling taverna in an old house with high ceilings. Wine from the barrel.

Dhimókritos, corner of Dhimokrítou and Tsakálof (Kolonáki), ☎ 210 361 3588. A pleasant old building with well-prepared food. Lunch and evening.

Dhelfí, Níkis 13 (Síntagma), ☎ 210 323 4869. Extensive menu; traditional Greek food.

Diána, Melissoú 1 and Krisíla (Pankráti), ☎ 210 701 8064, 210 752 1014. A quiet and pleasant backwater; unpretentious range of good dishes; pleasant service.

Dirós, Xenofóntos 10-12 (Síntagma), ☎ 210 323 2392, fax 210 323 3810. Good food and pleasant service, unspoiled by extensive recommendations. Best at lunchtime when quieter. Air-conditioned.

Dourambéis ☆, Ath. Dhilavéri 29 (Piraeus), ☎ 210 412 2092. Away from the waterfront and patronised by connoisseurs rather than tourists. Excellent fish.

Eden, Lissíou 12 (Pláka), ☎ 210 324 8858. Vegetarian. Old mansion with terrace.

Ennéa Adhélfia (Nine Brothers), Sotíros 48, Plateía Kanári (near Zéa harbour, Piraeus), ☎ 210 411 5233, 210 411 5273. Tables outside in pedestrianised street. Large range of dishes. Fast service.

Fátsio ☆, Evfroníou 5 (Hilton), ☎ 210 721 7421. Excellent Constantinopolitan cuisine. Get there in good time: the best dishes disappear quickly. Lunch all year; dinner in winter only.

Fílippou, 19 Xenokrátous (Kolonáki), ☎ 210 721 6390. A sound eating place, with tables outside in the summer. Lunch.

Ideál, Panepistimíou 46, ☎ 210 330 3000. Large reasonably priced city-centre restaurant, with neo-Art Deco ambience. Greek, Turkish and European dishes.

O Ilías, Stasínou and Telesílis (Pankráti), ☎ 210 722 3400. A good popular taverna.

Kalíva, Vassiléos Pávlou 60 (Kastélla, Piraeus), ☎ 210 412 2593. A lovely terrace overlooking Tourkolímano, and much cheaper than the waterside restaurants. Not much fish though.

Karavítis, Arktínou/Pavsaníou (Pankráti), ☎ 210 721 5155. An old-style taverna with garden. Good for casseroles.

Kentrikón, Kolokotróni 3 (Síntagma), ☎ 210 323 2482. Wide range of Greek dishes. In arcade near the National Historical Museum. Grander than most and service can be supercilious. Lunch.

Kioúpi, Plateía Kolonakíou 4 / Skoufá, ☎ 210 361 4033. In a basement on the upper side of Kolonáki square. Good value (especially in this expensive area) traditional cuisine. Lunch, and evening till late.

Klimaratiá, Klepsídhras 5 (Pláka), ☎ 210 321 6629. A pleasant, unpretentious taverna in a quiet shaded street.

Léfka, Mavromikhaïli 121 (Exárkhia), ☎ 361 4038. A lovely old-fashioned taverna with a walled courtyard for the summer. Get there well before 21.00 to be sure of a table.

Mandráki, Aktí Themistokléous 40, Piraeus (Zéa harbour), ☎ 210 451 3216.

Overlooking the sea. Wide range of fresh fish and vegetable dishes, all well-prepared. The mussel pilaf is recommended.

Megarítis, Ferekídhou 2/Arátou (Pangráti), ☎ 210 701 2155. An old-fashioned taverna with a terrace, as well as some tables on the pavement.

Oikeío, Ploutárkhou 15 (Kolonáki), ☎ 210 725 9216. Charming small café-restaurant, with some tables outside in the summer. Imaginative salads; good house wine.

Oikonómou, Troön/Kidhandhídhon (Petrálona), ☎ 210 346 7555. A real, simple, old-fashioned taverna, with good food in basic surroundings.

Plátanos, Dhioyénous 4 (Pláka), ☎ 210 322 0666. As the name suggests, under a plane tree, and in a quiet square near the Museum of Greek Folk Music. A good place for summer lunch.

Rodhiá, Aristíppou 44 (Likavittós), ☎ 210 722 9883. Upmarket but not particularly pricey taverna with a small open terrace.

Rozália, Valtetsíou 58 (off Plateía Exarkhíon), ☎ 210 330 2933. In pedestrianised street: courtyard shaded by trees. Good *mezédhes*, to choose from a tray.

Sigálas, Plateía Monastirakíou 2 (Monastiráki), ☎ 210 321 3036. Established 1879. Huge barrels of retsina line the walls.

Simpósio ☆, Erekhthíou 46 (Acropolis), ☎ 210 922 5321. An attractive tree-studded courtyard, convenient for the Odeion of Herodes Atticus.

Skalákia, Aiyinítou 32 (Ilíssia), ☎ 210 722 9290. Most of the dishes are grilled, plus some starters and salads, but good quality and not expensive.

Strofí, Rovértou Gálli 25/Propilaíon (Acropolis), ☎ 210 921 4130. Good-quality Greek food in a family-run establishment with a lovely rooftop view of the Acropolis.

Théspis, Thespídhos 18 (Pláka), ☎ 210 323 8242. A nicely situated Pláka taverna with a pleasant shady dining area. The food is fairly modest (good selection of *mezédhes*) but if you want a meal in the middle of touristy Pláka, it's reasonable.

Tría Adhélfia, Elpídhos 7 (Plateía Viktorías), ☎ 210 822 9322. A reliable taverna, a little out of the centre.

Vassílaina, Aitolikoú 72 (Ayía Sofía, Piraeus), ☎ 210 461 2457. Long known for its large range of courses (brought to you in succession) and the service.

Virínis, Arkhimídhous 11 (Pankráti), ☎ 210 701 2021. Wide range of *mezédhes*. Garden.

Vizantinó, Kidhathinaíon 18 (Pláka), ☎ 210 728 1000. A long-established restaurant-taverna.

Tís Xanthís, Irínis Athenaías 5 (Lófos tou Stréfi, Exárkhia), ☎ 210 882 0780. Sound food and a lovely setting for the summer, with views over northern Athens from tables on the roof.

Xínou, Angélou Yéronda 4 (Pláka), ☎ 210 322 1065. A very traditional and mildly upmarket taverna with very good food. Music at the table can be noisy and obtrusive. Closed at weekends and for some of the summer.

Yerofínakas ☆, Pindhárou 10 (Centre), ☎ 210 362 2719. An old-established expense-account restaurant with a good reputation and interesting food. Expensive.

Zafíris, Dhionissíou Areopayítou/Propilaion 2 (Acropolis), ☎ 210 921 5182, fax 210 923 1836. Long-established restaurant (originally in Pláka) specialising in game. Pleasant atmosphere. Good food and service.

Ouzerí

The Ouzerí serves a range of *mezédhes* (especially seafood), traditionally with oúzo, but usually also wine, beer and soft drinks. They can be relatively expensive but are often colourful and provide good food. Many of the better ones are to be found near Omónia, especially in Odd. Themistokléous and Emm. Benáki. Piraeus is also a good place to hunt—especially along the coast between the Naval College and Zéa harbour. For Psirí and Thisío, see Cafés p 39.

To Athinaïkón, Themistokléous 2 (near Kánningos), ☎ 210 383 8485. A nice atmosphere with high ceilings and marble-topped tables. Good quality and service.

Filóistro, Apostólou Pávlou 23 (Thisío), ☎ 210 342 2897, 210 346 7554. Pleasant roof-terrace with views of the Acropolis and Likavittós.

To Yeráni (also known as Ouzerí Koúklis), Tripódhon 14 (Pláka), ☎ 210 324 7605. Attractive, old-established ouzerí. Balconies. Many *mezédhes*, including flaming sausages! Good house wine.

Menu glossary

The following menu (*katálogos*) contains some of the simpler dishes and items to be found:

Orektiká ~ hors d'oeuvre

Dhiáfora orektiká ~ hors d'oeuvre variés (a selection of starters)
Taramosaláta ~ a paste made from the roe of grey mullet and olive oil
Dolmádhes yalantzí ~ stuffed vine leaves served hot with egg-lemon sauce
Dolmadhákia ~ cold stuffed vine leaves
Eliés ~ olives

Soúpes ~ soups

Soúpa avgholémono ~ egg and lemon soup
Soúpa apo khórta ~ vegetable soup
Maghirítsa ~ tripe soup generally with rice (Easter speciality)
Psarósoupa ~ fish soup

Zimárika ~ pasta and rice dishes

Piláfi sáltsa ~ rice with sauce
Spagéto sáltsa me tirí ~ spaghetti with sauce and cheese
Makarónia ~ macaroni

Psária ~ fish

Strídhia ~ oysters	*Kalamarákia* ~ baby squids
Sinagrídha ~ sea bream	*Kolioí* ~ mackerel
Barboúnia ~ red mullet	*Lithrínia* ~ bass
Marídhes ~ whitebait	*Xifías* ~ swordfish
Astakós ~ lobster	*Khtapódhi* ~ octopus
Garídhes ~ prawns	

Ladherá ~ dishes cooked in oil

Khórta ~ vegetables or greens	*Arakás* or *Bizéllia* ~ peas
Patátes tiganités ~ fried potatoes	*Domátes yemistés* ~ stuffed tomatoes
Fasolákia ~ green beans	

Avgá ~ eggs
Omelétta Zambón ~ ham omelette
Avgá 'brouillé' ~ scrambled eggs
Avgá 'á la Russe' ~ eggs with Russian salad

Entrádhes ~ entrées
Arnáki fasolákia ~ lamb with beans
Moskhári ~ veal
Kokkinistó ~ meat stewed with oil and
   tomato
Sikotákia ~ liver
Gourounópoulo psitó ~ roast sucking-
   pig

Kotópoulo ~ chicken
Papí ~ duck
Tsoutsoukákia ~ meatballs in tomato
   sauce

Skháras ~ grills
Souvlákia ápo filéto ~ shish kebab (see p 32)
Keftédhes, keftedhákia skháras ~ grilled meatballs
Brizóles moskharíssies ~ veal chops
Païdhákia khiriná ~ pork cutlets

Salátes ~ salads
Domáta saláta ~ tomato salad
Maroúli ~ lettuce
Radhíkia ~ radishes
Kolokithákia ~ courgettes (zucchini)
Angoúri ~ cucumber

Ankináres ~ artichokes
Melizánes ~ aubergines (eggplant)
Piperiés ~ green peppers
Russikí ~ Russian salad

Tiriá ~ cheeses
Féta ~ soft white goat's milk cheese
Kasséri ~ hard yellow cheese

Graviéra ~ Greek gruyère
Roquefort ~ blue cheeses generally

Gliká ~ sweets
Khalvás ~ halvas
Baklavás
Kataïfi   } see p 33
Galaktoboúreko

Yiaoúrti ~ yoghurt
Karídhia me méli ~ walnuts with honey
Rizógalo ~ rice pudding

Froúta ~ fruits
Mílo ~ apple
Banána ~ banana
Akhládhi ~ pear
Portokáli ~ orange
Kerásia ~ cherries
Víssina ~ black cherries

Fráoules ~ strawberries
Dhamáskina ~ plums
Rodhákina ~ peaches
Veríkoka ~ apricots
Pepóni ~ melon
Karpoúzi ~ watermelon

Other
Psomí ~ bread
Voútiro ~ butter
Aláti ~ salt
Pipéri ~ pepper
Moustárdha ~ mustard

Ládhi ~ oil
Xídhi ~ vinegar
Zákhari ~ sugar
Paghotó ~ ice-cream
Lemóni ~ lemon

Soft drinks

Ghála ~ milk
Neró ~ water
  éna potíri ~ a glass
  éna boukáli ~ a bottle
  pagoméno ~ iced
Kafé ~ coffee
  ellinikó ~ Greek
  fíltro/Gallikó ~ filter coffee
  eprésso ~ espresso
  kapoutsíno ~ cappuccino
  Nés ~ Nescafé
  frappé ~ frappé

Mé/khorís ghála/zákhari ~
  with/without milk/sugar
Tsáï ~ tea
Tsáï tou vounoú ~ 'mountain tea'
  (made from mountain herbs)
Khamomíli ~ camomile
Portokaládha ~ orangeade
Lemonádha ~ lemonade
Kóka-kóla ~ Coca-Cola
Khimós ~ fruit juice (may or may not
  be freshly pressed)

Cafés

The traditional Greek *kafeneíon* is an austere establishment, usually thronged with male patrons for whom it is both local club and political forum. Such places are slowly disappearing or being modified in various ways: they serve coffee, soft drinks and a limited range of alcoholic drinks. Coffee is almost always served in 'Turkish' fashion in tiny cups, with the grounds. It is drunk heavily sweetened (*varígliko*), medium (*métrio*) or without sugar (*skhéto*).

Coffee shops and open-air cafés (see list below) are more western in style.

Aígli, Záppio Gardens. Next to the Záppion hall and an open-air cinema. Quite grand and on the pricey side but nicely away from the traffic.
Aliktó, Plateía Ayías Irínis 6 (behind the church of Ay. Irini in Aiólou). A pleasant, quiet café near the flowersellers.
Anna Ríska, Ermou 26 (near Síntagma). Upstairs café in a clothes shop. No character, but a comfortable place to put your feet up.
Brazíl, Vourkourestíou 1, near the corner with Stadhíou (Síntagma). A well-established shop with good coffee.
Café Néon, corner of Dhórou (in Omónia). A splendid neoclassical building with a modernised self-service café. Also a branch in Síntagma.
Centre of the Hellenic Tradition, Mitropóleos 59 (upstairs, in arcade near Cathedral). Coffee, oúzo—and an excellent selection of Greek handicrafts on sale.
Dhiónissos/Zonar's, opposite approach road to Acropolis. A café-restaurant in an interesting building facing the Acropolis approach. Pleasant terrace and lots of outside seating. Car park. Another branch on the top of Mt Likavittós is less attractive.
Dhióskouri, Dhioskoúron 13, in the higher reaches of Plaka, shaded by trees and overlooking the ancient agora. A good place to stop on the way to/from the Acropolis.
En Dhelfís ('At Delphi'), Dhelfón, near Skoufá 75. A pleasant café with a few tables on a pedestrianised street near the French Archaeological School.
Hóndos Centre, Omónia. Top-floor café in a department store. Utilitarian, but great views.
Kallimármaro, literally under the shadow of the Stadium.

Kotsólis, Adhrianou 112 (Pláka). An old family concern which has been beauti-fully refurbished. Photos and mementoes line the walls. Spotlessly clean, excellent quality, friendly and attentive service. Some delicious cakes and sweets. Highly recommended.

Likóvrisi, Plateía Kolonakíou 8. The best of a series of quite expensive cafés on the upper side of the square. A good vantage point for watching the locals —and a surprisingly nice place to eat in the evening.

Loumbardhiáris, by the church of Ay. Dhimítrios (p 132) on Mouseion Hill. Lovely situation among pine and olive trees. Avoid the filter coffee, however.

Oasis, on edge of Záppion Gardens, nearly opposite the end of Filellínon. Shady and well-positioned.

Oikeío, Ploutárkhou 15 (Kolonáki). Pleasant café/restaurant with a few tables on the pavement.

Palaiá Voulí, Plateía Kolokotróni (Stadhíou, near Síntagma). A nice, though quite expensive, mainly open-air café under trees and awnings by the side of the National Historical Museum. A good place to rest when exhausted.

Other café stops when sightseeing include (if you have a ticket) the new rooftop terrace of the *Benáki Museum* (museum and café open till midnight on Thursday, when a buffet meal is available—booking essential, ☎ 210 367 1030); a shady garden café on the edge of the *National Garden* (a few metres down Iródhou Attikoú, opposite the Benáki), very popular on Sunday mornings; and the little known café in the basement of the *War Museum* (next to the Byzantine Museum in Vasilíssis Sofías)—not that wonderful but very well situated.

Large squares are often lined with cafés and can be interesting places to sit: you could try Kolonáki Square (p 215) and surrounding streets—Tsakálof, Milióni etc or Plateía Exarkhíon. Thisío (p 135; Plateía Thisíou, off Apostólou Pávlou and streets around) has become a lively area, as has newly-fashionable Psirí (p 172) where the cafés and ouzerís are more trendy than traditional. In Piraeus there are numerous cafés overlooking Zéa harbour and further along towards Néo Fáliro.

A word of **warning**: if you like good filter-coffee (café fíltro or gallikó), it's worth checking what you are going to get, since such coffee is often kept stewing on a hotplate until undrinkable. Only a few places (e.g. Palaiá Voulí) bring you a cup-filter or cafetière.

Zakharoplasteía

Properly these are confectioners, selling a wide range of traditional and modern cakes and sweets. Sometimes they have a few tables and serve drinks as well.

For **cakes**, try the following (only *Mondiál* and *Vársos* have tables and serve drinks):

Asimakópoulos, Kharilaóu Trikoúpi 82 (Exárkhia).
Au Délicieux, Kanári 17/Sólonos (Kolonáki).
Delice, Vasiléos Alexándrou 3/Vrasídha 13 (Hilton).
Mondiál, Patriárkhou Ioakím 31 (Kolonáki).
Miké, D Soútsou 8/Dhorilaíou (Plateía Mavíli).
Vársos, Kassavéti 5 (Kifissiá).

Money

There is no limit to the amount of currency you can bring into the country but you cannot take out more than €10,000 unless it has been previously declared on arrival.

The euro
The euro replaced the drachma as the official unit of currency in Greece on 1 January 2002. The drachma ceased to be legal tender on 1 March 2002. The euro (€), worth 340.75 drachmas, is subdivided into 100 leptá (or cents). There are notes of value 5, 10, 20, 50, 100, 200 and 500 euros; coins of 1, 2, 5, 10, 20 and 50 lepta, also 1 and 2 euro.

Cash machines are quite common in Athens, usually available in small towns, but rare elsewhere. They are the easiest way of getting money with major credit cards (prime your account before leaving home to avoid paying interest), or an appropriate local account. Most British bank or building society **cash cards** can also be used in machines abroad through the Plus, Cirrus or other networks. These have the advantage of allowing withdrawals direct from a home account, but you should check on the level of commission charges before leaving home. If you are depending on cash cards for funds it is advisable to carry more than one.

Travellers' cheques are an easy way of carrying funds, although they incur commission at both ends.

Major **credit cards** are accepted for purchases by a large number of shops, restaurants, etc in Athens but are still sometimes regarded with suspicion, especially in more remote places.

If you require an **emergency transfer** of funds, banks can be unhelpful and slow, but there are other providers such as *Western Union* (UK enquiries ☎ 0800 833 833, www.westernunion.com, email moneytransfer@westernunion.com). Such services are not cheap.

Bureaux de change are operated by some travel agents, and hotels will often change money, though it is advisable to check the rate and commission charges.

Post offices also change money and are very useful in out-of-the-way places.

There are numerous **banks**. Standard hours are 08.00–14.00 (13.30 Fri); closed Sat and Sun. Several branches near Síntagma Square are **open additional hours**: *National* (Ethnikí), Karayeóryi Servías 2 (Mon–Thur 15.30–17.30, Sat 09.00–15.00, Sun 09.00–13.00); *Commercial* (Emborikí), Panepistimíou (Venizélou) 11 (open till 15.30 Mon–Thurs, till 15.00 Fri).

For complicated transactions you may need to go to bank head offices. *Alpha Credit Bank* (Písteos), Stadhíou 40; *Bank of Greece* (Trápeza tis Elládhos), Panepistimíou (Venizélou) 21; *National Bank of Greece* (Ethnikí), Aiólou 86; *Commercial Bank of Greece* (Emborikí), Sofokléous 11; *Ionian* (Ioникí), Pesmazóglou/Panepistimíou (Venizélou).

Telephones, postal and internet services

Telephones

Athens area code 010 until 1 October 2002, when it becomes 210 (p 11 for further details and information about changes to other codes). Area codes are always used, even when dialling within an area.

Dialling Athens from UK 00 30 + 210 (or 10 before 1 Oct 2002) + number
Dialling Athens from USA 011 30 + 210 (or 10 before 1 Oct 2002) + number
Dialling UK from Greece 00 44 + area code (omit the first digit) + number
Dialling USA from Greece 001 + area code (omit the first digit) + number

Useful numbers

Police (Emergency) 100; **Fire** 199; **Ambulance** 166.
The **Tourist Police** (171) will advise in any emergency.
Lost property. For general lost and found, ☎ 210 647 6000 (Police HQ, Leofóros Alexándras 173); for items left in buses and taxis (brought in on Monday mornings), ☎ 210 528 4000.

Making calls

Greek telephone and telegraph services are run by a public corporation, the OTE (Organismós Tilepikinoníon Elládhos; referred to as 'ó, té'). Calls can be made from its offices (Patisíon 85, open 24 hrs; Stadhíou 15, Sólonos 53 and Kratínou 7, open from 07.00 or 08.00 to 22.00 or midnight), but **long-distance calls** can also be made from most hotels, many kiosks and any other telephone which has a meter (*metrití*) attached.

The charge per unit is fixed—lowest at OTE, slightly higher at kiosks and shops, highest in hotels. International calls are, at present charges and exchange rates, about 25 per cent more expensive than in the UK. The cheap rate periods are 22.00–06.00 (UK); 23.00–08.00 (USA); 15.00–17.00 and 22.00–08.00 (Greece). For operator-controlled calls dial 132 (Greece), 161 (international); telegrams 155; time 141 (in Greek); directory enquiries (Greece) 131, (international) 161.

Local calls can be made from most phones, in shops, kiosks, etc, on payment of the small charge. Public phone boxes now almost always accept **phone cards** (usually 100 units), which can be purchased from many shops and kiosks. Other cards (including the useful OTE *Khronokárta*—€12 for 500 units) give access via a special code.

Postal services

For post offices, look for ΤΑΧΥΔΡΟΜΕΙΟ, Takhidhromío; yellow signs ΕΛΤΑ, for Elliniká Taxidhromía (Greek Postal Services). Ordinary post offices are open Mon–Fri 07.30–14.00; closed Sat, Sun.

The main Athens post office is at Aiólou 100 (**Map 3,6** just out of Omónia Square) and has longer hours: Mon–Fri 07.30–20.00, Sat 07.30–14.00, Sun 09.00–13.00. The branch in Síntagma Square (on the corner with Od. Mitropóleos) is open similar hours.

Normal post boxes are yellow (at larger post offices those for ΕΣΩΤΕΡΙΚΑ, internal mail, and ΕΞΩΤΕΡΙΚΑ, external mail, are separate); Express boxes (at post offices only) are red. Postage stamps (normally 10 per cent surcharge) are obtainable at some kiosks and shops as well as post offices.

For mail, a transit period of between two and four days to the UK is normal but there can be considerable delays to post (especially postcards) in the summer season and internal mail is not exempt from problems. The charge for express letters is reasonable and usually ensures delivery in the UK two days after posting. A registered letter is '*éna sistiméno grámma*'. There is a transit period of one week to the USA and Canada.

Correspondence marked POSTE RESTANTE (ΠΟΣΤ ΡΕΣΤΑΝΤ) may be sent to any post office and collected by the addressee on proof of identity (preferably passport). A small fee may be charged. Do not use 'Esq.' in an address.

Parcels are not delivered in Greece. They have to be collected from the post office, where they are subject to handling fees, customs charges where appropriate, and often to delay.

Internet cafés

These are quite common in Athens (best to check hours by telephone). Three central establishments are:

Bits and Bytes, Akadhimías 78 (Kánningos end, not far from Omónia), ☎ 210 382 2545/6, 210 330 6590

Museum Café, Patisíon 46 (by National Archaeological Museum), ☎ 210 883 3418

Sofokléous Internet Café, Stadhíou 5 (in arcade; close to Síntagma), ☎ 210 324 8105

 Language and transliteration

The impossibility of achieving consistency in the transliteration of Greek into English has long been recognised. In this book modern (i.e. post-Independence) names and place names are transliterated according to the phonetic system codified by the Permanent Committee on Geographical Names (E. Gleichen and J. H. Reynolds, *Alphabets of foreign languages*, PCGN. for British official use, London, 1951, pp 52–56). This, together with the accentuation, gives the non-Greek speaker a reasonable chance of understanding and being understood when receiving or asking for directions.

Ancient names are transliterated according to a more conservative convention closer to that traditionally employed by Classical scholars. Here I have usually preferred a version nearer to the ancient Greek rather than the strictly latinised system (e.g. *k* rather than *c*, *o* rather than *u*, *ai* rather than *ae*). This has been arbitrarily modified when either a strictly English form (Corinth as opposed to Corinthus) or the latinised form (Aeschylus rather than Aiskhylos; Boeotia/ Boiotia; Acropolis and Attica for Akropolis and Attika) is likely to be more familiar to the reader. When consulting reference works for further information, readers should bear in mind that these (e.g. *Oxford classical dictionary*, 3rd edn, 1996) mostly use fully latinised forms (e.g. Lycurgus rather than Lykourgos).

The use of two different systems concurrently inevitably produces some inconsistencies between ancient and modern (e.g. respectively *ch* and *kh* for the Greek χ). But, in the case of place names, it does highlight the fact that a modern centre with an ancient name is not necessarily in the same location as its predecessor. The names of ancient places are printed in italics at their first main appearance. Ancient names, if accented, have been given their modern stress, since this may help in asking directions.

Travellers should bear in mind that, until the relatively recent designation of Demotic Greek as opposed to Katharévousa (formal Greek) as the official language, place names had often both a Katharévousa and a Demotic form (Αι Αθήναι, Η Αθήνα—for Athens). Formal versions of place names may occasionally linger on old signs; likewise the final -v (n) of neuter names.

All place names decline, like other nouns, often producing a change of stress as well as of inflexion. Some places have their more familiar spoken form in the accusative (given, where important, in the text; e.g. Elefsína).

Street names are in the genitive when called after a person, e.g. Ermoú (Street of Hermes), or when leading to a place, e.g. Patisíon (to Patísia).

As in English, a **church** may be called by the name of its saint in the nominative or genitive.

Oddities arise where a modern Greek name is itself a transliteration from Roman characters. Βερανζέρου has to be rendered Veranzérou, in spite of the fact that the spoken name bears little resemblance to the French original— Béranger. For good measure, if you find yourself in Οδός Τζώρτζ, it will be difficult to appreciate that the street was named after Sir Richard Church, since the Greek has been re-transliterated as 'George'!

Modern Greek

Some knowledge of modern Greek is very useful, especially off the beaten track, and certainly helps you make contact with ordinary people. On the main tourist routes you will always find someone who can understand English.

A good introduction to modern Greek is D. A. Hardy, *Greek language and people* (BBC publications, 1983 and many reprints; cassettes available but not essential).

A knowledge of the Greek alphabet, at least, is highly desirable, since some street names, bus destination plates, etc are not transliterated.

The Greek alphabet now, as in later classical times, comprises 24 letters: Αα, Ββ, Γγ, Δδ, Εε, Ζζ, Ηη, Θθ, Ιι, Κκ, Λλ, Μμ, Νν, Ξξ, Οο, Ππ, Ρρ, Σσ (ς when final in lower case), Ττ, Υυ, Φφ, Χχ, Ψψ, Ωω.

Vowels There are five basic vowel sounds in Greek to which even combinations written as diphthongs conform: α is pronounced very short; ε and αι as e in 'egg' (more open, when accented, as in the first e in 'there'); η, ι, υ, α, οι, υ have the sound of ea in 'eat'; o, ω as the o in 'dot'; ου as English oo in 'pool'. The combinations αυ and ευ are pronounced av and ev when followed by voiced consonants (af and ef before unvoiced consonants).

Consonants are pronounced roughly as their English equivalents with the following exceptions: β = v; γ is harder before a and o, softer before other vowels (more like the y in 'your'); γγ is usually the equivalent of ng, γκ of the English g in 'guard'; δ = th as in 'this'; θ as th in 'think'; before an i sound λ resembles the lli sound in 'million'; ξ has its full value always, as in 'ex-king'; ρ is always rolled; σ (ς) is a sibilant as in 'oasis'; τ is pronounced half-way between t and d; φ = ph or f; χ akin to the Scottish ch, a guttural h; ψ = ps as in 'lips'. The English sound b is represented in Greek by the double consonant μπ, d by ντ. All Greek words of two syllables or more have one accent which serves to show the stressed syllable. In the termination ον, the n sound tends to disappear in speech and the ν is often omitted in writing.

Use of Greek. Names, words and expressions are given in Greek where this may be a help in reading signs, etc.

Useful words and phrases

Remember that raising your voice at the end of a phrase can turn a couple of words into a question and avoid tangling with unfamiliar verbs. Asking 'to mousío?', 'the museum?' is equivalent to 'Where is the museum? Please tell me how to get there.'

General

né	yes (informal)
málista	yes (formal)
ókhi	no
endáxi	all right, okay
í-né (two syllables)	he / she / it is / they are
sas parakaló	please

Greetings etc
It is polite to use the plural (as given below) when addressing strangers.

Khérete	greetings, hello, goodbye
addío	goodbye (more informal)
kaliméra	good day
kalispéra	good evening
kaliníkhta	good night
kalós sas vríkame	well met (conventional reply to the greeting *kalós orísate*, welcome)
ti kánete?	how do you do?
pos ísthe?	how are you?
kalá efkharistó, ké sís?	well, thank you, and you?
étsi k' étsi?	so-so
yásas	literally 'your health'
sto kaló	keep well
perastiká	may it pass / may things improve (to console people in illness or distress)

Shopping

Note that is polite to greet shopkeepers, and people in general, with 'good day' or 'good evening' (see p 45).

tha íthela	I should like
póso káni aftó	how much is that?
póso ékhi	how much is it?
pió fthinó	cheaper
eínai fthinó / akrivó / oraío / áskhimo	it is inexpensive, expensive, nice, unattractive
m'arési	I like it
dhen m'arési	I don't like it
ipárkhi se állo khróma / mégethos?	do you have it in another colour / size?
megálo	large
mikró	small
pió	more
takhidhromío	post office
grammatósima	stamps

Refreshment

For menu details see Food and drink, p 37)

thélo káti na fáo	I want something to eat
thélo káti na pió	I want something to drink
ti ékhete	what have you got?
zestó	hot
krío	cold
éna katálogo	a menu
to logariasmó	the bill

Hotels

xenodhokhío	hotel
éna dhomátio	a room
monó / dhipló / dhíklino	single / double / twin
mía vradhiá / dhío vradhiés	one night / two nights

Getting around

poú eínai ... to mousío / Metró / leoforío yiá ...?,	where is ... the museum / Metró / bus for...?
póso makriá í-ne ...?	how far is ...?
pósi óra?	how long?
póte ékhi leoforío yiá ...?	when is there a bus for...?
dhexiá	right
aristerá	left
evthía	straight on
penínta / ekató / dhiakósia métra	fifty / a hundred / two hundred metres
éna khiliómetro	a kilometre
me ta pódhia	on foot

For finding ancient sites etc

yiá	to / towards
ta arkhaía	'ancient things' / antiquities
to kástro	any fortified height
tis anaskafés	excavations
to froúrio	medieval castle
tin ekklisía	the church
to monastíri	the monastery

Emergencies

voíthia	help
astinomía	police
grígora	quickly
ponáo	I'm in pain
iatrós	doctor
farmakío	chemist
nosokomío	hospital

Numbers

Éna	one	*exínta*	sixty
dhío	two	*ebdhomínta*	seventy
tría	three	*ogdhónta*	eighty
téssera	four	*enneнínta*	ninety
pénde	five		
éxi	six	*ekató*	one hundred
eptá	seven	*dhiakósia*	two hundred
okhtó	eight	*triakósia*	three hundred
enneá	nine	*tetrakósia*	four hundred
dhéka	ten	*pentakósia*	five hundred
		exakósia	six hundred
endheka	eleven	*okhtakósia*	eight hundred
dhódheka	twelve	*enneakósia*	nine hundred
dhekatría	thirteen		
dhekatéssera	fourteen	*khília*	one thousand
		dhío khiliádhes	two thousand
eíkosi,	twenty		
eíkosi éna	twenty-one	*éna ekatomírrio*	one million
triánda	thirty	*dhío ekatomírria*	two million
saránda	forty		
penínda	fifty		

Written numbers

Although Arabic numerals are normally used and always understood, an alternative system is sometimes found, usually for low numbers (to c 25). This is based on the letters of the Greek alphabet. Each symbol can stand for either the cardinal or the ordinal number, thus KA' is either 21 or 21st.

A' = 1, B' = 2, Γ' = 3, Δ' = 4, E' = 5, ΣΤ' = 6, Z' = 7, H' = 8, Θ' = 9, I' = 10, IA' = 11, IB' = 12, K' = 20, KA' = 21, KB' = 22, etc.

Additional information

Advice on visiting archaeological sites, museums and churches

Ancient remains of any significance are signposted and, except in rare instances, the sites enclosed. There are usually (but not always) admission charges, varying according to the importance of the place. Students are allowed free entry on production of an ISIC (International Student Identity Card), supported by proof of nationality of an EU member state.

At major sites, where the number of visitors in the tourist season can be a serious distraction, it is a good idea to arrive at opening time, before the coach parties.

Photography (hand cameras) is allowed on archaeological sites and in museums (no flash), with the exception of unpublished finds.

ΑΠΑΓΟΡΕΥΕΤΑΙ/Απαγορεύεται (*apagorévetai*) means 'forbidden'.

Set fees (not cheap) are charged for using tripods, etc.

Visitors' safety on sites is their own responsibility. Surfaces may be slippery, excavation trenches unfenced and heights unrailed.

Finding sites Assistance beyond that given in the text can usually be canvassed on the spot—see p 47 for phrases.

Opening hours of sites and museums vary by season and the importance of the site. A list of current opening hours of major sites and museums in Athens and elsewhere is available from the Tourist Organisation and can be found in some monthly travel guides and newspapers.

Virtually all sites and museums which charge an entrance fee now supply useful leaflets with historical information—and plan(s), where appropriate.

Normal hours are 08.30–15.00. For smaller sites/museums, it is advisable to reckon on opening hours of 08.30–14.00. The most important places may close in season as late as 20.00 (museums) and 19.00 (sites). Monday is **closing day**, but major institutions will either remain open, or open three or four hours later than on other days. Museums not belonging to the state have different arrangements.

Sites and museums are closed on 1 January, 25 March, Good Friday morning, Easter Day and Christmas Day. Hours are restricted on Christmas Eve, New Year's Eve, 2 January, 6 January, the last Saturday of Carnival, Thursday in Holy Week, Easter Tuesday.

Orthodox churches and monasteries with formal visiting hours are usually open c 08.00–12.00 and 16.00–19.00, unless they are administered as ancient monuments, in which case the hours for archaeological sites apply.

If a church is closed, enquire for the key locally: it is often kept by a neighbour. If the church is isolated, try the priest in the nearest village.

Antiquities regulations Laws are strictly enforced. Importation of antiquities and works of art is free, but these articles should be declared on entry so that they can be re-exported. Except with special permission, it is forbidden to export antiquities and works of art dated before 1830, which have been obtained in any way in Greece. If a traveller's luggage contains antiquities not covered by an export permit, the articles are liable to be confiscated, and imprisonment and prosecution may follow. It is an offence to remove any object, however seemingly insignificant, from an archaeological site.

Note that the use of metal detectors is strictly forbidden in Greece.

Diving and underwater photography are not permitted in most parts of Greece (leaflet from the NTOG) and attempts to locate, photograph or remove antiquities are strictly forbidden.

Airline offices
British Airways, Themistokléous, Glifádha, ☎ 210 353 1168, fax 210 890 6510.
Olympic Airways, Singroú 96, ☎ 210 926 7306, fax 210 926 7154; Kotopoúli 3 (Omónia Square); for telephone bookings, ☎ 210 966 6666.
Air France, Vouliagménis 18, Glifádha, ☎ 210 960 1100, fax 210 960 1457.
Lufthansa, Zirídhis 10, Maroússi, ☎ 210 617 5200, fax 210 610 8989.
Qantas, as British Airways.
Virgin Atlantic, Panórmou 70, ☎ 210 690 5300, fax 210 699 5840.
Easyjet, ☎ 210 967 0000 (best on the web at www.easyjet.com).
KLM, Vouliagménis 41, Glifádha, ☎ 210 960 5000, fax 210 964 8868.
Avro/Monarch, Kallirróis 89, ☎ 210 923 8011, 210 923 8997.

Booksellers
Athens is full of interesting and useful bookshops. The **Stoá tou Vivlíou** (p 138), off the Stoá Orféos between Panepistimíou and Stadhíou, is a pleasant arcade with numerous booksellers (and a café). There are many bookshops, including second-hand, at the lower end of Ippokrátous, near the University.

Andrómeda is an excellent specialist classics and archaeology bookshop, at Mavromikhaïli 46–50, ☎ 210 360 0825, fax 210 339 0469.
Dhodhóni, Asklipíou 3, ☎ 210 363 0312, 210 363 7973, fax 210 323 9246. Good for Greek books.
Efstathiádhis, Akadhimías 84, ☎ 210 383 7439 have books (translated into various languages) on Greek flowers, birds, cookery, etc.
Ekdhotikí Athinón, Akadhimías 34, ☎ 210 360 8911, fax 210 360 6157, specialises in archaeological and historical books, including guides, most of which are extensively illustrated and translated into English.
Eleftheroudhákis, Panepistimíou 17 (with café), ☎ 210 331 4180/3, fax 210 323 9821. A new six-storey western-style emporium, with a wide selection of Greek, English and other books. Further branches at Níkis 20 (Síntagma) and elsewhere.
Foliá tou Vivlíou (in arcade), Panepistimíou 25–29, ☎ 210 322 9560, fax 210 323 9246, has both Greek and foreign books.
Kardhamítsa, Ippokrátous 8, ☎ 210 361 5156, is good on the ancient world and has a number of guides.
Kaufmann, Stadhíou 28, also Voukourestíou 11, ☎ 210 322 2160, fax 210 323 0320. Similar to Pantelídhis (below).

Mélissa, Navarínou 10, ☎ 210 361 1692, fax 210 360 0865, is the retail outlet of a publishing house which produces beautifully illustrated books, especially on architecture and art history, many of them translated into English.
Pantelídhis, Ameríkis 9-11, ☎ 210 362 3673, 210 363 9560, 210 362 9763, fax 210 363 6453, is a well-established shop specialising in foreign books.
Papasotiríou, Stournára 35 and elsewhere, ☎ 210 332 3300, fax 210 384 8254, has some nice books on art, topography and travel.
Protoporía, Gravías 3–5, ☎ 210 380 8283, fax 210 330 2648, is good for Greek books; also publishes the Erevnités series of guides to museums.
Road Editions, Ippokrátous 39. see above p 17. Guidebooks and a good series of maps.
Vivlía yia ólous (Books for all), Aiolou 104 (1st floor), ☎ 210 321 8934, 210 325 0650, fax 210 321 4941, www.books4all.gr. Large stock; will order any book published in Greece and give you a 20 per cent discount.

The official bookshop of *TAPA*, the publications division of the Antiquities Service of the Ministry of Culture is in the stoa at Panepistimíou 57, ☎ 210 324 2840); stock includes their excellent series of site guides. Open 09.00–14.30. See also Select bibliography pp 89–90.

Crime and personal security
The crime rate in Greece is the lowest in Europe, but unfortunately is on the increase (theft particularly). Beware of pickpockets on crowded buses and trolley buses, in the flea market, and at major sites and attractions.

The easiest method of reporting crime is to contact the Tourist Police (☎ 171; 07.00–23.00) who will advise on the action to be taken. Otherwise dial 100 or contact the nearest police station.

If you intend to make a claim on your holiday insurance, you must report any loss, as soon as possible, to the police station in whose area it took place, and get a reference number and police confirmation form.

Embassies and consulates
Australian Dhimitríou Soútsou 37, Athens (**Map 7,2**), ☎ 210 645 0404, fax 210 644 3633.
Canadian Yennadhíou 41, Athens (**Map 7,5**), ☎ 210 727 3400, fax 210 727 3480.
UK Od. Ploutárkhou 1, Athens (**Map 7,5**), ☎ 210 727 2600, fax 210 727 2720, www.british-embassy.gr, email info@fco.gov.uk.
US Leofóros Vasilíssis Sofías 91, Athens (**Map 7,4**), ☎ 210 721 2951/9, 210 721 8400/1, fax 210 675 6282.

Equipment
Strong suncream, a sunhat and great care in exposure to the sun are vital, particularly in the summer. Sunglasses are useful all year round.

A pocket compass can come in handy, since many directional indications in the Guide are given by compass points. A small pair of binoculars is also highly recommended. A torch is useful. Some form of mosquito repellent may be needed: small electrical devices are available from chemists and supermarkets, or packs of combustible coils (*spirales*).

Health

A private insurance policy is advised. Although Greece has a **reciprocal arrangement** with the UK National Health Service (get form E111, from British post offices, if you wish to take advantage of this), it may involve lengthy bureaucratic procedures. If you do use it, with your E111, you will need to acquire a Health Book from your local office of **IKA** (Idhrima Koinonikón Asfalíon, Social Insurance Service: for the central IKA Office ☎ 210 522 1159—or seek advice from Tourist Police).

Hospitals (☎ 106 or 166 for duty hospitals) will treat emergency cases without question.

Most **chemists** are open Mon, Wed 08.30–14.00; Tues, Thur, Fri 08.30–13.30, 17.00–20.00. Emergency opening hours of duty chemists are displayed in pharmacy windows, listed in the press and can also be obtained by dialling 173. In smaller communities the pharmacist, if there is one, will always dispense in an emergency.

Most problems are caused by unfamiliar climate and food, or over-exposure to the sun, and precautions can be taken accordingly. Sunblocking creams should always be used in summer. Plain boiled rice is good for upset stomachs. Chemists can often advise on other medicines. Animal bites should be treated immediately.

Learned and other institutions

American School of Classical Studies, Souidhías 54, ☎ 210 723 6313/4, fax 210 725 0584.
Benakios Library, Anthímou Gázi 2, ☎/fax 210 322 7148.
British Council, 17 Kolonáki Square, with library, ☎ 210 369 2333, fax 210 363 4769.
British School at Athens, Souidhías 52, ☎ 210 721 0973, fax 210 723 6560.
College of Music (Odheíon), Vasiléos Yeoryíou 17/Vasiléos Konstantínou/ Riyíllis, ☎ 210 725 7600.
Directorate of Antiquities (Ministry of Culture), Bouboulínas 20, ☎ 210 820 1100.
Deutsches Archäologisches Institut, Fidhíou 1, ☎ 210 382 0270, 210 382 0092.
École Française d'Athènes, Dhidhótou 6, ☎ 210 361 2518, 210 361 2521.
Foreign Press Service, Zalokósta 3, ☎ 210 368 1000 (many lines).
Gennádhion Library, Souidhías 61, ☎ 210 721 0536, 210 725 8829, fax 210 723 7767.
Greek Archaeological Society, Panepistimíou (Venizélou) 20, ☎ 210 362 6042, 210 362 5531.
Hellenic-American Union (American Library), Massalías 22, ☎ 210 360 7305, 210 362 9886, fax 210 363 3174.
Institut Français d'Athènes, Sína 29, ☎ 210 326 4301-5.
Municipal Library, Odhós Kleisthénous, ☎ 210 727 3700, 210 722 9811/5.
National Gallery (Ethnikí Pinakothíki), Vasiléos Konstandínou 50, ☎ 210 721 1010, 210 723 5857.
National Library, Panepistimíou, ☎ 210 361 4413, fax 210 361 1552.
National Research Centre, Vasiléos Konstandínou 48, ☎ 210 722 981.
Parliament Library, Parliament Building, ☎ 210 322 7958.

Leisure and sport

Art galleries Private galleries are numerous, and the works shown are often interesting and of a high standard. Two of the best known are *Ora*, Xenofóntos 7 and *Zígos*, Iofóntos 33. *Athinórama* carries a full list (see also *Now in Athens*, Newspapers, pp 20, 54–55).

Theatres

Winter season (Oct–May): *Ethnikó* (National Theatre Company), Ay. Konstandínou ☎ 210 522 0585; *Olimpía* (Lirikí Skiní), Leof. Akadhimías 59, opera and ballet, ☎ 210 361 4433; *Arts* (Tékhnis), Odhós Stadhíou 44, ☎ 210 322 8706; and many others.

Summer season (June–Sept): *Athens Festival* in the Odeion of Herodes Atticus, and other outside venues, including Likavittós theatre; also in the suburbs of Khalándri and Víronos. See *Athinórama* and daily press. *Festival Booking Office*: Stoá Spiromilíou (Stadhíou 4, between Stadhíou and Panepistimíou—Síntagma end), ☎ 210 322 3111/9; Mon–Sat 08.30–14.00, Sun 10.00–13.00.

Son et lumière Lighting of the Acropolis viewed from the Pnyx (p 133), ☎ 210 322 7944. Early April – end Oct; nightly in English .

Folk dances (Dora Strátou) in the Philópappos Theatre (pp 100, 131), ☎ 210 324 4395 (day), 210 921 4650 (from 19.30). May to September.

Classical concerts The *Mégaro Mousikís*, Vasilíssis Sofías/Kokkáli ☎ 210 728 2333, www.megaro.gr, has a regular programme. Booking may be done by telephone, with a credit card, or at the box office (Mon–Fri 10.00-18.00, Sat 10.00–14.00, Sun 18.00–20.30). There is also an in-town booking office at Omírou 8, open Mon–Fri 10.00–16.00. In summer there are concerts at the *Odeion of Herodes Atticus* (Athens Festival, also opera and ballet); and recitals at *Parnassós Hall* (Od. Khr. Ladhá).

Popular music Apart from public concerts, you can hear it in nightclubs (e.g. *Apanemía*, Thólou 4, Pláka; *Esperídhes*, Thólou 6), from around 21.30. There is normally no entrance charge but to compensate drinks are expensive (c €6). Also at costly nightclubs along the coast towards Glifádha.

Rebétika The traditional music of the dispossessed (comparable in content with the American blues) is enjoying a new popularity. The last of the really famous old-timers, Sotiría Béllou, died in 1997 and the surviving establishments are mostly both expensive and very noisy. The same system of payment applies as at nightclubs, though charges are rather higher. Programmes do not begin until c 23.00 and the main singer rarely appears before half past midnight. The most genuine of these centres is the *Stoá ton Athanáton*, Sofokléous 19, ☎ 210 321 4362. Similar music can be heard from enthusiastic groups intent on recreating the genuine music, in a nightclub setting, at such centres as *Rembetikí Istoría*, Ippokrátous 181, ☎ 642 4937.

Dhimotikí Mousikí (Folk Music) *To Armenáki*, 1 Patriárkhou Ioakím, Távros (music from the islands), *Kríti*, Ay. Thomás, Ambelókipi (Cretan music). Look out for public concerts by Greece's leading singer, Dhómna Samíou.

Cinemas These are numerous and cheap, showing a good variety of Greek, European, American and other films. There are several in Stadhíou and Panepistimíou. Open-air summer cinemas are common and pleasant.

Sport
Tennis Athens Tennis Club, Leof. Olgas (members only); at EOT beaches (Alimos, Flísvos, Voúla, Vouliagméni).
Swimming (in Athens) at Hilton and Caravel Hotels (expensive).
Golf at Glifádha, ☎ 210 894 6820.
Sailing information from Sea Horse, ☎ 210 895 6733.
Horse racing at Fáliron Delta (bottom of Singroú; to move to Markópoulo before 2004), see daily papers.
Motor racing Acropolis Rally (late May) for touring cars, starts and ends in Athens; Autumn Rally in November.
Football (mostly Sunday afternoons) at the Olympic Stadium (PAO, or Panathenaïkós); Karaïskákis Stadium, Néo Fáliro (Olimpiakós); Néa Filadhélfia (AEK, or Athlitikí Enosis Konstantinoúpolis).

Olympic Games 2004
Press office, ☎ 210 200 4000.

Manners and customs
Appointment times are often elastic in Greece, and it is best to confirm whether or not a meeting arranged is an 'English rendezvous', i.e. one to be kept at the hour stated. The **siesta** hours after lunch (c 15.00–18.00, or 19.00 in summer) should not be disturbed by calling or telephoning.

Manners are quite formal and **conventions** should be observed. You shake hands at meeting and parting and always enquire 'how are you?'.

In direct contrast to English custom, personal questions showing interest in a stranger's life, politics and money are the basis of conversation in Greece, and you should not take offence at being asked directly about your movements, family, occupation, salary and politics.

Unless you are close friends—and often even then—it is usual for the bill for **a meal out** to be paid by the host; the common foreign habit of sharing out payment round the table is looked upon as mean and unconvivial.

It is not good manners to fill a wineglass, nor to drain a glass of wine poured for you. Pour it half full and keep it topped up. Glasses are often touched with the toast '*stin iyá sas*', to your health, generally shortened in speech to the familiar '*yásas*' or '*yámas*' (our health), or, to a single individual, '*yásou*'.

Payment must never be offered for any **hospitality**, but Greeks always bring presents (sweets, cakes, flowers, wine, a present for a child) when invited to another's house, and most foreigners would wish to follow suit.

When visiting a Greek home you may formally be offered preserves with coffee and water, an old tradition which is becoming less common: this should not be refused. Even the poorest people in Greece are exceptionally hospitable. It is important to remember this and not abuse the kindnesses offered.

The '**volta**', or evening stroll, universal throughout provincial Greece (often focused on the main square or the harbour), has no fixed venue in Athens, but is evident nonetheless.

Fasting in Lent is taken seriously by many people, and special foods are prepared.

National holidays and festivals

Public holidays are: New Year's Day; 6 January (Epiphany; Blessing of the Waters); Katharí Dheftéra ('Clean Monday'), the Orthodox Shrove Day at the beginning of Lent; 25 March (Independence Day); Good Friday; Easter Monday; 1 May; Ascension Day; 15 August (Assumption of the Virgin Mary); 12 October (Anniversary of Liberation in 1944; hoisting of National Flag on Acropolis); 28 October ('Okhi' Day, commemorating the Greek 'no'—OXI—to the Italian ultimatum of 1940); Christmas Day; 26 December (St Stephen).

Church and other festivals in Athens: Blessing of the Waters at **Epiphany** (6 January) in Plateía Dhexamení after procession from Ay. Dhionísios the Areopagite just to the south; Feast of **Ay. Dhionísios** (3 October).

25 March, 12 and 28 October (see above) are all marked by church services and processions.

The pre-Lenten **Carnival** reaches its climax, after three weeks of festivities, on the Sunday before Clean Monday. There are processions and student revels, particularly in Pláka.

Easter sees the procession with the *Epitáfios* (bier) on the evening of **Good Friday**; ceremonial lighting of the Paschal candle and release of doves, in front of churches at midnight preceding **Easter Sunday**—the conventional greeting is '*Khristos anésti*' (Christ is risen) and the reply '*Alíthos anésti*' (He is risen indeed). This is followed by candlelight processions and 'open house', with *mayirítsa* (see menu) served. Roasting of Paschal lambs and cracking of Easter eggs on morning of Easter Day.

Newspapers

The English-language *Athens News* and *Hellenic Times* are both published weekly on Fridays. The former is better for announcements. The *Herald Tribune* (daily) includes an English-language supplement provided by the Greek newspaper *Kathimeriní* with mainly Greek news.

Foreign newspapers are obtainable at central kiosks in Athens from around 20.00 on the day of publication (and the following day at other major tourist centres) at two to three times the normal home price.

Odyssey, a well-produced monthly magazine in English, has articles on various aspects of Greek life and culture and useful information about entertainment, restaurants and basic services in the capital.

The weekly *Athinórama* (ΑΘΗΝΟΡΑΜΑ; Thursdays, in Greek) has comprehensive information about all forms of entertainment (including gastronomic) in Athens, for those with some knowledge of Greek.

Non-orthodox churches in Athens

English, St Paul's, Odhós Filellínon 29, ☎ 210 721 4906
American, St Andrew's, Sína 66, ☎ 210 645 2583
Roman Catholic, St Denis, Panepistimíou (Venizélou) 24, ☎ 210 362 3603.

Prices

The cost of living in Greece is much closer to that of western Europe than used to be the case, but in some respects (e. g. restaurant meals, fruit and vegetables) it is substantially less. For the last few years the exchange rate has favoured most visitors. It is unclear what effect the introduction of the euro may have.

Public toilets

These are often underground, in squares and parks, and the standard is very variable. Cafés, restaurants and bars always have toilet facilities.

Shipping offices

Strintzis Lines, Amalías 48, ☎ 210 322 6400, 210 322 6800, fax 210 322 9193; *Minoïkés Grammés*, Vas. Konstandínou 2 (near Stadium), ☎ 210 746 4850, 210 752 0540.

Most are in Piraeus (p 233), including *Hellenic Mediterranean Lines* at Plateía Loudhovíkou 4, ☎ 210 422 5341, fax 210 422 5317.

Flying Dolphins Hydrofoils for Aíyina, etc. Tickets can be booked by telephone (210 419 9000) with a credit card and collected at the port, or obtained from *Minoïkés Grammés* (see above).

Shopping

Opening hours

Most shops (summer) 08.00–13.30 and 17.30–20.30 on Tues, Thur and Fri; 08.00–14.30 only, on Mon, Wed and Sat; (winter) 09.00–20.00 on Tues, Thur and Fri; 09.00–15.00 on Mon, Wed and Sat.

Supermarkets have a special status, opening Mon–Fri 08.00–21.00, Sat 08.00–18.00, closed Sun.

Chemists, see Health, p 51.

Certain shops (e.g. dry cleaners) never open in the evening or on Sat. Note that shop hours are liable to revision.

The **períptero** (kiosk), developed from a French model, is a familiar site in Greek towns and villages. Selling newspapers, reading matter, postcards, cigarettes, chocolate, toilet articles, films, postage stamps, etc, some are open for about 18 hours a day.

Undoubtedly the most lively and colourful shopping district is the market and bazaar area of Monastiráki, centred on Odhós Iféstou (p 145), by the Metró station, and Plateía Avissinías. **Note** especially the Sunday morning **flea market**. Backgammon boards, kilims, silver jewellery, ceramics, leather and copper goods, and a vast array of Greek cotton clothing are amongst the items on sale—not to mention books, pictures and 'antiques' of various kinds.

Not to be missed is the weekly **street market**, or *laikí agorá* (people's market). There is bound to be one in your neighbourhood. Ask for information, or try those in Kallidhromíou (above National Museum, Saturday), Arkhimídhous (behind Stadium, Friday) or Xenokrátous (Kolonáki, Friday). These sell mostly fruit, vegetables and flowers and the sights, smells and sounds are a real treat, even if you don't want to buy.

Off the other side of Monastiráki Square from Iféstou, Od. Pandrósou has a lot of tourist shops. Amongst the lower-quality clothing can be found some good cotton garments (*Esterel* at no 89). At no. 3 is *Stavrós Melissinós*, the poet-sandalmaker, who has been composing both verses and good-quality sandals and shoes since 1954. Adhrianoú is also a busy shopping street (another *Esterel* at no. 110) and Pláka in general can be pleasantly scoured for clothes and small souvenirs. *Níkos Birlirákis* has a sign outside his shop, down a passage at no. 4,

Plateía Mitropóleos, selling headscarves and neckchiefs, some in traditional designs. His stock is much depleted from former days, but there may be something you like and he should be encouraged!

Gánas at Mitropóleos 54 has a good selection of traditional Greek *floccati* (sheepswool rugs) and other rugs and carpets.

Better-quality mementoes can be got from the *National Welfare Organisation* at Ipatías 6, on the corner of Apóllonos near the Cathedral. The shop has a superb selection of handicrafts from all parts of Greece. Particularly good value (and easily portable) are the cushion covers, with designs borrowed from the folk tradition, and Byzantine and Hellenistic art. Not far away, the *Centre of the Hellenic Tradition* (p 39) has some good handicrafts.

Several **museums** sell books, postcards and reproductions of items in their collections. The *National Archaeological Museum* has a basement shop with cards, books, videos and a large selection of casts and reproductions: the casts are excellent but mostly expensive and hard to transport. The *Benáki* (p 221) has a splendid range but is rather expensive; the *Folk Museum* (p 171) has a small selection of reproductions, including ceramics and shadow puppets, while its sister-museum (of *Popular Greek Art*) in the Tsistaráki Mosque (p 145) has a few attractive and reasonably-priced plates. The *Goulandrís Cycladic Museum* (p 224) is another source of reproductions, including of the marble figures and vases. The little-known *Centre for the Study of Traditional Pottery* (p 172) has some fine modern pottery (including functional kitchenware) made in traditional style, as well as other items.

A short distance out of the centre, at Khariláou Trikoúpi 75, the *Anastasía Faltaïts* shop, based on a workshop on the island of Skíros, has a large selection of intriguing and imaginative small gifts, only some of which have a specifically Greek flavour.

For CDs etc the ubiquitous *Metrópolis* shops (one at Panepistimíou 54) have a good selection of Greek (and foreign) music, both contemporary and traditional, though you need to battle your way through a wall of sound. For a more traditional selection and much more pleasant surroundings, visit *Xyloúris*, in arcade at Panepistimíou 39, kept by the charming widow of the famous Cretan singer, Níkos Xyloúris.

For more down-to-earth shopping or, more likely, shop- and people-gazing, try the streets round the central meat and fish market, either side of Athinás.

Time and calendar

Greece uses Eastern European Time (2 hours ahead of GMT). Note that Greek πμ (*pm*) = English am; and Greek μμ (*mm*) = pm.

All moveable festivals are governed by the fixing of Easter according to the Orthodox calendar.

Weights and measures

A metric system of weights and measures was adopted in Greece in 1958, and is used with the terms of its French source substantially unaltered. Thus *métro* (metre), *khiliómetro* (kilometre), etc. Some liquids are measured by weight (*kiló*), not in litres. The standard unit of land measurement, the *strémma*, equals a quarter of an acre.

BACKGROUND INFORMATION

History

Prehistory

Palaeolithic remains have been found in Attica (e.g. Pikérmi, Brauron, Kítsos cave), while the slopes of the Acropolis have been occupied since the **Neolithic** period, and other Neolithic sites in Attica are known (e.g. Néa Mákri, Zágani, Kítsos cave). **Early Bronze Age** settlements (e.g. Ayios Kosmás, Tsépi Vraná) are widely spread. They had contacts with the Cyclades, a link which still existed in the **Middle Bronze Age**, when Aíyina (*Aegina*) was also an important centre.

In the **Mycenaean** period (Late Bronze Age) there was a palace on the Athenian acropolis which must, like its counterparts in other areas of Greece, have been the administrative centre of a district, perhaps Attica. This could be the source of the later tradition of a 'synoikism' (union) of the towns of Attica in the time of the legendary Theseus.

The causes of the decline of Mycenaean civilization are unclear, though it is often attributed to the so-called 'Dorian Invasions'. These may have involved the arrival in southern Greece either of foreigners, or of other Greeks from further north (cf. the Slav invasions of the 6–7C AD). At this time many Greeks migrated to new homes in or beyond the Aegean. But Attica was much less affected by these changes than other parts of Greece, and the Classical Athenian claim to be autochthonous (the original native inhabitants) may be true.

From c 1000 BC, and more especially after c 800 BC, archaeology indicates that Athens not only shared in the growing material prosperity of Greece but set the standard, for example in the production of decorated pottery. During this period the Phoenician alphabet was adopted (? late 8C) to express Greek in writing. This was probably the real historical context of the synoikism of Attica under Athens.

The Archaic period

The 7C sees increasing contacts with foreign parts (Orientalising phase), and in the 7C and 6C, like many Greek states, Athens was ruled by tyrants. In 632 BC an attempt to seize power by **Kylon** was thwarted; the archon Megakles and the whole Alkmaionid family in perpetuity were banished for allowing the murder of his associates while in sanctuary. This led to an unsuccessful war with Megara, his father-in-law's city.

At the beginning of the 6C, **Solon**, a man of noble family but sympathetic to the poorer members of the community and trusted by both, introduced sweeping social and economic reforms (see Politics in Classical Athens, p 65) and encouraged foreign commerce. He inspired the conquest of Salamis from Megara soon after 570 BC. Instrumental in this campaign was **Peisistratos**, whose triumph encouraged him to try to seize power as tyrant. Only after three attempts did he finally succeed in establishing himself when, after ten years' exile in

Thrace, he returned in 546 BC to land at Marathon and defeat his opponents at Pallene in Attica. Peisistratos was succeeded in 528 by his elder son, Hippias.

The **rule of the Peisistratids** was probably the most benign of all the Greek tyrannies. A 10 per cent tax was levied, but was used to make loans to poor farmers to extend agriculture, as well as to finance an extensive programme of public works. The water supply was improved and the fountain-house of Enneakrounos built in the Agora. The huge Temple of Olympian Zeus was begun and the Old Temple of Athena built (or rebuilt) on the Acropolis. Peisistratos encouraged the editing of an improved text of Homer for recitation at the Panathenaic Festival and the first dramas were introduced as part of the Great Dionysia. These festivals were instituted or reorganised and the Panathenaic (refounded in 566 BC) became as prestigious as the great festivals at Olympia and Delphi. **Hippias** acted as patron to the poets Anakreon and Simonides. At this time too Athenian black-figure pottery ousted its Corinthian rival in the export market and Attic sculptors were prominent.

Abroad, the Peisistratids developed a network of international alliances in the pursuit of peace and prosperity. Only in the northeast (including the islands of the northeast Aegean) were they more aggressive, holding Sigeion (against the opposition of Lesbos) as a family fiefdom on the Asiatic side of the Hellespont, and encouraging the aristocratic family of Miltiades to rule the Thracian Chersonese (the Gallipoli peninsula) on its European side. Colonies were established in the Hellespont.

Although the tyrants retained the support of the citizens through most of their reigns, the atmosphere turned sour after the assassination in 514 BC of Hippias' brother Hipparkhos by Harmodios and Aristogeiton (who later became folk heroes). Hippias' opponent Kleisthenes, head of the powerful **Alkmaionid family**, obtained the support of the Delphic Oracle and thus of the Spartans. The latter sent an army under King Kleomenes and expelled Hippias in 510 BC.

Democratic institutions were now further developed. In this process Kleisthenes was prominent (see Politics in Classical Athens, p 66).

The Persian Wars

The early years of the 5C BC were dominated by the threat from Persia. In 498 BC Aristagoras of Miletos instigated a rebellion of the Greek cities of Asia Minor against the Persian king Darius (the '**Ionian revolt**'). Only Athens and Eretria (in Euboea) answered his call for help. Twenty Athenian ships took part in the burning of Sardis in the first season of the campaign. After the defeat of the Ionians in 494, **Darius** dispatched a huge army and fleet to exact revenge. They were accompanied by the aged Hippias. Eretria was sacked. Heading for Athens, the Persian army was met at **Marathon** (August or September 490) by 9000 Athenians and 1000 Plataians, and decisively defeated by the inspired tactics of **Miltiades**.

Xerxes, Darius' successor, sent a massive force by both land and sea against Greece in 480, but Athens had used the intervening years wisely, to prepare a large and effective navy, financed by a lucky strike in the silver mines at Lávrion. Although Athens was sacked after the Persians broke the pass of **Thermopylai** in the face of heroic Spartan resistance under Leonidas, she was instrumental in the Greek naval victory at **Salamis**. The remnant of the Persian force was finally defeated at the **Battle of Plataia** in 479.

Athens emerged from the Persian Wars remarkably confident and forward-looking. She led the **Delian League** of Greek cities which united to prevent further Persian threat and to free their fellow Greeks from Persian domination. As time passed this confederation was gradually transformed into an Athenian empire over which Athens exercised firm control. At first the cities had contributed ships to a common fleet. This arrangement was later commuted to a money tribute to Athens. In 454 BC the treasury of the league was moved from Delos to the Athenian acropolis and funds were diverted to the treasury of Athena. Under Perikles (see below) the Athenians put much of the resources towards new buildings on their acropolis to replace those destroyed by the Persians.

The Age of Perikles and the Peloponnesian Wars

The middle years of the century saw the First Peloponnesian War between Athens and her empire, on the one hand, and Corinth, Aegina, Boeotia and Sparta, on the other. A period of peace from 446 came to an end in 431 BC. The great **Peloponnesian War** (431–404 BC) is presented by the historian Thucydides as the inevitable outcome of Spartan suspicion of growing Athenian power.

The most famous and influential Athenian of the years preceding the war had been **Perikles** (c 495–429 BC), who was related through his wife to Kleisthenes and belonged naturally to the democratic wing of Athenian politics of which he became the leading figure c 461. He led numerous military campaigns and encouraged the Athenians to build up their influence abroad by founding colonies. He was prime mover of the mid-5C reconstructions of buildings earlier destroyed in the Persian invasions. A remote and austere character, he seems to have been upright as well as clever and accusations of dishonesty were probably unjustified. After his death in 429 Athens was, at least in the opinion of Thucydides, led by lesser men.

In the later phase of the Peloponnesian War, an ill-fated 'Sicilian Expedition' (415–414 BC), urged on by the flamboyant democratic politician **Alkibiades** (ward of Perikles) and aimed at establishing Athenian control of Sicily, was the prelude to the disastrous defeat of the Athenian navy by the Spartan Lysander at Aigospotamoi on the Hellespont in 405. The humiliating conditions of peace forced on Athens in 404 included the destruction of her fortifications. For a brief time even democracy was eclipsed in a coup d'état of the **Thirty Tyrants**, a group of Athenian oligarchs appointed by Lysander to execute reforms and govern the city. **Thrasyboulos** restored the constitution in 403, marring its record by the execution of the great philosopher Sokrates (399).

The 5C BC saw a **flowering of Greek art and letters**. The design and decoration of the Parthenon, and the Acropolis project as a whole, were under the supervision of **Pheidias**, one of the most famous sculptors of all time. **Polygnotos** and others produced wall-paintings for the city's public buildings. Athens attracted visiting philosophers (**Zeno** of Kition, **Anaxagoras** of Miletos), orators and the historian **Herodotos**, who variously stimulated the young **Sokrates** to take up philosophy and **Thucydides** to write history. The famous names of Greek tragedy were active—**Aeschylus**, **Sophokles** and **Euripides**. Throughout the years of war **Aristophanes** (fl. 427–387) was writing comedies which reflect the concerns of the time.

The fourth century, Macedon and the Hellenistic period

Athens recovered rapidly from the Peloponnesian War. The general **Konon** won a great victory against Sparta at Knidos (on the coast of Asia Minor) in 394 BC. Assisted by Thebes, Athens re-established her naval leadership with a **Second Maritime League**, organised in 378. The 4C was the age of the philosopher **Plato** (428–347), the military historian **Xenophon** (c 430–354) and the orator Isokrates (436–338).

A new danger now appeared in the person of **Philip II**, king of the rising power of Macedon in northern Greece. He conquered the northern cities of Amphipolis (357) and Potidaia (356), and Methone in 353. Spurred on by the oratory of **Demosthenes** (383–322), Athens took up the role of champion of Greek liberty, but was finally defeated at the Battle of Khaironaia in 338.

Alexander the Great inherited the throne of Macedon from his father Philip and created a vast Hellenistic territorial empire stretching as far as India. As a subject city he treated Athens favourably. His Macedonian tutor, the philosopher **Aristotle**, taught in the Athenian Lyceum. An unsuccessful Athenian bid for independence on Alexander's death (323 BC) led to the imposition by the usurper Kassander of a collaborating governor, **Demetrios of Phaleron** (318–307). A brief liberation by Demetrios Poliorketes, claimant to the Macedonian throne, was followed by alternating freedom and subjection to Macedonia. After defeat in the Chremonidean War (266–263), Athens endured a Macedonian garrison until 229, although her democratic institutions were respected. Supremacy in science had now passed to Alexandria, but Athens was still the centre of philosophical teaching. The dramatist **Menander** (342–291) was the leading exponent of New Comedy.

The Romans

Perseus, king of Macedon 179–168 BC, was first enemy then ally of the Romans. Losing confidence in him, the Romans declared war in 171 and were finally victorious at Pydna (near modern Kateríni in Macedonia) in 168 BC. Under Roman rule Athens continued to flourish, retaining many privileges when the Roman province of Akhaia was formed out of southern Greece after 146 BC.

Athens joined the expanding empire of **Mithridates** (king of Pontus in Asia Minor), opposed to Rome. In 86 BC the city was captured by the Roman general **Sulla**, who razed the fortifications, looted treasures and curtailed its privileges. Nevertheless, the city later received a free pardon from **Julius Caesar** for siding with Pompey, and from Antony and Augustus after supporting Brutus, who removed there after the murder of Caesar on the Ides of March 44 BC. Athens continued to be the fashionable seat of learning in the ancient world, attracting the sons of rich Romans, including **Cicero** and **Horace**.

In AD 54 **St Paul** preached 'in the midst of Mars' hill' (Acts xvii 22). The emperor **Hadrian** (reigned AD 117–38), under whom the historian **Plutarch** was procurator (imperial agent) of Akhaia, frequently lived in the city and adorned it with imperial buildings. His example was followed by **Herodes Atticus** (p 278) in the time of the Antonine emperors, when the city was visited by **Pausanias** (p 85), who wrote a detailed and accurate account of his travels in Greece and the things he saw and was told. Athens remained the centre of Greek education until an Edict of the emperor Justinian in AD 529 closed the pagan schools of philosophy.

Early Christian, Byzantine and Medieval history

The **Early Christian** period can be reckoned to begin either with the birth of Christ or in AD 330, when the emperor Constantine moved his capital from Rome to the Greek city of Byzantium, renaming it Constantinople. The Empire divided into Eastern and Western branches in 395. Under Constantine, Christianity became accepted in the Roman empire and it is from this point that the older architectural forms and artistic media begin to be adapted to suit Christian rites and beliefs. The term **Byzantine** is often applied to the Eastern empire after the reforms of Heraclius in AD 629.

The Agora of Athens was destroyed by the **Goths** (Heruls) in AD 267. The Gothic king Alaric's capture of the city in 396 seems to have caused less damage to its monuments. In the reign of **Justinian** (527–65), or earlier, many temples were consecrated to Christian use and modified. Athens was sacked c 580 by **Slavs**. Under the **Byzantine Empire** it dwindled to an unimportant small town. The emperor Constans II wintered in the city in 662 on his way to Sicily, and Theodore of Tarsus studied here before becoming Archbishop of Canterbury (669–90). Basil II, the Bulgar-slayer, celebrated his victories of 1018 in the Parthenon.

After the fall of Constantinople to **Frankish Crusaders** in 1204, the Greek provinces north of the Isthmus of Corinth were controlled by Boniface III, Marquis of Montferrat, with the title of King of Thessalonica. Boniface granted Attica and Boeotia to Otho de la Roche, a Burgundian knight, with the title of Grand Seigneur of Athens and Thebes. A century of peaceful and prosperous Frankish rule improved the lives but not the influence of the Athenians. Trading privileges were granted to **Genoese and Venetian merchants**. The English chronicler, the widely travelled Matthew Paris of St Albans (c 1199–1259), records a visit to Athens by Master John of Basingstoke (d. 1252) as a student. In 1258 Guy I de la Roche accepted the title of Duke from King Louis of France; the magnificence of the Athenian court of this period is noted by the Catalan chronicler Ramon Muntaner, who himself served in the Catalan Grand Company. On the death of Guy II in 1308, the duchy passed to his cousin Walter de Brienne. Walter's designs on Byzantine territories joined the rulers of Constantinople, Neopatras (at modern Ipáti, near Lamía) and Epirus in league against him. He called to his aid the **Catalan Grand Company**, an unreliable mercenary force originally formed in Sicily and subsequently active in Asia Minor, in theory at least, on behalf of the Byzantines. Later unable to get rid of them, Walter precipitated the disastrous battle of Kopaïs (in Boeotia), where in 1311 the Catalans totally destroyed the power and nobility of Frankish Greece.

Athens and Thebes were now controlled by the Grand Company, who elected Roger Deslau, one of the two noble survivors of Duke Walter's army, as their head. After pursuing a career of conquest in north Greece, they approached Frederick of Aragon, king of Sicily, in 1326, with the result that his second son Manfred became duke and for 60 years the Duchy of Athens and Neopatras (as it was now styled) was misgoverned from Sicily by avaricious General Commissioners. In 1386 the Siculo-Catalans fell foul of Nerio Acciaioli, governor of Corinth, a member of that family which was 'plebian in Florence, potent in Naples, and sovereign in Greece' (Gibbon). Nerio seized Athens, Thebes and Levadia, and in 1394 received the title of Duke from Ladislas, king of Naples. Captured by a band of Navarrese troops, he bought his ransom by rifling all the churches in the lands under his control. In the late 14C Albanian settlers were moved into Attica and other parts of Greece to counteract rural depopulation and, in some cases, as mercenaries.

Ottomans and Venetians

Under Nerio's son Antony, Athens, protected by Venice, enjoyed 40 years' peace, but Antony's weak cousin and successor Nerio II (1435–51) held his duchy as a vassal of the **Ottoman Sultan**. During his reign Athens was twice visited by Ciriaco de' Pizzicoli (better known as **Cyriac of Ancona**), a merchant, antiquary and emissary. The illustrated diaries of his extensive travels and discoveries, which have partly survived, if rarely in their original form, give unique insights into lost monuments. **Demetrios Chalkondyles** (1424–1511), the Renaissance scholar who published the *editio princeps* of Homer, was an Athenian. When Nerio's widow and Pietro Almerio, the Venetian governor of Nauplia and her new husband, seized the dukedom, the Athenians complained to the Sultan, who replaced Almerio by Franco Acciaioli, a nephew of Nerio. Franco banished his aunt, the ex-duchess, to Megara and had her murdered there, whereupon Pietro complained to the Porte (Ottoman government). Sultan Mehmed II ordered Omer, son of Turahan (an important Ottoman commander), to seize the Acropolis, and annexed Attica to the Ottoman Empire in 1456.

Nearly 400 years of **Turkish rule** followed, a peculiar result of which was the rehabilitation of the **Orthodox Church**, so long dispossessed by Rome. Athens was visited in 1672 by Père Babin, a French Capuchin, who drew the earliest extant plan, and in 1675 by Francis Vernon, who sent back to the Royal Society the first English account of the city. The same year Lord Winchilsea, then ambassador to the Porte, acquired some architectural fragments. In 1676 came Jacques Spon and George Wheler (p 116). In 1687 the Acropolis was besieged by the Venetians under Francesco Morosini, and the Parthenon was shattered. From then until 1821, the condition of Athens under the Turks is picturesquely described by Gibbon, who accuses the Athenians of his day of 'walking with supine indifference among the glorious ruins of antiquity'. The worst period of tyranny was under the governor Hadji Ali Haseki in 1775–95. After the appearance of *Antiquities of Athens* (1762–), **travellers to Athens** became more numerous. The volumes, funded by the Society of Dilettanti, were compiled by the Scot James Stuart (1713–88) and the Englishman Nicholas Revett (1720–1804), both painters, architects and draughtsmen. They visited Athens together between 1751 and 1755 and produced elegant and accurate drawings of the monuments, which were highly influential on western neoclassical architecture.

The War of Independence and modern Greece

In 1821, soon after the outbreak in Patras (in the Peloponnese) of the War of Independence, the Greek general Odysseus seized Athens and the Acropolis. In 1826–27 the Acropolis, besieged by Reshid Pasha, was bravely defended by the *klepht* (irregular soldier) Gouras and, after his death, by the French general Fabvier, but the city was devastated in street fighting. Vain attempts to raise the siege were made by General George Karaïskakis and, after his death in 1827, by Admiral Cochrane and General Sir Richard Church. On 27 May 1827, the

Acropolis was taken by the Turks and held until 12 April 1833. In 1834 Athens became the capital of liberated Greece. A hereditary monarchy was imposed on Greece by the mediating powers (Great Britain, France and Russia), and **Otho**, son of Ludwig I of Bavaria, became the first king. Many aspects of the new state, both organisational and physical (its architecture for example), were influenced by ideas and officials from Otho's homeland. The remainder of the 19C and early 20C saw the dominance of the 'Great Idea' (uniting of all Greeks in a new state with its capital at Constantinople), the gradual enlargement of Greece's territory with the decline of the Ottoman Empire, and uneasy relationships between conservative and liberal forces which impeded the development of a settled system of government.

The World Wars and after

During the First World War the city was occupied by British and French troops after some opposition by Royalist elements of the pro-German government, following which Eleftherios Venizelos was reinstated as prime minister. In 1923 the population was hugely swollen by the exchange of Greek and Turkish nationals after the Greek defeat in and expulsion from Asia Minor, which saw the end of the 'Great Idea'.

Greece joined the Allies in the Second World War. On 27 April 1941, German forces entered the capital unopposed after a campaign lasting three weeks, and Athens remained in their hands until October 1944, her people suffering great deprivation. In December 1944 (the events are referred to as 'tá Dhekemvrianá') open Communist revolution broke out in the Thisío area after a demonstration had been fired on by police earlier the same morning in Síntagma Square. After bitter street fighting British troops, with reinforcements, landed at Fáliro and eventually restored order. At a conference called by Churchill on Christmas Day an armistice was arranged whereby Archbishop Dhamaskinos became regent.

The recovery of Athens, and the whole of Greece, was retarded by the Civil War, between strongly polarised pro- and anti-Communist interests, and complicated by Greece's isolated position as the only non-Communist state in the Balkans, which did not end until 1950.

A military junta, established by coup d'état on 21 April 1967, was finally brought down in July 1974. Konstandinos Karamanlis, a leading politician in voluntary exile, returned to streets thronged with cheering crowds, to lead an interim government. Student demonstrations the previous year, centred on the Polytechnic and brutally ended by the police, had crystallised opposition, but the crucial factor was the deposition by the junta of Archbishop Makarios, president of Cyprus. This precipitated a Turkish invasion and subsequent occupation of the north of the island, an event which caused enormous human misery and has bedevilled relations between Greece and Turkey ever since.

The re-establishment of democratic government was soon followed by a referendum on the future of the monarchy as a result of which Greece became a republic. The years since 1974 have seen regular changes of government in free elections. In 1981 the PASOK party formed Greece's first socialist government. In the same year the country joined the EEC and her orientation was fixed firmly in the direction of western Europe. The liberalisation of the political system and the return of Greek families which had gone into exile behind the iron curtain during the civil war have both contributed to greater social cohesion.

Greece's increasing economic prosperity is undoubted although not universally shared. But the long-standing problems with Turkey, especially over the Cyprus issue, and the present instability of neighbouring Balkan countries, leave her with complex political problems.

Politics in Classical Athens

Classical Athens is known for the **democracy** which flourished in the 5C and 4C BC, but that system took centuries to evolve. Its development is described in detail by Aristotle in the *Constitution of Athens*, written in 320 BC.

Early Athens and the reforms of Solon
The Athenians believed that they, and other city states, had once been ruled by a monarchy (perhaps down to the 11C BC). Whatever the truth of this, by the 7C BC Athens was governed by an aristocracy. The three organs of government were: an **Assembly** (*Ekklesia*) of adult male citizens; the **Council of the Areopagos**, an advisory council of ex-magistrates; and the magistrates in office. By the late 7C there were nine of these executive magistrates, or **archons**, elected annually; originally there had been only three. Both the archonship and membership of the Council are believed to have been monopolised by the nobility (Eupatrids).

By the late 7C rule by aristocracy was under threat. In several neighbouring states (Corinth, Megara, Sikyon) aristocracies had been replaced by popular dictatorships, known as **tyrannies**. Although Kylon did not succeed in making himself tyrant of Athens in c 632 BC (see History, p 58), popular Athenian discontent forced the aristocracy to publish the laws for the first time in 621 BC. This was the **law code of Draco**, which later became a byword for its 'Draconian' severity. Meanwhile serious economic problems were driving Athens towards crisis. We know of the plight of the Hektemoroi, a depressed class of poor farmers, paying rent in kind to their richer neighbours or creditors. Mortgages proliferated and many people were enslaved for debt.

Violent revolution was prevented by the election of **Solon** as principal archon in 594 BC, with a mandate to procure the necessary reforms and to codify Athenian law in full. His sweeping measures included the cancellation of debts and removal of mortgages; a ban on the future enslavement of debtors; and the promotion of olive cultivation so that high-quality oil could be exported in exchange for corn to feed the poor. In politics, Solon replaced birth with wealth as the qualification for office. The citizens were now divided into four classes on the basis of wealth. The archons were chosen from the top two of these. Solon removed the right to draw up the Assembly's agenda from the Areopagos council and gave it to a new **Council of 400**, whose members were selected by lot. Other important democratic measures were (a) the creation of a **Court of Appeal**, in which juries of several hundred ordinary citizens could overturn the verdict of a magistrate in a court of the first instance; and (b) empowering citizens to prosecute a magistrate for misdemeanours at the end of his period of office.

Solon's concern for justice shines through his poetry (he was the first known Athenian author) and he was later remembered as a founding figure in Athenian democracy. But his compromise solutions could not contain the social and political conflicts of the succeeding generation. In 560 BC Athens came under the rule of the 'tyrant' Peisistratos.

The tyranny and the reforms of Kleisthenes

In the 560s Attica was deeply divided by the struggles of three rival political factions, the 'Plain', the 'Coast' and the 'Hill'. These most likely represented respectively the rich plains close to Athens itself, the southeastern part of Attica with sea on both sides, and the northeastern area round Marathon and Brauron (literally 'over the hills' as viewed from Athens). **Peisistratos**, the political leader who dominated the 'Hill' faction, combined personal charm with a high degree of political astuteness. Appealing beyond his own regional power-base to the poor in Attica as a whole, he seized power twice, and twice lost it, finally building up many alliances abroad during a ten-year period of exile. In 546 BC he secured his position.

Democracy established

After some unrest following the end of tyranny in 510 BC (see History, p 59), Kleisthenes trumped his rivals in the bid for popular favour by introducing an important series of reforms in 508–507 BC. Up to this time the Athenians, like other Greeks in the Ionian cities, had belonged by birth to one of four age-old 'tribes'. Kleisthenes sidelined these by introducing ten new tribes based upon place of residence. These were made the basis of the army and of representation in a new **Council of 500** (the *Boule*) which replaced Solon's Council of 400. The interest of the new **tribes** (*phylae*) is that each contained a cross-section of the citizens, since each had three parts (*trittyes*, or Thirds) located respectively in the city area (*asty*), the coastal area (*paralia*) and the inland parts of Attica (*mesogaia/mesogeion*). Each *trittys* contained a number of **demes** (villages or wards). These originally numbered 139, later more. Each deme had a deme assembly and deme magistrate, and each was represented in the Council of 500 at Athens by councillors selected by lot (50 from each tribe), serving for a year only at a time, up to a total of two years. The importance of this was that the Council, which performed a vital role in deliberating in advance of the Assembly and in advising it, now consisted of citizens drawn evenly from Attica as a whole;

Ostracism

Kleisthenes introduced the safety-valve of ostracism as a final safeguard against ambitious politicians who might destabilise the system. Each year the Athenians had the chance to remove one of their number from Attica. The citizens assembled in the Agora, each having written on a piece of broken pottery (*ostrakon*) the name of a fellow-citizen: provided that there was a quorum of 6000 votes, the 'winner' went into exile for ten years. There are numerous surviving *ostraka* in the Agora and Kerameikós museums.

yet the use of lot and the restricted tenure of office ensured that the Council could not build up any dangerous professional expertise which might lead it to dominate the Assembly of all citizens which had the final and authoritative voice in political decisions.

The fifth century BC: refinements to democracy

The framework which Kleisthenes had instituted was extended with increasing confidence during the 5C. In 487 BC, lot was first used as part of the election process for archons and in 457 the archonship was opened to the third class of citizens. In 461 the ancient Council of the Areopagos lost its residual political influence (becoming a homicide court) and about the same time, or earlier, large jury-courts became normal courts of first instance rather than mere courts of appeal. A major innovation in the mid-century was the introduction of pay for jurymen, members of the Council and magistrates. This allowed even the poorest Athenians to serve in these capacities, as well as attending the all-important Assembly which met in the open air on the Pnyx, roughly every nine days. The most important political leaders were now the ten generals (one from each tribe) who commanded the army, and figured prominently as speakers and advisers in the Assembly. But here too it is striking how Athenian democracy reserved power for the ordinary citizen: the Assembly was given the formal opportunity ten times a year to dismiss any of its magistrates, and the generals were expected to acquiesce when the Assembly ignored their advice and instructed them to carry out policies of which they did not approve. Under this system the Athenians defeated Persian invasions and built up an empire.

Topography

This summary should be read alongside the description of Athens as seen from the top of Likavittós (p 217), the best overall view of Athenian topography.

Prehistoric Athens

In the Neolithic and Early Bronze Age, small groups of settlers lived within reach of the Acropolis fortress. The Mycenaean royal city was also focused on the Acropolis, where a 'Cyclopean' wall—called by later writers the Pelargikon, or Pelasgikon—enclosed the palace complex, with an outer extension mainly on the west. Other evidence of occupation has been found to the south, as far as the River Ilissós. There were chamber tombs of the same period on the north and west slopes of the Areopagos hill, and in the area which later became the Agora.

Evidence from graves of the Sub-Mycenaean and Proto-Geometric periods (c 1075–c 900 BC) shows a gradual spread of occupation towards the northwest, where the Kerameikós became the main necropolis.

The Archaic city

It is not certain whether or not the palace of the Peisistratids was located on the Acropolis but it is clear that, during the 6C, the hill was converted to exclusively religious use and the population resided entirely in the lower city. The Pnyx and Mouseion hills were already occupied by houses in the 6C, when the Agora was (p 93) evidently northeast of the Acropolis, but even before the Peisistratids the popular Kerameikós quarter (the term includes the area of the later Agora) was becoming a centre of Athenian life and, from the time of Solon, it was the meeting-place of the Assembly, the site of the Altar of the Twelve Gods and the offices of the archons. There was probably a city wall at this time (it is mentioned in an ancient source) but no archaeological evidence of the structure has ever been found.

Classical Athens

The Acropolis and much of the lower town were destroyed by the Persians in 480 BC. After the Battle of Plataia (479), the statesman Themistokles, who had begun to fortify Piraeus as early as 493, began a city wall on a course which lasted till the time of Hadrian. Thucydides records its hasty erection with whatever material was at hand, a report confirmed by archaeological discoveries. The walled circuit defines the heart of the city, but the major gymnasia and several important shrines were outside it.

Since Athens grew piecemeal over a long period, no overall plan of the kind adopted in Piraeus was possible there, and the narrow crooked streets remained. Kimon finished the walled circuit; and the two Long Walls, connecting Athens with Piraeus, were completed under Perikles. Of the 15 city gates located, the names of ten are known but not certainly identified. In the 440s the master builder Kallikrates completed the Phaleric Wall (p 220).

Many of the great monumental buildings of ancient Athens dated from the third quarter of the 5C when Perikles' plans to replace the buildings destroyed by the Persians on the Acropolis and elsewhere came to fruition. The Academy, embellished by Kimon, became a favourite Athenian promenade. In 404 the walls were demolished at the Spartan command, and the Long Walls never rose again. Konon rebuilt the enceinte in 393, according to Xenophon, and Lykourgos (338–326), a leading Athenian statesman, completed, rebuilt or embellished much of the city, modifying the Pnyx for the Assembly's use. The walls were shortened about this time by the erection of the Diateichisma (a new *Cross-wall* on the Mouseion and Pnyx), and the city flourished with gradual modifications until the Roman sack of 86 BC.

Roman imperial Athens

It is not certain whether Hadrian extended the walled circuit, but Hadrianoupolis, to which the Arch of Hadrian gave access, was certainly an extension of the older town to the east, beyond the line of the Themistoklean wall. Here were gymnasia, thermae (baths) and other standard manifestations of Roman rule. Under Augustus a new market had been built east of the Agora; Hadrian added a huge library in the same area. He also built a reservoir on Lykabettos, fed by a new aqueduct bringing water from Mt Parnes. A generation or so later Herodes Atticus founded his Odeion and re-seated the decaying Stadium in marble. In the middle of the 3C AD the city wall was rebuilt and

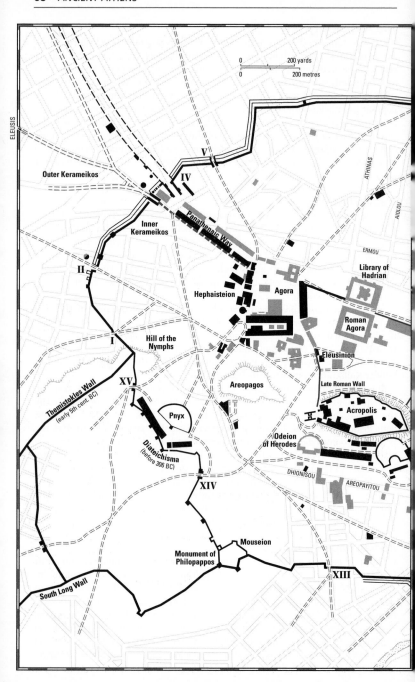

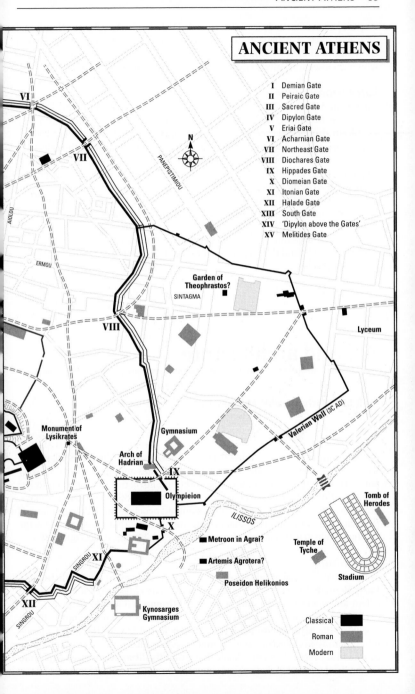

ANCIENT ATHENS

I Demian Gate
II Peiraic Gate
III Sacred Gate
IV Dipylon Gate
V Eriai Gate
VI Acharnian Gate
VII Northeast Gate
VIII Diochares Gate
IX Hippades Gate
X Diomeian Gate
XI Itonian Gate
XII Halade Gate
XIII South Gate
XIV 'Dipylon above the Gates'
XV Melitides Gate

PANEPISTIMOU

AIOLOU

ERMOU

Garden of
Theophrastos?
SINTAGMA

Lyceum

Monument of
Lysikrates

Gymnasium

Arch of
Hadrian

Valerian Wall (3C AD)

Olympieion

ILISSOS

Tomb of
Herodes

Metroon in Agrai?

Temple of
Tyche

Artemis Agrotera?

SINGROU

Poseidon Helikonios

Stadium

Kynosarges
Gymnasium

SINGROU

Classical
Roman
Modern

extended somewhat to the east (the so-called Valerian Wall). After the Heruls had destroyed most of Athens in 267, the Athenians lost confidence in the Roman army and withdrew behind the Late Roman (or post-Herulian) Wall (p 220), which enclosed a relatively small area on the north slope of the Acropolis.

Later topography
Christian Athens remained clustered round the Acropolis, round whose lower slopes the Rizókastro wall was later built in the 11C (?). After 1204, the **Frankish dukes** had their palace in the Propylaia. The **Ottomans** fortified the south slope of the Acropolis; their wall called Serpentzes turned the Odeion of Herodes Atticus into a redoubt. The later Turkish town was lightly walled by Hadji Ali Haseki in 1778–80, its northern line based on the ruins of the ancient circuit.

Modern Athens owes its basic inner plan to the Bavarian architects of King Otho. The core of this plan is a huge triangle, pointing north, with Ermoú as its base and Piraiós and Stadhíou its sides. The larger triangle is divided into two equal halves by Athinás. Omónia is at the apex, Síntagma at the eastern point.

The largely unplanned suburban development is due to the massive influx of refugees in 1923 and the extensive migration of people from country districts in more recent years.

Art and architecture

by R.L.N. Barber and K.M. Skawran

(Note: *NAM* = National Archaeological Museum)

Most visitors to Athens are attracted by the monuments of her Classical past, of which ample remains survive on archaeological sites and in museums. The city and surrounding area also have important and attractive Byzantine churches and collections. Greek folk art is represented by some excellent museum displays. From the 19C and 20C Athens has outstanding neoclassical buildings, many of them newly restored, and the later architecture is not without interest. Today the city has a rich artistic life, with many galleries, exhibitions, concerts and plays.

Beginnings
The earliest archaeological discoveries in Athens go back to the **Neolithic** and **Early Bronze Age** phases (c 6000–c 2200 BC, *Agora Museum*) but are limited in extent and interest. In the time of the first **Minoan palaces** in Crete (c 2200–c 1700 BC), the Greek mainland was still a cultural backwater, but with the advent of the **Mycenaean period** (c 1550 BC)—the time of Homer's heroes—monumental architecture and a much richer material culture appear in continental Greece. The remarkable finds from the **Shaft Graves at Mycenae** (in the Peloponnese) include objects imported from Crete and elsewhere and are

the first major witness to the wealth of Mycenaean society; they can be seen in the *NAM* in Athens. The beehive-shaped **tholos tombs** in the Athens suburb of Menídhi, at Marathon and at Thorikós are examples of the Mycenaean architectural achievement. Parts of the massive **fortifications** of the time can still be seen on the Acropolis, though nothing now survives of the palace which once stood there. In spite of the destruction of the Mycenaean palaces, possibly as the result of internal conflicts, about 1200 BC, Mycenaean civilisation continued to flourish (finds from Peratí, *Brauron Museum*) until a terminal decline set in c 1100 BC. Greece then entered a **Dark Age** of depopulation and material decline, for which the main evidence is pottery and finds from cemeteries (**Sub-Mycenaean** and **Proto-Geometric**, *Kerameikós Museum*).

Although the Proto-Geometric period (c 1025–c 900 BC) shows clear artistic revival in more precise pottery forms and decoration, as well as in some other aspects of material culture, it is convenient to set the end of the Dark Ages in a historical sense at about 800 BC (the **Late Geometric period**). There are now more substantial and widespread signs of recovery and development, such as numerous dedications and the building of some temples in major sanctuaries, and the (re)invention of writing. From this point the history of Greek material culture can be discussed in terms of its principal forms of expression.

Ancient Greek pottery

Pottery (see also pp 209–213) is frequently used by archaeologists purely as a tool for dating, but in Greece much of it is of greater interest for its aesthetic qualities and/or iconography.

Each stage (Early, Middle, Late) of the **Geometric period** (c 900–c 725 BC) has its own distinctive features, but in general Geometric pottery is characterised by precision of shape and decoration and care in suiting the motifs to the structure and form of the vessel. In the best examples a visual harmony is created, unsurpassed in the history of vase-painting. In the Late Geometric period scenes with figures, themselves geometricised, became more popular. Some of them may represent incidents from the poems of Homer, which were particularly influential at this time. The larger vases are enormous and were used as grave markers, a function which is reflected in the scenes of funerary ritual with which they are often decorated (*NAM, Kerameikós Museum*).

Towards 725 BC the orderliness of the Geometric style began to break down under the influence of new motifs and stylistic features derived from the East Mediterranean. The so-called **Orientalising phase** (c 725–c 625 BC) is symbolic of the newly expansionist stage of Greek cultural development. Most Athenian Orientalising vases (the local style is called **Proto-Attic**) are decorated with large figured scenes, often with animals or exotic creatures (sirens, etc). Athenian vase painters used an outline technique with painted interior detail, while Corinthian artists (**Proto-Corinthian**) quickly developed the black-figure method. In this the figure is painted in black silhouette, sometimes with other colours added on top, and the details are incised. Corinthian vases, often very small and with a correspondingly precise miniaturist style of decoration, dominated the market at this period and were frequently exported to other Greek states (including Athens) and abroad.

Towards 600 BC (**Archaic period**) Athenian artists adopted the Corinthian black-figure technique but used it for their own large-scale narrative scenes—

subjects drawn from the Trojan War or other mythological cycles (e.g. the Labours of Herakles). In the hands of its masters (Exekias, the Amasis Painter 550–530 BC; *NAM*), the **Attic black-figure** style is notable for a magnificent stately elegance and exquisite detail.

From c 530 this technique was gradually superseded by that of **red-figure** in which the background was painted black and the figures left reserved in the natural colour of the clay, the interior detail being painted in with a brush of goat's hair. Although less imposing than black-figure the new technique allowed a more natural representation of figures and encouraged the depiction of many scenes from everyday life (athletics, parties, etc) in addition to those of traditional mythology. Some 5C red-figure vases show the influence of contemporary wall painting (e.g. in the use of variable ground-lines, ill suited to vase painting) of which nothing else has survived. Towards 400 BC the style became more florid and ornate (added white paint, gilding) and the subject matter often rather trivial (boudoir scenes). During the 4C vase painting virtually died out in Athens, though it continued to flourish in the Greek colonies of the west (southern Italy, Sicily).

A striking and attractive group of 5C Athenian vases (*NAM*) which does not fall into any of the above categories, is decorated in a **white-ground** technique. This was particularly applied to the tall *lekythos* shape, used especially for funerary rituals and often decorated with appropriate scenes (offerings at the tomb). The ground of the vase is coated white, the figures and other elements drawn in outline and broad washes of colour applied for hair, garments, etc.

In the **Hellenistic period** (c 330–c 50 BC) decorated pottery is usually made in moulds with ornament in relief (Megarian bowls, *Agora Museum*).

Ancient Greek sculpture

Sculpture was made in large and small scale, in the round and in relief, and in a range of materials (stone, terracotta, metal, even wood—though little of the latter has survived). Until the end of the Classical period most sculpture served religious functions and it was only in Hellenistic times that the erection of statues of famous mortals became common practice.

Archaic Down to c 650 BC all surviving figures are small, though there may have been larger pieces in wood which have not survived. They are usually offerings from sanctuaries. Human figures may represent the deity to whom they were dedicated or be symbolic worshippers; animals probably indicate the desire of the donor to provide the deity with a valuable gift.

After c 650 BC comes the development of **monumental** stone (then bronze) sculpture, the most familiar **Archaic** types being the male *kouros* (*NAM*) and the female *kore* (*Acropolis Museum*). The forms are relatively static over a long period (to c 480 BC): the kouros is naked and usually standing rigidly, one foot advanced, the hands by the sides; the kore also stands upright, but is often holding out an offering (fruit, or a small animal or bird), sometimes clutching her garment and pulling it tight over the legs. The artistic interest of the naked kouros is concentrated on the anatomy; that of the kore in the careful treatment of the drapery, frequently with added colour. Formal patterning of both anatomy and drapery gradually gives way to greater naturalism, though the development is unlikely to have been as regular as is often implied.

These figures had a limited range of **functions**. Some were cult statues, for example the Piraeus kouros (*Piraeus Museum*), one of very few bronzes to have survived. More often they were offerings in sanctuaries where they may have acted as symbolic servants or worshippers. Many stood in cemeteries as grave markers. Some of the male figures are gigantic (Sounion kouros, *NAM*).

Classical By the early 5C, some figures (Kritian Boy, *Acropolis Museum*) show a much more naturalistic pose and treatment of hair and musculature. The earliest phase of Classical sculpture, often termed the **Severe Style**, is represented by the ambitious but slightly awkward bronze Poseidon (or Zeus) in the *NAM*. The spectacular achievements which quickly followed can be exemplified by the figures from the **Parthenon** pediments (*Acropolis Museum*; *British Museum, London*; casts in *Centre for Acropolis Studies*) where complex poses, realistic anatomy and spectacular drapery effects are achieved at will. Particularly striking drapery effects are seen in the Nike Balustrade (c 400 BC; *Acropolis Museum*). Yet Classical sculptors made little effort to show feeling through facial expression, and the features of the figures remain calm and idealised, in whatever action they are engaged (copy of Diadoumenos of Polykleitos, *NAM*).

Hellenistic Some features of Hellenistic sculpture have their roots in developments of the 4C, such as a greater expression of feeling and physical character. But Hellenistic sculptors were the first to make full-blown efforts at emotional realism, including portraiture, and to show a willingness to tackle non-idealised everyday subjects (Horse and jockey, *NAM*; bronze portrait from Delos, *NAM*). The diversity of Hellenistic work includes many pieces directly derivative from the Classical tradition, though the subjects can be rather frivolous and fussy (Pan and Aphrodite, *NAM*) or else presented with a baroque extravagance (Lykosoura figures by Damophon, *NAM*).

Archaic kore—the 'Peplos kore'. From the Acropolis.

Roman The work of Roman sculptors is at first largely derived from Hellenistic prototypes (though note also the reliefs in the Greek Archaic style in the *Piraeus Museum*) and in general served roughly the same purposes. But the forms and style were strongly influenced by certain functions unfamiliar to the Greeks—for imperial propaganda (statues of emperors in military dress and official portraits) and for funerary ritual (commemorative figures). Although these led at times to a deliberate harking back to Greek style, at others they resulted in a harsh realism ('verism') in the depiction of individuals, of which there is little sign in earlier Classical art. As well as using traditional technical approaches sculptors explored the effects to be achieved through deep cutting with the drill, polished surfaces and contrasts between the two.

In the Late Roman period certain stylistic features—frontality, simplification, unnatural proportions—anticipate aspects of Byzantine art.

Relief sculpture Most of the works so far mentioned have been in the round. Relief sculpture follows the same general course as far as stylistic development is concerned but some examples and formats are worthy of particular mention. Greek temples were often decorated with sculpture (see Ancient Greek architecture, pp 76–77). The Acropolis Museum contains a fine series of early **pedimental sculptures** showing experiments, not only in the representation of form, but also in solving the difficult problem of filling the triangular field in a satisfactory way. The Archaic three-bodied monster is colourful, its fishy tail filling the declining height of the pediment; the Introduction of Herakles is static and highly Archaic; the Athena and fallen giants of the late 5C Gigantomachy is much more compositionally successful. The frieze and metopes of the Parthenon (*Acropolis Museum; British Museum, London*) show the mature Classical style in other formats. The peaks and edges of pediments were often decorated with freestanding sculptures (*acroteria*), such as the Nike (*Victory*) from the Stoa of Zeus (*Agora Museum* colonnade).

Much of the relief sculpture to be seen in Athens is in the form of **grave stelai** (i.e. tombstones; *Kerameikós Museum, NAM*) and **votive or record reliefs** (*NAM, Brauron Museum, Eleusis Museum*). Archaic stones are tall, narrow and have one (or two) figures only. Later stones are lower and broader and can accommodate more figures. They are often topped by ornate finials. The depth of relief is very low in the Archaic period but can be so deep in the 4C that the figures are virtually in the round. Later examples were often contained in a temple-like frame. The most familiar motif on Classical gravestones is of the dead bidding farewell to the living with a handshake. Record reliefs commemorated (and sanctified) treaties between states and other formal agreements. Votive reliefs were set up in sanctuaries as offerings to deities and often depict the deities themselves (Apollo, Artemis and Leto, *Brauron Museum*) or scenes of ritual (sacrifices to Asklepios, *NAM*; sacrifices to Artemis, *Brauron Museum*). Asklepios is sometimes depicted in the act of healing (*Piraeus Museum*).

Ancient Greek architecture

Athens and Attica have some excellent examples of Classical buildings. The most complete are the Hephaisteion (Theseion) on the edge of the Agora, the temples and Propylaia on the Acropolis and the stoa at Brauron. The Hellenistic Stoa of Attalos in the Agora has been completely rebuilt.

The two main orders (styles) of Greek architecture (see overleaf) are the **Doric** (baseless columns, two-part capitals, plain architrave, metope and triglyph frieze) and **Ionic** (moulded column bases, volute capitals, three-stepped architrave, continuous frieze, also frequent use of subsidiary mouldings). The **Corinthian** order, which was particularly popular in the Roman period, is essentially the same as Ionic, though the capital is formed of acanthus leaves. Other variations are less important.

The most common form of the mature Classical **Temple** (e.g. the Hephaisteion in the Athenian Agora) was rectangular with a surrounding *pteron* (colonnade) of six columns on the front and 13 on the sides (the corner columns are counted each time). Earlier temples tended to be longer and narrower. The interior (the complete building unit, within the colonnade, is called the *sekos*) consisted of a porch (*pronaos*), *cella* (the main room where the cult statue stood, the position of the base being often still visible) and a back room (*opisthodomos*), which balanced the porch in the plan but did not communicate with the cella. There are, however, numerous variations in plan and proportions.

Sculptured decoration was applied in differing degrees—to some or all of the metopes of Doric buildings, to the frieze of Ionic ones and in the pediments of both. In addition there were often acroteria (see above).

Of the Acropolis temples, the **Parthenon** (Doric) is large (8 x 17 columns) and has an unusual Ionic-type continuous frieze, peculiarly set within the colonnade; the temple of **Athena Nike** (Ionic) is minute, has only one room and no external colonnade, columns only at the front and rear (prostyle) and a sculptured frieze; the **Erechtheíon** (Ionic) is a most unusual shape, but its style is clearly Ionic and a continuous sculptured frieze of white marble figures on a background of darker stone united the disparate elements of the structure. The construction of the Parthenon was carried out with the aid of numerous sophisticated technical refinements (e.g. a barely visible convexity of the floor, reflected also in the entablature; minute inward inclination of the columns) which helped to produce a subtle visual effect.

Most of the buildings of which substantial remains survive are temples but the **Propylaia** to the Acropolis is an example of a (very elaborate) entrance system, which may also have incorporated a ritual dining-room. Although its façades were Doric, use was made of Ionic columns in the interior and elaborate ceiling decoration (coffers).

The **Stoa** was a common building unit in both city and sanctuary architecture. In its simplest form a plain rectangular structure with a frontal colonnade (earliest form of the Royal Stoa, *Agora*), it sometimes had wings (later form of Royal Stoa, Stoa of Zeus, *Agora*). There might be a second, internal row of columns and rooms at the back. The stoa in the Sanctuary of Artemis at Brauron was shaped in the form of the Greek letter Π and had ritual dining-rooms behind. The Hellenistic Stoa of Attalos (*Agora*) was two-storeyed and had Doric and Ionic, as well as Pergamene features. Its restored state allows you to experience the stately atmosphere of this grand building and appreciate the relief given by the shaded colonnade from the summer heat.

There are several **Theatres** in Athens and Attica. Built theatres developed gradually, often in locations originally chosen because their natural features supplied the basic requirements. These were a sloping hillside on which the audience could sit and flat ground below where the chorus could dance and sing and (later) the actors perform. The **Greek theatre** was composed of three basic elements—the auditorium (*cavea*), the circular choral area (*orchestra*) and the stage building (*skene*). Open passages (*parodoi*) between the auditorium and the stage provided access for spectators. In the **Hellenistic and Roman theatre** the orchestra became semicircular and the stage structure was linked to the auditorium to form a single building unit. In larger theatres the cavea was divided horizontally by passageways (*diazomata*) and vertically by stairways into wedge-shaped blocks of seats (*cunei*).

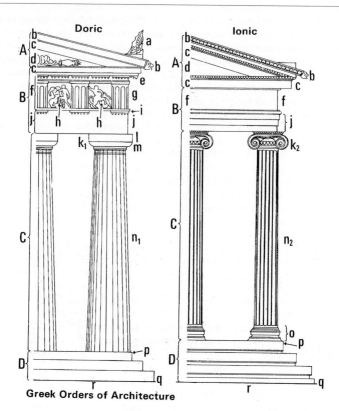

Greek Orders of Architecture

A. Pediment
B. Entablature
C. Column
D. Crepidoma (the whole of the stepped platform)
a. Acroterion
b. Sima (gutter)
c. Geison (cornice)
d. Tympanum (the triangular wall enclosed by cornices)
e. Mutules (projecting slabs) & guttae (round projections) - below horizontal cornice
f. Frieze
g. Triglyphs
h. Metopes

i. Regulae (projecting slabs) & guttae - below frieze
j. Architrave (or epistyle)
k₁ Capital (Doric)

k₂ Capital (Ionic) with volutes
l. Abacus
m. Echinus
n₁ Shaft with flutes separated by sharp arrises
n₂ Shaft with flutes separated by blunt fillets
o. Base
p. Stylobate (top step of crepidoma on which columns and building rest)
q. Euthynteria (bottom step of crepidoma, immediately above stereobate)
r. Stereobate (foundations below crepidoma)

Corinthian Capital

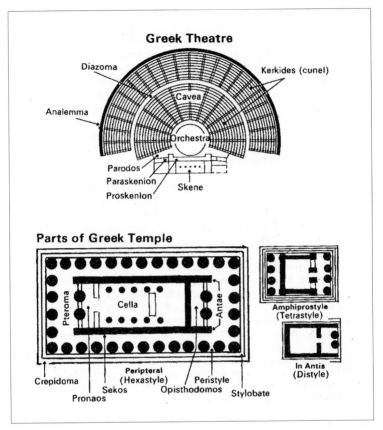

Greek Theatre

Diazoma

Kerkides (cunei)

Analemma

Cavea

Orchestra

Parodos

Paraskenion

Proskenion

Skene

Parts of Greek Temple

Pteroma

Cella

Antae

Amphiprostyle
(Tetrastyle)

In Antis
(Distyle)

Crepidoma

Peripteral
(Hexastyle)

Sekos

Pronaos

Peristyle

Opisthodomos

Stylobate

In the earliest Greek theatres there was no raised stage. The backdrop to the action was simply a building (skene) in which the actors changed and on which scenery could be mounted. Later a raised stage platform (*proskenion*) was introduced, projecting from the front of the building at first-floor level. The side projections of this, which formed the outer sides of the *parodoi* and had steps up to the main *proskenion*, are the *paraskenia*.

In Roman times, the backdrop to the stage (*scaenae frons*) became extremely high and elaborate and was extensively decorated with statuary.

Less common building types are the **Telesterion** (Ritual Hall) at Eleusis and the **Tholos** and **Prison** in the Agora. Although many **Roman buildings** used monumental masonry similar to earlier Greek, a distinctively Roman technique can be recognised at many sites where there are remains of this period (Baths in the Olympieion). An interior mass of concreted rubble is faced with courses of thin brick. The strength and flexibility of this type of masonry allowed much more ambitious architectural forms than had been possible with the traditional post-and-lintel system. The bath buildings with their high vaulted ceilings are a case in point.

Greek mythology in sculpture and vase-painting

Although ancient Greek artists gradually became more interested in depicting scenes of everyday life and although there is a strain of portraiture from the Classical period, the subject matter of art was much more often mythological in content. This is almost always true of the sculptural decoration of buildings.

The rich and varied mythology of Greece not only provided colourful and exciting narrative but was a source of moral teaching, and also used to transmit symbolic messages. For instance, in the battle of the mythological Centaurs and Lapiths (p 118), the uncivilised Centaurs could stand for the heathen Persians defeated by the civilised 5C Greeks. After democracy replaced tyranny as the style of government in Athens at the end of the 6C BC, the hero Theseus was promoted as its new symbol (replacing Herakles who was especially associated with the Peisistratids).

Stories connected with the 12 Olympian gods, each with his or her own colourful biography, are frequently depicted (e.g. Athena springing fully armed from the head of Zeus, on the Parthenon pediment), as are the exploits of heroes such as Herakles and Theseus. The figures are recognised by their attributes (distinctive items of clothing, or accessories—e.g. the winged sandals of Hermes or Perseus, the club and lionskin of Herakles) or by the contexts in which they are shown (Theseus decapitating the Minotaur).

Of the infinite fund of characters and stories, two groups can be chosen as illustrations: the **Trojan War** and the exploits of Herakles. Greek legend tells of the war fought against the city of Troy (in the northwest of Asia Minor). The prime cause was the abduction of Helen, daughter of Menelaus, king of Sparta, by Paris, son of the Trojan king Priam. A great expedition was assembled under the leadership of Agamemnon, king of Mycenae. Forced to offer for sacrifice his daughter Iphigeneia (see Brauron, p 256) to secure favourable winds for the voyage to Troy, he set sail with the Greek armada. The vicissitudes of the war, which lasted ten years and involved famous heroes (Achilles, Ajax, Hector, etc), are described in Homer's epic poem, the *Iliad*, written down in the 8C BC but depending on much earlier oral sources. A second epic poem, the *Odyssey*, recounts the exploits of the Greek hero Odysseus whose return from Troy was delayed by adverse winds and numerous exotic adventures.

Herakles was a hero, not a god, who came from Tiryns in the northeast Peloponnese and had famous strength and courage. He was forced by King Eurystheus of Argos to perform 12 fearsome tasks (the 'Labours'), all of which were at various times depicted in Greek art. One of the most common is his struggle with the lion which had been terrorising the people of Nemea. In his other labours, he is regularly shown wearing the skin of the conquered lion—as well as carrying a club, another hallmark. His protectress Athena is often standing by, lending her support.

Early Christian and Byzantine architecture and art

Christian art in Athens and its surroundings developed from the 5C AD. The empress Eudokia, wife of Theodosius II (408–50), was an Athenian and saw to it that many buildings destroyed by the barbarians (e.g. Hadrian's Library) were restored.

By the middle of the 5C Christianity was established. This was a period of great building activity in which churches were erected and temples, like the Parthenon, converted into churches. Fragments of 12C frescoes from the Panayia Athiniotissa can still be seen today on either side of the entrance to the Parthenon (from the 10C to 12C the church served as the Mitropolis, or Cathedral, of Athens). The Asklepieion was transformed into the church of Ayy. Anaryiri, while the Hephaisteion later became the monastery of Ay. Yeoryios. Fresco fragments assigned to the 11C have survived from it, as well as an inscription.

Churches

Early Christian Typical of the early period are the large three-aisled wood-roofed **basilicas**, long halls based on a Roman building type. Near the Temple of Olympian Zeus in Athens are the sparse remains of two three-aisled basilicas; the foundations of another are situated nearby, close to the Kolimvitírio (swimming-pool) bus stop on Leofóros Ardhittoú. This latter, the Basilica of the Ilissos, was lavishly decorated and fragments of its beautiful mosaic floor can be seen in the Byzantine Museum. Basilican ground plans can be better appreciated on sites at Glifádha and near Brauron.

Variants of the basilican type, often small in scale, can be found throughout Attica; domed basilicas were also common.

Byzantine Not much has survived from the 7C–9C, a period often referred to as the Dark Ages. Attacked from the north and south, the Greek population suffered also pestilence and earthquakes. Crete was conquered by the Arabs in 823, while Athens lost its geographical importance. Thebes became the administrative and economic centre of Greece. Between 726 and 843 the Byzantine empire was further torn by the bitter conflict over the cult of icons (the Iconoclast Controversy). Figural imagery was banned and much existing church decoration was destroyed.

Under the Macedonian dynasty (867–1056) the situation improved. In 961 Crete was freed from the Arabs and in 1018 Basil II reconquered the Balkans from the Bulgars. The record of church building during the 9C attests the progress of ecclesiastical rehabilitation to which the final restoration of the use of icons had given new impetus.

From the 10C to the 12C a number of well-known bishops, like Michael Choniates (in Athens between 1182 and 1204), contributed significantly to the flowering of art in Athens. From early travellers' accounts we know that Athens and its surrounding area boasted some 300 churches. Many of these were destroyed in fighting during the War of Independence, or demolished after 1832, when the city expanded and archaeologists excavated numerous sites in Athens in their search for antiquities.

By the 9C the **domed-inscribed-cross** church plan (see Dhafní, p 263), typical of the Middle Byzantine period, had been established. Within a square hall, usually of modest size, the small central bay is covered by a dome carried on four piers or, ideally, columns. From its sides extend four barrel vaults which form the arms of the cross. The (lower) bays which fill the corners of the square are roofed by vaults (or small domes). The whole is preceded by a *narthex* or vestibule on the west, and screened on the east from the sanctuary. This was tripartite, consisting of the central *bema* with the altar, flanked by the *prothesis* (north) and the *diaconicon* (south). The sanctuary screen originally consisted of a stone *templon*, with waist-high panels (*thorakia*) but open above. The later *iconostasis* (lit. 'icon stand'), usually wooden and often carved and painted, had a solid upper zone which carried icons.

From the second half of the 10C builders made use of the **cloisonné** technique in which individual squared stones were enclosed with tile-like bricks in both horizontal and vertical joints. This kind of masonry was usually found in the upper courses of the façade, in the dome and around the windows. It frequently formed simple geometric patterning and pseudo-Cufic ornamentation (derived from a decorative form of Arabic script).

Although the form of the domed-inscribed-cross church remained remarkably constant, minor variations of the type can be found in and around Athens.

The oldest of the Athenian churches based on the inscribed cross plan is **Ayy. Apostoli** (c 1000) below the Acropolis. Built over a nymphaion of the 2C BC, it is characterised by four large and four half-domes, which create a feeling of lightness and spaciousness in the interior. The skilful application of the cloisonné technique on the façade attests the sophistication of the builders.

The monastery of **Sotíra Likodhímou** (the present Russian Church), built before 1030 AD, is of the large dome type better known from the **Monastery of Dhafní** (c 1080). The dome here covers the whole span of the square *naos* (body of the church), the corners of which are bridged by squinches to form the octagonal base of the large dome.

The **Kapnikarea** (c 1050) is characterised by harmonious and elegant proportions. These are particularly evident on the eastern front, where the cloisonné style is effectively used to break the verticality and flatness of the façade.

The church of **Ayy. Theodhori** in the centre of Athens (c 1070) is of heavier proportions. Its exterior decoration includes terracotta slabs with pseudo-Cufic ornamentation.

Belonging to the 12C is the **Gorgoepikoös** church (the Little Mitropolis or Ay. Eleftherios) which is best known for its sculptural ornamentation and plastic simplicity. Here the tile articulation of the façade has been replaced by marble slabs with a variety of relief images.

The once famous **Monastery of Kaisariani** on Mt Imittós has a large unadorned façade and a tall, narrow dome supported by four columns. This type of groundplan is widely represented in Attica (the monasteries of Asteri and St John Kinigos on Imittós and the Omorfi Ekklisia).

Decoration

One of the major developments following the overthrow of the Iconoclasts was the establishment of a standard programme for the distribution of religious images in church decoration.

No complete cycle of frescoes or mosaics has survived, but the mosaics in the Monastery of Dhafní are an indication of church decoration at the height of the Middle Byzantine period.

The most sacred areas—the dome and higher vaults and the sanctuary—were reserved for the holiest personages. The bust of Christ **Pantokrator** was the most favoured image for the summit of the dome. His presence formed the centre, formally and spiritually, around which the rest of the images in the church were arranged in a strictly hierarchical manner. He is accompanied in the zone below by a **Celestial Host**, while the **Prophets** feature between the windows of the drum and the **Evangelists** commonly in the pendentives (at Dhafní scenes from Christ's life are represented here). The narthex usually had its own heavenly zone.

Almost invariably the conch of the apse was reserved for the **Virgin**, either enthroned with the Child on her lap (Dhafní) or standing with the child on her arm, or alone with arms upraised.

The **Communion of the Apostles** was usually depicted on the wall below the conch of the apse, with the **bishops** of the church shown in the lowest register of the apse wall. **Deacons** appeared just outside the sanctuary. The **Ascension** normally fills the bema vault, while the rest of the scenes of Christ's life—usually limited to 12 major episodes of the Festival Cycle (**Dodekaorto**)—were depicted on the vaults and upper surfaces of the walls.

Subordinate cycles of Christ's Passion, the infancy of Christ, Christ's miracles, the life of the Virgin or a favoured saint, were sometimes added to the decorative programme of the church.

Holy physicians were regularly admitted to the sanctuary, while holy monks, female martyrs and canonised emperors were commonly relegated to the narthex. Sacred warriors and martyrs figured in the nave in relatively high positions where such were available, while half-figures and busts of saints in medallions decorated the undersides of arches. This hierarchical system of images had to be suitably adjusted for the basilican type of church (Sicily). No such examples have survived in Athens or its vicinity.

Icons

Although the term can be used of images in any size or medium, it is most often applied to painted wooden panels of various sizes. These form part of the furniture of every church, many homes and all museums with Byzantine collections. The subjects of the decoration are sacred personages of all kinds, either on their own or as participants in events, usually drawn from the New or Old Testament.

Properly, icons are devotional aids, not themselves the objects of worship, though not infrequently they are regarded as having magical powers. Stories of miraculous discovery are common. The earliest surviving icons are of the 10C and they are still made today. As in fresco painting some image types are standardised (the Virgin Odegetria, Brephokratousa, etc) and some individuals (Ayios Nikolaos, Ayios Pandeleimon) can be recognised from their features, independently of the contexts in which they are depicted.

In churches the major icons are permanently set on the iconostasis or displayed on stands in the body of the church. The arrangement of icons on the iconostasis is more or less standard—Christ immediately to the right of the central door with, beyond him, Ayios Ioannis Prodhromos (John the Baptist); to the left is the Virgin, then the patron saint of the church. The icon(s) on display in the body of the church may relate to the current feast day or to the patron.

Sculpture and other arts

Stone sculpture was less prominent in the Byzantine than in the Classical world and, in any case, its survival rate has been poorer. The most commonly found sculptures are in the form of decoration applied to parts of church interiors, such as column capitals or pulpit panels. The subjects are mainly geometric patterns, symbolic motifs (the cross), vegetation, occasional birds or animals. The natural forms are stylised, and the compositions frequently have an elegant and appealing simplicity entirely suited to their context.

Figures in the round are very rare but there are occasional relief scenes, some of them from sarcophagi which continued to be used for burials into the 7C or 8C. At first pagan imagery (Herakles, *Byzantine Museum*) may be employed alongside Christian but pagan motifs are more popular when they suit Christian symbolism (the Good Shepherd).

Devotional plaques and metal vases or panels may be decorated with figured scenes, and ecclesiastical jewellery is ornate. Silks and vestments may also carry figures. The best known type of Byzantine pottery, with simple incised scenes (not normally religious) and a greenish-yellow glaze on the visible surface has the same kind of direct appeal as the sculpture.

The Byzantine and Benáki museums are the most important for Byzantine antiquities—with pottery, metalwork, church plate and furniture, in addition to icons, wall-paintings and sculpture. (Note also the *Kanellopoulos Museum*.)

Post-Byzantine and Modern art and architecture

Before Independence

The term Post-Byzantine signifies that stage of art and architecture which, although closely adhering to the Byzantine tradition, postdates the destruction of Constantinople by the Turks in 1453 and predates the liberation of Greece from Ottoman rule in the early 19C. Many of the smaller **churches** in the Attic countryside were built and painted in this period, older buildings were sometimes repainted. Some individual painters are known: in Attica the work of G. Markou of Argos is particularly prominent.

The period discussed here encompasses both Frankish and Ottoman intervention in Greece. Although the country as a whole has many fine examples of Frankish (especially castles) architecture, it is not well represented in the area of Athens. The time of **Frankish** domination here (c 1204–1460) is chiefly marked by the remains of **towers**. One such on the Acropolis was demolished in 1874, though it can be seen in earlier illustrations; another at Eleusis met a similar fate (1960). There is a good surviving example on the road from Markópoulo to Brauron and others at Kaisarianí and Oinóë (Marathon). The Cistercian cloister at Dhafní is a rare piece of original ecclesiastical architecture of this period, although many earlier buildings (the Parthenon, Erechtheion and Theseion) were re-used as churches at the time.

From the **Ottoman** period (1460–1830) Athens preserves the **Tsisdharaki Mosque** at Monastiráki and, nearby in Pláka, the Fetihe mosque, the Medresse gateway and a fine bath-house (the **Loutró Aéridhon**). Frankish and Ottoman **material culture** is not well represented in museums, but there is some material in the Benáki and Agora museums.

Neoclassical architecture and architects

From the establishment of the Greek monarchy in 1833, the dominant style of public architecture was neoclassical, promoted by a series of outstanding architects attached to the Bavarian court. Some exceptionally fine buildings of the 19C and early 20C can be seen throughout Athens (see descriptions of Odd. Panepistimíou, Stadhíou), many of them recently restored. Their architectural features are often directly inspired by the Classical, but some also make use of Byzantine (Eye Hospital) and other forms. Details of ancient architecture (column types, antefixes, sculptural motifs) were copied, but used in combinations often quite different from the original. From public buildings their use was transferred, albeit to a much lesser extent, to private villas and other buildings.

Leading architects A number of names will crop up frequently in this Guide in descriptions of the streets of Athens. Some biographical details are given below.

The Hansen brothers were Danish. **Christian Hansen** (1803–83) came to Athens in 1833. He taught architecture in Athens and helped in the rebuilding of the Temple of Athena Nike on the Acropolis. His neoclassical designs included the University. He subsequently left Greece for Austria and eventually died there. **Theophilos Hansen** (1813–91) arrived in Athens in 1839 and taught architecture and drawing, eventually becoming Professor of Architecture. He designed the Academy and shared in work on the National Library, as well as numerous other projects. In 1843, when foreign staff were dismissed from their teaching posts in Athens, he left Greece for Vienna.

Born in Thessaloniki, **Lísandros Kaftanzóglou** (1811–85) studied in France and Italy and was widely honoured in Europe. From 1844 he worked in Greece and was the first director of the Polytechnic. A devoted adherent of the neoclassical style, he was responsible for many public buildings, both in Athens and other parts of the country.

Stamátis Kleánthis (1802–62) came from the area of Kozáni in Macedonia. He was a member of the Sacred Brigade at Dragashan in 1821. He adopted the name of the ancient philosopher because they shared a need to support themselves. Having studied in Berlin and subsequently won various prizes for architecture, he came to Greece in 1828 and was involved in the first attempts at creating a new town plan for Athens. His designs included the Villa Ilissia (now the Byzantine Museum) and the Palace of Rhodhodháfnis at Pendéli, both for the Duchesse de Plaisance (Plakentía)—p 249.

Edward Schaubert (1804–68) was a German from Breslau. He came to Greece in 1828 and was later appointed state engineer by Kapodhístria. A friend of Kleánthis, he collaborated with him on the original town plan of Athens. He worked on the plans of Piraeus, Megara, etc, and contributed to other projects.

The last major German architect was **Ernst Ziller** (1837–1923), from Dresden, who subsequently adopted Greek nationality. Having worked for Theophilos Hansen in Vienna, he came with him to Athens. He accompanied Schliemann to Troy and conducted excavations of his own in Athens. From 1872 he was Professor of Architecture at the Polytechnic. His numerous designs, which included the house of Schliemann, favoured Renaissance features.

Public and apartment buildings of the early to mid-20C show that the influence of Classicism, although less evident in details, is retained in the rhythm. Modernist architecture makes its appearance between the wars, especially for blocks of flats. There are occasional examples of period styles, as in the Art Deco Rex cinema.

The Folk tradition; Contemporary art

The **Folk Culture** of Greece has attracted increasing interest in recent years and there are excellent collections in Athens (*Museum of Greek Folk Art; Benaki Museum, City of Athens Centre for Folk Art and Tradition, Museum of Costume*) which are of particular interest for their attractive textiles, **embroideries** and garments demonstrating different regional traditions. Woodwork, metalwork, etc. are also represented.

For **contemporary art**, in which Athens is rich, see the section on art galleries (p 52) and the entries on the Ethnikó Mouseío Sígkhronis Tékhnis, the Frisíras Museum and the Pierídhis Gallery (Glifádha) in the main text. The Ethnikí Pinakothikí has some work of later 20C artists.

Primary sources for ancient history

The most accessible translations of ancient texts are in the Penguin Classics and Loeb series; the latter have parallel Greek/Latin and English.

Herodotos (c 500–c 425 BC). The 'father of history'. Born in Halikarnassos (a Greek city of Asia Minor); widely travelled in the Greek world. Wrote a discursive history (in nine books) of the Great War with Persia.

Thucydides (c 460–c 400 BC). Athenian soldier and writer. Produced a history of the Peloponnesian War in eight books. Highly regarded as more scientific and objective than most ancient historians.

Xenophon (428/7–c 354 BC). An Athenian, who fought with other Greeks in the campaigns of Cyrus against Artaxerxes of Persia. Wrote about this expedition (*Anabasis*) and (*Hellenica*) about Greek history after the period covered by Thucydides.

Polybius (c 200–c 118 BC). Born at Megalopolis (southern Greece). Captured and deported to Rome after the Battle of Pydna. Witnessed the destruction of Carthage. Contributed to the administration of Greece after 146. Wrote a universal history in 40 books of which about one-eighth survives. Important for the early relations of Rome with Greece.

Plutarch (L. Mestrius Ploutarkhos; c AD 50–c 120). From Khaironaia in Boeotia (central Greece). Lived for a time in Rome. A prolific writer, his series of *Lives of famous men* contains much of historical interest.

Pausanias (c AD 150). A Greek from Asia Minor. Wrote a *Description of Greece* in ten books (Book 1 includes Athens and Attica). This contains highly informative discussions of ancient sites, buildings and works of art, with numerous digressions into mythology, history, etc.

Arrian (Flavius Arrianus) (c 2C AD). From Bithynia (Asia Minor). Wrote a history (the *Anabasis*) of Alexander, also of his successors, though little of the latter has survived.

Other sources which provide useful historical and archaeological information are the Attic comic playwright **Aristophanes** (c 457–c 385), the philosopher; **Aristotle** (384–322 BC), born at Stagira in Thrace and later a pupil of Plato in Athens, whose *Constitution of Athens* explains the political structure of Athenian democracy (its bodies can be related to the buildings which housed them in the Agora); **Demosthenes** (384–322 BC), the Athenian orator; and the geographer **Strabo** (64/63 BC–AD 21+), a Greek from Pontus, who visited Rome and Egypt and wrote a discursive *Geography* of the world in 17 books: this includes much material on Greece and Italy.

Inscriptions   In antiquity many important records (decrees, treaties, financial accounts, holders of office, etc) were inscribed on stone. The study of these plays an important part in the reconstruction of ancient history. The Epigraphical Museum in Athens (p 213) has an informative and well-organized collection; see also B.F. Cook, *Greek inscriptions*, 1987 (British Museum).

Select bibliography

Athens—ancient and modern

K. Andrews, *Athens*, Methuen (Cities of the World Series), London, 1967. Not easy to obtain but one of the best books ever written about Greece: a sensitive and finely written appreciation of Athens and its people.

K. Andrews, *Athens alive*, Hermes, Athens, 1979. Excerpts from writers about Athens between AD 7 and 1940.

John M. Camp, *The archaeology of Athens*, Yale University Press, New Haven, 2001.

M. Chatzidakis, *Byzantine Athens*, Pekhlivanidhis, Athens, n.d. Short and useful but hard to find.

W.W. Davenport et al., *Athens*, Time-Life Books, Netherlands, 1978. Good pictures.

Osbert Lancaster, *Classical landscape with figures*, John Murray, London, 1947 and reprints.

M. Mackenzie, *Turkish Athens*, Ithaca Press, Reading, 1992. Useful on a badly documented period.

A. Mikhalópoulos, *The museums of Athens*, Erevnités, Athens, 2001 (Vol. 1 of series *The museums of Greece*). Includes Attica.

L. Mikhelí, *Unknown Athens*, Dromena, Athens, 1990. Also other works on Athens, Monastiráki, Pláka, Piraeus.

Pausanias (tr. P. Levi), *Guide to Greece* Vol. 1, Penguin, Harmondsworth, 1971. Note also a very fine five-volume Modern Greek edition of this work, published in Athens by Ekdotike Athenon. Vol. 1 has numerous illustrations of sites and monuments in Athens and Attica.

D. Sicilianos, *Old and new Athens*, Putnam, London, 1960. Contains much interesting information.

J. Travlos, *Pictorial dictionary of ancient Athens*, Präger, New York, 1971.
R.E. Wycherley, *The stones of Athens*, Princeton University Press, Princeton, 1978. A readable account of the archaeology of the ancient city.

Greek Ministry of Culture, *Athens from the end of the ancient era to Greek independence*, Athens, 1985. Greek and English parallel text with illustrations.
Greek Ministry of Culture, *Historical map of Athens*, Athens, 1985. Useful.

Those with some knowledge of modern Greek may find interesting a two-volume work on the street names of Athens, which is extremely useful as a biographical and historical dictionary: Μ. Βουγιούκα, Β. Μεγαρίδης, Οδωνυμικά, Demos of Athens, Athens, 1997 (3rd edn). Available from bookshop of the Cultural Centre in Panepistimíou.

Attica

Robin Barber, *A guide to rural Attika*, 1999. Privately published, in traditional Blue Guide style. From author (robin_bar@hotmail.com), Hellenic Bookservice or Oxbow.
C. Bouras et al., *Churches of Attica*, Athens, 1970. Good on the small churches of the region.
H.R. Goette, *Athens, Attica and the Megarid: an archaeological guide*, Routledge, London, 2001. A detailed archaeological guide, with many site and building plans.
L.D. Loukopoulou, *Attika*, National Bank of Greece, Athens, 1973. Old but still useful.
J. Travlos, *Bildlexicon zur Topographie des antiken Attika*, Wasmuth, Tübingen, 1988.

Guidebooks to individual sites are mentioned in the main text.

Many useful articles (some with English summaries) on topics not covered elsewhere can be found in the proceedings of a series of conferences on the culture of southeastern Attika—Επιστημονική Συνάντηση Νοτιοανατολικής Αττικής Α' etc, various places, 1985–.

Prehistory

Sinclair Hood, *The arts in prehistoric Greece*, Pelican History of Art, Harmondsworth, 1978.
Peter Warren, *The Aegean civilizations*, Phaidon, Oxford, 1989 (2nd edn).

History

A.R. Burn, *A traveller's history of Greece: the Pelican history of Greece*, Penguin, Harmondsworth, 13th rev. edn, 1982.
J. Campbell and P. Sherrard, *A history of modern Greece*, Cambridge University Press, Cambridge, 1968.
R. Clogg, *A concise history of Greece*, Cambridge University Press, Cambridge, 1992.
P. Lock, *The Franks in the Aegean*, Longman, London, 1995.
W. Miller, *The Latins in the Levant*, J. Murray, London, 1908.

Early travellers
Pausanias (see p 85).
R. Stoneman (ed.), *A literary companion to travel in Greece*, Penguin, Harmondsworth, 1984.
F.M. Tsingákou, *The rediscovery of Greece: travellers and painters of the Romantic era*, Thames and Hudson, London, 1981.

Art, architecture and archaeology
E. Bastea, *The creation of modern Athens: planning and myth*, Cambridge University Press, Cambridge, 2000.
Ch. Christou, *The National Gallery: 19th and 20th century Greek painting*, Ekdotike Athenon, Athens, 1992. See also Ethnikí Pinakothíki entry (p 229).
Commercial Bank of Greece, *Neoclassical buildings in Greece*, Athens, 1967 and reprint.
P. Hetherington, *Byzantine and Medieval Greece*, John Murray, London, 1991.
R. Krautheimer, *Early Christian and Byzantine architecture*, Pelican History of Art, Yale University Press, New Haven, 4th edn, 1986.
A.W. Lawrence (5th edn, revised by R.A. Tomlinson), *Greek architecture*, Pelican History of Art, Yale University Press, New Haven, 1996.
D. Philippides (ed.), *Urban housing of the '30s: modern architecture in pre-war Athens*, Nereus, Athens, 1998.
C.M. Robertson, *A shorter history of Greek art*, Cambridge University Press, Cambridge, 1981.
L. Rodley, *Byzantine art and architecture: an introduction*, Cambridge University Press, Cambridge, 1994.
F. Sear, *Roman architecture*, Batsford, London, 1982.
D.E. Strong, *Roman art*, Pelican History of Art, Yale University Press, rev. edn., 1988.
D. Talbot Rice, *Art of the Byzantine era*, Thames and Hudson, London, 1963.
L. Welters, *Women's traditional costume in Attica, Greece*, Peloponnesian Folklore Foundation, Nafplio, c 1986.

The most comprehensive book on modern Greek architecture is only available in Greek: Δ. Φιλιππίδης, Νεοελληνική Αρχιτεκτονική, Melissa, Athens, 1984.

British School at Athens/Society for the Promotion of Hellenic Studies, *Archaeological Reports*. An annual, and somewhat technical, survey of recent discoveries in Greece and its ancient colonies. The best source of up-to-date information. Enquiries to the Secretary, Hellenic Society, Senate House, Malet St, London WC1H 7HU, ☎ 020 7862 8730, fax 020 7862 8731.

Social anthropology
R. Hirschon, *Heirs of the Greek catastrophe: the social life of Asia Minor refugees in Piraeus*, Oxford University Press, Oxford, 1989. An erudite and moving book.

Flora and fauna
T. Akriotis and G. Handrinos, *Birds of Greece*, Helm, London, 1997.
A. Huxley and W. Taylor, *Flowers of Greece and the Aegean*, Chatto and Windus, London, 1977.

Food and drink

Miles Lambert-Gocs, *The wines of Greece*, Faber, London, 1990.

Kh. Paradhíssi, *The best book of Greek cookery*, Efstathiádhis, Athens, 1977.

Maps

For Athens street plans, and maps, see Practical information p 17.

Classical texts in translation; mythology

For the extensive *Penguin Classics* and *Loeb* series of translations, see pp 84–85. Apart from Pausanias' travelogue mentioned above, some sample works with relevance to places and topics discussed in this book are Aristotle, *Constitution of Athens*; Sophocles, *Oedipus at Colonus* (set near the Academy) in *The Theban plays* (Penguin); Euripides, *Iphigeneia in Tauris* (connections with Brauron); Aristophanes, *Acharnians* (the people of Akharnai); Menander, *Dyskolos* (The bad-tempered man; set near the Cave of Pan on Mt Parnes); Aeschylus, *Persae* (The Persians; the Persian wars); Herodotos, *Histories*; Thucydides, *The Peloponnesian war*.

Lucilla Burn, *Greek myths*, British Museum Press, London, 1990.

Modern Greek literature in translation

Apart from the novels of Níkos Kazantzákis and poetry by Constantine Kaváfis and the Nobel prize-winners George Seféris and Odysséas Elítis, relatively little modern Greek literature is available in English. The new series of translations put out by the Athens publishers *Kedros* (G. Gennadhíou 3, Athens 106 78, ☎ 210 380 9712, 210 380 2007, fax 210 383 1981, 210 330 2655) is thus very welcome. The books should be obtainable in the UK from the shops recommended or, in case of difficulty, from the British distributors—*Central Books*, 99 Wallis Rd, London E9 5LN, ☎ 020 8986 4854, 020 8533 5821. US distributors: *Paul & Co. Publishers Consortium Inc*. PO Box 442, Concord, MA 01742, ☎ 508 369 3049, fax 508 369 2385; credit card orders (toll free) 1-800-288-2131. There are over 30 titles on the list at present. Unless otherwise stated those in the following small selection are part of the Kedros series:

Evgenía Fakínou, *Astradení*. Small-island and Athenian city life are contrasted in this tale of a little girl whose family are forced to move.

Margeríta Limberáki, *Three summers*. A charming story of three sisters growing up in prewar Athens.

Didó Sotiríou, *Farewell Anatolia*. A tragic but gripping account of the Asia Minor Greeks and their expulsion from Turkey in 1922–23.

Kóstas Tákhtsis, *The third wedding wreath*, Hermes, Athens. A woman recalls her three marriages, in the process giving many insights into Greek history and society before, during and after the Second World War.

Strátis Tsírkas, *Drifting cities*. A sweeping trilogy, set in Jerusalem, Cairo and Alexandria but exploring human and ideological conflicts in Greece from 1941.

Booksellers

For bookshops in Athens, see Practical information pp 49–50.

Ministry of Culture and TAPA publications are mostly available from bookshops at Panepistimíou 57 (in arcade) and in the National Archaeological Museum; Bank publications from (National Bank of Greece) 12 Thoukidhídhou (Plaka) or 2 Karayeóryi Servías (Síntagma), or (Commercial Bank) 45 Mitropóleos.

Bookshops in the UK

The *Hellenic Bookservice*, 91 Fortess Rd, Kentish Town, London NW5 1AG, ☎ 020 7267 9499, fax 020 7267 9498, www.hellenicbookservice.com, email hellenicbooks@btinternet.com; *Zeno*, 6 Denmark St, London, WC2H 8LP, ☎ 020 8446 1986, fax 020 8446 1985; *Oxbow* (Classics and Archaeology only), Park End Place, Oxford OX1 1HN, ☎ 01865 241 249, fax 01865 794 449, www.oxbowbooks.com, email oxbow@oxbowbooks.com.

Bookshops in USA

The *Foundation for Hellenic Culture*, Inc, 7 West 57th Street, New York, NY 10019, ☎ 212 308 6908, fax 212 308 6908, www.hri.org/FHC; *Have Book, Will Travel Inc.*, 124 Deer Run Road, Wilton, CT 06897, ☎ 203 761 0604, fax 203 762 0148, email havebook@aol.com.

(illegible)

ATHENS

1 • Síntagma to the Acropolis

Starting from Síntagma, one of the main squares of central Athens, you can take in the Russian Church (Byzantine 11C), the English Church (19C) and the Jewish Museum. The large and shady National and Záppion Gardens are pleasant places to stroll or sit. Beyond is the impressive Arch of Hadrian. Dipping into the edge of Pláka (Old Athens) to see the fine Monument of Lysikrates (4C BC), you come out below the South Slope of the Acropolis, with several important sites, including the Theatre of Dionysos and the prettily situated Asklepieion. Opposite will be the new Acropolis Museum. The walk ends at the striking Odeion of Herodes Atticus, venue of Athens Festival performances, just below the ascent to the Acropolis.

- **Distance on foot**. Maps 8,1–2; 5,4. About 1.5km, without detours. Amalías is busy, Dhionissíou Areopayítou for pedestrians only.
  Access by bus. No. 230 (every 20 mins weekdays; 30 mins, Sun) from Akadhimías to Síntagma (stop in Amalías for Russian Church, etc. Next stops: Makriyiánni (in Singroú), Iródhio (in Rovértou Gálli, for Acropolis South Slope excavations and Odeion of Herodes Atticus); Acropolis; then Thisío, etc.
  Note. Bus route may change with road closures.
  Metró (less convenient, except for S Slope). Akrópolis station (Line 2) for S Slope (100m from station), Odeion (500m), Acropolis (700m).

Síntagma to the Arch of Hadrian
You leave Síntagma (p 140) by Leofóros Vasilíssis Amalías (Queen Amalía Avenue), usually known simply as Amalías.

Next to the former palace are its extensive gardens, lush and green amid the dry heat of the city. Laid out (1839–60) by Queen Amalía, in 1927 they became the **National Garden** (Ethnikós Kípos; open daily to sunset; leaflet in Greek, with plan, from Botanical Museum; see below). There is a pleasant small café near the corner of Vasilíssis Sofías and Iródhou Attikoú and the barracks of the ceremonial guard.

Subtropical trees are watered by a channel that succeeds the ancient aqueduct of Peisistratos; peacocks and waterfowl populate the serpentine walks, streams, ornamental ponds and bridges. There are a small zoological compound and aviary, a children's playground and a library. A charming small pavilion (1857) houses the Botanical Museum (closed at time of writing, ☎ 210 721 5019 for information), with an imaginative display of all the trees, plants and shrubs in the gardens. The statuary includes busts of the poets Solomós and Valaorítis, and of Count John Kapodístrias (first governor of an autonomous Greece, 1828–31).

Antiquities found in the grounds include an Early Christian basilica, Roman baths and parts of the Valerian city wall. Architectural fragments from these are scattered here and there (some next to the café) but are generally difficult to locate in the labyrinth of paths. Behind the palace, close to the main entrance from Vasilíssis Sofías, is part of a Roman villa with geometric mosaics.

The impressive inscription from the Hadrianic reservoir (p 215) on Likavittós is behind hedges near the entrance behind the Záppion Hall. It is about 25m from the small children's library (ΠΑΙΔΙΚΗ ΒΙΒΛΙΟΘΗΚΗ), if you follow a line leaving the library to your left and the nearby bust of Eynard, the French philhellene, to your right.

On the right of Amalías (access also from Filellínon) the solid **Russian Church** of Sotíra Likodhímou (or St Nicodemus; open 07.00–10.00 daily) overlooks a small square. The largest surviving medieval building in Athens, it was founded shortly before 1031 by Stefan Likodemou (d. 1045). Its monastic buildings, ruined by an earthquake in 1701, were demolished in 1780 to provide material for Hadji Ali Haseki's city wall. Damaged by shellfire in 1827, the church remained derelict until restored by the Russian government in 1852–56. Its wide dome rests on squinches. The exterior has a terracotta frieze. The detached belfry is a 19C addition; its great bell was a gift of Tsar Alexander II.

Beneath the church and square (special permission from the church authorities required to visit) are remains of a **Roman Bath** (2C AD) which was probably adapted for worship in the Early Christian period. An inscription (1C BC) from the Lyceum Gymnasium (p 225) was found near the church, suggesting that the bath belonged to the Lyceum.

Just beyond is the **English Church**, St Paul's, an undistinguished Gothic building designed by C.R. Cockerell but built (1839–41) by Christian Hansen (p 83) who altered the original plans. Inside (north) are a British funerary monument (1685), originally in the Hephaisteion, and a painted window to Sir Richard Church, British hero of the Greek War of Independence, with an inscription by Gladstone. The east window commemorates the victims of the 'Dílessi murders' (of Lord Muncaster and others by brigands, in 1870).

At Níkis 39 (below Filellínon) is the **Jewish Museum** (Mon–Fri 09.00–14.30, Sun 10.00–14.00, closed Sat), founded in 1977 to illustrate the heritage and history of the Jewish community in Greece, whose origins go back to the 3C BC.

The **Záppion Gardens** continue the National Garden but are divided from it by an avenue. Left of the entrance is a sculpture of Pan (I. Dhimitriádhis) and, in the central avenue, a statue of I. Varvákis, founder of the Varvákeion high school (p 146). The showy **Záppion Hall** (Theophilos Hansen, p 84, 1874–88; renovated 1959–60), was founded as a national exhibition centre. The entrance portico projects from a handsome neoclassical façade. The building behind is semicircular. The open interior court is surrounded by a lofty circular colonnade. In front of the Záppion are statues of its founders and, beyond, a large café (pleasant but expensive).

> **Evángelos** (1800–65) **and Konstandínos** (1813–92) **Záppas** came from Epirus but amassed their fortune in Romania. They endowed various schools and foundations for Greek communities in Greece and beyond. Evángelos was particularly interested in the re-establishment of the Olympic Games. Konstandínos was responsible for the Záppion, and left the family wealth to the Greek state.

Almost opposite the end of Filellínon a **Roman bath** (c 300 AD, refurbished 5–6C AD), found in recent excavations for the Metró, is soon to be opened to the public. Past the gardens, Amalías meets (left) Leofóros Vasilíssis Olgas, their southern boundary (p 185). On the corner is a sentimental 19C sculpture group (by Chapu and Falguière) of *Byron and Hellas* (bus/trolley stop Agalma Víronos).

A few metres along from the junction and just within the garden the foundations and some remains of mosaic floors of a large **Roman building** can be seen. This consisted of a semi-circular unit attached to a colonnaded court (five column bases), which can itself be traced further into the gardens. The bath (above) clearly belonged to the same complex, which may have been a **Gymnasium**. Several marble thrones here are perhaps from the Stadium.

The Arch of Hadrian

On the far side of Olgas is the now isolated **Arch of Hadrian**, a gateway of Pentelic marble erected by Hadrian c AD 132 to mark the limit of the ancient city and the beginning of his Novae Athenae (New Athens) or Hadrianoupolis. It stands in front of the Olimpieion (Sanctuary of Olympian Zeus, p 185). The structure is 18m high, 12.5m wide and 2.3m deep, with an archway 6m across. The piers of the arch had Corinthian columns (traces survive). Above the arch, the attic consists of a portico of four Corinthian columns, with three bays. Over the central one is a pediment. The two façades have contrasting inscriptions. The northwestern (facing the Acropolis) reads 'This is Athens, the ancient city of Theseus'; the southeastern (facing the Olimpieion) 'This is the city of Hadrian and not of Theseus'. The gate is some distance west of the line of the Themistoklean wall. It was incorporated into the 18C Turkish enceinte.

At the far end of Leofóros Olgas rises the leafy hill of Ardhittós (*Ardettos*), by the Stadium (p 190).

The Lysikrates Monument and the eastern edge of Pláka

On the other side of Amalías from the Arch of Hadrian, you can take Od. Lisikrátous, with some pleasant older buildings, west into Pláka, the remainder of which is described below (p 164). On the right is the church of **Ay. Aikateríni** (11C) in a palm-shaded garden. Ancient columns there are probably part of the façade of an earlier (6C) church. Between the church and the road are parts of the foundations of the peristyle court and walls of a Roman building, with two Ionic columns and part of their entablature re-erected. More of the structure has been found in Od. Galánou, close by.

At the end of Lisikrátous ran the ancient Street of the Tripods. Recent research (*Hesperia* 1998; *BSA* 1999) has shown that the **first agora** of Athens and other important buildings (Prytaneion, Theseion, Anakeion) were in this area. The street name survives in Od. Tripódhon where no. 28, a fine neoclassical building, incorporates part of a choregic monument.

The **Street of the Tripods** was called after the ancient practice of dedicating to the god Dionysos the bronze tripod-cauldrons won by victorious choregi in competitions for choral lyric. The *choregos* was a wealthy citizen who undertook the expense of training choruses for choral and dramatic competitions. The tripods were put either in the theatre precinct or in the street 'of the Tripods' which ran round the east end of the Acropolis hill from the Prytaneion to the Theatre of Dionysos. They were set on top of sculptures or small buildings. Pausanias mentions a satyr of Praxiteles which was such a sculpture (the figure is lost but a torso in the Louvre may be a copy), but makes no mention of the Monument of Lysikrates. The foundations of several other such monuments excavated between 1921 and 1955 and in 1980 have been recorded but covered over again.

At the end of Od. Lisikrátous is the **Monument of Lysikrates**, the most spectacular survivor of the choregic dedications. It consists of a circular setting of six monolithic Corinthian columns with curved panels between (only the three with a frieze of tripods are original), the whole forming a round drum. The entablature above is crowned by a marble dome. On top is a finial of acanthus leaves which supported the tripod. The superstructure is of Pentelic marble apart from the curved panels which are Hymettian. The three-stepped base of Hymettian marble rests on a 4m high foundation with a cornice: these elements are of Piraeic and Eleusinian stone, respectively.

The inscription on the architrave reads: 'Lysikrates of Kikyna, son of Lysitheides, was choregos; the tribe of Akamantis won the victory with a chorus of boys; Theon played the flute; Lysiades of Athens trained the chorus; Euainetos was archon.' The last reference dates the event to 334 BC.

The frieze shows the story of Dionysos and the Tyrrhenian pirates, whom he turned into dolphins.

The interior of the monument was not for use—the columns are unfinished and there are no windows. The missing panels were removed in 1669–1821, when the structure was incorporated into a French Capuchin convent. At that time it was known as the Lantern of Demosthenes, from a belief that the orator prepared his speeches there. Byron, one of many English visitors to the convent, is said to have used it as a study: he wrote part of *Childe Harold* there in 1810–11. The convent was occupied and accidentally burned down during the occupation of Athens in 1826 by the Ottoman general Omer Vrioni. The monument was disengaged and restored in 1892, with French financial support.

Beside the Lysikrates Monument are foundations of two others among a mass of later remains. The Street of the Tripods continued in a curve to the formal entrance (not yet located) of the Sanctuary of Dionysos, with its theatre. Further sections of the street and the foundations of more choregic monuments (also Roman burials and the remains of an Early Christian basilica) have been found; the terminal stretch of the street is just south of the Odeion of Perikles.

From beside the Monument of Lysikrates, rather than returning to the busy road, you can climb up Od. Epimenídhou on to the lower slopes of the Acropolis, and then descend Thrasíllou. At the top of Epimenídhou, up to the right, you can see in the Acropolis rock-face the cave which contained a shrine of Aglauros, daughter of Kekrops. Between Thrasíllou and the Theatre of Dionysos (right) are the minimal remains of the Odeion of Perikles (p 98).

You join the broad pedestrianised Od. Dhionissíou Areopayítou (in the area called Makriyiánni), named after St Paul's convert Dionysios the Areopagite, and turn right. The street runs along the southern foot of the Acropolis. Opposite is the **Centre for Acropolis Studies** (closed at time of writing), which will become (by 2004?) the core of a new Museum complex housing all the finds from the Acropolis including, it is hoped, the Elgin marbles. The building itself, sometimes called the Weiler building after its designer Lieutenant W. von Weiler, was constructed in 1836 as a military hospital (restoration completed 1988). The walls include some ancient material.

In streets off to the left are the Swedish (in Od. Mitsaíon) and Italian (Parthenónos) Archaeological Schools and, between them (Kariatídhon and Kallispéri 12) the sleek (1995) **Ilías Lalaoúnis Museum of Jewellery** (Mon, Thur, Fri, Sat 09.00–16.00; Wed 09.00–21.00; Sun 11.00–16.00; closed Tues; shop; attractive café; special provision for disabled visitors). The contents, on three floors, represent the work, chiefly in precious metals and stone, of the internationally renowned Greek jeweller, whose infinitely resourceful and imaginative creations draw on the natural world, technology and children's designs, as well as extensively on ancient art from Greece and elsewhere. There is a video theatre and practical demonstrations of various techniques are given.

The South Slope of the Acropolis

Right of the main road (near the corner with Thrasíllou) is the entrance to the South Slope **archaeological site** (see Acropolis plan, pp 106–107; open Tues–Sun 08.30–15.00, closed Mon). This covers an extensive area, pleasant and wooded, and contains interesting features.

Straight away you cross the line of the boundary wall of the **Temenos of Dionysos Eleutherios**. Its formal entrance (propylaia) from the Street of the Tripods to the east, has not been found.

The worship of Dionysos Eleutherios

This was introduced into Athens in the 6C BC from Eleutherai in Boeotia. The festival of the Great Dionysia, instituted by Peisistratos, eclipsed an older festival, the Lenaia, held in the marshes. This involved competing choruses of actors dressed as satyrs, in goatskins, who danced round the altar of the god and sang their goat-songs (tragodies). These dithyrambic contests were the ancestors of Attic tragedy.

Foundations, in breccia, are of a small 4C **temple** (pronaos + cella) which was built to rehouse the chryselephantine statue of Dionysos seen by Pausanias. Only its base remains. Nearer the theatre are slight remains of another **temple**, of the 6C BC. To the southeast are foundations, either of the great **altar**, or of a large votive offering. At the east entrance to the theatre, on the opposite side of the passageway from the retaining wall of the auditorium, are fragments of an epistyle on three low concrete supports, with a worn inscription: this belonged to a choregic monument in the form of a gateway across the road. Its original position is unknown.

The Theatre of Dionysos

Originally (6C BC) the Theatre of Dionysos had no permanent buildings. An intermediate structure, in which the masterpieces of Aeschylus, Sophokles, Euripides and Aristophanes were performed, was succeeded by the stone-built (342–326 BC) version of Lykourgos. Extensive modifications in Hellenistic and Roman times involved the re-use of earlier material and make tracing the history of the structure extremely complex (see A.W. Pickard Cambridge, *The theatre of Dionysos in Athens*, Oxford, 1946). A useful guidebook, available at the site, is T.G. Papathanassopoulos, *The sanctuary and theatre of Dionysos*, Athens, 1995. Readers unfamiliar with the architectural terms may find the theatre diagram on p 77 helpful.

The only surviving structure from the 6C BC is a terrace wall. At that time there would have been a circular orchestra on the low flat ground, the spectators sitting on the hillside above. By the beginning of the 5C the audience probably had wooden stands, later in an auditorium of banked earth. Retaining walls were built to support the sides of the auditorium, probably under Perikles. A stone wall retained the terrace of the orchestra, and supported a wooden skene. Below this (south) a stoa was constructed, with an open colonnade on the south, and linked to the auditorium on the north by a flight of steps.

In the course of the 4C reconstruction of Lykourgos, the cavea was rebuilt in stone in a form similar to that visible today. A permanent stone skene was erected, flanked by paraskenia with columns. At this point plays continued to be acted at orchestra (floor) level but, in Hellenistic times, when dramatic acting took precedence over the ritual choral dance, a raised stage was added, supported by a stone proskenion. At the same time the paraskenia were taken back and the parodoi widened to improve access to the auditorium. The orchestra was curtailed to a semicircle.

The skene and stage were rebuilt again, possibly by T. Claudius Novius c AD 61. At some point the Roman stage was extended over the parodoi to meet the auditorium. A marble barrier was erected round the orchestra to protect the audience during gladiatorial contests which were now held there. Later on (?3C AD) the Bema of Phaedrus (see below) was added in front of the Roman proskenion. Still later, the reliefs on the bema were truncated and cemented over when the orchestra became a watertight basin for mock sea-battles (*naumachiae*).

Even in Classical times the theatre was used also for other purposes. The presentation of crowns to distinguished citizens, the release of orphans from state control on reaching their majority and other ceremonies might be curtain-raisers to the plays. Golden crowns presented by independent foreign states and the tribute of subject states were displayed in the theatre. There were annual cock-fights from after the Persian Wars. The Assembly could meet here instead of on the Pnyx—as happened occasionally in the 5C (Thuc. VIII 93) and regularly after the 3C. After capturing Athens from the Macedonians in 307 BC, Demetrios Poliorketes put on a military display in the theatre to overawe the Assembly.

In the 5C–6C a church was built in the east parodos. The wall of the Rizókastro, a fortification erected round the lower slopes of the Acropolis in the ?11C (p 129), ran through the theatre. Many stone seats from the stadium were used in its construction.

The **auditorium** now has roughly the form of the Lykourgan reconstruction when, on the west, an outer wall of poros was added to the original buttressed wall of breccia. At the same time the retaining wall on the east was extended to the rock above, its irregular line to avoid the Odeion of Perikles. The cavea has 25 surviving tiers of seats, divided into 13 cunei by narrow stairways. The upper parts are only partly preserved. Originally there were probably 64 rows divided by a diazoma into two sections of 32. Above the second the Peripatos (see below) acted as another diazoma. A further series of 14 rock-cut rows may have been a later addition. Although Plato, in the *Symposium*, estimates the capacity of the theatre as 30,000, it seems unlikely to have held more than 17,000.

Apart from the front row, the **seats** were made of Piraeus limestone. The backs of each were hollowed to take the legs of the spectators behind. The front row consisted of 67 fine sculpted **thrones** in Pentelic marble, probably dating from the Lykourgan period. Sixty of these were found in the theatre, 14 in situ; the rest have been replaced as far as possible in their original positions. Each carries the name of the priest or dignitary for whom it was reserved. Some inscriptions were later altered.

The most elaborate is the central **throne of the priest of Dionysos Eleutherios**, an armed chair with lion's-claw feet, opposite the altar in the middle of the orchestra. On the back are worked two satyrs supporting a yoke with a hanging bunch of grapes. On the front is the owner's name with, above, two kneeling male figures in Persian dress, each grasping a griffin by the neck with one hand and wielding a scimitar in the other. On each arm is a winged youth conducting a cock-fight. The large plinth behind this throne supported the throne of Hadrian.

The area in front of the seats drained into a channel which runs round the orchestra.

The theatre contained numerous **statues** of tragic and comic poets, orators, statesmen, philanthropists and Roman emperors. At the northwest corner of the skene is the base of one of these, of the playwright Menander, by Kephisodotos and Timarkhos, sons of the great sculptor Praxiteles; others can be seen under a shelter at the eastern edge of the site.

The **orchestra** now has a form quite different from that of the Classical period. The present semicircular shape is from the Roman rebuilding under Nero. At that time it was paved with marble slabs, with the central rhombus of smaller coloured pieces. The Lykourgan drainage channel was covered with slabs. Both these and the marble barrier protecting the auditorium were pierced with drainage holes, later blocked up as was the water channel, when the theatre was used for naumachiae.

The latest Roman stage-front is represented by the so-called **Bema of Phaedrus**, about half of which survives, damaged. The name comes from a dedicatory inscription now on top of the four steps in the centre, not in its original position. Nothing is known of Phaedrus. The decorative reliefs (2C AD) show scenes in the life of Dionysos. The westernmost has the god installed in his theatre on a fine throne, the Acropolis and Parthenon in the background. The crouching sileni (satyr-like figures) were inserted later. When discovered in 1862 they were still covered with cement from the waterproofing described above.

Behind the Bema are the foundations of earlier stage buildings. The Hellenistic proskenion is flanked by paraskenia (some truncated columns survive). Further back you can see the outline of the long Periklean stoa. The remains between the two are confused by late walls built to support the Roman skene.

Around the Theatre

The scanty and obscure remains of the **Odeion of Perikles** lie to the east of the theatre. Built before 446 BC, it was burnt down in 86 BC during the sack of Athens by Aristion, a general of the ambitious king of Pontus, Mithridates. Aristion feared that the Roman general Sulla might use the roof timbers for siege engines. It was rebuilt in marble to the original plan by Ariobarzanes II, king of Cappadocia (65–52 BC). Excavations (Greek Archaeological Service, 1914–31, and in recent years) showed it to have been rectangular (rather than circular as suggested by Classical references which compared it with the tent of Xerxes). The large hall, terraced on the south side, had nine rows of ten columns in the interior and a pyramidal roof, with a lantern. The venue of music contests in the Panathenaic Festival, it was supposed to be the best concert hall in the Greek world. Rehearsals of tragedies performed in the Theatre of Dionysos at the Great Dionysia were also held there.

Above the theatre, a cave opening in the sheer upper face of the Acropolis rock contains a church of the **Panayía Khrisospilótissa** (Our Lady of the Golden Cave), with some faded paintings. The rock round the mouth of the cave has been cut to a vertical face. Until 1827, when it was destroyed by Turkish artillery, the entrance was masked by the **Choregic Monument of Thrasyllos** erected in 320 BC by one Thrasyllos, who dedicated the cave to Dionysos. It consisted of a Doric portico on two steps. Three marble pilasters supported the architrave, with the dedicatory inscription. Above this was a frieze of 11 carved wreaths. The tripod stood on the cornice. Fifty years later Thrasykles, son of Thrasyllos, was president (*agonothetes*) of the Games and added two further dedications from victories of his own in similar contests: these are still visible. A seated figure of Dionysos, found above the monument and now in the British Museum, was a Roman addition.

The two Corinthian columns above the cave also supported votive tripods. The cuttings for their feet can be seen from above on the Acropolis (Wall of Kimon). A sundial to the right, of Pentelic marble, is mentioned in the Vienna Anonymous (a Greek writer's description of a visit to Athens c 1460, now in Vienna).

West of the Theatre

There are ancient remains on two terraces. The upper one, retained by a massive wall buttressed by a series of some 40 arches, supported the **Peripatos** (c 5m wide; lit. 'a place for walking'), the main highway round the Acropolis. Steps lead down to it from the top of the Theatre. If, however, you approach from below by climbing up along the side of the Theatre, you pass (left) the rectangular foundations of the **Choregic Monument of Nikias** (319 BC), demolished soon after AD 267 to provide material for fortifications. The stones were used in the Beulé Gate (see p 129) where part of the inscription is still visible. The full text read 'Nikias, son of Nikodemos of Xypete, dedicated this monument after a victory as choregos, with boys of the tribe of Kekropis; Pantaleon of Sikyon played the flute; the Elpenor of Timotheos was the song; Neaikhmos was archon.'

The arches of the Peripatos terrace were formerly hidden by the huge **Stoa of Eumenes**, which extended for 163m from just west of the theatre of Dionysos to the (later) Odeion of Herodes Atticus. The external Doric colonnade had 64 columns. The socle of the back wall is in Hymettian marble.

The Stoa was built by King Eumenes II of Pergamon (197–159 BC) as a shelter and promenade (Vitruvius V, 9, 1). Recent study (M. Korres) has shown close technical connections (similar marble, masons' marks) with buildings at Pergamon itself, and parts of the structure may have been prefabricated there. In Roman times access to the much later Odeion of Herodes Atticus was provided by two doors. The Stoa continued in use until the 3C AD when material from it was used for the Late Roman fortification wall. In 1687 the Turkish fortification called Serpentzes incorporated both it and the Odeion.

Above the Stoa (east end) and the Peripatos, immediately to the west of the upper levels of the Theatre of Dionysos, is the **Asklepieion**, one of the most attractive of the lesser-known sites of Athens, beautifully situated among cypress trees, in a quiet and secluded setting. It was dedicated in 418 BC by one Telemakhos of Akharnai, on a site already sacred to a water god. The wooden buildings of the 5C sanctuary were replaced by a new precinct in the 4C. This was rebuilt in the 4C AD after destruction. The most conspicuous remains within the temenos are now those of a large Byzantine church of the 5C or 6C AD, probably of Ayy. Kosmas and Damian, Christian successors of the pagan deity of healing.

> ### The cult of Asklepios
> The worship of Asklepios, which spread from the main centre at Epidauros, was introduced to Athens after the plague of 429 BC. The sick were treated by a ritual in which patients washed in the sacred spring, offered sacrifice at the altar and then retired to a hall (*abaton*) where they slept (incubation). The ritual atmosphere induced dreams through which the god Asklepios effected treatment. Appropriate dedications were subsequently made. In Athens these included votive tablets (examples in National Archaeological Museum) to Asklepios and his daughter Hygiaea, showing the part of the anatomy treated, as well as larger stelai (scenes of the god visiting patients in their sleep, etc).

The Sanctuary contains remains of a **stoa** against the cut rock-face. This had 17 Doric columns on the exterior; the interior was divided into two aisles by a further row of columns. The stoa was probably two-storeyed, with the abaton, or *enkoimeterion* upstairs. The north gallery is connected by a short passage with a **spring chamber** cut into the rock. This is now a chapel (locked) which continues the sacred character of the place. At the west end of the stoa, probably under a baldachin roof, was the *bothros*. This pit was either for sacrifical offerings to chthonic deities, or the home of the snakes sacred to Asklepios. In front of the stoa are foundations of a small temple in antis, with a portico of four columns at the front. On the south side are a *propylon* (an inscription mentions its repair in the 1C BC) and a small stoa of the Roman period.

To the west are foundations of a 5C stoa with ritual dining-rooms. Nearby is the old spring house of fine Archaic polygonal masonry, antedating the Asklepieion and later altered by the Turks. To the south is a huge cistern, probably Byzantine.

West of the Asklepieion, the sanctuaries mentioned by Pausanias have disappeared beneath the Turkish fortifications. A path follows the general direction of the Peripatos, through confused remains, round the top of the Odeion where an access gate to the Acropolis is normally closed.

You return to the site entrance, leave the enclosure and continue along the street to a flight of steps which leads up to the towering remains of the **Odeion of Herodes Atticus**, one of the landmarks of Athens. Access to the interior is permitted for performances only, but plenty is visible from outside, both at street level and from above.

One of the last great public buildings of ancient Athens, the Odeion was erected in honour of Regilla, wife of Herodes Atticus (p 278), who died in AD 160. It was a typical Roman theatre, seating 5000–6000.

Excavation of the interior in 1858 showed that it had been destroyed by fire. The discovery of murex shells suggested that in Byzantine times there was a factory here for Tyrian purple dye. The Turks incorporated the Odeion into the Serpentzes redoubt, but without altering its basic form. It is now used for orchestral, dramatic and operatic performances at the summer Athens Festival. Don't miss the experience of attending one of these (see p 52).

The massive façade survives to its second storey, in places to the third. Originally there was a portico in front (a mosaic was excavated and covered again). Entrance to the auditorium is by vestibules (traces of mosaics) at either side. These lead either to the parodoi or, by stairways, to the upper levels. The stage back wall (scaenae frons) has the standard three doors, also eight niches for statues. Three steps remain of the east stairway which connected the orchestra with the stage. The steeply rising auditorium, retained by a thick limestone wall, was once roofed with cedar. The cavea (c 78m across) is divided by a diazoma. Below are five cunei, above ten. The seating was entirely restored in Pentelic marble in 1950–61, when the orchestra was repaved in blue and white slabs.

Between the Odeion and the road, to either side of the modern stairs, are remains of various periods, excavated by the Greek Archaeological Service in 1955–59 in advance of roadworks. These include Roman houses, a cistern (right, on ascent) with columns supporting the roof and (left) traces of a sanctuary of the Nymph (in her aspect of the Bride), identified by a boundary stone. Vases (*loutrophoroi*) found here date from the mid-7C BC: such vessels were used in wedding ceremonies and afterwards dedicated in the sanctuary. Beyond are two more (vaulted) Roman cisterns, with hydraulic plaster.

Just beyond the Odeion, at the end of Dhionissíou Areopayítou, is a busy junction. To the right a drive (no vehicles; car park opposite by the Dhiónissos restaurant) climbs to the Acropolis entrance. Ahead a paved avenue (pedestrians only) and paths ascend the Mouseíon Hill, with access to the tomb of Philópappos (p 131) and the Pnyx (Son et Lumière; **Map 4,4**).

The **Dora Strátou Folk Dance Theatre** (p 52; **Map 4,6**), on the far side of the hill, can be reached from here: it is also accessible from Od. Arakínthou, off Singroú or Kallíróis, or from Thisío via Odd. Akámantos (traffic lights, opposite the Hephaisteion) and Stisikléous; also Petrálona electric railway station (500m).

Between the Pnyx and the Acropolis the main road continues as Leofóros Apostólou Pávlou (to be pedestrianised), curving down (c 1km) to Thisío and the west entrance to the Agora (p 135).

2 • The Acropolis

In spite of the vast expansion of modern Athens, the ancient Acropolis (plan pp 106–107) still dominates the city, as it does the expectations of visitors. Trudging the crowded pavements below, how often you glance up and see the refreshing green of its slopes and the elegant marble columns, high against the sky. On the site, the spectacular mass of the Parthenon and the exceptional elegance of the Erechtheíon and Nike temples are outstanding, and the surrounding views spectacular. The Museum is one of the best in Greece.

The extensive restoration work in progress, certain to continue for several years to come, means that some of the buildings are disfigured by cranes and scaffolding and parts of the site are inaccessible.

Note. Readers may find the discussion and illustrations of architectural features on pp 75–78 useful in following the descriptions of buildings on the Acropolis.

- **Access on foot**. By paths from the south side of the Agora (pp 148, 163); through Pláka (p 169) or from the Odeion of Herodes Atticus (p 100).
  Warning. The approach stairway and surface of the Acropolis are extremely slippery in places. It is absolutely essential to wear non-slip shoes.
  Access by bus (best). No. 230 from Akadhimías or Síntagma to Acrópolis stop.
  Metró. Akrópolis station (Line 2), then 700m walk. The station has beautifully lighted casts of some of the Parthenon sculptures, and other displays.
  Opening. 08.00–18.30 daily (16.30 in winter). Note that the **museum** does not open until 11.00 on Mondays. The site and museum are often very crowded and it is best to get there at opening time.
  Facilities. Refreshments (no food allowed on the site) and post office below ticket office; lavatories below ticket office and by museum.
  Further reading. M. Brouskari, *The Acropolis museum: a descriptive catalogue*, 1974, detailed; S. Casson, *Catalogue of the Acropolis museum* (vol. I), 1912; G. Dickens, *Catalogue of the Acropolis museum* (vol. II), 1912; H. Payne and G.M. Young, *Archaic marble sculpture from the Acropolis*, 1936.
  Guidebooks. Those by M. Brouskari are particularly recommended.

The Acropolis hill
At 156m above sea-level (91m above the lower town), and with a surface area of c 320 x 128m, the hill is composed of semi-crystalline limestone and red schist. The sides are steep and largely inaccessible: even the normal approach from the saddle on the west ends in a final steep ascent.

History of the Acropolis
Traditionally connected with the Pelasgians ('the mythical prehellenic inhabitants of Greece', *Oxford classical dictionary*), the site of a fortified Mycenaean settlement, then perhaps the residence of the early kings, the Acropolis was regarded as an essential military strongpoint by the tyrants of the Archaic period. After the fall of the Peisistratid dynasty at the end of the

6C BC, it became exclusively a sanctuary. Following the Persian sack in 480 BC came the greatest period of construction (c 450–430 BC), under Perikles. To this belong all the major buildings surviving today. The site was described by Pausanias (I 22—see Select bibliography, p 86) on his visit to Athens in the 2C AD and his account is still valuable and interesting.

The natural defensive advantages together with the existence of springs attracted settlers to the hill from the Neolithic period. In the Early and Middle Bronze Age there was a narrow stepped approach to the northeast. In later Mycenaean times (c 1250 BC) there was a palace on the Acropolis, in the area of the Old Temple of Athena. In the same period a Cyclopean circuit-wall of defence was built, its main gateway defended by a massive bastion, now hidden beneath the Temple of Athena Nike. Towards 1200 BC a deep underground spring chamber (excavated but not accessible) was constructed on the north side, reached by eight precipitous flights of steps. This provided the citadel with a secret water supply. Some Mycenaean houses have been excavated on the north slope of the hill, and tombs of the same period below.

There is literary but no archaeological evidence for a wall called the Pelasgikon (after the Pelasgi) or Pelargikon (after the storks who nested there) which was built at some later date on the west slope. Also known as the Enneapylon, after its nine gates, this was dismantled in 510 BC, after the fall of the Peisistratids. The Delphic Oracle forbade use of the compound it enclosed but this injunction was ignored by refugees during the Peloponnesian War. According to some authorities the Pelargikon proper is the Mycenaean circuit-wall, while the circuit just described is the 'Outer Pelargikon'.

There is very little evidence for activity on the Acropolis between the Mycenaean and Archaic periods (12C–6C BC). However, the survival of cults (Erechtheus, Kekrops; p 121f.) which apparently have Prehistoric origins suggests that it continued to be a focus of ritual activity, and the existence of a Geometric-period temple has been assumed.

Pedimental sculpture and some architectural remains of four small Archaic buildings—possibly but not certainly temples—have been found on the Acropolis. The earliest of these (Herakles and Hydra pediment, see Museum) is c 580 BC. Other pedimental sculptures, found between the Parthenon and the south wall of the Acropolis (Gigantomachy with central Athena; Animal combat; Herakles and Triton; Three-bodied daemon, or 'Bluebeard'), are often assigned to the mid-6C Old Temple of Athena, whose foundations can be seen between the Parthenon and the Erechtheíon.

Inscriptions use the name Hekatompedon ('hundred-footer') both in reference to a temple on the Acropolis earlier than the Parthenon and to the cella of the Parthenon itself. Because of the latter use, some have assumed that the name must refer to an earlier temple on the Parthenon site. Others think it means the Old Temple of Athena, in view of its proximity to the Parthenon.

Ruin and rebuilding   After the Greek victory over the Persians at the Battle of Marathon (490 BC) and the opening of new marble quarries on Pentelikon (p 249), a new temple (the 'Older' or 'Pre-Parthenon') was begun on the site of the later Parthenon, probably at the instigation of the archon Aristides. The scheme involved extending the surface area of the Acropolis with new retaining walls and fill, the latter including material from the demolished

Hekatompedon. This, together with the other buildings, was largely destroyed in the Persian sack of 480 BC.

Some repair work, perhaps including reconstruction of the opisthodomos of the Old Temple of Athena for use as a treasury, was done after the final defeat of the Persians at the Battle of Plataia in 479 BC. But an oath was taken after the battle to leave the sanctuaries in ruins as a reminder of Persian barbarism and a warning for the future. The north wall, however, was reconstructed, since the Mycenaean wall there was no longer usable after the Persian attack. In the new wall remains of both the Old Temple of Athena and the Older Parthenon were formally incorporated. These can still be seen. On the south, there were further extension and infilling, and Kimon used the spoils of the Battle of the Eurymedon (460 BC) to finance a massive south wall. This was later completed by Perikles in the form which still survives, with a bastion 18m high.

Following the signing of a peace treaty with the Persians at Susa in 448 BC, Perikles took the decision to rebuild on a monumental scale. The Parthenon was finished in 438 BC and the Propylaia started. The Temple of Athena Nike and the Erechtheíon followed. The latter was not finished until 395 BC and the subsequent demolition of the restored opisthodomos of the Old Temple of Athena in 353 BC marks the completion of the project.

The Acropolis changed little from the time of Perikles until the death of Augustus in AD 14. Alexander the Great attached shields to the Parthenon as votive offerings and Antiochus Epiphanes added a gilded image of a gorgon's head (*gorgoneion*) to the south wall. Sulla's siege in 86 BC affected only buildings on the South Slope. The round Temple of Rome and Augustus was constructed in 27 BC, to the east of the Parthenon.

About AD 52 the Roman emperor Claudius began a grandiose embellishment of the approach, with a monumental staircase. Hadrian enriched various shrines. The construction of the Beulé Gate in the 3C AD marked a new period of defensive building in response to the barbarian invasions which were threatening Greece.

Decline and destruction The ravages of the barbarians, the anti-Pagan edict of Theodosius (AD 429) and the conversion of the temples to churches by Justinian all contributed to the decline of the Acropolis of pagan antiquity. Under Justinian it became again a military stronghold with a defended water supply. Some time before AD 900 the famous bronze statue of Athena Promakhos (p 109) was removed to the Byzantine capital in Constantinople to adorn the hippodrome.

In 1204 the Acropolis was first captured by the Marquis of Montferrat, then plundered by Otho de la Roche (p 62). In 1387 it was captured by Nerio Acciaioli after a long siege and, after his death when the succession was disputed, by his son Antony (in 1403 after a siege of 17 months). Under Antony, the Propylaia was converted into a Florentine palace. In 1458 Franco, the last Duke of Athens, surrendered the Acropolis to Omer (p 63), having held out for two years after the rest of Attica had been annexed to Turkey.

As the use of cannon became more common, the Acropolis defences were remodelled. In 1640 or 1656 lightning struck a powder magazine in the Propylaia, causing the first serious damage. After 1684 the Temple of Athena

Nike was removed to make way for a new battery. On 21 September 1687 the Venetian army under Francesco Morosini landed at Piraeus and, two days later, two batteries opened fire on the defences in front of the Propylaia. After an explosion in the Parthenon a fire raged on the Acropolis for 48 hours. The Turks surrendered on 3 October but reoccupied the Acropolis in April 1688. For the next hundred years the ancient remains were incorporated in a maze of houses and narrow streets. In 1822 the Turks surrendered to the Greek insurgents but, under Reshid Pasha, recaptured the Acropolis in June 1827, retaining it until 1833. From 1833 until 30 March 1835 a Bavarian garrison was stationed on the Acropolis to provide a guard of honour for the newly independent Greece.

Lord Elgin

In 1801 Lord Elgin, then British ambassador to Turkey, obtained permission in a *firman* (permit) to fix scaffolding, to excavate, to make casts and drawings, and to take away pieces of stone with inscriptions or figures. The 'Elgin marbles' thus acquired, comprising most of the surviving original sculptural decoration of the Parthenon, and some other material, are now mostly in the British Museum in London. A campaign to have these works returned to Greece, inspired particularly by the late Melína Merkoúri, when Greek Minister of Culture, has won considerable support in the UK.

Excavations After the expulsion of the Turks in 1833, demolition of Frankish and Turkish structures began. In 1835 one of the regents commented that 'the archaeologists would destroy all the picturesque additions of the Middle Ages in their zeal to lay bare and restore the ancient monuments'. This is exactly what has happened.

In 1853 Beulé discovered the gate which is now named after him. In 1874 Burnouf found the Klepsydra spring and in 1875 Schliemann demolished the Frankish tower. From 1876 to 1885 Kavvadhías and Kawerau excavated on behalf of the Greek Archaeological Society, in many places to bedrock. Work has gone on almost continuously ever since, with numerous publications.

One important figure who excavated on the Acropolis, at further sites mentioned in this book and at many other places in Greece and beyond, was the German archaeologist Wilhelm Dörpfeld (1853–1940). An architect by training he first took part in the excavations at Olympia, later becoming architect to and then director of the German Archaeological Institute. He worked both for Schliemann and for the Greek authorities and was responsible for several significant discoveries and publications.

Recent restoration

Damage to the Acropolis monuments has three main causes: internal deterioration of the marble because of the use of iron clamps and supports in the 19C restorations; chemical changes caused to the surfaces by sulphurous pollution from central heating and car exhaust emissions; and wear to surfaces by the passage of millions of visitors. Measures to counteract all these have been taken. Restoration work on the buildings involves the replacement of all iron elements by titanium and reincorporating into the structures architectural fragments which have been identified. The proper positions of these are located with the aid of a computer program. The remaining original sculpture is being removed to a controlled museum environment and replaced with casts. Work on the Erechtheíon took nine years and was completed in 1987. That on the Parthenon started in 1983 and, although expected to take around 12 years, is not yet finished. The Propylaia (work started 1986) and Temple of Athena Nike (1994) are also being treated.

Note The following description contains a full account of the remains, although not all are directly accessible.

The approach and Propylaia

In the Archaic period the ceremonial approach to the Acropolis may have been along the south side of the hill. In the Classical period it was by the Panathenaic Way, which crossed the Agora, climbed the hill and ended in a straight, steep 1:4 climb to the Propylaia. The present visitors' route is oblique, emerging between the Beulé Gate (p 129) and the façade of the Propylaia.

The **approach** to the Propylaia was frequently modified. The Late Archaic **ramp** of the Panathenaic Way is represented by a few courses of its northern retaining wall, in polygonal masonry, on the axis of the Propylaia. In the time of Perikles the ramp was widened to the full width of the central section of the Propylaia. When Pausanias visited Athens, apart from a central path for sacrificial animals, the earlier approach had been covered with a broad **marble staircase** 73m long. The part of the stair between the wings of the Propylaia was built by Claudius in AD 52; the lower section was finished much later. Today the path zigzags up the hill on a line resembling the Mycenaean and Medieval approaches rather than the Classical ramp.

Propylaia

Still a grand and imposing entrance to the Acropolis and retaining much of its original effect, the Propylaia consisted of a central gate-building inset between two flanking porches at right-angles. The southern of these was curtailed, perhaps to avoid encroachment on the territory of adjacent sanctuaries; the northern had independent functions. The material was almost entirely Pentelic marble, apart from the foundations and some decorative elements in black Eleusinian stone.

Origins The precise form of the original plan is uncertain since there are indications that the building was unfinished when construction stopped at the beginning of the Peloponnesian War in 432 BC. The axis of the Propylaia is exactly parallel to that of the Parthenon, the only known example of such deliberate architectural interrelationship before the Hellenistic period. The complex overlaid an earlier entrance system on a different alignment, probably of the time of Peisistratos (mid-6C BC). Construction of the Classical building began in 437 BC to the plans of Mnesikles, an architect who is otherwise unknown, although the Erechtheion has sometimes been attributed to him. The cost was met by grants from the treasuries of Athena and Hephaistos, the sale of old building material, house rents, private subscriptions and grants from the treasurers of the Delian League (p 60). Perikles ran into political difficulties over the building programme, and was accused of squandering the funds of the Delian League on embellishing the Acropolis.

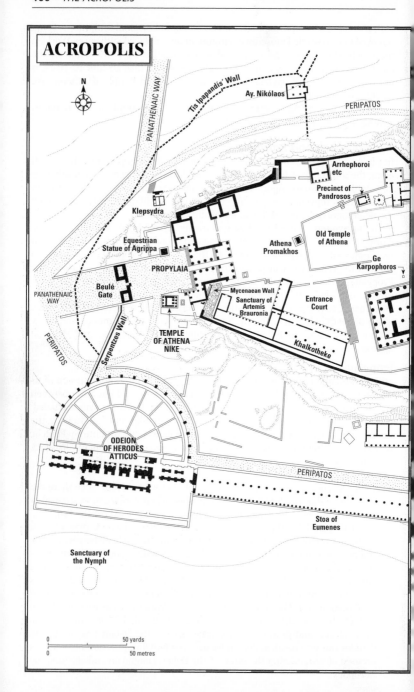

ACROPOLIS

N

'Tis Ipapandis' Wall

PANATHENAIC WAY

Ay. Nikólaos

PERIPATOS

Klepsydra

Arrhephoroi
etc

Precinct of
Pandrosos

Equestrian
Statue of Agrippa

Athena
Promakhos

Old Temple
of Athena

PROPYLAIA

Ge
Karpophoros

Beulé
Gate

PANATHENAIC
WAY

PERIPATOS

Mycenaean Wall

Entrance
Court

Sanctuary of
Artemis
Brauronia

Serpentzes Wall

Khalkotheke

TEMPLE
OF ATHENA
NIKE

ODEION
OF HERODES
ATTICUS

PERIPATOS

Stoa of
Eumenes

Sanctuary of
the Nymph

0   50 yards

0   50 metres

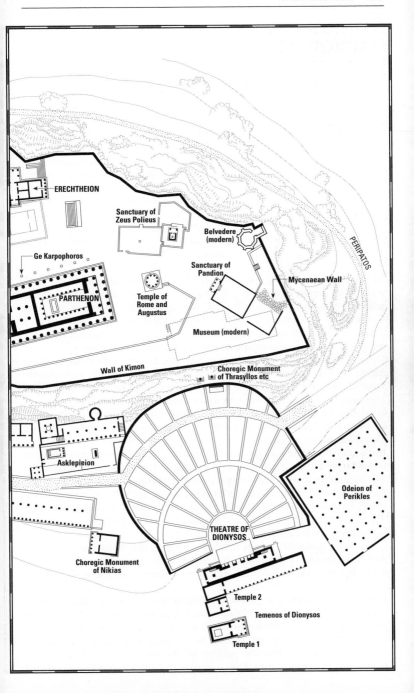

Later history The ancient Propylaia were converted into a Byzantine episcopal palace, with a church of the Taxiárkhis, presumably in the 9C when Athens became a metropolitan see. The building remained almost intact until the 13C, when the Frankish dukes of Athens (whom Shakespeare had in mind when he made Theseus the Duke of Athens in *A midsummer night's dream*) demolished the north wing and used the remainder as their chancery. Nerio Acciaioli had his palace here and erected the Frankish tower (27.5m high) on the south side. The Turks put a cupola over the central vestibule and used it as a magazine. The Aga (Ottoman commander) made it his official residence. In the 17C a stroke of lightning exploded the magazine, the architraves of the east portico fell and broke and two Ionic columns collapsed. The west façade and the fine coffered ceiling were demolished in the Venetian bombardment of 1687. A Turkish bastion was later constructed between the bastion of the Temple of Athena Nike and the south wing. Some of the columns were used to make lime. Further damage was done in 1827. K. Pittákis removed the Frankish and Turkish additions, except the tower which was taken down at Schliemann's expense in 1875. The central hall was reconstructed in 1909–17; the wings after 1945.

The **central gate-house** is a rectangle of 23.7 x 18.2m wide with, at each end, a portico of six Doric columns and a standard Doric entablature. There was no sculpture although some may have been intended. The columns of the outer façade stand on a foundation of four steps, while those of the inner rest on a simple stylobate, an indication of the upward slope of the rock beneath. The interior columns are also slightly shorter (by c 25cm) than the outer.

The **portal** is two-thirds of the way down the length of the building, at the higher level of the east façade. It has five doorways, originally with massive wooden doors; the middle one largest, the outer pairs progressively smaller. The approach to the main doorway is by a paved **ramp** (continuing the Panathenaic Way) bisecting the steps and landings which give access to the side doors. Between the west entrance and the four side steps (the topmost of black Eleusinian stone) which rise to the portal, the ramp was lined on each side by three tall (10.2m) Ionic columns with elegant capitals. Each row was topped by a massive architrave block, reinforced by an iron bar let into its upper surface. The columns supported a stunning high coffered **ceiling** (lauded by Pausanias), the individual elements painted with stars. Below the portal some steps (now covered) cut at an oblique angle to the ramp are remains of an **earlier gateway**. The porch between the portal and the inner façade is relatively shallow and without interior columns.

The north and south **wings** which project from and frame the west façade each have façades of three Doric columns in antis and a Doric architrave and frieze, but the roofs were hipped. Although the façades are identical, what lies behind each is quite different.

In the north, there is a shallow vestibule behind the portico, then a square room entered by a door (slightly off-centre), with a window to either side. This room was called the **Pinakotheke** (Picture Gallery) by Pausanias from the contents he saw. The rough surface of the walls indicates panel-paintings rather than murals. The odd position of the door (which would suit the positioning of dining couches) has suggested to some scholars that its original function may have been as a ritual dining-room, a standard feature of Greek sanctuaries, in which sacrificial meals were consumed by the official participants. The joist sockets from the upper storey later added by the Dukes of Athens are visible.

In the south, there is no room behind the façade and even the shallow porch is incomplete. The back wall stops behind the third column from the east and the anta is a single pillar rather than a thickened wall-end. The eastern end of the back wall is slightly chamfered so as not to interfere with the surviving section of the Mycenaean wall behind.

The truncated form of this wing is probably due to the need to respect the integrity of pre-existing sanctuaries—that of Artemis Brauronia which was bounded by the Mycenaean wall, and that of Athena Nike (p 110). The later Frankish tower was built over the south wing.

If you pass through the Propylaia on to the surface of the Acropolis itself you can look back and see the evidence for parts of the building apparently planned but never constructed. These would have been two large **halls**, inward of the north and south wings just described. The space available for each is c 21 x 12m, making the total width of the Propylaia exactly equal to the length of the Parthenon. To proceed with these additions some agreement with the authorities of the neighbouring sanctuaries would have been necessary. The fact that the projecting **bosses**, around which ropes were looped to lift the building blocks, were never removed is usually taken as an indication that the building was not finished, but it is conceivable that they were simply left as a decorative device. A cornice round the two walls of the putative north hall, an anta at the southeast, and a projection at the northwest all suggest that construction was actually started; and there is an anta at what would have been the northeast corner of the south hall.

L-shaped foundations, partly overlain by the south wall of the existing south wing and between it and the Mycenaean wall, are from the earlier layout of the area. They belong to an exedra which flanked the earlier Propylaia and was used as a grandstand for the Panathenaic procession. This may have been the site of the famous Hekatompedon inscription, cut in 485 BC on the back of an earlier metope, which listed various activities forbidden to visitors to the Acropolis.

The small trapezoidal enclosure to the south was a precinct of the Graces, probably associated with the worship of Hekate of the Tower, whose famous triple image by the sculptor Alkamenes was seen near here by Pausanias.

A circular base, to your right immediately on leaving the Propylaia, belonged to a statue of Athena Hygiaea (of health), and has traces of her feet and spear.

The **Sacred Way** (now largely protected by concrete) is marked by transverse scores in the rock to give a better foothold on the climb towards the Parthenon, a rise of about 12m. In Classical times, only the west pediment of the Parthenon would have been visible. The precinct would have been approached through a propylon in the boundary wall of the entrance court (see below).

The immediate focus of attention would have been the gigantic (9m high) bronze **Statue of Athena Promakhos** (Champion) by Pheidias. There are fragments of its poros base and the crowning egg-and-dart moulding about 30m in front of the Propylaia.

The nature of the figure, dedicated in 458 BC to record Athenian valour in the Persian wars, is known from a medieval description by Niketas Choniates (12C) and from copies on contemporary medals. The goddess was standing; her right arm resting on her spear; in her left a shield decorated with scenes of the battle of Lapiths and Centaurs. These were designed by Parrhasios and made by Mys. The name Promakhos became current in later times to distinguish the figure from the Athena Parthenos in the Parthenon and the Athena Polias in the Erechtheion. The spear blade and helmet crest could be seen from well out to sea (as far, it is suggested, as Sounion).

The statue was later removed to Constantinople, and was there destroyed in a riot in 1203, because of a belief that Athena's apparently beckoning hand (the spear had by now disappeared) had summoned the Crusaders from the west.

In the angle of the walls of the unfinished southeast room of the Propylaia you can see (best from the sanctuary of Brauronian Artemis—p 112) a good section of the **Mycenaean Circuit-wall**. It consists of two faces of large, undressed and irregularly shaped stones with a filling of rubble and clay. Over the whole circuit its thickness varies from 4.5m to 6.7m. Behind this some foundations are all that survive of the pre-Periklean Propylaia.

The Temple of Athena Nike

The Temple of Athena Nike (Athena of Victory), beyond the section of Mycenaean wall, is an exquisite structure, tiny and elegant in its Ionic style. Although adjacent to the Propylaia, the best view is from within the Acropolis, by the boundary wall to the south of the Propylaia.

The temple stands on a platform 8m high projecting west from the south wing of the Propylaia. The core of this platform is a bastion of the Mycenaean wall, which still exists beneath the later facing.

Origins The bastion became a sanctuary of Athena Nike, with an altar, in the time of the Peisistratids. This was destroyed in the Persian sack of 480 BC. In 449 BC a new *naïskos* (miniature temple) was decreed to mark the peace concluded with Persia, and Kallikrates was commissioned as the architect. In 448 BC the bastion was faced with poros. A long-held theory that the inscription recording the 449 decree refers to the temple rather than the naïskos now seems less persuasive. If true, however, there would have been a gap of over 20 years between decree and construction.

Later history The Turks demolished the temple in 1686 in order to clear the bastion as an artillery emplacement. The material from it was used to build another gun position above the Beulé Gate. A closely similar temple by the River Ilissós (p 189), certainly designed by the same architect, was drawn and later published by Stuart and Revett in the late 18C. With the help of these drawings the Athena Nike temple was painstakingly reconstructed by the architects Ross, Schaubert and Christian Hansen in 1836–42. In 1936–40 it was again dismantled and rebuilt in the course of repair work on the bastion. Further conservation is in progress, and the original sculptures are being replaced with casts.

The Temple of the Athena Nike on the Acropolis

The three-stepped stylobate measures 5.5 x 3.5m. The building, in Pentelic marble, is tetrastyle and prostyle, with an almost square cella and a very shallow porch at either end. The column shafts are monolithic. A **frieze**, possibly designed by Agorakritos, ran right round the building. Four of the original 14 slabs are in the British Museum in London, the rest in the Acropolis Museum. The swirling 'calligraphic' drapery, characteristic of late 5C sculpture, is evident but details of the subject matter are uncertain. On the east are gods and goddesses, mostly female, with Peitho (*Persuasion*), Aphrodite and Eros at the south corner. On the other sides are scenes from the Battle of Plataia (479 BC) with Athenians fighting (west) Boeotians and (north and south) Persians. The normal convention that mortals were not depicted in the sculptural decoration of sacred buildings was not broken here if the troops victorious in such a crucial battle were regarded as heroes (i.e. more than mortals), as the victors of the Battle of Marathon certainly were (Parthenon sculptures, p 120).

Inside the temple was a marble statue of the goddess, which reproduced a wooden predecessor, probably destroyed by the Persians. Athena held a pomegranate (emblem of fertility and peace) in her right hand and, in her left, a helmet symbolising her warlike aspect. In antiquity confusion arose about the identity of this figure because Nike (Victory) was usually depicted with wings. Since this statue of Athena had none, the temple came to be known as that of Nike Apteros (Wingless Victory), and Pausanias retails a popular idea that the Athenians had plucked Nike's wings to stop her flying away.

Winged Nikai, attending Athena, were, however, depicted on the lovely panels of a **balustrade** (topped by a bronze screen) surrounding the temple platform, itself surfaced with marble. They include one of the best known late 5C reliefs, the so-called *Sandalbinder*, showing a Nike adjusting her sandal (Acropolis Museum). Some of the slabs are thought to be by Paionios who made the famous *Nike* at Olympia.

A block of marble at the top of the steps to the temple has marks of an equestrian statue and an inscription recording its dedication by the cavalry in 457 BC. The artist was Lykios of Eleutherai, son of the better known Myron. The block was later inverted and used as a base for a statue of Germanicus on his visit to Athens in AD 18. This event is recorded on another inscription, below the block.

The return of Theseus

This is the spot on the Acropolis from which, according to legend, Aegeus kept watch for the return of his son Theseus from the expedition against the Minotaur in Crete. Theseus had promised to hoist a white sail if he had been successful, instead of the usual black. He forgot to do this and Aegeus, sighting the black sail and thinking his son dead, threw himself off the cliff.

In the space to the east of the Mycenaean wall was the **Sanctuary of Artemis Brauronia**, intimately connected with a sanctuary of the same name in the Attic countryside (p 256). The precinct is roughly triangular, its entrance on the long north side, with rock-cut steps. In this form it dates to the 4C BC. On the south was a stoa with two projecting wings, recalling the sanctuary at Brauron itself; on the east a further detached stoa. Inscriptions recording the storage of votive offerings include copies of ones found at Brauron, from where valuable offerings were removed to Athens at the beginning of the Peloponnesian War.

Between this sanctuary and the Parthenon are the entrance court to the latter (north) and the Khalkotheke (south). The triangular **Entrance Court** to the Parthenon may have been created as part of Mnesikles' commission to tidy up the Acropolis. Rock-cuttings suggest that it was entered from the Sacred Way to the north by a propylon. To the west its boundary was the Brauronian sanctuary, to the east the stepped retaining wall of the Parthenon terrace. Nine of its steps were rock-cut and seven others built of poros (fragments survive). Numerous votive offerings were erected on them, as cuttings for 38 stelai show. In front of the steps at the west end stood a bull dedicated by the Council of the Areopagos.

The south side of the court was closed by the **Khalkotheke** (Storehouse of Bronzes). This building, of c 450 BC, is a slightly imperfect rectangle c 41 x 14m. A colonnade, which encroached on the Parthenon steps, was later added to the north. On its inner north wall are five fragments of a long statue base, with inscriptions. These show that the artists of the works were Sthennis and Leochares (350 BC). Roman inscriptions on the south face indicate that the base was later appropriated for figures of Drusus, Tiberius, Augustus, Germanicus and Trajan. Pausanias records other statues round here and fragments of bases can be seen.

Northwest of the Propylaia

Note. The first part of this description down to '...from the Older Parthenon', p 112, is at present inaccessible and you must proceed straight to the Erechtheion. On the way, opposite the seventh column of the Parthenon peristyle, a barred surround protects a rock-cut dedication to Fruit-bearing Earth (ΓΗΣ ΚΑΡΠΟΦΟΡΟΥ). Here stood a personification, apparently rising from the ground, of Earth praying for rain to Zeus. Between here and the Erechtheion are the foundations of the Old Temple of Athena (p 120).

Left beyond the Propylaia is the projecting anta of the unbuilt north hall. Another projection, from the far end of the Pinakotheke, also signals the original intention. The chapel of the Frankish dukes which later occupied this area was demolished in 1860. Crossing an ancient drain, three large cisterns (probably Justinianic, c AD 530), you reach the Acropolis wall. From the next angle a flight of steps (Classical period) goes down north.

A little further on are remains of the Ottoman phase of a second stairway. In front of this are the poros foundations of a small square building (8.50 x 8.50m) with four columns in the façade, identified with the **House of the Arrhephoroi** (lit. 'bearers of secret things') mentioned by Pausanias.

The *Arrhephoroi*, who had to be female, from aristocratic families and between seven and eleven years of age, were chosen by the King Archon. Their duties included weaving and carrying the peplos for Athena's statue and a rite whose details are unknown. This involved carrying down to the sanctuary of Aphrodite in the Gardens, via a secret stair and an underground passage, an unspecified burden. Here they exchanged it for another, which they carried back.

The stairway descends to the east and then turns to enter a cave. Research here (1937) revealed not, as expected, traces of the activities of the Arrhephoroi but remains of a **Mycenaean Stairway** and **Spring Chamber** (neither accessible), created in the late 13C BC to provide the Acropolis with a protected water supply. The stairway, partly rock cut and partly constructed from wood and stone, dropped 33.5m to a natural spring, below the floor of the cave.

At this point (good view also from below) the outer face of the Acropolis wall incorporates architectural members from the Old Temple of Athena and, further on, from the Older Parthenon.

You walk between a Byzantine cistern, which abuts on the Acropolis wall, and the Erechtheion, and climb a flight of steps to a platform. From here there is a good view over the city to the north but, more immediately, of the interior of the **circuit-wall** which was exposed when the artificial fill (containing sculptures) was excavated. Built into the wall, at both ends of the steps, are column drums and stylobate blocks from the Older Parthenon.

In the next deep excavation, a rock gully contains the remains of the stairway which led down from the postern gate in the Mycenaean wall. You can also see the original slope of the rock.

A little further on are poros capitals and column drums from the Old Temple of Athena, some of them reddened by fire.

At the east end of the site is a **Belvedere** (view) where the Greek flag is ceremonially raised and lowered at sunrise and sunset. A plaque with an inscription in Greek commemorates the removal of the Nazi flag on the night of 30 May 1941. Below are the tiles roofs of Pláka.

Between the Belvedere and the Parthenon, a rock-cut platform may be the site of the Precinct of Zeus Polieus. In front of the Parthenon are architectural members of the circular Monopteros of Roma (city goddess of Rome) and Augustus (27 BC). A monopteros consists only of columns with no interior structure. The conical roof rested on nine Ionic columns. The dedicatory inscription on the architrave was recorded by Cyriac of Ancona (p 63) in 1456.

Behind the museum you can see a good stretch of the Mycenaean Wall. This abuts on the barely visible remains (c 35 x 15m; the best preserved section is in the basement of the museum) of the Sanctuary of Pandion, a legendary king of Athens. The open air precinct, rebuilt in the 5C, was divided into two parts, with a propylon at the west.

Continuing along the **Wall of Kimon** you see the Mouseion Hill in the foreground, capped by the monument of Philópappos (p 132). In the distance is the sweep of Phaleron Bay.

A deep triangular cutting contains the secondary cross-wall of the rectangular **Ergasterion**, a temporary workshop erected during the construction of the Parthenon and later subdivided. Two other excavations have walls of earlier phases mainly belonging to terracing for the foundations of the Parthenon's predecessor. Between the two is a display showing the roofing system of the Parthenon.

You are now back at the Parthenon Entrance Court.

The Parthenon

In spite of a chequered history, much of the Parthenon is well preserved. Built on the highest point of the Acropolis, its marble columns catch the eye from all parts of the city below. From close at hand, both the monumentality and the subtlety of its architecture are evident. More than any other Greek temple, the Parthenon incorporates refinements of design and construction to give visual life and excitement to what might otherwise have been solid and simple mass. But its splendid ancient exterior had two features which have now largely vanished—extensive sculptures and colour, which was applied both to the figures and to some of the architectural members. Some figures also had bronze appendages. Except for the wooden roof, the whole structure was of Pentelic marble.

Built between 447 and 438 BC as the central feature of the new Periklean Acropolis, the Parthenon was designed to contain a colossal new chryselephantine statue of Athena by Pheidias and to celebrate the Greek triumph over the Persians. The overseer of the whole project, both architecture and sculpture, was Pheidias. The two architects were Iktinos and Kallikrates. Although it is impossible for one man to have created all the sculptures which decorated the building, and indeed the hands of various different sculptors can be identified, it is usually assumed that Pheidias was responsible for the overall design and that the style in general reflects his own.

The name Parthenon (Παρθενών), which means the 'chamber of the maidens' (i.e. the priestesses of Athena), originally applied only to the western room of the building. It came to be used (first in the speeches of Demosthenes) for the whole building. The statue, in fact representing Athena Polias (guardian of the City), acquired the title Athena Parthenos. Before this the temple may have been known as the Hekatompedon, after a predecessor on the site (p 102).

In spite of the physical and visual dominance of the Parthenon, it was the Erechtheion which had the greater ritual importance. The Erechtheion succeeded the Old Temple of Athena as the home of the oldest and most important cult statue of Athena, and that to which the Panathenaic procession was directed.

The Parthenon's predecessors At least four temples seem to have been constructed on this site and recent investigations (M. Korres) have suggested that the location of the first of these may have been influenced by the existence of an even earlier shrine in the area of the north colonnade. Rooftiles of the late 7C BC may be from the **first Archaic temple**, while to the **Hekatompedon** may belong parts of entablature (outside the museum at its north corner) and some surviving poros architectural members, at present stacked in a rectangle between the south side of the museum and the Acropolis wall. These members show that the building to which they belonged was peripteral and c 30m long. The uncertainty about its identification stems from the fact that these remains could belong to the Old Temple of Athena (p 120). The Hekatompedon was replaced by the **Older** or **Pre-Parthenon**, which was apparently begun at about the time of the Battle of Marathon. The terrace was artificially extended using material from the older temple as infill. A massive stereobate (masonry foundation), measuring 76.8 x 31.4m, is up to 22 courses high in places. By the time of the Persian sack of the Acropolis in 480 BC, the marble stylobate had been laid on top, also the lower drums (not yet fluted) of the columns (6 x 16) and one course of masonry of the interior building. Marks of the Persian fire destruction can still be seen, both under the later stylobate (on the west side, near the north angle) and on material built into the north wall (p 113). This building represents an important step in large-scale construction in marble and the remains show that many elements (and some of the material) of its sophisticated design were re-applied to the Parthenon itself.

The Parthenon In a slightly different position from its predecessor, the Parthenon also has a different column arrangement (8 x 17) and is both wider and shorter than the pre-existing base. As a result the older foundations project 4.3m on the east and 1.7m on the south while, on the north extra foundation courses had to be laid.

Work on the building started in 447 BC. In 438 BC the statue was dedicated at the Great Panathenaic Festival. In 435 BC the first treasure was stored in the opisthodomos and in 434 BC the first inventories recorded. The last sculptures were completed in 432 BC.

Alexander the Great embellished the building with gilded bronze shields (p 117). Demetrios Poliorketes turned the west portico into a residence for himself and his seraglio. Later, in 296/95 BC, he laid siege here to Lakhares, an Athenian general who set himself up as tyrant and decamped with treasures from the sanctuary and gold fittings from the statue to pay his troops. For most of the Roman period things continued as before but, by the 5C AD, the statue had been removed. In the 4C AD a colonnade was incorporated into the cella, made of material taken from a Hellenistic building elsewhere in the city.

Later history In the 6C AD the Parthenon was converted into a church. Under Justinian it was dedicated to Ay. Sofía. Later it became the Cathedral of Athens, named for the Mother of God (Theotókos). For this new function, the entrance was at the west, the opisthodomos of the temple becoming a porch and the Parthenon proper the narthex of the church. The back wall of the original cella was pierced by three doors, two of them giving access to staircases up to women's galleries which were erected over the colonnade. The walls of the former cella were frescoed and the roof barrel-vaulted. The pronaos of the temple was made apsidal to receive the altar. Bishops were buried in vaults beneath the floor. In the Byzantine period a bell-tower was constructed at the southwest angle of the opisthodomos.

From 1204 to 1458 the Parthenon became the Latin cathedral of the Frankish dukes. When later converted into a mosque, the Byzantine bell-tower became the minaret.

The most serious damage to the building occurred in the course of Venetian attempts to take Athens from the Turks. In 1687, at 19.00 on 26 September, a mortar placed by Morosini on the Mouseion Hill was fired by a German lieutenant. It hit the Parthenon which the Turks had been using as a powder magazine. Most of the cella and frieze were destroyed in the explosion which followed, as well as 14 columns (eight on the north and six on the south) and their entablature. The building was thus split into two. When Morosini took the Acropolis, he attempted to remove the horses and chariot of Athena from the west pediment, but they fell and were smashed.

Nevertheless there are some excellent records of the building and its sculptures before the 1687 destruction. In 1674 Jacques Carrey, a draughtsman attached to the Marquis de Nointel, French ambassador to the Ottoman Porte, made over 400 drawings of the sculptures. These are now in the Bibliothèque Nationale in Paris. Jacques Spon and George Wheler were the last foreigners to see the building intact (1676). A French physician and an English naturalist, they met in Italy and together visited Greece and Turkey, separately publishing accounts of their experiences (1678, 1682).

In 1787 the Comte de Choisseul Gouffier took a detached segment of the frieze to France. In 1801 Lord Elgin was granted a permit by the Turkish authorities 'to remove some blocks of stone with inscriptions and figures'. The work, overseen by the artist Lusieri, included removal of most of the frieze, 15 of the southern metopes, the figures from the pediments, etc. In 1816 these 'Elgin Marbles' were sold to the British Museum.

As a result of its complex history the Parthenon now incorporates fragments of at least 40 other structures.

Restoration Restoration of the building began in 1834–44. After an earthquake in 1894 N. Balános re-erected some sections of architrave and capitals in the west façade. In 1921–30, in spite of considerable opposition, he reconstructed the north colonnade, with new columns of Piraeic stone covered with concrete. They are similar in appearance to the originals but cannot be confused with them. Five of the capitals, however, were replaced in

Pentelic marble. The west colonnade was partly reroofed with copies of the original coffers in order to protect the remaining blocks of the frieze (now removed). Casts made in Elgin's time show how much these sculptures have deteriorated since. The current programme of restoration started in 1983.

The exterior architecture

The **crepidoma** of the Parthenon consists of three marble steps. On the south side, the steps of its predecessor are visible below.

There are 46 Doric columns in the **colonnade** in an octastyle arrangement (8 x 17) which is only paralleled by the earlier Temple G at the Greek colony of Selinus in Sicily. Each column (base diameter 1.9m; height 10.4m) consists of 10–12 fluted drums of varying height.

Immediately above the columns the **architrave**, originally plain, was adorned with gilded bronze shields, perhaps by Alexander the Great in 334 BC, after the Battle of Granicus—14 on the east and eight on the west. Between them the names of the dedicators were inscribed in bronze letters. A later inscription on the east front has been deciphered from the marks left by the nails. It recorded an honour conferred by the Athenians on the Roman emperor Nero. On the north and south sides the architrave had bronze pegs for hanging garlands on festival days.

The exterior has a normal **Doric frieze**. The cornice was a slab projecting above the frieze, topped by a moulding. On the underside were *mutules* and *guttae*. At the ends of the building it provided a platform for the figures in the pediments.

On the apex of each pediment, 18m above the stylobate, was a palmette **acroterion**.

The **roof** (see display on south side of building, towards the west end) was wooden but the tiles were Pentelic marble. Palmette antefixes covered the joins between tiles at the edge of the roof. There was an ornamental lion's head at each corner, but no gutter and waterspouts.

Colour played a part: mouldings were decorated with drawn and painted motifs; triglyphs and *guttae* were painted dark blue; the ceilings had deep blue coffers with gilt stars. The British Museum has a coloured reconstruction of part of the building.

Greek architects modified the severe angles of their structures in various ways. These **refinements**, usually invisible to the naked eye, give life to the buildings and avoid an over-solid feel. Although some such refinements were adopted quite early in the history of Greek temple building, the Parthenon is exceptional in making use of most of them in combination.

The spaces between the columns are not uniform. The corner columns are thickened. The spacing of the triglyphs is also adjusted so that each end triglyph coincides with the corner of the building. Horizontal and vertical members are very slightly removed from the true. The pavement of the building is convex (you can see this by standing at a corner and looking along the top step) and this curvature is reflected in the entablature. The columns incline slightly inwards and have a convex swelling (*entasis*) designed to counteract the optical illusion which makes straight tapered shafts appear concave.

The introduction of various Ionic features (such as the famous frieze—p 119) represents refinement of a different kind, modifying the severity of the basic Doric style.

The exterior sculpture

In the **east pediment** was the *Birth of Athena* but little of this scene survived the construction of the Byzantine apse (fragments in *Acropolis* and *British Museums*). Pausanias records the subject, and the decoration of a Roman *puteal* (well-head) in Madrid (*Museo Arqueologico*) was apparently copied from the central scene. In the **west pediment** was the *Contest of Athena and Poseidon* for the possession of Attica. The figures were mostly destroyed by Morosini but the composition is largely preserved in Carrey's drawings.

There were 92 sculptured **metopes**, varying in quality and clearly the work of several different hands. Some were lost in the Morosini bombardment. Apart from some fragments in the Acropolis and Vatican Museums, there are 15 in the British Museum and one in the Louvre, all from the south series whose subject was a famous mythical battle between Lapiths and Centaurs.

> ### Battle of Lapiths and Centaurs
> This legendary combat took place at the wedding of King Peirithoös of Thessaly, when his people, the Lapiths, were attacked by the wild and licentious Centaurs (half-horse, half-human) who attempted to carry off their women. In Classical Greek art, the subject was used as an allegory of the conflict between the civilised Greeks and the barbarian Persians.

There were 41 other metopes on the building until recently but all have now been replaced with casts. On the east front was a *Gigantomachy* and on the west an *Amazonomachy*. The metopes seems to have been deliberately damaged, perhaps in the 6C–8C AD. A large part of one of the south metopes was found built into a wall in the Theatre of Dionysos in 1989.

As well as the coloured backgrounds to the sculpture mentioned above, much detail was also **painted** on to the figures, especially details of dress. Exposed flesh was polished but left plain. Metal accessories such as weapons were attached.

The interior architecture

The interior is not accessible.

The ambulatory within the colonnade is 4.3m wide on the flanks and 6cm more at the ends. It has drainage channels. The ceiling had marble coffers. The building (*sekos*) stands on a raised socle, two steps above the stylobate. Instead of the normal Doric temple plan of pronaos, cella and opisthodomos, the Parthenon has a shallow pronaos and opisthodomos, with the remainder of the structure divided into two rooms—the cella, which contained the statue, and the Parthenon proper.

The **pronaos** and **opisthodomos** are identical except that the columns in the latter, perhaps made from drums originally destined for the Pre-Parthenon, are 5cm thicker. In each case a porch fronted by six columns precedes a door into the interior. The wall between the pronaos and cella probably had windows; the columns and antae of the opisthodomos have traces of the grating which closed it off from the ambulatory. At the southwest corner, below pavement level, is the base of the Turkish minaret, and a rough staircase climbs to the pediment. Byzantine inscriptions (left pillar) and fragments of fresco (right of doorway) belong to the time when the opisthodomos was the church porch.

The **cella**, whose name of *Hekatompedos naos* (100-foot temple) was presumably inherited from an earlier building, is rather less than 100 Attic feet in length. It had a two-storeyed colonnade round three sides. There are marks showing the positions of some of the original columns, but the more obvious remains are those of Hellenistic columns from another building, which were inserted in the Parthenon after it was damaged by fire. When the temple was converted into a church, all the columns were removed and the west wall of the cella, originally plain, was pierced by three doors.

Barriers between the lower columns of the colonnade formed an ambulatory from which Pheidias' chryselephantine Statue of Athena Polias could be viewed. The position of the statue's **base** is clear, where plain Piraeic stone contrasts with the marble of the rest of the floor.

Details of Pheidias' statue (which later acquired the name of **Athena Parthenos**) can be recovered from smaller-scale ancient reproductions and from descriptions. The former include the Varvakeion and Lenormant figures in the National Archaeological Museum, and the Strangford shield in the British Museum. The core of the figure was wooden; the surface gold. The face, hands and feet were of ivory; the pupils precious stones. The whole, including base, was 11.9m high. The figure stood upright, wearing a dress reaching to the feet. On her breast was an ivory Medusa (on the aegis). In her right hand she held a crowned Victory about four cubits (c 1.7m) high; in her left, a spear. The helmet was topped by a sphinx, with griffins in relief on either side. These represented the winged beasts which fought with the Arimaspi for gold (Hdt. III 1 16). On the goddess's sandals was depicted the Battle of Lapiths and Centaurs. On the outside of the shield, which rested against the figure, was the battle of the Athenians with the Amazons. Representations of both Pheidias and Perikles were included, something which was regarded as impious and punished by the Athenians (Plutarch, *Life of Perikles*). On the inside was a Gigantomachy. At Athena's feet was a serpent, perhaps Erichthonios (p 121). The pedestal had scenes of the birth of Pandora.

The dress and other additions of solid gold, weighing in total between 40 and 50 talents (c 1300kg), were removable in times of crisis (Thuc. II 13).

A plain wall, without doors, divided the cella from the other room; this was the actual **Parthenon**, which gave its name to the whole temple (see above). It ran the full width of the building, but was only 13.1m long. Three of its walls survive. Four Ionic columns (traces on the floor) supported the roof.

The interior sculpture

Round the outside of the sekos, 11.9m above floor level, ran a continuous **Ionic frieze**, one of the best known features of the building. Of the total length of 159.5m, 75.3m are in the British Museum, 53.6m in Athens. Other parts were drawn by Carrey. Another 13.7m are completely unrecorded and some of the surviving elements were damaged in the 1687 explosion.

About one-third of the north side and five slabs of the south are in the Acropolis Museum (p 114). Most of the remainder are in London, apart from parts of the east scene (three slabs and some fragments in the Acropolis Museum; eight in the Louvre).

The height of the frieze is 99cm. The maximum depth of the relief, which was increased from bottom to top to improve visibility, is 5.7cm. The changing scenes, viewed successively between the columns of the peristyle, imparted a feeling of the movement and forward impetus of the procession.

The **subject** has usually been taken to be the *Panathenaic procession* (see overleaf) since many of those known to have participated appear in the frieze and the incidents shown are appropriate. There are, however, some omissions, and what should be the climax scene of the presentation of the peplos on the east is oddly downplayed. Nor was it the practice to depict mortal themes in temple decoration. Such difficulties have led to suggestions that this is a special version of the procession in which the participants may be either those in the first (legendary) festival, or heroic Greeks (possibly the dead of the Battle of Marathon) being received into divine company on the occasion of Athena's great festival. This interpretation is supported by the seated deities on the east who welcome the leaders of the procession in a way which recalls other scenes of apotheosis in Greek art. The Marathon dead were certainly regarded as heroes and thus more than mortal and fit to be depicted in the decoration of a temple. Although there are difficulties with this explanation too, and a count of participants which produces the same total (192) as the Athenian dead in the battle is highly suspect, some interpretation on these lines (a divine or heroic Panathenaia) seems the most likely.

The **Festival of the Greater Panathenaia** was, according to tradition, founded by Erichthonios and renewed by Theseus. It was refounded in the archonship of Hippokleides (566/65 BC) and turned into a major festival by Peisistratos. It was held every four years on the anniversary of the goddess's birthday in the month of Hekatombaion (August). Apart from sacrifices, it included athletic, musical and equestrian contests. The prizes were Panathenaic amphorae filled with tax-free olive oil from the sacred olive trees. The central feature of the festival was a **procession** in which was carried a new peplos for the old wooden statue of Athena Polias, originally in the Old Temple of Athena, later in the Erechtheíon, on the Acropolis. The garment (apparently woven by the Arrhephoroi, p 113), was ceremonially carried through the streets of the city on a 'ship' (p 147), manned by priests and priestesses wearing golden crowns and garlands of flowers (Philostratos, *Vit. Soph.* II 7). Specific groups, such as Athenian citizens, envoys from allied states and resident aliens had special roles to play in the ceremony. The route began at the Pompeion, by the Dipylon gate in the Kerameikos, and followed the Panathenaic Way through the Agora to the Eleusinion on the lower slopes of the Acropolis, then past the Pelargikon to the Pythion (a cave-shrine of Apollo in the north face of the Acropolis), where the ship was 'moored'. The procession probably halted near the Parthenon for the victors in the Panathenaic games to be presented with their amphorae. There followed a sacrifice at the altar and the deposition of the robe in the Erechtheion.

Between the Parthenon and the Erechtheíon, you can see the foundations of a temple, generally known as the **Old Temple of Athena**. The building, on the same site as a predecessor, belongs to the later 6C BC (possibly 529 BC). Two column bases, no longer in situ, are thought to come from an even earlier temple, of the Geometric period. Pedimental sculptures (Acropolis Museum) of a Gigantomachy with a central Athena probably belong to the Archaic building (east end); also an animal combat (west) which may have been flanked by the three-bodied Daemon on one side and Herakles wrestling with Triton on the other.

The building was amphidistyle (two columns at each end), or perhaps prostyle, in antis, with a colonnade of 6 x 12 columns. The eastern cella, which had two rows of columns, may have belonged to Athena Polias; the western, which was tripartite, to Poseidon-Erechtheus, Hephaistos and the hero Boutes (see p 124).

The temple was partly destroyed in the Persian sack of 480 BC, when some of its remains were built into the north wall of the Acropolis. The opisthodomos seems to have been rebuilt as a treasury; it is probably that referred to in the Kallias decree (a financial decree of ?434/33 BC) and could be the 'megaron facing west' which Herodotos describes as having smoke-blackened walls. Demosthenes says that it was dismantled in 353 BC.

In the area of the Old Temple of Athena was the Mycenaean palace, of which only some terrace walls have been traced.

The Erechtheíon

The true successor to the Old Temple of Athena was the Erechtheíon (finished 395 BC; plan, p 123), one of the most unusual, original and elegant of Greek temples. Like the Parthenon it came to be called after only one of its functions. Standing about halfway along the north side of the Acropolis, its odd layout was caused by the need to respect pre-existing cults in the area.

The temple contained various **exotica**. Apart from the ancient wooden statue and its golden lamp (p 124), there were a wooden figure of Hermes, said to be an offering of Kekrops, a folding chair made by the mythical craftsman Daidalos and some Persian spoils from Plataia. These included the corselet of Masistius (commander in Xerxes' army), made of gold links, and the sword of Mardonius, son-in-law of Darius.

Legend In the reign of Kekrops, the legendary first king of Athens, Athena and Poseidon competed for possession of the Acropolis (Hdt. VIII 55; Apollodorus III 14). Poseidon offered a 'sea' called Erechtheís; Athena an olive tree. Although Athena was adjudged the winner, the two were reconciled and were worshipped together. According to another myth, Erichthonios, son of Hephaistos and Earth, was placed by his foster-mother Athena in a chest and given into the care of Pandrosos, daughter of Kekrops. Erichthonios, who had serpent attributes, grew up to expel Amphiktyon and become king of Athens. There is inevitably much confusion over the detail of these stories but the sacred tokens which were venerated in Classical times—Athena's olive tree and the marks of Poseidon's trident, where he struck the rock and the 'sea' gushed forth—probably date from before the time of Homer. At some point Poseidon and Erechtheus became identified with each other.

The group of cults on the north side of the Acropolis which centred on the worship of Athena and Poseidon-Erechtheus may have grown up in the Mycenaean period since they are in the vicinity of the Mycenaean megaron (see above). According to Dionysos of Halikarnassos, the olive tree was in the Pandroseion (see below), and Pausanias puts Poseidon's well of seawater within the Erechtheíon. The Kekropeion (Tomb of Kekrops, see below) was close by and there were sacred snakes in the precinct. There is no archaeological evidence for a combined temple on the site earlier than the Erechtheion.

History The Erechtheion was part of the Periklean building programme on the Acropolis. It is sometimes attributed to Mnesikles. Construction was delayed by the Peloponnesian War but inscriptions show that it was nearly complete in 409 BC and probably finished in 406 BC. However, it was then damaged by fire (Xenophon, *Hellenica* I 6 1) and not rebuilt until 395 BC at the earliest. In the Augustan period there was another fire and the rebuilding incorporated some new features. In the 6C AD it was converted into a church and the original interior virtually destroyed. In 1463 it was turned into a harem for the wives of the Turkish commandant of the Acropolis. Elements were removed by Lord Elgin in 1801. It was besieged on various occasions during the War of Independence.

Excavation and restoration In 1838 K. Pittákis cleared some of the wall. In 1842–44 Paccard restored the Caryatid porch. On 26 October 1852 the upper part of the west façade was blown down in a violent storm. In 1903–09 the exterior was virtually rebuilt by N. Balános. A new programme of conservation and restoration, begun in 1979, was completed in 1987.

Architecture

So that the structure could encompass the various cults which were already established on the site of the Erechtheion, the temple spans an abrupt change in ground level (the foundations of the south and east walls are nearly 2.7m higher than those of the north and west) and the plan of the building is highly unusual. The change of level can be easily appreciated from the need to climb a flight of steps from the north porch to the east front. The functions of the Old Temple of Athena (cults of Athena and Poseidon-Erechtheus), as well as some others, were accommodated in the higher-level chambers, with those of earlier cults below and in the attached open-air precinct.

East end Behind the Ionic façade (six prostyle columns) at the east end, the layout is a plain rectangle with two projecting porches—the Caryatid porch on the south, and the north porch with foundations at the lower level. The west end of the building has a small basement entrance only; on the upper part the bases of engaged columns approximately reflect the entrance level on the east. Structural and visual unity was provided by the pediments, uniform at east and west, and the frieze.

The white marble figures on the frieze were set against a background of dark Eleusinian limestone and ran all round the building except where interrupted by the roof of the north porch, whose own frieze zone was treated similarly. The sculptures were attached by bronze clamps. The holes for the fittings are visible and fragments of the figures survive, but the subject is unknown. Decorative elaboration of the architecture was provided by such elements as gilt bronze ornaments and coloured glass inlays on the capitals, and painted mouldings. The coffers of the portico ceilings were painted blue with gilt bronze stars.

The Ionic columns (base diameter 0.8m; height 6.7m, including bases and capitals) of the eastern façade stood on a stylobate of three marble steps. The pediment had no sculpture. The north corner column was removed by Elgin. The wall behind the portico, which had a doorway and two windows, was pulled down to make way for the Byzantine apse. The south anta survives; the north (without its capital which is in the British Museum) was reconstructed in 1909.

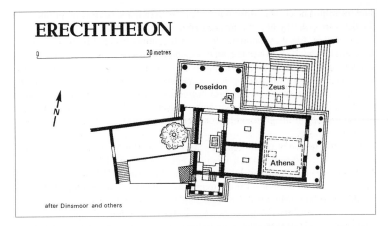

after Dinsmoor and others

The **Caryatid porch** projects from the south side of the building, at the same level as the east façade. Limited access from outside was provided by narrow steps at the east. Inside, an L-shaped stairway connected with the western cella. On the marble parapet (1.8m high), which partly overlaps the foundations of the Old Temple of Athena, six female figures instead of columns support the entablature. These Caryatids (the originals now replaced by casts) had libation bowls in their missing right hands. In pose and style they closely resemble the figures at the head of the procession on the Parthenon frieze, directly opposite. This is probably deliberate and intended to reflect the fact that the ultimate destination of the procession was the Erechtheion. Although the floor has gone, the coffered ceiling is well preserved.

West end From the east façade, you descend steps beside the temple to reach the north porch and west front of the building. The space between the steps and the temple was paved and probably had a ritual function. The **North porch**, one of the most sophisticated pieces of Greek architectural design, has six tall Ionic columns, four in the façade and one behind on each side. The west side projects a little beyond the façade of the building. It has a fine coffered ceiling, a richly decorated inner doorway and elegant minor mouldings. Much of the superstructure and the doorway date from a Roman reconstruction after a fire. Within the porch, a gap was left in the floor to show marks in the rock, perhaps of a thunderbolt, in a crypt below. There was a corresponding opening in the roof, according to the belief that places struck by lightning should be left open to the sky. By the gap stood the altar of the Thyechoös, a priest who offered honey cakes to Zeus Hypatos, and is known to have had a seat reserved for him in the theatre. Here may have been the tomb of Erechtheus and, because of his serpent associations, perhaps also the home of the snake (Hdt. VIII 41; Plutarch, *Themistokles* 10).

The guardian serpent
In the words of Herodotos (Penguin translation, p 537), 'The Athenians say that the Acropolis is guarded by a great snake, which lives in the temple; indeed they believe so literally in its existence that they regularly put out honey cake for it to eat.'

The mouldings of the **doorway**, Augustan copies of the originals, are particularly fine. The inner linings are Byzantine additions.

The west façade, blown down in 1852, was restored in 1904 to the form it had acquired by the 1C BC. Over the high wall of the basement is a row of columns engaged in a low wall. The open spaces above the wall were closed by wooden grills, except above the Kekropeion—presumably for some requirement of the cult. The column bases are original but everything else belongs to the Roman renewal. The south block of the entablature is a copy: the original, with Turkish inscriptions, is on the ground in front of the west façade.

Outside the west end of the building were two further sacred areas. The first, reached from the north porch where it extends beyond the end of the main building, was the **Pandroseion** (precinct of Pandrosos). Its precise limits are uncertain but it contained a small temple and the sacred **olive tree** of Athena. Herodotos relates that it sprouted again after being burnt down by the Persians. The present tree was planted by the archaeologist Bert Hodge Hill on 22 February 1917 (Washington's birthday) near an ancient copper waterpipe which he had excavated. He thought its function was to supply water to something of special importance, probably the olive. To the south again was the **Kekropeion** (precinct of Kekrops). Here was the tomb of Kekrops, most likely at the southwest corner of the Erechtheion where the temple foundations were modified to avoid disturbing an earlier structure. It was spanned by a huge block c 4.5 x 1.5m.

The original arrangement of the **interior** of the Erechtheíon, of which virtually nothing survives, has been a matter of endless dispute. The eastern cella, probably the main chamber with the venerated olive-wood **statue of Athena Polias**, was at a higher level than, and separated by a wall from, the rest of the interior. In the western cella were three **altars**: for Poseidon-Erechtheus, Hephaistos and the hero Boutes, as well as the thrones of their priests (those of Hephaistos and Boutes, both fragmentary but inscribed, have now been set up outside on stones at the east end of the Old Temple of Athena). Pausanias mentions portraits on the wall of the Boutad family from which the priests of the cult were drawn.

Ancient references suggest that the **statue** depicted the goddess standing and armed (Aristophanes, *Birds* 826–31), and holding a round shield with a gorgoneion (Euripides, *Electra* 1254–7). The Dresden Athena has been thought a copy of the figure. This was the statue to which the peplos carried in the Panathenaic procession was offered. In front of it burnt a golden lamp made by Kallimakhos with a special asbestos wick that needed oil only once a year, and a chimney in the form of a bronze palm tree. The lamp was tended by elderly widows. During the siege of Athens by Sulla in 86 BC, Aristion let it go out (Plutarch, *Sulla* 13).

Evidence of the **sea called Erechtheïs**, below the antechamber, has been obliterated by a medieval or Turkish cistern. The 'sea' was perhaps covered with marble tiles and seen through a *puteal* (well-head). When the south wind blew it gave off the sound of waves.

The Acropolis Museum

Carefully designed so as not to interfere with the skyline of the Acropolis, the museum contains all the objects discovered on the site since 1834, apart from most of the vases and bronzes, which are in the National Museum. It is particularly rich in Archaic sculpture and, although sometimes overcrowded, is one of the most exciting collections in Greece. The arrangement is roughly chronological.

The **vestibule** has a variety of sculptures. No. 1333 is a stele with a relief scene of *Athena* (representing Athens) and *Hera* (representing Samos) and the text of a treaty (405 BC) between the two states: this was defaced under the Thirty Tyrants (p 60) and re-engraved later in a changed political climate. A fine head of *Alexander the Great* (1331) may be by Leokhares, c 330 BC. The famous *Hermes Propylaios of Alkamenes* (430 BC) is copied in a Roman herm (2281). Bases (1326, 1338) of votive offerings have relief decoration. *Portrait of philosopher* (1313), 5C AD. No. 1358 is *Prokne*, perhaps a copy of the first figure from the Prokne and Itys group by Alkamenes which was seen by Pausanias. Itys was killed by his mother Prokne and served up as a meal to his father Tereus, in revenge for his abusing Prokne's sister, Philomela.

Rooms I–III have exciting and colourful **6C pedimental sculptures** from buildings on the Acropolis. They illustrate early developments in the medium: a trend from lower to higher relief, extensive use of paint, careful choice of compositions to suit the triangular shape of the pediment and the use of mythological subjects.

Room I Fragments (552, 554) of a marble leopard may be from the metopes of the Hekatompedon. A pedimental group (1) has *Herakles fighting the Hydra*, with Iolaos his charioteer: the crab was sent by Hera to impede Herakles. The group of a *Lioness attacking a bull* (4) may have been the central part of the west pediment of the Hekatompedon, flanked by the serpent figures in Room II. The *Head of a running gorgon* (701) was possibly the acroterion of the east pediment of the Hekatompedon.

Room II Two sides of a pediment, perhaps the eastern from the Hekatompedon, whose centre may have been the fighting lions in Room III: (36) *Herakles wrestling with Triton* and (35) *Three-bodied monster* with a serpent's tail. The heads are dramatic and the tail highly colourful. The creature may carry a political message of the unity of the Athenian state, since each figure is holding a symbol of one of the three groups into which the citizens were divided—a water symbol for the people of the shore, corn stalks for those of the plain, and a bird for the hill people. Pieces of serpents (2, 37, 40)—see Room I. Part of pediment (9) showing the *Introduction of Herakles to Olympos*: Iris presents the hero (wearing his lionskin) to Zeus, who has Hera seated beside him. The *Moschophoros* (Calf-bearer; 624; illustration p 127) is a votive statue showing a man carrying an animal for sacrifice. The *Olive-tree pediment* (52), with an unusual architectural background, must have belonged to a very small building. The subject is not certain but may be the ambush of Troilos by Akhilles in the Trojan War. A case of terracotta figures near the entrance exemplifies the dedications of ordinary citizens.

Room III Large group (3) of *Two lions attacking a bull*, perhaps from the Hekatompedon (see above). Korai include 619 in a distinctive East Greek style (cylindrical body and lightly incised drapery), best known from the island of Samos. Another (677) is probably Naxian since it mixes eastern and western Aegean elements, and the face strongly resembles that of the Naxian sphinx from Delphi.

Room IV includes most of the **korai**. Dedicated as votive offerings, they were damaged in the Persian sack and afterwards ritually buried, only to be recovered in the excavations of 1882–86.

Korai

Always draped, korai often hold small offerings (birds, fruit, animals). The *peplos* gave way in time to the *chiton* (tunic; often worn with a *himation*, a cloak) as the most popular garment. At first efforts were concentrated on decorative treatment of the dress, later sculptors became interested also in showing the form of the body beneath. Many have the characteristic 'Archaic smile' which may be deliberate, or the result of problems in working the transition from mouth to cheek. It dies out as the treatment of features becomes increasingly naturalistic.

The room has three sections. In the first is a votive relief (581) showing worshippers bringing a sacrificial animal to Athena. Three works perhaps by the same sculptor (the Rampin master) are the famous *Peplos kore* (679), a *Horseman* (590; the head is a cast of the 'Rampin' head in Paris; the join was recognised by Humfry Payne in 1936) and a fragmentary kore head (654). A fourth work is in the National Museum (38: stele fragment with *discophoros*—discus carrier). Another *Horseman* (606), part of a display of Archaic riders, wears Scythian or Persian dress. Votive reliefs include one (702) of *Hermes, the Three graces and a Boy*.

The second section has a fine *Kore* (675; illustration p 127) made by a sculptor from the island of Chios, with much of the original colour preserved; also *Scribes* (629 etc). Some of the pieces in this room carry marks of fire from the Persian sack. The third section has several interesting korai dated to the later part of the 6C; also a seated figure thought to be the Athena by Endoios which was seen by Pausanias.

In **Room V** are striking figures from the *Gigantomachy* (c 525 BC) which filled the east pediment of the Old Temple of Athena. In 631 Athena advances, wearing her aegis; two falling giants fill the corners. The *Kore of Antenor* (671) c 525 BC is associated with a base bearing the signature of the sculptor Antenor and of the dedicator, a potter called Nearkhos. Antenor probably made sculptures also for the Temple of Apollo at Delphi, where kore figures are very similar in style. A fragment of sculpture on the top of an inscribed column (6206) illustrates a favoured way of displaying votive sculpture in sanctuaries.

In an alcove is the striking **frieze from the Temple of Athena Nike** (p 111).

Room VI has sculptures of the **severe style** (from c 480 BC) which saw a definite break with Archaic pattern and exuberance and the adoption of more Classical qualities of physical naturalism and restraint. The *Kritian boy* (698) is

*The Moschophoros (Calf-bearer) and an archaic kore (no. 675);
both from the Acropolis, now in the Acropolis Museum.*

the best-known example of the earliest Classical naturalism. Note also the ***Blond
Head*** (689). The so-called ***Mourning Athena*** (695) is an elegant votive relief
showing the goddess. There is a rare example (67) of a painted ***pinax*** with a
running warrior. An interesting votive relief (1332) shows a seated potter
(presumably representing the dedicator) holding two cups.

In **Room VII** are fragments of the **Parthenon pediments** and models showing
possible reconstructions. The composition of the **west pediment** (***Contest of
Athena and Poseidon***) is reasonably certain; that of the East (***Birth of Athena***)
less so. Most of the eastern figures still surviving in Carrey's day (p 116) are now
in the British Museum. Here you can see, from the **east pediment**, *Heads of
horses* from Athena's and Poseidon's chariots (882, 884); a ***Seated goddess*** (U;
1363); ***Hermes*** (H; 880); ***Selene*** (N; 881); ***Kekrops and daughter*** (B, C; in case,
14935); part of torso of ***Poseidon*** added to cast of another fragment in London
(M; 885); torso possibly of ***Kephalos*** (V; 887); ***Procris*** (?), reclining, draped (W;
14936). Also here is (705), a metope with ***Centaur abducting a Lapith woman***.

Room VIII has substantial sections of the **Parthenon frieze** (arranged in sequence, and with explanatory diagram). Most is in London but parts that were blown off by the 1687 explosion and later buried escaped Lord Elgin. Pieces recently removed from the building will be added after conservation.

The Acropolis Museum has 13 of the 42 slabs showing the procession on the **north side**: horses and riders in various poses; marshals; chariots, one with an *apobates* (soldiers in armour who jumped on and off chariots in a ritual competition); musicians; carriers of *hydriai* (water-jars); men with sacrificial rams and heifers. The few slabs from the **south side** mostly have horses and riders. The three slabs from the **east side** include an excellent one of three of the seated deities—Poseidon, Apollo and Artemis.

In the same room are the 13 surviving slabs from the **parapet of the Temple of Athena Nike**: *Winged Victories* in various poses. No. 973 is the well-known *Sandalbinder*, where an awkward pose is entirely redeemed by the composition of the drapery, whose texture is itself exceptionally subtle. No. 972 (to the right) is thought to be by Paionios, sculptor of the famous *Nike* at Olympia.

Room IX contains four of the six original **Caryatids** from the Caryatid porch of the Erechtheion (one is in London, one being conserved).

The Beulé Gate and Klepsydra

To leave the site, you return to the Propylaia and descend towards the Beulé Gate. Halfway down from the Propylaia is a landing, with a terrace extending to the right. Partly blocking access to the terrace is the so-called **Monument of Agrippa**. This consisted of a quadriga set on a tall (8.8m) podium of Hymettian marble, with base and cornice mouldings in poros. The conglomerate foundation steps would not have been visible. The monument had a curious history which can be traced through marks and inscriptions on the monument itself, further inscriptions on the landing below, and references in Plutarch and Dio Cassius. Originally it recorded a Pergamene victory in the Panathenaic games and carried a chariot group including the Pergamene king Eumenes II. The second chariot group, including Marcus Agrippa, was erected after his third consulship in 27 BC.

Behind the Agrippa Monument, the terrace (Periklean; now inaccessible) lies below the north wing of the Propylaia. From it Late Roman steps (inaccessible) descend through a Byzantine doorway, down a gulley, to Klepsydra.

The landing just above the Beulé Gate is the only point where you can get some view of the steep north slope of the rock and a hint of the site of the interesting Klepsydra spring, also partly visible from Pláka (p 169).

Klepsydra, originally a spring in a small natural **cave**, attracted the settlers of Neolithic times. First called Empedo, it was a shrine of the Nymphs by the Classical period. About 460 BC a well-house with a deep draw-basin was constructed inside the cave and, beside it, a court of which the paved floor and a wall survive. Part of the well-house roof collapsed in the 1C BC, though the well was still accessible in 37 BC when Mark Antony was instructed by the Delphic Oracle to take with him to Parthia a bottle of water from Klepsydra. A further collapse occurred in the reign of Claudius but the spring continued in use. Later in the Roman period a **well-house** was constructed over the collapsed cave, a shaft sunk down to water level, and the whole sealed with concrete. The **stairway** to the bastion above was built at this time and access was then possible only from the Acropolis (see below). A lower cistern was built later (6C) to take the overflow. During the building of the Roman well-house the court went out of use and was subsequently covered by the Late Roman Wall.

In due course the well-house was transformed into a **church** of the Ayy. Apostoli (Holy Apostles), and decorated with frescoes. The Byzantine door above may be contemporary. By 1822 the ancient and Byzantine remains were covered, although the spring still fed a Turkish fountain lower down the hill. Lack of water forced the Turkish capitulation in 1822. The Greek forces subsequently rediscovered the Klepsydra source and repaired it. General Odysseus Androutsos enclosed it in a bastion in 1826 (demolished 1888) and, with the aid of this supply, the Greeks withstood the siege of 1827. In 1897 Kavvadhías excavated the paved court. The main investigations were by American archaeologists in 1936–40. For other monuments on the north slope of the Acropolis, see p 169.

The **Beulé Gate** was named after the French archaeologist who discovered it in 1853. Part of the Late Roman defensive system (see p 220; also 160, Agora; p 165, Hadrian's Library), and erected c AD 280 at the expense of F. Septimius Marcellinus, it consists of a trilithon portal in a marble wall inset between two projecting towers. It incorporates material from the Choregic Monument of Nikias (p 98), part of whose inscription can be read above the lintel outside; the rest of the text is higher up. On the inner side is a slab with two victor's wreaths.

Just inside the Beulé Gate are four fragments of an architrave with doves, fillets and an inscription. These belong to the shrine of Aphrodite Pandemos which stood below the southwest corner of the hill.

Byzantine (?) and Ottoman fortifications

The path down from the gate runs parallel with remains (left) of a Turkish wall (called **Serpentzés** after a Persian word for fortification) which linked the Beulé Gate with the Odeion of Herodes Atticus (the point where it is best preserved). In this wall was a gate into the fortified area (redoubt) thus created below the south face of the Acropolis, making use of the Odeion and the Stoa of Eumenes. The name Serpentzés is also applied to the redoubt as a whole.

In the 18C another wall was built by the Ottomans to protect the Acropolis approach. Later called Tis Ipapandís, from a church on its course, it ran from the east side of the gate into Serpentzés to the church of Ay. Nikolaos (p 169), which became a tower defending its lower gate (on the north side of the hill). A gate below the Beulé, together with the western part of the wall, has not survived.

Earlier, perhaps in the 11C, another wall, the Rizókastro, ran round the foot of the Acropolis hill at the level of the Theatre of Dionysos (p 96). This has been located at various points.

3 • The hills of Athens: the Areopagos, Mouseion, Pnyx and Hill of the Nymphs

The sites included in this chapter provide a mixture of Classical associations, pleasant rambles and excellent views, ranging over most of the ancient city. The Pnyx, setting of the Classical Assembly, is an exciting surprise, with a fine prospect of the Acropolis.

- **Distance on foot**. The route described is roughly circular and about 1.5km in total. It begins and ends at the Areopagos, close to the Acropolis (p 101), and could also be combined with seeing the Agora (p 147).
  Access by bus. No. 230 (see Acropolis) from Akadhimías or Síntagma to Acropolis stop.

The Areopagos
This low hill (**Map 5,3**; 115m) immediately west of the entrance to the Acropolis, is joined to it by a saddle. There is a good view over the Classical Agora.

Background and history
The name Areopagos may come from the tradition (Euripides, *Electra* 1258) that Ares was tried here by the other gods for the murder of Halirrhothios, son of Poseidon. Alternatively it may mean 'Hill of the Curses' (*arai*).

In his play *The Eumenides* (458 BC; 681–706) Aeschylus described the legendary trial of Orestes on the Areopagos for the murder of his mother Klytemnestra, and the foundation by Athena of the court of the Areopagos and a sanctuary of the Eumenides (Furies) on the very spot where the trial of Orestes took place. He also located the camp of the Amazons here in their legendary attack on Athens in the time of Theseus.

According to tradition, the Cave of the Furies lay below the northeast brow of the hill. The precinct of the cave was a recognised sanctuary for murderers and fugitive slaves. This right of asylum was abused by the killers of Kylon's fellow-conspirators (p 58). It was the custom for those acquitted by the Areopagos court to sacrifice at the cave. The tomb of Oedipus, regarded as essential to the safety of Athens, was within the precinct.

In historic times, the Persians encamped on the hill when they besieged the Acropolis in 480 BC (Hdt.VIII 52).

The 7C council of elders became known as the **Council of the Areopagos**, to distinguish it from later councils. Its original and most important function was criminal justice, particularly cases of murder and manslaughter, but in pre-democratic Athens it became the governing body of the state (p 65). The archons were either members ex officio or, according to Plutarch (*Life of Perikles*), became members after their period of office expired. At that time the Assembly of the people merely endorsed the decisions of the Areopagos.

Solon transferred the administrative and legislative powers of the Council to the Assembly, but made the Areopagos protector of the constitution and guardian of the laws, with control over magistrates and censorship. Under Ephialtes (461 BC), both the latter were transferred to the Assembly, and the jurisdiction of the Areopagos was once again limited to cases of homicide. The implication of the story of the Eumenides (previous page) is that such cases were its proper functions.

In the 4C BC the Areopagos dealt also with crimes of treason and corruption. Notable cases were those of the deserters after the Battle of Khaironaia in 338 BC, of Demosthenes in 324 BC and of the 4C courtesan Phryne who charmed the court when argument failed. It continued in existence under the Roman empire.

In AD 51 **St Paul** (Acts xvii 22–34; text on a **bronze plaque** to the right of the steps) 'in the midst of Mars' hill', described his religion to the Council. In the process he converted one of their number, Dionysios, who became St Dionysios the Areopagite and patron saint of Athens.

Rock-cut steps lead up to the summit of the hill which was artificially levelled. You can see beddings cut in the rock for a small Ionic temple of the 5C BC. Pausanias (I 28 5) says that 'the unwrought stones on which the accused and accusers stand are called respectively the Stone of Injury and the Stone of Ruthlessness' (see Euripides, *Iphigeneia in Tauris* 961).

Taking a path downhill by the bronze plaque, you pass enormous boulders which must be the collapsed roof of the **Cave of the Furies**. On the far side of these, on a level platform believed by some to be the setting of the court's sessions, you can see the foundations of the 16C church of **St Dionysios the Areopagite**. Lower down the north slope four Mycenaean chamber tombs (early 14C BC; no longer visible) were explored in 1939 and 1947. Some fine contents (Agora Museum) suggested royal or aristocratic burials.

The slopes to the west have never been fully investigated, though Dörpfeld found houses and a street (towards Leofóros Apostólou Pávlou; p 136) which he mistakenly identified as the Panathenaic Way. From the Areopagos you can reach the Agora by a path.

At the southwest corner of the Acropolis hill Leofóros Dhionisíou Areopayítou terminates at a roundabout, beyond which its continuation, Leofóros Apostólou Pávlou, curves down to Thisío. On the far side of these roads lie, respectively, the Mouseion Hill, with the Tomb and Monument of Philópappos; the Pnyx; and the Hill of the Nymphs.

Mouseion Hill

To reach the Mouseion Hill (**Maps 4,6; 5,5**) you descend the Acropolis approach road to Leofóros Dhionisíou Areopayítou. On the far side, by the Dhiónisos Restaurant, paths and a road (no vehicles) mount the tree-clad slopes. The road can also be used to approach the Philópappos theatre (p 131) on the far side of the hill.

According to a Greco-Roman tradition, the name is derived from Musaios, the poet-disciple of Orpheus. More likely it came from a shrine of the Muses located here.

The hill has played a strategic role in the fortunes of Athens. The **Themistoklean Wall** ran up its gentle east slope, followed the top of the sheer south face (visible traces) and joined the southern long wall near its western extremity. The later *Diateichisma* (cross-wall; see overleaf) ran northwest from the summit. In 294 BC Demetrios Poliorketes built a fort here to command the Piraeus road; it changed hands four times in the ensuing campaign. It was from the Mouseion in 1687 that Morosini bombarded the Acropolis. At the end of November 1916 Greek royalist forces occupied the area, and fired on allied troops on 1 December. It was again a key point in the military coup of 21 April 1967.

In the area enclosed by the walls of Themistokles and the Diateichisma were the **ancient demes** of *Koile* and *Melite*. There are numerous remains, including houses (many of them partly or wholly rock-cut) and pear-shaped cisterns 4–6m deep, mostly of the 5C. The area, then entirely within the city walls, became overpopulated at the time of the Peloponnesian War, with an influx of people from the countryside (Thuc. II 14) but it was deserted before the end of the 3C BC. In Roman times the earlier structures were used as tombs. In the bottom of the valley are traces of a rutted ancient road which led southwest from the Ayios Dhimítrios gate (see below).

Walk up the paved road to the 16C church of **Ay. Dhimítrios Loumbardhiáris**. The name (from *loumbárdha*, cannon) comes from a miracle attributed to the saint in which a Turkish cannon situated on the Acropolis was struck by lightning at the very moment it was about to open fire on his congregation. There are some surviving Byzantine frescoes. Restoration of the building and the attractive refurbishment of the surrounding area (including an outdoor cafeteria, whose setting is its main attraction) was the work (1951–57) of the leading architect Dhimítris Pikiónis, his students and local artists.

Opposite the church are remains of the north tower of a **gate** in the Diateichsma, incorrectly described as the Dipylon above the Gates after a 4C inscription. Its south tower was excavated in 1936 and re-covered. Further over is the misnamed **prison of Sokrates**, probably a large rock-cut house. The levelled rock-face has slots for the wooden beams of the roof of other rooms in front.

By the tower a paved path (signed) ascends to the Philópappos monument. This path follows the **Diateichisma**, whose lower courses are visible for most of the way. It was built at the end of the 4C BC after the destruction of the Long Walls had made Themistokles' original cross-line untenable. The **Fort of Demetrios Poliorketes** on the summit of the Mouseion Hill was later joined on to it. Remains of a tower of this fort are visible at the top of the Diateichisma c 70m north of the Philópappos tomb (there are foundations of another lower down to the north-east).

On the bare summit, above the tree line and with a fine panoramic view, especially at sunset, is the **Tomb of Philópappos**. It was built in AD 114–16, probably by his family, in honour of C. Julius Antiochus Philópappos, a prince of Commagene (north Syria) who held the highest offices of state in both Athens and Rome.

The tomb was seen intact by Cyriacus of Ancona in 1436. Of Pentelic marble, it has a slightly convex façade 12.2m high. The façade, facing the Acropolis, has a sculpted frieze showing Philópappos as consul (AD 109) driving his chariot. Above this, four Corinthian pilasters frame three niches. The central one has a statue of Philópappos as an Athenian citizen of the deme of Besa; the left contains his grandfather Antiochus IV Epiphanes, the last king of Commagene, who was dethroned by Vespasian. According to Cyriacus, the right niche contained Seleukos I Nikator, the Macedonian founder of the dynasty. On the left central pilaster, inscribed in Latin, is the deceased's *cursus honorum* (cycle of public office) in Rome; on the right, in Greek, were his princely titles. Traces of the tomb chamber survive behind the façade.

The Pnyx

On the opposite side of Ayios Dhimítrios rises the hill of the Pnyx (**Map 4,4**; 109m), in Classical times popularly called the Rocks. This is accessible in a few minutes by a path (also serving the Son et Lumière auditorium) above the church, which skirts the boundary fence of the site. You get in by the third gate in the fence. The Pnyx itself is nearly 30m below the summit on the northeast side. Not much visited, this is one of the surprises of Athens. It is quiet, the site itself is impressive, and there are fine views of the Acropolis and over Athens. The other side of the hill (with seats) looks out to Fáliro Bay and Piraeus.

The Pnyx, meeting-place of the Assembly, was firmly identified by the discovery in the 19C of a boundary stone inscribed ΟΡΟΣ ΠΥΚΝΟΣ (boundary of the Pnyx). The site was investigated by K. Kourouniótis and Homer Thompson between 1930 and 1936.

The word 'Pnyx' (η Πνύξ, gen. Πύκνος) means a place where people were tightly packed (πύκνος, crowded); the hill of the Pnyx was one of the most densely populated parts of ancient Athens.

With the establishment of democracy under Kleisthenes at the end of the 6C BC, the Assembly changed its venue from the Agora to the Pnyx, perhaps symbolically now above rather than below the Areopagos. Here the great statesmen of the 5C and 4C, among them Aristides, Themistokles, Perikles and Demosthenes, held their audiences. The Prytaneis (see Agora, p 154) presided over the Assembly. The citizens (5000 were needed for a quorum) were hustled towards the Pnyx by Scythian archers who held cords daubed with wet red paint across the Agora and neighbouring streets to hurry up the participants and prevent abstention. Arrivals were scrutinised at the entrance to ensure that they were qualified. Non-citizens were only allowed to attend with special permission. People marked with red paint forfeited their allowances.

The archaeological site

The essential features of the Pnyx were an **auditorium** and speaker's **rostrum**. There were three periods of construction. Around 500 BC the auditorium faced north (towards the Agora) and the rostrum south, an arrangement which fitted the lie of the land. Under the Thirty Tyrants (403 BC; see p 60) these arrangements were reversed, with the rostrum facing inland, because, according to Plutarch (*Themistokles* 19 4), they thought oligarchy less distasteful to farmers than to mariners. The retaining wall of this period was excavated in 1930–31 and is visible in an open trench. Most of the remains belong to the third period, originally thought to be Hadrianic, but now attributed to a comprehensive plan (p 134) of Lykourgos for the embellishment of the site in the 4C BC. But the buildings planned to accompany the new auditorium were never finished and the Assembly seems to have migrated to the Theatre of Dionysos (Thuc. VIII 93).

In this final form the Pnyx consisted of a huge semicircular artificial terrace, its ends abutting onto a striking vertical rock-face, also man-made. From the centre of this projects the speaker's rostrum (bema). The terrace (circumference 198.5m) is retained by a massive wall of trapezoidal blocks quarried from the rock-face: a section 4.5m high, representing about a third of the original, survives at the centre of the arc. The wall retained an earth filling which reversed the natural slope of the ground (now restored with the passage of time). The **entrance** was by a flight of steps (visible in a fenced trench) which ascended through the wall at the north, opposite the bema. Remains of a second wall, concentric with and about 10m within the retaining wall, were found in excavations: this belonged to the second period. There is no evidence for any seating in the auditorium.

The line of the rock-face is divided into two sections which meet at an angle in the centre, where it is highest (4.6m). At the angle is the **bema** from which the speakers addressed the Assembly, a three-stepped platform (9.4 x 6.4 x 0.9m high) projecting from the rock. It was surrounded by a balustrade (sockets visible). The bema was crowned by a cube of rock (3 x 3 x 1.8m high) with a flight of steps at each side. Round the base of the rock was a ledge for votive or legislative stelai. Twelve metres to the east of the bema a large **niche** in the rock is surrounded by over 50 smaller ones. Twelve marble stelai (now in the British Museum) were found below by Lord Aberdeen in 1805, and others since. Most of them are dedications of the Roman period by women to Zeus Hypsistos (highest).

On the opposite side of the bema, a flight of steps gave access to the terrace above. On this broad levelled terrace, above the rock-face, in the centre and on the axis of the bema, is a bedding, probably for a monumental **altar**. This is flanked by rock-cut benches, possibly the seats of the Prytaneis. Further back, another bedding may mark the site of the **heliotropion** (sundial) put up by the astronomer Meton in 433 BC, and there are bases of other monuments.

At a higher level are beddings for the foundations of two large stoas, the west 148 x 18m, the east 21.5 x 6m. The latter is on a different alignment and, in its second form, designed to harmonise with a third (central) building, perhaps a propylon. Dating from 350–325 BC, they have usually been taken as representing the scheme of Lykourgos to provide ancillary accommodation for the Assembly.

Soon after these buildings were begun, it was decided to run the Diateichisma through the site, although the first wall was quickly replaced by another, of white poros, with towers, traces of which can be seen to the south and west. This may have strengthened a weak point in the circuit at the time (c 200 AD) the outer cross-wall and the Long Walls were finally abandoned.

Hill of the Nymphs

A few minutes north of the Pnyx, and reached by a continuation of the same path, is the Hill of the Nymphs (**Map 4,4**). The name is modern, borrowed from a dedication to the Nymphs carved on a rock in the garden of the Observatory. Its slopes are peppered with ancient foundations, in the midst of which stands the little rock-cut church of **Ay. Marína**, dwarfed by its multi-domed modern partner. The church has frescoes in several layers (13C and earlier). Some early 20C paintings have been conserved and redisplayed on canvas panels. On the rock below the church is a 6C retrograde inscription (the writing goes right to left) 'ΟΡΟΣ ΔΙΟΣ', or boundary of Zeus, and the foundations of a 5C Temple of Zeus have been identified. At the edges of the slope are remains of rock-cut buildings. Excavations are in progress.

The first Athens Observatory as it looked in the 19C

On the summit of the hill are the pleasant buildings of the original Athens **Observatory** (Asteroskopío; not open to visitors), founded by Baron Sínas in 1842 and designed by Th. Hansen. A second building with a larger telescope was added in 1905, and a seismological station in 1957. The main Athens observatory is now at Pendéli (p 249).

Behind the Observatory is a radio station. To the right (c 70m) the Little Pnyx, a rock-cut Assembly area, has disappeared beneath modern houses. Traces of the northern Long Wall were found close by. A long depression to the west, partly filled, is sometimes identified with the ancient *Barathron* (place of execution).

You return past the Observatory and descend to Leofóros Apostólou Pávlou in the area now known as **Thisío**, after the name first given to the famous temple described on p 149. Left, on the other side of the main road, opposite a major junction with Od. Akámantos, is the small Plateía Thisíou (bus stop on the 230 route; cafés with good views of the Acropolis), with a secondary entrance (08.30–15.00, or 17.00 in high season; closed Mon) to the Agora excavations.

The main road continues to drop northwest, past public gardens, and sweeps round to the right. On the bend, at the junction with Od. Poulopoúlou, the road ahead takes you straight to the large church of Ay. Athanásios, west of which are some traces of the ancient wall. Beyond the church, a bridge over the electric railway comes out opposite the entrance to the Kerameikós (p 173).

Further sections of the **ancient wall and gates** have been found in surrounding streets. On Iraklídhon (at the junction with Erisíkhthonos) a section is preserved in the middle of the pleasant pedestrianised street. The Piraeus gate was close by. Like the Dipylon, it had an interior court. A recently discovered stretch of wall is to be preserved in the basement of Poulopoúlou 37.

At the bottom of Iraklídhon (no. 66) a former hat factory has been well converted into the **Melína Merkoúri Cultural Centre** (09.00–13.00 and 17.00–21.00; closed all day Mon, and Sun evening), named after the late Greek actress and Minister of Culture. The permanent display consists of reconstructions of traditional shops with appropriate contents; the Centre also hosts temporary art exhibitions.

Suburbs of the ancient city

As you face Plateía Thisíou (previous page), up to your right and opposite the Cinema Thisíon, a gate gives access to the lower slopes of the Areopagos. To your left the fencing of the Agora site terminates in a sharp triangle. Between that point and the Agora proper are a domestic and industrial area of ancient Athens and the prison (see plan of the centre of Ancient Athens, pp 150–151).

Right of the Areopagos Gate is an area excavated by Dörpfeld (p 104) in 1892–97 (for a lead into the references see American School of Classical Studies, *The Athenian agora XIV: The agora of Athens* by H.A. Thompson and R.E. Wycherley, p 181, n. 52). Some of Dörpfeld's identifications, most importantly those of the temple of Dionysos in the Marshes (*Limnai*) and of the Enneakrounos (pp 59, 163), have proved inaccurate. Some of the remains are now beneath the modern road.

Although partly overgrown and little visited (features which give added appeal, especially when spring flowers are in bloom), these excavations give some idea of the situation and character of ancient Athens away from the public centres. This indeed is their main interest since the building remains are undistinguished.

To reach the exposed area you must first cross a few metres of the rocky hillside. The buildings excavated cluster around an **ancient road**, possibly the main street of the deme of Melite. The Dörpfeld excavations uncovered a stretch of about 230m reaching to the modern roundabout by the Acropolis approach road.

To the right of the road, heading south, was a **lesche** (club-house), identified as such by inscriptions. This is now beneath Leofóros Apostólou Pávlou, just before the point where the ancient street emerges to view. Opposite, a triangular precinct (Dörpfeld's Dionysos sanctuary) has a small temple, or heroön, base (perhaps supporting the statue of Herakles by Agelades mentioned by the Scholiast to Aristophanes, *Frogs* 501), and wine-press. In the 2C AD the religious fraternity of the Iobacchoi built their club-house or **Baccheion** over part of the site. Fragments of the substantial walls of this latter are now the most obvious feature. On the far side of the side road which bounds the Herakles sanctuary to the east, in the angle it makes with the main street, is the 4C courtyard **House of the Greek Mosaic**, often illustrated in reconstruction, where good pebble mosaics were found in the *andron* and its anteroom (wheel pattern). To the right of the principal road the fine **House of Aristodemos** (4C and later) with a peristyle court (this can be made out) had a record of two mortgages, for 1000 and 210 drachmas, inscribed on its front wall in 4C lettering. There are some remains of a local water supply system, which have no relation to the Enneakrounos, as Dörpfeld thought. Opposite again are indistinct remains of the **Amyneion**, a small shrine to the hero Amynos, an assistant of Asklepios. Inside were a temple, and a well fed by a conduit from the water supply. The playwright Sophokles held the priesthood of this shrine.

The road continues southeast to a major junction. From the Amyneion a footpath climbs to your starting-point at the Areopagos.

4 • Omónia and Síntagma

In and around these two squares, at the heart of Athens, are many of the city's public buildings. Omónia is commercial and popular; Síntagma, with the Greek Parliament in the former Royal Palace, political and aristocratic. They are connected by two long streets, Od. Stadhíou and Od. Panepistimíou. Plateía Kolokotróni (off Stadhíou) has a fascinating National Historical Museum in the fine 19C Parliament building. King Otho's modest first palace, now a Museum of the City of Athens, is nearby in Plateía Klafthmónos. Panepistimíou contains the elegant neoclassical (19C) National Library, University and Academy. Both streets have a wide variety of shops and other fine buildings, many of them recently restored.

- **Distance on foot**. Maps 3,3–6; 7. The walk from Omónia to Síntagma by Stadhíou, returning by Panepistimíou, is about 2.6km.
  Access by bus/trolley bus. There is no circular route but both streets (one-way) can be surveyed from public transport: Stadhíou by taking bus no. 155, or trolleys nos 2, 4, 7, 11 or 15 (stops in Stadhíou) or 1, 12, 22 (stop in Aiólou)—and alighting in Síntagma; Panepistimíou by boarding in Leofóros Amalías, by the National Garden, or in Vasilíssis Sofías, and alighting either just above Omónia or at the following stop (Politekhnío), near the Polytechnic in Patisíon.
  Metró. Omónia–Síntagma (Line 2) with intermediate stop at Panepistímio (the old University in Panepistimíou)

Omónia

Plateía Omonías (Concord Square) is always called simply Omónia. The name, which derives from the reconciliation of two conflicting 19C political factions, applies also to the immediately surrounding area. The Omónia bus terminals, for instance, are actually in the surrounding streets. The square is a hub of Athenian life in more ways than one. A commercial centre, it has numerous shipping and travel agencies and large hotels. The square is always full of people, often gathered in lively circles (*pigadhákia*, little wells), vociferously discussing issues of the day. The attractive neoclassical buildings which reflect Omónia's history and status have recently been redecorated. These include the elegant neoclassical National Bank of Greece (Ethnikí Trápeza tis Elládhos, ΕΘΝΙΚΗ ΤΡΑΠΕΖΑ ΤΗΣ ΕΛΛΑΔΟΣ) on one corner of Panepistimíou, the former Hotel Bánghion (1890) and the Mégas Aléxandros building (1889), both by Ziller, to either side of Athinás, and the Café Néon opposite.

Omónia is a major crossroads and several important streets radiate from here: Panepistimíou from the upper side of the square, then (anti-clockwise) Patisíon, Tríti Septemvríou, Ayíou Konstandínou, Piraiós (officially Panayí Tsaldári), Athinás and Stadhíou. Down Ayíou Konstandínou, on the right past a square with a huge church (Kaftanzóglou, 1869–93) of the same name, is the imposing neoclassical National Theatre. Down Piraiós are the Municipal Gallery and Plateía Koumoundoúrou (p 172).

Patisíon leads towards the National Museum and Athinás towards Monastiráki and the Acropolis. Panepistimíou and Stadhíou are described below.

Stadhíou

Od. Stadhíou runs from the southeast corner of Omónia, to Síntagma; traffic is one-way in that direction. Od. Panepistimíou, described below, is parallel but with the traffic flow reversed.

Long, broad, busy and tiring to walk, but otherwise a pleasant and interesting street, Stadhíou has some good shops and arcades and an interesting range of buildings (a restoration programme is in progress)—as well as its share of indifferent modernity. It is named after the Stadium, on which it is aligned, even though that monument lies invisible, another kilometre beyond Síntagma, the other side of the National Garden. Stadhíou was renamed after Churchill from 1945 to 1955.

Leaving Omónia, you first cross the narrow and pedestrianised Aiólou, with a fine view of the Acropolis rising in the distance to the right. On the left is Od. Emmanouíl Benáki, named after a former head of the Greek community in Alexandria and later Mayor of Athens; he was a major public benefactor (d. 1929) and father of the great collector Andónis Benáki. Between here and Odd. Santarósa and Arsáki is the former state **printing-press** (1836, with many later alterations), a modest two-storeyed building, now being restored. A plaque on the wall (temporarily removed) commemorates the centenary (1925) of the death of the Italian philhellene Santorre Santarosa, fighting at Pylos in the War of Independence. Next is the imposing **Arsákion extension** (Ernst Ziller, 1900; for the Arsákion itself, see description of Panepistimíou, p 143), white with silver cupolas and a restrained use of Classical motifs. Running through this to Panepistimíou is the airy **Stoá Orféas** (shops, café) and, off it, the attractive **Stoá tou Vivlíou** (Book Stoa). This pleasant arcade, entirely occupied by good bookshops, has seats, a café and an open-air terrace. You can also reach the Book Stoa via the next street, Od. Pesmazóglou, which has a rich and elegant neoclassical **Ionian Bank** (Ionikí Trápeza, ΙΟΝΙΚΗ ΤΡΑΠΕΖΑ). Next, a massive modern building (1986–90) of the **Alpha Credit Bank** (Alfa Trápeza Písteos, ΑΛΦΑ ΤΡΑΠΕΖΑ ΠΙΣΤΕΩΣ), entirely faced in marble, completes the architectural triad begun by the Ionian Bank and Arsákeion extension—from thoroughgoing neoclassicism, to more subdued Classical references, to a completely plain exterior whose adherence to the Classical tradition shows only in its proportions and rhythm. Next is the neoclassical National Bank of Greece.

Halfway along, the broad pedestrianised Od. Koraï (access to Panepistímio Metró) opens to the left, with a view of the the university and other buildings on the far side of Panepistimíou. At Koraï no. 4, down a staircase to the Asty cinema, a former Gestapo interrogation chamber is kept as a memorial (ΧΩΡΩΣ ΙΣΤΟΡΙΚΗΣ ΜΝΗΜΗΣ) but is normally closed.

The broad axis of Koraï is continued on the lower side of Stadhíou with the trees and lawns of Plateía Klafthmónos (underground car park). The square, with a bronze group (1988) of entwined figures representing National Reconciliation by V. Dhorópoulos, has several interesting features. In the basement of Dhragatsaníou 6, on the Omónia side (enter the arcade and descend the staircase by the lifts) you can see a substantial and impressive section of the ancient **city wall**. In the west corner of the square is one of the most attractive Byzantine churches in Athens, **Ayy. Theódhori**. An inscription in the west wall indicates a foundation date of 1049 or 1065; another, above the west door, records rebuilding in stone with brick courses and Cufic decoration in the 12C. On the opposite side of Klafthmónos, a mansion (1833–34) at Paparigopoúlou 5 looks modest among the massive later accretions but was loaned by its owner to be the first **Palace of King Otho** (p 64). It is now an attractive **Museum of the City of Athens** (Mon, Wed, Fri, Sat, Sun 09.00–13.30). The original furnishings have been retained and the decoration restored. There is a good collection of prints. The ornate exterior of the building next door (no 7; 1859) is due to radical alteration in the early 20C.

Beyond Klafthmónos, down Od. Khrístou Ladhá to the right, the fashionable church of Ay. Yeóryios (Kaftanzóglou, 1845–49) occupies most of Plateía Karítsi. Opposite it are the rooms of the prestigious **Parnassós Literary Society** (founded 1865), with a small gallery of Greek artists (Mon, Wed, Fri 10.00–13.00): a plaque commemorates Greeks who were condemned here by a Nazi military court. At no. 2 (1st floor) is the **Venizélos Historical Museum** (09.00–13.00 daily), with an archive and mementoes of the statesman (1864–1936; see pp 64, 232).

Nearing Síntagma, you come to the **Palaiá Voulí** (Old Parliament), flanked by the Benákeios Library (State Archive; open Mon–Fri 09.00–13.30, 18.30–20.30; Sat 09.00–13.30). The attractive café at the side is a good place to take a breather. The Parliament building sits in the centre of **Plateía Kolokotróni**, named after the hero of the Wars of Independence and fronted by lawns and palm trees, its Doric-columned façade approached by a broad flight of steps. It was designed by Boulanger in 1858 for the National Assembly and completed in 1874, after alterations needed because of the suppression of the upper house. Theódhoros Dheliyiánnis (statue on south side), three times prime minister of Greece, was assassinated on its steps in 1905. The fine chamber is still sometimes used for lectures. The bronze equestrian statue of Kolokotrónis (1904) by the road is a copy of that by L. Sókhos in Návplio. At the northern corner of the square, on Stadhíou, is the fine **OTE Building** (A. Metaxás, c 1931).

The Palaiá Voulí now contains the worthwhile **National Historical Museum** (Tues–Sun 09.00–14.00; closed Mon) with material relating chiefly to the period 1453–1941, particularly the Wars of Independence and the monarchy. The good handbook (1994; in Greek and English) is a useful aid. The parliament chamber, with fine neoclassical decoration, can be viewed through glass doors and from the first-floor balcony. Interesting exhibits include the ceremonial sword of the Byzantine emperor Leo V (813–20; removed for conservation at time of writing); relics of the Battle of Navarino (modern Pílos, 1827), in which the Turkish fleet was decimated; and Byron's helmet and sword. Several impressive carved wooden figureheads from ships' prows include one from the first Greek steamship, the *Karteria*, which was captained by the British philhellene, Frank Abney Hastings (p 145). Paintings (all periods) include one (on wood) of the *Battle of Lepanto* (1571), probably by an eyewitness; David d'Angers' *Girl weeping for the death of Botsaris* (a hero of the War of Independence) and scenes (1836–39) from the war by Dhimítrios Zográfos commissioned by General Markiyiannis. Also a fine series of small watercolours of Athens and other parts of Greece, made in the first five years of Otho's reign by Ludwig Kölnberger. George I's study has been re-created. There is a display of regional costume, embroidery and traditional jewellery. The museum also has a library and extensive archives of historical documents and photographs.

On the other side of the main road, between Odd. Ameríkis and Vourkourestíou, stretches the back of the massive MTS building (described on p 141, from Panepistimíou). Within is the **Stoá Spiromilíou**—the entrance from Stadhíou is via ΣΤΟΑ ΧΡ ΒΥΖΑΝΤΙΟΥ (Stoá Khr. Vizantíou)—with shops and a booking office for the Athens and Epídhavros festivals.

Stadhíou curves right, to enter Síntagma by the National Bank of Greece.

Síntagma

Plateía Sintágmatos (Constitution Square), always called just Síntagma, is the formal centre of Athens. It is dominated on the east (upper) side, beyond Leofóros Amalías, by the Parliament Building (Voulí). The centre of Síntagma is pleasantly laid out with oranges, oleanders and cypresses. The bronzes, presented by Lord Bute, are good copies of ancient originals in Naples Museum. In the southeast corner (as well as from the Monastiráki-direction platform of Metró Line 3 in the station below) you can see the interesting installation Αίθριο (Aíthrio; 1999) by the sculptor G. Zongolópoulos, whose works often employ umbrella-shaped motifs.

In Classical antiquity there was a cemetery in the area of the square, which lay outside the city wall, between the Akharnian and Diocharous gates. An inscribed boundary stone found here points to the approximate location of the Garden of the Muses which was given c 320 BC by Demetrios of Phaleron to Theophrastos, Aristotle's successor at the Lyceum. Theophrastos bequeathed it to the school. Recent excavations in the advance of Metró construction (see displays in Síntagma station) have revealed more of the cemetery, part of a huge Roman bath and other finds which include the bed of the Eridanos river, ancient roads, the Peisistratid aqueduct and traces of the 1778 Ottoman city wall of Haseki. The Mesogaia Gate of this wall, which had part of the Hadrianic reservoir inscription (p 92) for its lintel (illustration in station), was at the southeast corner of Síntagma. The bath is being reconstructed at the university site at Zográfou.

The lower part of the square, where you enter, is busiest, with a post office and banks. From north to south, Odd. Karayeóryi Servías (which becomes Perikléous lower down), Ermoú (largely pedestrianised) and Mitropóleos, lively and exciting, head towards Athinás and Monastiráki. The far (south) side of the square, above Od. Filellínon, is occupied by banks and airline offices, the nearer side by hotels.

The **Voulí**, originally the **Royal Palace**, was designed by L. von Gartner and erected in 1836–42. The foundation stone was laid by King Ludwig of Bavaria. The style is plain neoclassical, with a Doric porch of Pentelic marble. The interior, originally decorated with paintings in the ancient Roman Pompeian style, was damaged by fire in 1910 and completely altered in 1935. From the balcony of the Palace, the constitution was proclaimed in 1843. Since the abolition of the Senate in 1862, the Greek Parliament has consisted of a single house.

In front, opening off Amalías, is a paved square with, below the palace, a **Memorial to the Unknown Soldier** (E. Lazarídhis, 1929–30). The relief, of a dying Greek, is modelled on a figure from the pediment of the Temple of Aphaia on Aíyina; the accompanying texts are from Perikles' funeral oration over the Athenian dead of the first year of the Peloponnesian War. Bronze shields commemorate Greek victories since 1821. From the memorial, a broad marble staircase ascends to the palace.

The **Ceremonial Guard** (changed on Sundays at 11.00 and well worth seeing, the process beginning at the barracks in Iródhou Attikoú, behind the Voulí) is provided by the three armed services in rotation. The personnel are members of the Presidential Guard, the only company of Evzónes remaining in the Greek armed services. The term literally means 'well-girded', and was originally used during the Wars of Independence, being later retained for light-armed troops. They are conspicuous for their traditional dress of white pleated kilt, fez and slippers with prominent bobbles.

The fine **Hotel Grande Bretagne** (Megáli Vretanía), on the corner with Panepistimíou, was built in 1842–43 by Th. Hansen for A. Dhimitríou and reconstructed in 1958, retaining some of the original features. From 1856 to 1874 it was the French School. In the Second World War it was the headquarters successively of the Greek, German and British forces. On Christmas Eve 1944, during Churchill's visit to the war-torn city, an attempt to blow it up from the sewers was narrowly averted.

Panepistimíou

To return to Omónia you turn down the side of the Grande Bretagne, opposite Leofóros Vasilíssis Sofías, into Od. Panepistimíou (University St). Officially, and on all street signs, it is called Eleftheríou Venizélou (ΕΛΕΥΘΕΡΙΟΥ ΒΕΝΙΖΕΛΟΥ). A busy main artery of the city, parallel to Stadhíou, it also contains several important buildings, serving particularly the intellectual and financial life of Athens.

In Od. Kriezótou (right; no. 3) is a museum of the paintings of N. Khatzikiriákou-Ghíka (p 231; normal opening 10.00–14.00, closed Tues; closed at time of writing, ☎ 210 362 6266 for information). To the left, after Od. Voukourestíou, is the enormous and rather forbidding **MTS** (Metokhikó Tamío Stratoú, Communal Army Fund) building (A. Cassandra and L. Boni, 1928–30). On its ground floor both the Pallás Cinema (entrance in Voukourestíou) and the former Zonar's Patisserie have fine Art Deco ornament.

Opposite is **Schliemann's House**, built by Ziller in 1870–81 for the famous 19C German archaeologist, and bearing the inscription ΙΛΙΟΥ ΜΕΛΑΘΡΟΝ (Palace of Troy). In 1928 the house became the home of the Areópagos (Supreme Court).

Heinrich Schliemann (1822–90) was born in Germany but made his money in France and the USA. Believing that the content of the Homeric epics had its basis in fact, he searched for their most important centres. He excavated Troy, Mycenae and Tiryns, with spectacular success, although his methods are nowadays derided.

Through the gate is a garden, with a copy of an Amazon, whose original may have been by Pheidias. A double stairway rises to the main entrance. The attractive Renaissance style of the building was castigated as 'an incurable leprosy' by the architect Lísandros Kaftanzóglou, a devotée of the neoclassical.

The splendid interior decoration includes mosaics with motifs based on finds from Schliemann's excavations at Mycenae and Troy and wall and ceiling-paintings copying Pompeian styles.

Since 1994 it has housed the **Numismatic Museum** (08.00–14. 30; closed Mon) whose displays cover the history of the collection and development of Greek coinage, the latter from technical, functional and iconographical points of view. Specialised themes include, for example, the Athenian Mint, Greek Colonisation and Coinage; Mythological Subjects. Information is available on computer and the museum has a web site (www.culture.gr/nm/presveis/).

On the corner of Omírou, is the **Archaeological Society** (Arkhaiologikí Etairía), founded in 1837, and roughly the equivalent of the English Society of Antiquaries. The society has a library, conducts excavations and research, and publishes impressive series of monographs and periodicals. The occasional lectures are open to the public, and publications of the society are sold (Floor 5).

Beyond is the **Roman Catholic Cathedral of Ay. Dhionísios** (the Areopagite, known in the western church as St Denis), in Italianate style, with an airy arcaded loggia. Designed by Leo von Klenze it was finished off (1870) by Kaftanzóglou, who also completed the Eye Hospital. On the other side of the road is the substantial Bank of Greece (Trápeza tis Elládhos, ΤΡΑΠΕΖΑ ΤΗΣ ΕΛΛΑΔΟΣ).

On the corner of Od. Sína is the **Ofthalmoiatrío** (Eye Hospital; Th. Hansen and Kaftanzóglou, 1847–51). This is in a different, Byzantine, style, with narrow arched windows and some use of cloisonné.

Sína is the southern boundary of a large open area occupied by three of the most striking public buildings of Athens, which is also an important bus terminus.

First of the major public buildings is the **Academy** (1859), Greece's most prestigious institution of learning, designed by Th. Hansen and funded by Baron Simon G. Sínas (1810–76). The title of baron was inherited from his grandfather (d. 1822), who was granted it by the Austrian state. Born in Epirus, he had been rich and influential in Vienna, where he founded the National Bank of Austria.

Faced in Pentelic marble, it has attractive formal gardens to the front and rear, the latter enclosed. The façade recalls the layout of the Classical Propylaia on the Acropolis but the order here is Ionic. Paint is extensively used to pick out the architectural details, the pediments are filled with sculpture and figures of Athena and Apollo (like the pediments, the work of Leonídhas Dhrósis) stand on top of tall columns to either side of the entrance. Although the overall effect is coldly and excessively ornate, individual features (pedimental sculptures, painted details, figures on columns) are a help in appreciating those aspects of ancient practice which they reflect but which are rarely preserved on archaeological sites. There are seated figures of Plato and Sokrates to either side of the entrance and a statue of Baron Sínas in the hall (all by Dhrósis).

Next, behind formal lawns, is the **University** (Panepistímio; Metró Line 2), now used only for formal occasions, its normal activities having been transferred elsewhere, in particular to the new Panepistimioúpolis (University City) complex at Zográfou, towards Kaisarianí. Other faculties, including Fine Art, are provided by the Polytechnic (Politekhnío) in Patisíon and Piraiós 258 (School of Fine Arts).

The Vallianós National Library in Od. Panepistimíou

A restrained neoclassical building with an Ionic portico in Pentelic marble and painted architectural details, it was built in 1839–42 by the Danish architect Ch. Hansen. The inner walls of the portico have frescoes depicting a variety of characters from ancient art, learning and mythology; above the entrance are personifications of subjects taught in the University, with King Otho in the centre. Before the building is a statue of Gladstone; in front of the façade are the poet Rígas and the patriarch Gregory; to either side of the steps, two heroes of Greek Independence, Kapodístrias and Koraïs.

Last is the **National Library** (Ethnikí Vivliothíki; Mon–Thur 09.00–20.00; Fri, Sat 09.00–14.00). Its massive façade, in the style of a Doric temple, stands between two side buildings and is approached by a curving double stairway. This encloses a statue of P. Vallianós, a native of the island of Kefallinía, who financed the building, constructed of Pentelic marble in 1887–91 to the design of Th. Hansen. The elegant main reading room, visible from the doorway, has Ionic columns.

The collection, formed from a combination (in 1903) of the National and University libraries, and now rapidly outgrowing the capacity of the building, contains over half a million books and 3500 manuscripts. The latter include two richly illuminated gospels (10C and 11C) from monasteries in Thessaly.

Beyond the library, Od. Ippokrátous, with numerous bookshops, forms the northern boundary of the area.

On the other side of the road is the **Arsákion**. The original building housed a girls' school and training college founded in 1836 by Apóstolos Arsáki (1792–1874), a native of Epirus who acquired wealth and status in Romania where he became a minister of the government. This moved to the suburb of Psikhikó c 1930. The neoclassical building, subsequently used for law courts and now the seat of the Council of State (Simvoúlio Epikratías), was designed by Kaftanzóglou (1848), who wrested the commission from Kleánthis. The extension (white) is described above on Stadhíou.

On the opposite side of the road from the Arksákion, at no. 40, the Mortgage Bank (Ktimatikí Trápeza, ΚΤΗΜΑΤΙΚΗ ΤΡΑΠΕΖΑ) of Greece occupies an attractive neoclassical building which has been imaginatively extended (A. Kalligás, 1980). Further down, the **Rex Theatre** (A. Cassandra and L. Boni, 1937) is conspicuous for its Art Deco style.

Panepistimíou curves left, crosses Patisíon and enters Omónia.

5 • Omónia and Síntagma to Monastiráki

The two walks suggested follow different streets in each direction. Both take you to Monastiráki Square, convenient for Pláka and the ancient Agora. The area bounded by Mitropóleos, Athinás and Stadhíou has been pedestrianised, with the exception of arterial streets. Only service vehicles are allowed access.

Omónia to Monastiráki
Aiólou, with an ever-present view of the Acropolis at the far end, has shops, colourful street traders and a flower market. It passes through Plateía Dhimarkhíou (Kotziá), with some fine buildings and an archaeological site. In Monastiráki, on the edge of Pláka, is a branch of the Museum of Greek Popular Art and close by are the tourist shops and flea market of Pandróssou, Iféstou and Plateía Avissinías.

- **Distance on foot**. Maps 3,5–8; 6,7. Via Aiólou (pedestrianised), returning by Athinás, a total of about 2km.
  Metró (Line 1): Omónia to Monastiráki (station not yet open), one stop, 3 mins.
  Bus (Athinás only). Nos 035 (ΚΑΤΩ ΠΕΤΡΑΛΩΝΑ), 731 (ΑΝΩ ΠΕΤΡΑΛΩΝΑ), both directions.

Leaving Omónia, by Stadhíou, you immediately turn right into the narrower Aiólou. Street vendors, cafés and the gradually expanding vista of the buildings of the Acropolis, above its green northern slopes, make this the most attractive approach on foot.

You soon enter Plateía Dhimarkhíou (or Kotziá) with fine and varied neoclassical buildings in good repair. On your left is the splendid headquarters of the National Bank of Greece (Ethnikí Trápeza tis Elládhos, ΕΘΝΙΚΗ ΤΡΑΠΕΖΑ ΤΗΣ ΕΛΛΑΔΟΣ); opposite, beyond Athinás, is the more severe Dhimarkhíon (town hall; p 146). The south side of the square is occupied by the **Melá Mansion** (Ziller, 1884), formerly the main post office, now yet another building of the National Bank of Greece, with art exhibitions. The centre of the square (underground car park), once filled with cafés and flower sellers, is now mainly surfaced in concrete. In the west part, facing the Dhimarkhíon across Athinás, there was a theatre (Ziller, 1888; funded by Singrós) until 1938. Its foundations were revealed in the excavations which preceded modern reconstruction, but have now been covered. The area towards Aiólou is an **archaeological site**. Finds from the site, which lies just outside the ancient Akharnian gate, included numerous burials of many different periods, three roadways and—most impressive—a series of well-preserved Roman potteries, with kilns, cisterns, settling tanks, etc.

Street traders line the route. You cross Od. Sofokléous, with the **Stock Exchange** (Khrimatistírio, ΧΡΗΜΑΤΙΣΤΗΡΙΟ; no admission) a few metres to the left. On the left side of Aiólou is the ornate church of the **Panayía Khrisospiliótissa** (D. Zézos, ?1857). The street is enclosed by tall buildings on either side. Also on the left, dominating a pleasant small square with a colourful market of nurserymen, is **Ay. Iríni** (Kaftanzóglou, 1847), probably on the site of an Early Christian building. The church has an outstanding choir.

Crossing Ermoú, with the Kapnikaréa church (p 147) a few metres to the left, you reach Mitropóleos. Turn right for Monastiráki. At the far end of Aiólou is the octagonal Tower of the Winds, from which the street takes its name (Aiolos was the god of the winds), then the slopes of the Acropolis. The north porch of the Erechtheion faces you, high above, backed by the Parthenon.

Monastiráki Square is disrupted at present by work on the Metró. The church of the *monastiráki* (little monastery) of the Pantánassa (Virgin Mary), a few steps down from the middle of the square, is a 10C aisled basilica (restored 1911).

Dominating the square at the far left side, is the former **Mosque of Tsistarákis** (1759), erected by a voivode (Ottoman governor) of that name. Incorporated in the building are a column from the Olympieion and other ancient remnants. A plain building, fronted by an open arcade approached by steps, it has an octagonal dome. The minaret was demolished after 1821. At one time a prison, the mosque was turned into a museum in 1918 and reorganised in 1958 as a **Museum of Greek Popular Art** (10.00–14.00; closed Tues). Although now a branch of the main Museum in Kidhathinaíon (p 171), it contains a fine collection of modern Greek pottery of the first half of the 20C, bequeathed by the late Professor V. Kiriazópoulos. The interior is pleasantly light and airy. The painted mihrab (prayer niche) of the mosque is intact and a few fragments of other frescoes remain. There is good original carving in the cupola. The pottery on the ground floor is mainly decorative work, some of it very fine, accompanied by histories of the artists, most of whom were refugees from Asia Minor. On the balcony, added at the time of the mosque's conversion into a museum, are displays of regional styles; most of the pieces are functional.

The museum is on the corner of Od. Pandróssou, a narrow street running up towards the cathedral. Originally part of the **Turkish Bazaar**, it is now full of shoemakers, antique dealers and tourist shops.

Opposite the museum, by the **Metró Station** (Lines 1 and 3, the latter's platforms not yet in service), an interesting building in its own right though scandalously neglected, the narrow Od. Iféstou (named after Hephaistos, the ancient deity of metallurgy) still resounds to the activities of metalworkers. It takes you to Plateía Avissinías (**Flea Market**, Sun mornings), close by the main entrance to the Agora. Iféstou continues as Od. Astingos, named after the English philhellene Frank Abney Hastings (1794–1828) who fought valiantly in the 1821 revolution and contributed funds to the Greek cause. He died from wounds suffered fighting at Aitolikó (1828); his funeral oration was given by Trikoúpis (p 190).

You can return to Omónia from Monastiráki by the broad, busy and exciting

Od. Athinás. At first the shops mainly sell ironmongery and tools. Halfway along on the right is the Central Market (Kentrikí Agorá), thronged with traders' stalls selling meat, fish and other commodities. The streets around are packed with small food shops of various kinds and specialities, their contents spilling over on to the pavements, far more colourful, and often cheaper, than the featureless supermarkets. The market building itself (undergoing restoration) is called Varvákeios after the educational institute endowed by **Ioánnis Varvákis** on the opposite side of Athinás, which was burnt down in 1944. Varvákis (1745–1835), a sea captain from the eastern Aegean, became wealthy and prominent in Empress Catherine's Russia. He devoted most of his riches to philanthropic enterprises in Greece and Russia. It was in this area that the *Varvákeion Athena* was found (National Archaeological Museum).

Athinás passes through the west side of Plateía Dhimarkhíou. The **Dhimarkhíon** (ΔΗΜΑΡΧΕΙΟΝ, town hall) to the left was designed by P. Kálkos in 1874 and altered in the early 20C. The interior (access may be allowed) is decorated with extensive frescoes of mythological and historical figures (1937–40) by Fótis Kóntoglou (p 230) and of the history of the city of Athens (1938–39) by G. Gounarópoulos. Beyond, you re-enter Omónia.

Síntagma to Monastiráki

Between Síntagma and Monastiráki are, in Mitropóleos, the old and new Cathedrals and the archbishopric; in Ermoú, the lovely 11C university church of Kapnikaréa.

• **Distance on foot**. Via Mitropóleos, returning by Ermoú, a total of 1.6km. Most of Ermoú is for pedestrians only.
  Access by bus. 025, 026, 027.
  Metró (Line 3; one stop). Section not operational at time of writing.

Leaving Síntagma by Mitropóleos, you pass (left) the Ministry of Education, dwarfing the tiny post-Byzantine church of Ay. Dhínamis beside it.

Further down, fronted by a spacious square, stands the huge and ugly **Cathedral** (Mitrópolis), built in 1840–55 from the remains of 72 churches, most of which were ruined in the War of Independence. Across a small paved square to the east is the tomb and a statue of Gregory V, Patriarch of Constantinople, brought here from Odessa in 1871, 50 years after his execution by the Sultan for failing to prevent the Greek uprising.

In front of the main (west) door is a much larger marble-paved square, occasionally used for concerts. A statue of Archbishop Dhamaskinós (1891–1949), who was Regent from 1945, is in a prominent position; another statue portrays Konstantinos Palaiologos, the last Byzantine Emperor (reigned 1449–53).

Behind (south of) the cathedral is the tiny (12 x 7.5m) **Old Cathedral**, originally dedicated to the Panayía Gorgoepíkoös ('quick to answer prayers'). After the expulsion of King Otho it was called Ay. Elefthérios (*eleftheria*, freedom) and is also sometimes known as the Mikrí Mitrópolis (Little Cathedral). Although the church is supposed to have been founded by the Byzantine Empress Irene c 787, the present structure dates from the 12C. Its fabric consists entirely of Classical masonry, some inscribed, and of material from a church or churches of the 6C–7C. Over the door at the west is the **Attic State Festival Calendar frieze**, removed from a building of the 2C–3C AD. Each festival is represented by a figure or symbol, signs of the zodiac showing the chronological sequence. One of the Maltese crosses, added in Christian times, has defaced a unique depiction of the ship which carried Athena's robe in the Panathenaic procession. Its wheels are visible to the right of the second cross from the left.

Beyond, in Od. Filothéis, the modernised church of Ay. Andréas is attached to the **Archbishop's Palace** and the offices of the Metropolitan of Athens, since 1864 the senior figure in the independent Greek Orthodox Church.

The Little Mitrópolis

Mitropóleos continues to Monastiráki. You can return to Síntagma by the largely pedestrianised **Ermoú**, a busy shopping street with an emphasis on fashion and textiles—more fashionable towards Síntagma.

Its main feature is the small and charming church of **Kapnikaréa**, round which the street divides to form a small square. The significance of the name is unknown. The building (including narthex and north parecclesion) is probably late 11C, with the exonarthex a slightly later addition (see plan of Dhafní). The four columns supporting the dome have Roman capitals. In 1834 Ludwig of Bavaria saved the Kapnikaréa from demolition. It was subsequently restored by the University and is its official church. The interior fittings and decoration are mostly modern, with frescoes by Kóntoglou (1955).

6 • The Hephaisteion (Thiseíon) Temple and the ancient Agora

The Hephaisteion or Temple of Hephaistos and Athena (**Maps 4,2; 5,1**), still sometimes known as the Thiseíon, is well preserved and nicely situated among trees overlooking the Agora. It gives a better idea than the more elaborate buildings on the Acropolis of the standard form of the Classical Greek temple.

No visitor with any feeling for ancient Athens as the source of democracy will want to miss the Agora where it was first put into practice and which formed the heart of the Classical city state. The site itself is open and pleasant. The Hellenistic

Stoa of Attalos has been fully restored and offers first-hand experience of a common ancient building type. In addition, it now contains a well laid-out and easily digestible museum. Nevertheless, the Agora as a whole is hard to understand because of numerous successive building periods, and most of the buildings are poorly preserved.

• **Entrances and access**. There are three entrances to the Agora (the site includes the Hephaisteion): (1) at the southwest corner of Plateía Thisíou (bus stop after the Acropolis on the no. 230 route from Akadhimías or Síntagma; nos 035, 731 from Omónia), off Leofóros Apostólou Pávlou; (2) from the north side by a bridge over the railway line from Od. Adhrianoú, about halfway between Monastiráki and Thisíon Metró stations and a 250m walk from each; (3) on the south near the church of Ayy. Apóstoli, accessible by paths from upper Pláka and the Acropolis. The description below starts from (1).
Opening. 08.30–15.00 (17.00 high season). Closed Mon.
There are **lavatories and drinking water** in the Stoa of Attalos, at the north (railway) end.
Layout. The upper gallery of the stoa of Attalos (normally closed) has six plans showing the topography of ancient Athens at different periods, and five stages in the development of the Agora. These are augmented by a model showing the Agora at the time of its greatest extent (2C AD).
Guidebooks. An excellent *Guide to the excavations and museum* (4th edn, 1990; available at the site) is published in English by the American School of Classical Studies; also a series of booklets (Athenian Agora Picture Books) explaining various aspects of the site, its buildings and finds. This series includes a shorter guide to the Agora (no. 16, new edition in press). A good overall study is John M. Camp, T*he Athenian Agora: excavations in the heart of Classical Athens*, Thames & Hudson, London, 1992 (corrected reprint).

Visitors hoping to get a clear picture of the Athenian Agora of the Classical period will need to make an effort of the imagination—and should try to get a distant view of the site, perhaps from the Acropolis or the Pnyx. Inevitably much of the visible construction belongs to later periods. The Roman Odeion of Agrippa and the remains of the 4C AD 'Palace' are particularly prominent, filling the centre of a square which was largely empty in the 5C BC. Although Kimon is known to have planted trees in the Agora in the 5C, there are unlikely to have been as many as now.

Discovery and excavation

The approximate location of the Agora was worked out as early as 1859–62 from references in ancient texts and the archaeological identification of the Stoa of Attalos by the Greek Archaeological Society. There were occasional excavations by Greek and German archaeologists between 1859 and 1897, at points where there were surface indications and when the cutting for the railway line was made across the north part of the site in 1890–91. In 1931–40 the American School of Classical Studies, with the financial backing of John D. Rockefeller, began systematic excavations under Prof. T. Leslie Shear. Since 1946 these have been continued by Prof. Homer Thompson, Prof. T. Leslie Shear Jnr and Prof. John McK. Camp.

The area round the Hephaisteion was investigated in 1936–37 and the peristyle and cella excavated in 1939.

When the zone between the railway and the Acropolis–Areopagos was declared an archaeological zone, about 350 19C houses were expropriated and demolished and it was excavated to Classical, and in some cases Prehistoric levels, involving the removal of some 300,000 tons of deposit. In 1970 excavations in a further expropriated area north of the railway line revealed the Stoa Basileios (Royal Stoa) and, in 1980, on the further side of Od. Adhrianoú, the Stoa Poikile (Painted Stoa).

The Hephaisteion

Crowning the low tree-clad knoll of Kolonós Agoraíos on the west side of the Agora is the Hephaisteion (Ancient Athens plan, pp 150–151; **1**), mentioned by Pausanias. The misnomer 'Thiseion' (or *Theseum*) is derived from the appearance of Theseus in scenes on the metopes and was used as early as the Vienna Anonymous. At that time it was thought to be the heroön built by Kimon to receive the supposed bones of the legendary Theseus recovered from Skyros c 475 BC. That real Theseum, which ancient sources suggest was on the north slope of the Acropolis, has yet to be found.

Background and history

The most complete surviving example of a Doric hexastyle temple, the Hephaisteion, together with some other buildings with similar architectural characteristics (the Temples of Ares in the Agora, of Nemesis at Rhamnous and of Poseidon at Sounion, as well as the recently located Temple of Athena Pallenis in Yéraka), may be the work of the so-called Theseum Architect. The suggested foundation date of 449 BC sets its construction at the beginning of the great period of rebuilding after the Persian wars. Appropriately since Hephaistos was the god of metallurgy, his temple was surrounded by metalworking establishments and shops.

Probably in the 7C AD, the Hephaisteion was adapted for use as a church by the addition of an apse. It was dedicated to Ay. Yeóryios. At that time it was given a concrete interior vault, and some extra walls were inserted into the east end. A later apse survived until 1835. Under the Ottomans, the liturgy was celebrated there only once a year and it acquired the nickname of 'Akamátis' (the 'idler'). The last services held in the church were a *Te Deum* to celebrate King Otho's arrival in the newly founded capital on 13 December 1834 and a centenary *Te Deum* in 1934.

The temple consists of a cella, with pronaos and opisthodomos, both distyle in antis, with a peristyle of 36 columns (6 x 13). Apart from the lowest step (in poros) the structure is entirely of Pentelic marble, the sculpture of Parian.

Exterior Apart from the roof and the sculptures, the exterior is extremely well preserved. In comparison with the Parthenon, the columns are slimmer and the entablature heavier, but there are similar optical refinements. The unusual form of the east colonnade, achieved by aligning the third column of the peristyle with the antae of the pronaos and carrying a sculptured frieze right across from one side of the building to the other, is a distinctive characteristic of works of the Theseum Architect (see above).

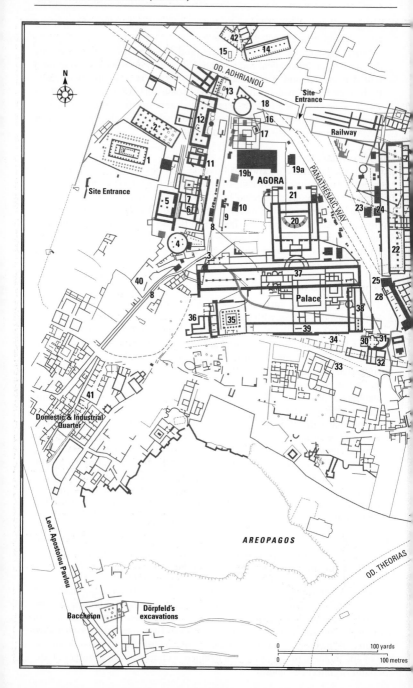

N

OD. ADHRIANOÚ

Site Entrance

Railway

42
15   14
13
18
16
17
12
11
19b   19a
1   AGORA
Site Entrance
5   7   21
6   10
20
9
4   8
3
37
40   Palace
8   38
36   35   39
34   30   31
32
33
41
Domestic & Industrial Quarter

AREOPAGOS

OD. THEORIAS

Leof. Apostolou Pavlou

Baccheion   Dörpfeld's excavations

0 _____ 100 yards
0 _____ 100 metres

ANCIENT ATHENS (CENTRE)

Hadrian's Library

Entrance

OD. AIOLOU

Stoa of Attalos

OD. DHEXÍPOU

OD. PANOS

OD. PELOPÍDHA

Gate of Athena

Medresse

Roman Market

Mosque

Latrine

Roman Market

Tower of the Winds

Agoranomion

27

26

Site Entrance

29

OD. PANOS

26

Klepsydra

ACROPOLIS

Key to numbers

1. Hephaisteion
2. Arsenal
3. Boundary Stone
4. Tholos
5. New Bouleuterion
6. Old Bouleuterion
7. Metróön
8. Great Drain
9. Eponymous Heroes
10. Altar of Zeus Agoraios
11. Temple of Apollo Patroös
12. Stoa of Zeus Eleutherios
13. Stoa Basileios
14. Stoa Poikile
15. Altar of Aphrodite Ourania
16. Peribolos of 12 Gods
17. Eschara
18. Starting line
19a. Altar of Ares
19b. Temple of Ares
20. Odeion
21. Palace

22. Stoa of Attalos
23. Bema
24. Donor's Monument
25. Tower
26. Late Roman Wall
27. Library of Pantainos
28. Water Mill
29. Eleusinion
30. Ay. Apostoloi
31. Nymphaion
32. Mint
33. S.E. Fountain House
34. South Stoa I
35. Heliaia
36. S.W. Fountain House
37. Middle Stoa
38. East Stoa
39. South Stoa II
40. Strategeion
41. Prison
42. Commercial Building

The 10 **metopes** of the east front show nine of the *12 Labours of Herakles*. Sculptured metopes continue down the north and south sides, four on each, with *exploits of Theseus*. The **pediment(s)** contained sculpture but only fragments survive, some in the museum.

Interior (no access). The fine coffered ceiling at the east end of the peristyle is still intact. This part of the building is emphasised as a separate and important compartment by the layout and the sculpture framing it—the frieze inside and the metopes on the outside, the latter continuing only as far as the limits of this eastern chamber.

The sculptured **frieze** at the east shows Theseus in heroic combat with his rivals, the sons of Pallas, in the presence of seated deities. It occupies three sides of the rectangular space immediately within the colonnade, running from one side of the peristyle to the other, passing above the entrance to the pronaos and returning on either side towards the front of the building. A frieze at the west end, above the entrance to the opisthodomos, has the Battle of Lapiths and Centaurs, with Theseus prominent and the Centaur Kaineus being hammered into the ground by a Lapith (he was invulnerable to ordinary methods of attack).

In the **cella**, the barrel vault, retained from the church of Ay. Yióryios, jars with the Classical architectural elements. The marble floor was ruined when graves were dug through it in the Middle Ages. An interior colonnade extended down both sides of the cella and behind the bronze cult statues of Hephaistos and Athena by Alkamenes, set up c 420 BC. Two blocks of the base, in Eleusinian limestone, have been restored to position. Some clay moulds, perhaps used in the casting of the statues, were found near the temple. The insertion of an interior colonnade seems to represent a change to the original plan, perhaps influenced by the Parthenon.

On the walls are sepulchral slabs (AD 896–1103), parts of a stone chronicle listing events between 1555 and 1880, graffiti of British visitors (1665) and memorials to others who died in Greece in the 17C–19C, when the building seems to have been used as a Protestant cemetery. That of George Watson (d. 1810) has a defaced Latin epitaph by Byron.

Between the 3C BC and 1C AD a formal **garden**, planted in sunken flower pots, was laid out round the north, south and west sides of the temple. It has been replanted with species thought to have been current in the area in antiquity (e.g. pomegranate and myrtle).

North of the Hephaisteion are slight remains of a large Hellenistic building, perhaps the State Arsenal (**2**).

The Agora

The Agora (originally 'assembly', then 'place of assembly' or 'market-place'; plan p 150) was the central public place of ancient Athens and the site of a whole range of communal activities. The headquarters of many of the institutions of government, law and religion, it was also a meeting-place for trade and business, on the one hand, and for intellectual discussion and social intercourse, on the other. St Paul (Acts xvii 17) met the Athenians daily in the Agora and talked to them. In earlier times it was used for athletic events (also later, at the Panathenaic festival) and dramatic competitions.

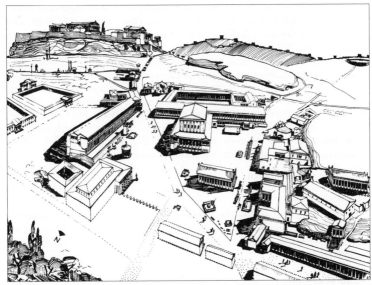

The Agora: reconstruction of the area in the 2C AD

History

The original Agora seems to have been northeast of the Acropolis (p 93). The new 'Solonian' Agora was developed from the 6C under Solon. From his time, burials in the area ceased and public structures, including the first meeting-place for the Council, were constructed in the southwest corner. The Peisistratid tyrants laid on a water supply. In the time of Kleisthenes (late 5C), the Great Drain was constructed and new buildings erected, largely to house bodies established as a result of his constitutional reforms. Many of these buildings were destroyed or damaged in the Persian sack of 480 BC, but were subsequently rebuilt and further additions made. Kimon is known to have embellished the site with plane trees. From the 4C BC it became progressively more crowded with sculptures.

Gradually the Agora began to turn into a colonnaded square. This trend was formalised in the 2C, when massive stoas were erected on the east and south sides. The Agora seems to have survived Sulla's sack in 86 BC. In the Roman period new or transplanted buildings encroached on the central area, previously empty, but the Agora retained its traditional functions. It was devastated in the Herulian raid of AD 267. When the Late Roman Wall was constructed, largely of material from destroyed buildings, most of the original Agora area was outside its circuit. When the older walled circuit was re-established in the 5C AD, part of the site was occupied by a large palatial residence which went out of use in the 6C. Alaric and the Visigoths in 395/96 and the Slavs in 582/83 further destroyed remaining buildings. Abandoned until the 10C, the area was covered with houses during Byzantine, Frankish and Ottoman times. The only surviving public monument of that period is the 11C church of Ayy. Apóstoli.

From the Hephaisteion, a path down through the trees comes out at the southwest corner of the main Agora square. Near the junction of the two branches of the Great Drain (p 155) is a **Boundary Stone** (**3**), inscribed, in 5C lettering, ΗΟΡΟΣ ΕΙΜΙ ΤΕΣ ΑΓΟΡΑΣ ('I am the boundary of the Agora'). The area so defined was a sacred precinct from which certain classes of convicts were debarred; people entering performed a purificatory rite. At a higher level, immediately to the south, is the stump of a marble pedestal (1C AD), probably the support of a holy-water stoup for that purpose.

The wall against which the boundary stone is set belongs to a row of houses and/or shops. In one of them hobnails and a cup inscribed with the name **Simon** were found. Diogenes Laertius records that Sokrates spent much of his time in this part of the Agora in the shop of a cobbler called Simon.

West side of the Agora

From the beginning, the west side of the Agora was the focus of state administration.

The circular foundation of the **Tholos** (**4**), discovered in 1934, provided the first certain fixed point for the topography of the ancient Agora, although the remains do not adequately reflect its original importance. Built c 465 BC, it was the Prytanikon.

> ### The Prytaneis
> The Prytaneis, whose headquarters was the Prytanikon, were the presiding members of the *Boule* or Council, who were available at all times to deal with emergencies. Aristotle records that the 50 officials sacrificed, held their deliberations and dined daily at the public expense. Their chairman (*Epistates*) and the third of his colleagues who were on duty at any one time also slept here (Aristotle, *Constitution of Athens* 44).

The building was the effective headquarters of Athenian government. A set of standard weights and measures (now in the museum) were also kept in the Tholos. A 6C courtyard building (Building F; see plan), which partly underlies the Tholos, may have been its predecessor but the alternative suggestion has been made that 'F' was a grand house, perhaps the palace of Peisistratos, superseded after the fall of the tyrants by the seat of an institution of the democracy.

The Tholos was also known as the *skias* (parasol) because of the shape of its roof. In the time of Augustus a porch was added to the original rotunda. The six columns (three stumps in situ) which supported the roof were removed during the Hadrianic period, and a single-span roof substituted. At the same time the 1C AD floor of mosaic chips was overlaid with marble slabs. The original floor of clay is 45cm below the present surface and, except for a few poros blocks, the outer wall is a restoration. To the north are traces of a small room (kitchen).

Northwest of the Tholos, on a platform cut into the Kolonos hill, are the foundations of the **New Bouleuterion** (Council House; **5**). Here the Council met, under the Prytaneis, to prepare legislation for the Assembly. This building belongs to the late 5C; a portico on the south side and an Ionic propylon on the west (facing the Agora) were added under Lykourgos, the two connected by a passage along what was originally the south front of the Old Bouleuterion.

The **Old Bouleuterion** (**6**), a square building whose foundations are now largely obscured by the Metróön, was constructed for the Council of 500 soon after its creation by Kleisthenes. It replaced an even earlier complex (some of it open-air) of Solon's time. When the New Bouleuterion replaced the Old, the latter was used as a public archive. Parallel with its north side was a small temple.

This temple was presumably dedicated to the Mother of the Gods, since worship was apparently continuous on this spot until a **Metróön** (Temple of the Mother of the Gods; **7**) was built on the site in the 2C BC. It consisted of four rooms and a colonnade facing the square. The building had a dual function, as sanctuary (second room from the south) and repository of state archives, perhaps with quarters for a superintendent at the north end. The mosaic pavement visible in one room dates from alterations in the 5C AD.

In front of the Metróön are a row of **statue bases** (those made of re-used material are of Christian date). From the 4C BC the number of statues displayed in the Agora, both of deities and of prominent citizens, increased substantially, and must have changed the appearance of the area. A headless **statue of Hadrian** here (the emperor identified from the corselet which carries a crowned Athena standing on the wolf which suckled Romulus and Remus, symbol of the captured taking the captor captive) was found in the Great Drain.

A few metres out, cut in the surface of the Agora itself and parallel to the front of the Old Bouleuterion, is the **Great Drain** (**8**), beautifully constructed in the late 6C BC of polygonal limestone. It channelled waters from the hills on the southwest into the Eridanos brook to the north. The two branches that flow into it near the boundary stone (p 154) were made in the 4C BC or later.

On the far side of the drain is the 4C **Monument of the Eponymous Heroes** (**9**; there may have been a predecessor in the area of the Middle Stoa). Its long base stands in a fenced enclosure. On the base stood statues of the ten legendary heroes chosen by the Delphic Oracle as founders of the ten tribes of Athens. It was extended several times after 307 BC, when additional tribes were created. It also carried two tripods. The side of the plinth was a noticeboard for official announcements and proposed legislation (Demosthenes XXIV 23).

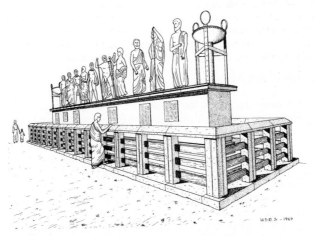

Reconstruction of the Monument of the Eponymous Heroes, Agora

A little further to the east is a 4C **altar** (**10**; possibly of Zeus Agoraios), known to have been moved in the 1C, probably from the Pnyx where a cutting for a monument of exactly the same size has been found.

Before the Metróön was built, rock-cut steps on the slope of the hill may have provided a meeting-place. Under the early Roman empire a grandiose stairway to the Hephaisteion was constructed here.

At this point there is a gap between the Metróön and the next structure, the **Temple of Apollo Patroös**, a small building (c 330 BC; **11**), tetrastyle in antis with walls in late polygonal masonry on conglomerate foundations. The two omphaloi, which had some ritual significance, may have stood in its porch. Inside was a statue of Apollo by Euphranor (an important 4C BC sculptor), now in the Stoa of Attalos.

Apollo Patroös, the epithet indicating the father (*pater*) of Ion, was especially worshipped by the Athenians, because of their Ionian descent. He was patron of the state administration. Before him magistrates were sworn and citizens registered.

There was an earlier (apsidal) temple of the 6C on the site, which was probably destroyed by the Persians, then left derelict for 150 years in accordance with the Plataean oath (p 103). The bronze cult statue for this 6C temple, a kouros figure, was cast in a pit immediately in front of the building. Fragments of the terracotta mould are in the museum.

Next are the foundations of a smaller and slightly earlier 4C temple, identified from an inscription on its altar as that of **Zeus Phratrios and Athena Phratria**, the deities of the ancestral religious brotherhoods (*phratries*). A porch was added to the east in the 2C BC.

Poros foundations, all that survive of the **Stoa of Zeus Eleuthérios** (**12**), stretch as far as the railway, which destroyed the stoa's north wing. A colonnade with a projecting porch at either end, it was built c 430 BC to honour Zeus as saviour of the Athenians from Persian domination. The external order was Doric, the interior Ionic. The wings had marble Nike figures as acroteria (one in the museum). Pausanias says that there were paintings by Euphranor inside. It was a meeting-place for private business; Sokrates discussed philosophy here with his friends. An annexe was added behind in the 1C AD. Piles of marble fragments in front mark the supposed sites of **altars** of the 6C and ?3C BC.

North side of the Agora

The northwest corner and north side of the Agora are beyond the railway line, mostly still concealed below later buildings. At the northwest corner, the **Panathenaic Way** (or Dromos), the road from the Dipylon Gate (p 174), entered the Agora between the Stoa Basileios and Stoa Poikile (p 157), then crossing the Agora diagonally to leave by the south end of the Stoa of Attalos, where the surface is gravel. Outside the Library of Pantainos (p 162) the road was paved in later times. It then climbed the Acropolis on a ramp. Post-holes along part of its course probably contained supports for stands for spectators of the Panathenaic procession and games. The road seems to have been extensively refurbished after the Persian sack. From the Dipylon to the Agora it was lined with stoas fronted by bronze statues. There was all the bustle of the most commercial part of the city (Lysias XXIX 20; Theophrastos, *Characters*). There too was the house of

Pulytion where Alkibiades acted the hierophant (priest) in the parody of the Eleusinian mysteries which preceded the mutilation of the herms (see below). Between the Pompeion (at the Dipylon) and the Stoa of Zeus (see p 156) was the sanctuary of Demeter, Kore and Iakkhos, with statues by Praxiteles (Pausanias I 2 4). A damaged monumental base (in museum), with the signature of Praxiteles, was found built into a wall north of the railway.

One of the most exciting postwar discoveries in the Agora (1970) was that of the **Stoa Basileios** (Royal Stoa; **13**) in which the Archon Basileus (King Archon) held his court. The best view is from behind and above the Stoa of Zeus. The building is clearly described in ancient sources (Pausanias I 3 1). In front was duly discovered the stone (*lithos*) on which the archons took their oath of office. A surprisingly small building, it was originally (c 500 BC, perhaps rebuilt after the Persian sack of 480) a plain rectangle, with a façade of eight Doric columns and four others in the interior. It survived, with alterations, to AD 400. In the late 5C BC porches were added at either end, probably to house new inscriptions with the statutes of Solon and Draco. Occasionally the Council of the Areopagos met here, and may even have heard St Paul. Sockets for herm-stelai can be seen at the north end. Many fragments of herms have been recovered, sometimes commemorating the periods of office of archons. A base in situ records prizewinners in the Epilenaia, a dramatic festival possibly held in front of the Stoa, where there are remains of stepped terracing and some 'thrones' (formal seats like those found in the front rows of theatres).

East of the Stoa was a small crossroads shrine of the 5C. In this part of the Agora was the **Orchestra**, also the **Leokoreion**, near which Hipparkhos was assassinated in 514 BC by Harmodios and Aristogeiton, while marshalling the Panathenaic procession. Statues of these so-called **Tyrannicides** stood in the Agora from c 505 BC. The first group, by Antenor, was plundered by the Persians in 480. A replacement was made by Kritios and Nesiotes (c 476). After the original was returned from Persepolis by Alexander the Great, both groups stood together in the orchestra of the Agora. Ancient copies give a good idea of the originals.

Between the Stoa Basileios and the Stoa Poikile (see below)was a group of **Herms**, with inscriptions, celebrating Kimon's victories over the Persians in Thrace in 475.

The mutilation of the Herms

On the eve of the Sicilian expedition in 415 BC the Athenian people were deeply shocked by the wholesale mutilation of these figures, an event which they saw as the prelude to a political coup and an ill omen for the expedition. Alkibiades was charged with responsibility, and also suspected of taking part in an impious parody of the Eleusinian mysteries (see above). Recalled from Sicily, he was sentenced to death in his absence. About 40 fragments of inscriptions listing his personal possessions, confiscated by the state and sold at public auction, have been recovered from the Eleusinion.

Another exciting discovery, again fitting in with ancient descriptions of the Agora, came in 1980 with the finding of the west end of the **Stoa Poikile** (Painted Stoa; **14**), best seen from Od. Adhrianoú, outside the Agora site compound. This was sometimes called Peisianaktios after its founder (c 460 BC) Peisianax, Kimon's brother-in-law. The philosopher Zeno taught here, his followers thus acquiring the name of stoics. The interior was decorated with battle scenes (Marathon, Troy, etc) by leading painters of the day, including Polygnotos, Mikon and Panainos, brother of Pheidias. The works were probably on wooden panels, held in place by spikes in the wall. Although Pausanias saw them, the paintings had disappeared by AD 402. Here also were displayed bronze shields (good example in the museum) captured from the Spartans at Sphakteria in 425 BC.

The **exterior** was in the Doric order, the interior Ionic. The building is 12.4m deep.

To the west massive square piers partly encroach on the steps of the Stoa. These probably supported a **gateway** across the narrow street leading off northwest. On this gate Pausanias saw a trophy set up by the Athenian cavalry to celebrate a victory over the Macedonian Pleistarkhos in 303/02 BC.

Further west are remains of a handsome altar (**15**) in island marble, built c 500 BC and repaired in the later 5C. Pausanias' text suggests that it should be part of the **Sanctuary of Aphrodite Ourania**. The Roman temple of the sanctuary, built on the site of a Classical house apparently used as a sculpture workshop, is nearby. Other houses of the Archaic and Classical periods have been found.

As well as the Stoa Poikile, this area of excavation produced finds from the end of the Neolithic period up to the 19C, including Mycenaean tombs. Some of the discoveries illuminate important episodes in the history of Athens, not least the Persian destruction of 480 BC. The small **Eridanos brook**, which flows through part of the area, partly underground even in antiquity, was canalised in a finely built channel, probably at the time the Stoa was constructed. The channel was subsequently doubled and, in Late Antiquity, columns from the Stoa's exterior colonnade were used to repair its middle wall. The German archaeologist Ludwig Ross traced some of its course via manholes in 1832 and found the columns, which have now been relocated by his American successors. A well-made terracotta pipeline is probably part of that mentioned in ancient sources as supplying water to the Academy.

A 4C AD destruction level here must be associated with the sack of Athens by Alaric and the Visigoths in 395/6, another with that by the Slavs c 582/83, after which the area was virtually abandoned for about 300 years. Above the ancient strata Byzantine houses were found (mostly 9C–12C) and a church (Ay. Nikólaos), with cemetery, built in the 10C–11C and destroyed in the War of Independence. In the Classical levels was a 4C **commercial building** with shops, one of which seems to have manufactured and sold terracotta figurines. It was eventually incorporated into Byzantine houses. These have now been removed and the building left in its Late Roman form.

An inscription naming a **Stoa of the Herms**, known also from other ancient sources to have been east of the Stoa Poikile but not yet discovered, was found in 1962.

Immediately east of the **Altar of Zeus** is a rectangular Late Roman building on massive concrete foundations, whose function is unknown. Its northeast angle overlies the **Peribolos of the twelve gods** (**16**), situated on the Panathenaic Way and largely destroyed by the railway. The gods to whom it belonged were a local Athenian grouping, not the 12 Olympians. Consisting of an altar within a fenced enclosure, it was erected by Peisistratos the Younger in 521 BC. A recognised place of sanctuary, it may be the Altar of Pity mentioned by

Pausanias. Road distances from Athens were measured from this point. The identification is clear from an inscribed statue base still in position against the west wall of the enclosure.

To the south, remains of an **eschara** (**17**) may be the Altar of Aiakos mentioned by Herodotos (V 89). East of the Peribolos, a line of stone sockets across the Panathenaic Way held wooden posts, part of the **starting mechanism** (**18**) for races originally run here during the Festival. Large postholes found nearby were probably for the supports of wooden seating (*ikria*) for spectators.

Central area of the Agora

South of the Peribolos and the Roman building, the outline of the **Temple of Ares** (**19b**) has been marked in gravel. There are some blocks of the superstructure at the west end and of the foundations at the east: these carry Roman masons' marks, showing that the building, which markedly resembled the Hephaisteion and is ascribed to the same architect, was removed to this site in the Augustan period, possibly from Akharnai. There are foundations of a large **altar** (**19a**) to the east.

South again, the structure known to 19C archaeologists as the Stoa of the Giants marks the northern side of two interrelated buildings, the **Odeion of Agrippa**, or Agrippeion, and a much later **Palace**. Apart from the Stoa of Attalos, the huge piers and their sculptures are the most eye-catching remains in the Agora.

An Odeion was endowed in 15 BC by M. Vipsanius Agrippa, son-in-law of Emperor Augustus. Shortly after Pausanias saw the building, its roof collapsed, but it was rebuilt on a smaller scale in the reign of Antoninus Pius (c AD 150), probably as a lecture hall. This was burnt down in the Herulian sack of AD 267 and much of its masonry used in the Late Roman Wall. About AD 400 the site of the Odeion was occupied by the court of a vast Palatial Residence (formerly thought to be a Gymnasium) which extends well to the south.

Although the **Palace** (**21**) is later in date than the Odeion it is best described first. The four massive piers with sculptures were part of the façade of the forecourt of the complex. This, which lay over the Odeion, can be traced by its rough wall. South of the Odeion site, and reached by a rectangular lobby and semicircular passage, is a square court with a bath unit on the west and a third small court on the east; this is surrounded by well-preserved rooms. The whole of this complex lies over earlier stoas (Middle Stoa, etc; p 163).

The **Odeion** (**20**), roofed by a single span 24.5m wide, was surrounded by a two-storeyed stoa (traces visible). The main entrance was from the south, contradicting the orientation of the Palace. Of its auditorium only a few marble seats remain, together with some of the polychrome paving of the floor of the orchestra. Remains of the skene have been buttressed with modern walling. When the Odeion was rebuilt in the 2C AD a cross-wall was inserted and the capacity of the auditorium considerably reduced; the stage building was turned into a portico whose façade was supported by the 'giants'. This façade is now marked by two seated figures (possibly philosophers) which were part of its decoration.

The 'giants', two of which are in fact Tritons copied from figures on the

Parthenon pediments, were made to decorate the original building. Also used in the second Odeion (see above), they were again re-used in the entrance façade of the 5C AD Palace.

You cross the **Panathenaic Way**, here with a stone water channel and the bases of various unidentified monuments.

The Stoa of Attalos

The Stoa of Attalos (**22**), massively impressive in its restored state, and now housing the Agora Museum, was originally erected by King Attalos of Pergamon (158–138 BC), as recorded in an inscription (recovered in 1861) on the architrave. Mentioned in ancient literature only by Athenaeus, it was used for promenades, for retail trade and for watching the Panathenaic procession and other events in the Agora. Because it subsequently formed part of the Late Roman defence system (pp 129, 165), enough of the Stoa's plan and architectural members were preserved to enable an accurate restoration (in 1953–56): additional materials were acquired from the same sources as the original. The façade is Pentelic marble; the remainder a creamy-coloured limestone from Piraeus. The costs were met by private donors in the USA.

Preceding the Stoa, on the same site, were Mycenaean and Proto-Geometric graves and later wells. The earliest building (late 5C BC) consisted of small rooms round an irregular court. Finds of bronze jurors' ballots and a voting box indicate that it was a court, perhaps the *Parabyston*, or Court of the Eleven, a petty sessions court for offenders caught in the act. Under Lykourgos, the building was superseded by another (59.5m square), presumably with the same function.

The Stoa of Attalos was sacked in AD 267 and its remains then partly incorporated into the Late Roman Wall (p 220). The north end survived to roof height and the rooms were filled with rubble. An oblong tower was constructed at the north end and another (smaller) in the middle. At the south were further towers either side of a gateway (below).

The **Stoa** was a two-storeyed building 116.4 x 20m wide. The exterior colonnade (45 columns) is Doric below, Ionic (half columns engaged either side of a pilaster) above; the interior Ionic below, Pergamene above. At the back of the portico on each floor were 21 rectangular rooms (for shops), each with a front door on to the portico and a narrow slit-opening in the back wall. The layout has been modified to some extent in the reconstruction.

The exterior staircase at the north end has been restored to its original plan. Below it, an arched opening, the earliest known use of a visible arch in an Athenian building, gives access to an exedra with a marble bench. The south end reflects the alterations which were made at the end of the 1C AD.

In front of the centre of the Stoa are a **bema** (**23**) and the **Donor's monument** (**24**). More than 100 blocks from the latter have been recovered from the dismantled Late Roman Wall. The monument resembled that of Agrippa on the Acropolis and carried a bronze quadriga at about the level of the second storey of the stoa. It was later rededicated to the Roman emperor Tiberius. Against the terrace wall to the north were other statues.

The Agora Museum

The ancient layout of the Stoa of Attalos has been modified to allow use as an excavation study centre and museum (ground floor).

Outside in the colonnade, the collection of sculpture has several interesting pieces (from south to north): S 2154, the probable cult statue of *Apollo Patroös* by Euphranor, 350–325 BC; S 33, 198, Herms, etc; S 1214, *Head of Triton* from the Odeion, c AD 150; section of Odeion stage front, c 15 BC; I 7154, Cave of Pan relief, inscribed, c 320 BC; S 429, Akroterion (?) figure from the Hephaisteion, c 420 BC; I 7167, Rider relief commemorating a victory won by the tribe Leontis in the *anthippasia*, the cavalry contest in the Panathenaic Games, c 365 BC; S 676, etc, reliefs from the frieze of the temple of Ares, c 420 BC; S 399, Apobates relief (contest in Panathenaic Games involving armed warriors jumping on and off chariots), early 4C BC; S 2370, *statue of ?Themis*, 3C BC; S 2436, *Portrait of Antoninus Pius* (138–61 BC); S 335, *Portrait of ?Aelius Verus* (d. 138 BC); S 347, *Portrait of Trajan* (98–117 BC); S 312, *Nike* akroterion from the Stoa of Zeus, c 400 BC.

Returning to the south end of the colonnade, you can see further monuments, set between the central columns, including I 7396, Votive stele of a shoemaker, with an illustration of the craft, 375–350 BC; S 270, *Head of ?Herodotos*, 2C AD; I 3244, 5509, 1024 are Record reliefs: the first of arbitration, 363/2 BC, the second a report of public auctioneers, 367/66 BC, the third recording thanks to the Prytaneis and Council officials of 260/59 BC; S 1654, *Nymph with water-jar*, 5C BC.

Inside (not all cases are described), a long gallery of exhibits is arranged in chronological order: **Cases 1–8** Neolithic to Mycenaean, including finds from Mycenaean tombs: bronze sword, outstanding ivory pyxis (cylindrical box) with relief of griffins and stags. Also a Canaanite amphora of c 1400 BC from one of the tombs. **Cases 9–11** Proto- and Early Geometric burial finds. **Case 12** Material from a Proto-Geometric potter's kiln. **Cases 13–18** Geometric pottery and finds, mainly from burials, including a row of model granaries on a chest. **Case 19** Orientalising pottery from a well. **Case 21** Offerings from a shrine dump of the mid-7C BC.

Case 22 Heads of herms (S 3347, 2499, 2425); also inscriptions with (I 2729) rules of the Library of Pantainos, (I 4809) tribute due to Athens in 421 BC by cities of the Hellespont; (I 4120) 6C BC eponymous archons, including the names of Hippias, Kleisthenes and Miltiades, for the successive years 525–523 BC, (I 3872) fragments of a base belonging to the second Tyrannicides group. **Case 23** Part of clay mould for casting the 6C cult statue of Apollo Patroös. **Case 29** Terracotta oil flask in the form of a kneeling athlete binding his hair with the victor's fillet, 540–530 BC.

Cases 26–28 Weights and measures standards. Bronze voting ballots. Water-clock for court use to measure time allowed for pleading (cf. Aristotle, *Constitution of Athens*). (I 3967) Part of a *kleroterion* for selecting jury members (slots for name-tags) by lot, using coloured balls. Numbered 28A is a relief (I 6254) with inscription of a law of 336 BC against tyranny (the scene shows Democracy crowning the Demos of Athens).

Cases 30–33 Black- and red-figure vases, many attributed to individual painters. The cups are particularly good (works by Epiktetos and the Chaireas Painter) and show how the figures are accommodated to the unusual circular field; also a fine calyx-crater by Exekias (**Case 31**), c 530 BC, with the

Introduction of Herakles to Olympos and Greeks and Trojans fighting over the body of Patroklos. Note also an alabastron by the Amasis Painter, c 550 BC. Signature of Gorgos, c 510 BC etc.

Case 36 *Head of bronze Nike*, c 430 BC, originally plated with gold and silver (traces behind ears and at back of neck). To the left, large bronze shield (34) captured by the Athenians from the Spartans at Sphakteria (Pylos), 425 BC, and crudely inscribed (ΑΘΗΝΑΙΟΙ ΑΠΟ ΛΑΚΕΔΑΙΜΟΝΙΩΝ ΕΚ ΠΥΛΟ, the Athenians from the Spartans, from Pylos). Below the shield are fragments of a bronze equestrian statue (36A) of Demetrios Poliorketes, set up c 300 BC and torn down c 200 BC. **Case 38** contains sherds of pottery (*ostraka*) used in ostracisms between 487 and 417 BC, including the names of Aristides the Just, Themistokles, Kimon and Perikles. **Case 42** A limited selection of coins from the Agora, from antiquity to the 19C AD. To the left, small-scale replicas of statues, including the 4C *Weary Herakles,* the 5C triple *Hekate* of Alkamenes and *Mother of the Gods* by Agorakritos. Right is (48) a 2C AD ivory copy of the *Apollo Lykeios* of Praxiteles.

The remaining cases (52, etc) contain Classical, Hellenistic and Roman pottery, terracottas and some bronzes, lamps from the 7C BC, various Roman portrait busts, a 2C AD copy of a Hellenistic satyr and a mosaic pavement (5C AD) from a house at the southwest corner of the Agora; (63) Byzantine and Ottoman pottery.

In front of the northern part of the Stoa is a circular foundation of the mid-2C AD, whose green marble columns probably supported a brick dome, the whole perhaps covering a statue.

South side of the Agora

Between the Stoa of Attalos and the Library of Pantainos (see below), a street led east to the Roman Market (p 166), through an arch with a small fountain. This rearrangement required some modifications to the Stoa.

Here are remains of a later **tower (25)**, one of two protecting a gate in the Late Roman Wall leading on to the same roadway. On the destroyed tower at one time stood a church of the Panayía Pirghiótissa. Beyond this point a part of the wall is well preserved.

The **Late Roman** (or Post-Herulian) **Wall (26)** in the Agora was part of a fortification which enclosed a rough square, with the Acropolis as its base and the north end of the Stoa of Attalos its northwest corner (pp 129, 160). The back rooms of the Stoa were filled with rubble to form part of the line. The use of material from buildings which had been partly destroyed in the Herulian sack of AD 267 is evident. An inscription attributes the construction of the wall to one Claudius Illyrius. Much of it has now been dismantled in order to recover inscriptions and architectural elements.

The Wall followed the line of the façade of the destroyed **Library of Pantainos (27)**. Erected before AD 102 at Expense of Titus Flavius Pantainos, who dedicated it to Athena Polias and the Emperor Trajan (the inscription from the lintel of the main door is exposed), this consisted of rooms—the most important to the east—round a peristyle court. The street front was a portico of nine Ionic columns; graffiti suggest the library attracted young readers. An inscription read 'Books shall not be taken out of the library and it shall be open from the first to the sixth hour.'

Along the outer face of the Late Roman Wall are some remains (well-built conduit) of a **watermill** (**28**) of the 5C–6C AD.

At the southeast corner of the site a **temple** with a hexastyle porch was built in the Augustan period with material brought from a Doric building at Thorikos.

Beyond the fenced site enclosure, the Panathenaic Way, with well-preserved paving of the 2C AD, continues upwards. About halfway up to the east (left) is the site of the **Eleusinion** (**29**), identified by reliefs, inscriptions and cult pottery (*kernoi*) of the worship of Demeter and Kore. This was the Athenian headquarters of the cult whose main centre was at Eleusis (p 265).

Near the southeast gate of the site is the pretty church of **Ayy. Apostoli** (**30**), restored to its form of c 1020 with the removal in 1954–57 of 19C additions. The dome was supported on four Roman columns: only one of those in place now is original. The paintings in the narthex are 17C, from the church of Ay. Spiridon which was originally over the Library of Pantainos; others are from Ay. Yeóryios in the Hephaisteion.

Below and to the east of the church are some rather disappointing buildings. A Nymphaion (**31**), a shrine to the Nymphs consisting of a semicircular fountain house, has been restored in a drawing made on the basis of surviving remains, but is virtually invisible. Its construction entailed the demolition of the north wall of a building of c 400 BC, thought to be the **Argyrokopeion** (Mint; **32**) of the ancient city. Only bronze coins have so far been found, but none of the silver 'owls' (illustration, p 260) for which Athens was famous. Next to (west of) the Mint are the more intelligible remains of the **Southeast Fountain House** (**33**), described by Pausanias as the Enneakrounos and probably built by Peisistratos in the later 6C BC. Rectangular in form, it had three columns in the entrance, and a draw-basin to either side.

The south side of the Fountain House borders a road, on the line of a Bronze Age predecessor. On the hillside to the left are remains of houses. The road ran along the the back of the **First South Stoa** (**34**) which, from the 5C to the 2C BC, dominated the south side of the Agora, with administrative offices and official dining-rooms. You can see some parts of the original interior walls of sun-dried brick. At the west end of the Stoa is the ground plan of an open yard with boundary wall which survived unchanged from the mid-6C BC to the sack of Sulla and may have been the **Heliaia** law court (**35**). In the 4C BC a water-clock, probably operated by a float on a column of water, was added to its north side. To the west is another fountain house (**36**).

In the 2C BC the layout of the south side of the Agora was completely redesigned with the construction of the **Middle Stoa** (**37**). The building had a central wall with colonnades opening to both sides. Over 137m long, it ran from the Panathenaic Way to the Tholos and was the largest structure in the Agora. In front of the Tholos it was raised on a high podium. The red conglomerate foundations are best seen at the west end, and elements of the poros colonnade, with unfluted Doric columns, at the northeast corner. The north terrace of the Stoa gave on to the Odeion (see p 159). In the Hadrianic period a small annexe of the Metróön was built against the podium opposite the Tholos.

The Hellenistic redevelopment of the area, much of which has been obscured by the Roman Palace (p 159), was completed by an **East Stoa** (**38**) and the realigned **Second South Stoa** (**39**), to form the 'South Square'.

The feeling of regular spaces formally enclosed by colonnades, so characteristic of Hellenistic architecture, is partly re-created by the restoration of the Stoa of Attalos.

West of the Middle Stoa and near the Tholos, where we began, are scanty remains of a large building which may have been the **Strategeion** (**40**), headquarters of the ten generals. Southwest of this, you can continue for c 100m on the line of an ancient road into an area of rather ill-defined buildings between the Agora proper and that of Dörpfeld's excavations (p 136).

One building with a distinctive plan, which you soon reach in this direction, has been identified—not without controversy—as the **State Prison** (*Desmoterion*; **41**) of ancient Athens, where Sokrates' death by drinking hemlock is described by Plato (*Phaedo*). Eight small 'cells' are set to left and right of a narrow entrance passage which leads to an inner yard. Left of the entrance a block of rooms (possibly two-storeyed) at an oblique angle to the passage could have belonged to the prison administration. Two of the 'cells' are linked, fitting the two-roomed setting of Sokrates' final hours. Small flasks found would have been suitable for hemlock.

This part of the ancient city was residential and industrial: there are remains of several courtyard houses of the Classical and Roman periods, and finds suggest the working of metal, marble and terracotta in the vicinity. The quarter should be considered together with Dörpfeld's excavations (p 136), to which of course it was joined in antiquity.

7 • Pláka ~ Old Athens

With its old houses and narrow, winding streets (stepped in the higher reaches and straggling up the slopes of the Acropolis), Pláka (**Map 5, 1–2**) has a delightful atmosphere. Lower down, many of the grander mansions have been well restored externally (though, paradoxically, the interiors have been often ruined). At the top, where the tiny ramshackle houses of Anafiótika cling to the hillside, you might be in an island village. It is pleasant to wander without following a set route. Near Monastiráki are some important ancient monuments—the Library of Hadrian, the Tower of the Winds and the Roman Market. The Museum of Greek Folk Music has a rich and fascinating collection and the Kanellópoulos Museum an outstanding and varied range of antiquities. There are plenty of restaurants and cafés, the most attractive those in the vicinity of Od. Panós or overlooking the Agora (Od. Dhioskoúron).

- **Access on foot**. The route described, starting from Monastiráki Square, is roughly 1.5km but you will want to make numerous short detours. Pláka can also be entered from Síntagma via Filellínon and Navárkhou Nikodhímou or Kidhathinaíon (where this walk ends); or from the area of Hadrian's Arch, via Od. Lisikrátous (p 93).
  Access by bus/electric railway. See pp 144, 146 for Monastiráki Square.

The name **Pláka** may come either from an Albanian word *pliaka* (old) or from a plaque (*pláka*) which once marked the crossing of its principal streets (Odd. Adhrianoú and Kidhathinaíon).

The area covers roughly the territory of the ancient deme of *Kydathenaion*, and was a centre of population in Byzantine times. It has no official boundaries but occupies the north and northeast slopes of the Acropolis, above Ermoú and towards Amalías (opposite the Olympieion). Formerly there were four separate districts—Rizókastro, Brizáki, Alíkokou and Anafiótika. In the Ottoman period much of it belonged to a district called Gorgópiko (p 146) after the Old Cathedral.

Lower Pláka

Leaving Monastiráki Square up Od. Areos (shops), past the Mosque of Tzistarákis (p 145), you come immediately on the left to the surviving part of the massive west façade and main entrance of the **Library of Hadrian** (plan p 151). Although the site is closed, it can be easily viewed by walking round the three sides defined by Odd. Areos, Dhexíppou and Aiólou.

Built c AD 132, on a site previously occupied by houses, the library complex consisted of a large court, probably with a garden and a pool in the centre. The entrance was to the west (on Areos), the main rooms to the east (on Aiólou). In Late Antiquity a quatrefoil building was erected in the centre of the court. This was later succeeded by an Early Christian basilica, then a Byzantine church.

The western part of the site also had a varied later history. The Late Roman fortification incorporated the south wall of the Library complex. The Byzantine church of Ayy. Asomati sta Skaliá was built over the steps (*sta skaliá*) on the north side of the entrance propylon in the late 13C, and graves were dug from the same period. The church was demolished in the 1840s. In the early Ottoman period, when the inhabited area was still within the Late Roman Wall, the propylon of the Library was one of the main gates of the town. In the 18C or earlier the residence of the Ottoman voivode (governor) was erected over the southwest part of the Library, with a courtyard and bath complex. Remains of the ornamental fountain from the court have been found southwest of the Library façade. Under King Otho there was a barracks. Much of the Library area used to be occupied by a bazaar through which passed Od. Adhrianoú. The line of the street is now interrupted by the excavations.

Of the **west façade and entrance** (Areos), the northern half of the façade is intact, as far as the north jamb of the central doorway. This consisted of a simple propylon (its north wall and forward column survive) approached by six steps. Either side of the propylon seven unfluted Corinthian columns of Karystos marble stood forward of the main wall, supporting an architrave which is indented between each pair of columns. The patch of mosaic visible between the north wall of the porch and the first column belonged to the church of Ayy. Asomati (see above).

Surrounding the **library compound** was a huge rectangular wall of poros (c 122 x 82m; parts surviving on all sides). Within was a cloistered court whose peristyle consisted of 'a hundred splendid columns' (Pausanias) of Phrygian marble. Three **recesses** opened off both the north and south sides—the central one rectangular, the flanking ones semicircular. The main block of five rooms was behind the eastern cloister (Aiólou). The central chamber, entered from the peristyle through a porch of four columns, housed the **library proper**. It is the back wall of this room which, buttressed by six Corinthian pilasters, impresses from Aiólou. A large central niche in the east wall, with four smaller ones to each side, contained the bookshelves, resembling the arrangement in the library at Pergamon. The other rooms were probably workrooms and repositories for archives, like those in the contemporary library at Alexandria.

The **interior of the court** was probably a garden, with a long reservoir or pool in the centre. About AD 410, under the governor Herculius, a quatrefoil-shaped building, either a lecture hall or a church, was built over the east end of the pool; the wall of its northeast angle stands to a height of about 2.7m and one of the semicircular foundations is visible (some mosaics were found). In the 7C this was replaced by a basilica (the four standing columns belong to this phase) which later became the Byzantine church of the Megáli Panayía. This survived, with modifications, until 1885.

In a small square off Dhexíppou, on the south side of the Library, is a **church of the Taxiárkhis** (Archangel) rebuilt after a fire in 1832. It has a revered icon of the Panayía Grigoroúsa (Ever Watchful). At a house in the street beyond, which he described as 'a splendid museum', the writer and politician Chateaubriand was received by Fauvel, the French consul, in 1806.

Continuing up Areos from the Library of Hadrian, you come to a small square where (Od. Pikílis, right) excavations have uncovered the ancient road from the Greek Agora to the Roman Market.

The Roman Market

To your left the **Gate of Athena Archegetes** (the epithet means 'first leader' or 'founder of a city') was the formal entrance. Slightly left of centre of the market's west wall, it consists of a Doric portico with four prostyle columns supporting an entablature and pediment. The side walls, which terminate in antae behind the end columns of the portico, run right through to the back wall of the colonnade of the inner court. Inside the vestibule so formed, two pairs of columns, between antae, form the entrance proper. A worn inscription on the architrave records the dedication to Athena Archegetes and credits the work as a donation of Julius Caesar and Augustus during the archonship of Nikias. On the central akroterion (both sculpture and its inscription now lost), was a statue of Lucius Caesar, son of Agrippa and Augustus' daughter Julia, who was adopted by Augustus in 17 BC and died in AD 2. The gateway must have been erected between these dates. On the north jamb is inscribed a well-known edict of Hadrian regulating the sale of oil and the related excise duty.

Walking along the edge of the market towards the entrance to the site you get a good idea of its character. Remember, however, that the north and part of the west side still lie unexcavated beneath roads and buildings.

The **market**, which incorporated an earlier Hellenistic compound, was a rectangle of c 111 x 96m. Inside the poros **outer wall** (early 1C BC), at least on the south side, was a **colonnade** to either side of a central block of rooms. Later, perhaps in the time of Hadrian, an Ionic peristyle was added inside. Its unfluted columns were in Hymettian marble; the bases, capitals and epistyle in Pentelic. The **central square**, bordered by a deep drainage channel, was later paved in marble (surviving in places). There was also access by a **southeast propylon** (down five steps), similar in plan to the Athena Gate, but smaller and later. It is neither on the central axis of the square nor exactly at right-angles to the wall. The lower part is well preserved, although the columns stand only to 2.4–3m. To either side were **shops** (five excavated; inscriptions give the names of the proprietors).

Just inside the **site** (08.30–15.00; closed Mon), but outside the market itself, are the foundations of a large public latrine of the 1C AD.

Beyond is the **Tower of the Winds**, properly the Horologion (lit. Hour-teller) of Andronikos Kyrrhestes. It was built in the 2C or 1C BC by the astronomer Andronikos of Kyrrhos (scholars

The Ottoman Medresse

disagree whether it is the Syrian or the Macedonian town of that name) and acted as a sundial, water-clock and weathervane combined. In Ottoman times it was used by dervishes as a *tekke* or house.

The octagonal tower is built of marble and set on three steps. The roof is a pyramid of marble slabs, retained by a round keystone. Each of the eight faces is set towards a cardinal point of the compass and decorated with a relief showing the wind which blows from that direction. On the northeast and northwest faces were porches with two fluted Corinthian columns with simple elegant capitals. Parts of the northwest entablature have been reassembled nearby. According to Vitruvius (I 6 4) the tower was originally topped by a bronze Triton holding a wand which pointed to the face of the prevailing wind.

The **eight wind-figures** are portrayed winged and floating almost horizontally through the air. Clockwise they are: north—*Boreas*, in a thick, sleeved mantle with folds blustering in the air; he blows a twisted shell; northeast—*Kaikias*, who empties a shield full of hailstones; east—*Apeliotes* with flowers and fruit; southeast—*Euros*, right arm wrapped in a mantle and threatening a hurricane; south—*Notos*, who empties an urn to produce a shower; southwest—*Lips*, driving before him the ornament from the stern of a ship, promise of a rapid voyage; west—*Zephyros*, who showers into the air a lapful of flowers; northwest—*Skiron* carrying a bronze vessel of charcoal, with which to dry up rivers. Beneath the figures of the winds the lines of eight sundials can be traced.

Projecting from the south face is a semicircular reservoir for the water which ran the clock's works. The interior has a white marble pavement with channels for a parapet, and other obscure markings.

Just to the south, arches of Hymettian marble on a massive base form the façade of a building dedicated to Athena Archegetes and the Divi Augusti (deified Roman emperors) in the 1C AD. Once thought to be the Agoranomion (office of the magistrates of the market), its function is not certain.

From here you can enter the court of the market by the southeast gate (above). In the corner of the site is a **Mosque** (15C; closed), probably the *Fetihie Cami* (Victory Mosque) built to celebrate the Ottoman conquest.

On the corner of Od. Aiólou, opposite the site entrance, are a gateway and cupola, all that remain of an Ottoman **Medresse** (seminary), founded by Mehmet Fakri in 1721 (inscription). Here, a century later, the *cadi* (Islamic judge) Haci Khalil dissuaded the Turks from a massacre of the male Greeks in Attica.

Close by at 1–3 Od. Dhioyénous is the **Museum of Greek Folk Music Instruments** and Centre for Ethnomusicology (most days 10.00–14.00, Wed 12.00–18.00, closed Mon), with a remarkable collection of instruments of all kinds, fascinating displays and a library. You can hear music involving the instruments shown.

At no. 8 Od. Kirrhístou (above Dhioyénous) is the Ottoman **bath house of Abid Efendi** (or **Loutró Aéridhon**; model in the Museum of Greek Folk Art), recently restored but not yet regularly open. A splendid monument, it has changing and bathing areas, and water and heating installations. Built before 1667, it was altered c 1870 and used until 1965.

Upper Pláka

You have a choice of ways up to the higher reaches of Pláka. Working your way back towards the gate of Athena you could climb the picturesque Od. Panós, stepped towards the top (restaurants), or choose the quieter Od. Dhioskoúron (cafés) overlooking the Agora. In this part of Pláka are several buildings restored by the Ministry of Culture and housing offices of the Archaeological Service.

At the top of Od. Panós, on the corner with Theorías, is the **Kanellópoulos Museum** (08.30–15.00; closed Mon), opened in 1976 (good guidebook by M. Broúskari, *The Paul and Alexandra Kanellopoulos museum*, 1985; available in English). The 19C mansion has been tastefully restored (note the painted ceilings) and the interior arranged functionally to display the rich and eclectic family collection of antiquities of all periods. In the **courtyard**, which may not be accessible, is Greek and Roman sculpture. The **ground floor** has a wide variety of Byzantine and Late Antique material including numerous fine icons (one by Michael Damaskinos, 16C). There are also fresco fragments, vases, bronzes, crosses, jewellery, coins, pottery, ivories, embroideries. Some of the material is from Egypt and the Middle East. In the **basement** (at present closed) are huge blocks of an Archaic wall. On the **ground-floor landing** are Coptic textiles, mummy portraits and a few pieces of Classical, Roman and Byzantine sculpture, including a head of Galerius, 4C AD. The **first floor** has prehistoric (good Early Cycladic, Minoan and Mycenaean material) and Geometric vases and bronzes; Sub-Minoan and Proto-Geometric figurines; Near Eastern and Cypriot objects, including faïence. On the **top floor** is a large collection of Archaic, Classical, Hellenistic and Roman objects: vases (including Argive, Boeotian, Corinthian and East Greek); major and minor sculpture (numerous terracottas); extensive collection of jewellery (including some Persian); coins; bronzes; a Roman marble cinerary urn.

Immediately above the museum is Od. Theorías (café). Opposite, on the other side of the boundary fence which prevents access to the North Slope of the Acropolis, are the ruins of a 17C church of Ayios Nikólaos (see also p 129).

Turning right will take you along the north slope and round to the Acropolis entrance, passing on the right (view) the path down to the Agora.

Along here you can see something of the inaccessible **North Slope of the Acropolis**, though the view is impeded by trees. In antiquity the area was known as the Long Rocks. From the Neolithic period there were primitive vegetation and fertility cults here: these survived into Classical times. A decree of 415 BC, restricting the erection of altars in the Pelargikon area, may represent an attempt to limit them. Investigations (1931–39) by the Greek Archaeological Society and American School of Classical Studies recovered much pottery and material apparently thrown down from the Acropolis, including inscriptions of the Erechtheion accounts, the Opisthodomos inventory and the accounts of the statue of Athena Promakhos, as well as some 200 ostraka (p 66) inscribed with the name of Themistokles, and a calyx-crater painted by Exekias.

At the west end, above the Klepsydra spring (p 128) are four **caves**. The first is merely a niche with rock-cut seats. The second, somewhat larger, contained a number of Roman tablets dedicated to Apollo Hypakraios by archons taking their oath of office. The third may be the Pythion (shrine of Apollo), where the Pythiasts (members of the sacred mission to the sanctuary of Apollo at Delphi who represented Athens at the festival there) watched for the flash of lightning from Mt Párnitha before starting the procession to Delphi. The narrow tunnel-like cave, above which there was later a chapel of Ay. Athanássios, is identified with the **Cave of Pan** (Euripides, *Ion* 938; Aristophanes, *Lysistrata* 911). Herodotos (VI 105) tells how the worship of Pan was revived after his appearance to the courier Pheidipiddes, on his way to seek Spartan help against the Persians in 490 BC. Further east were found reliefs with phallic and fertility emblems, also fragments of a frieze with Erotes, perhaps decoration of the precinct wall. A boundary marker of the Peripatos (p 98) is inscribed on a large boulder.

Looking up at the Acropolis you can see the striking remains of the entablature of the Old Temple of Athena and column drums from the Older Parthenon built into the wall (p 113).

Walking in the opposite direction (left) from the Kanellópoulos Museum along Theorías you come to the pretty **church of the Metamórfosis** (Transfiguration), known as Sotiráki (key from the church of the Panayía at the corner of Thrasivoúlou and Alibérti, down the hill). At this point you are below the level of the ancient Peripatos which separated the primitive sanctuaries on the higher slopes of the Acropolis from the seats of officialdom below.

Just below the Sotiráki church, at Od. Thólou 5, is the **Old University**, built under the Venetians and used as public offices by the Turks. It was first the private house of Kleánthis (p 84), who rebuilt it with a third storey in 1830 for the university, which functioned here 1837–41. It has recently been restored as a **Museum of the University** (open Mon, Wed 14.30–19.00; Tues, Thur, Fri 09.30–13.00; closed Sat, Sun), with a collection of manuscripts, books, photographs, paintings, medical instruments, etc, and displays relating to the histories of the various faculties. There is accommodation for seminars and educational programmes.

Keeping to the higher lane above the Old University, you reach the charming quarter of **Anafiótika** (with a church of Ay. Simeón ton Anafaíon) mostly built in the early 19C by immigrant workers drawn to Athens for the construction of the new capital. The first two houses were put up illegally by families from the island of Anáfi, and today the tiny ramshackle buildings, liberally decorated with flowers overflowing from pots of all kinds, reflect an informal island style.

You now begin to descend gradually eastwards. Below is Od. Pritaníou, called after the ancient Prytaneion (pp 93, 154). Although its exact site is unknown it was in this area. Here in a pleasant walled court is the **Metókhi tou Panayíou Táfou**, a monastic dependency of the Holy Sepulchre at Jerusalem. The monastery is traditionally associated with the Athenian orphan who became the Empress Irene (762–803), reigning alone in Byzantium after the death of her husband Leo in 797. The Sarandapíkhos family, to which she belonged, is said to have come from this district. It may, however, not be earlier than the 16C: the *katholikon*, Ayy. Anáryiri, was remodelled in the 17C. A few metres further, in the street below, is the 12C church of Ay. Ioánnis Theológos.

At the corner of Odd. Pritaníou and Epikhármou is the 12C Byzantine church of **Ay. Nikólaos Rangavás** (restored). You can wind your way down to Kirrhístou where, at the corner with Fléssa, are the rooms where Caroline, Princess of Wales, was entertained in 1816. Some slight remains on the north side of Kirrhístou have been tentatively identified with the Diogeneion, a gymnasium named after a 3C BC Macedonian general (p 207).

Carry on down to the touristy Od. Adhrianoú and turn right. In the vicinity of no. 88 and the junction with Mnesikléous have been found some remains of the **Pantheon**, a famous temple to all the Gods which was one of Hadrian's gifts to Athens. No. 96—now in a sorry state—was built under the Turks by the aristocratic Venizélos family, and may be the oldest surviving house in Athens. The name is commemorated in Od. Venizélou, which drops from here to the cathedral (p 146).

The Scottish historian George Finlay (1799–1875) lived in Adhrianoú in a house built c 1780. The primary school at the corner of Od. Fléssa, with a fine neoclassical porch, occupies the site of the Mosque of the Column which, for a short time in 1687, became the first Protestant church in Greece, for Morosini's Lutheran gunners.

Off to the left (via Navárkhou Nikodhímou), Od. Thoukidhídhou 9 is the **Hill Memorial School**, founded in 1831 by John Henry Hill (d. 1882), an American missionary. Opposite are excavated remains of a Roman peristyle building of the 2C AD which continued in use into the 6C. There are fine mansions at the junction of the two streets. In Od. Hill (right) there are some good buildings, those on the left restored to house the Institute of International Relations of Athens University. At the far end, in Od. Skholíou, is the Dora Strátou Dance Academy. At no. 6 Od. Khatzimikhaïli (left) is an interesting house (1924–27), which incorporates elements of traditional architecture, built by A. Zakhos for the famous Greek ethnographer Angelikí Khatzimikhaïli (1895–1965). Well worth a visit, it houses the City of Athens **Centre for Folk Art and Tradition**, with an outstanding collection of wood carvings, textiles, domestic equipment etc, and a library (Tues, Wed, Thur, Fri 09.00–13.00 and 17.00–19.00; Sat, Sun 09.00–13.00; closed Mon. The library is also closed on Sat and Sun).

Adhrianoú continues towards the Monument of Lysikrates (p 94) but you should turn left into Od. Kidhathinaíon. After a small square with cafés and eating-places you pass (right) no. 27 where King Ludwig of Bavaria stayed in 1835. Many of the neighbouring houses date from that period. Opposite (at no. 14) is the **Children's Museum** (Paidhikó Mouseío; Tues–Fri 10.00–13.00; Sat, Sun 10.00–14.00; closed Mon). More a series of educational games than a museum, its contents will probably appeal to most young children, and the staff are friendly, but the labelling is in Greek.

At Monís Asteríou (right), nos 3 and 7, is the new **Frisíras Museum of Contemporary European Painting** in two neoclassical buildings whose exteriors have been well restored though, as so often, the interiors spoiled to provide convenient exhibition space. The collection, which aims to show Greek art in its European context, as well as temporary exhibitions, has some excellent work (e.g. by Bouziánis, Móralis, Blake, Kitaj) but a good deal which will only appeal to progressive taste.

At no. 17 (right) is the **Museum of Greek Folk Art** (10.00–14.00; closed Mon; small shop with good ceramics and **embroideries**). This should not be missed. The ground floor has excellent island embroideries, with examples of the Dodecanesian bed-tent (*sperveri*); there are embroidered church garments including the surplice of Archbishop Chrysostomos of Smyrna, executed by the Turks when he refused to abandon his diocese in 1922. On the mezzanine is Çannakale and Italian **pottery** imported into Skíros; a display of **spinning and weaving equipment**, plus textile stamps; metal flasks; wooden bread stamps, bowls and cutlery; displays of shadow **puppets** and masquerade costumes and models. On the first floor are paintings by the Greek primitive artist **Theófilos** (p 231). Outstanding are his wall-paintings from a house on the island of Lésvos (Mitilíni) which have been installed here. There is also space for temporary exhibitions. The second floor has an extensive display of **metalwork**, including jewellery, body ornament, vessels, weapons and church plate. On the third floor are numerous pieces of **traditional costume**, also some 'Rhodian' plates. Pieces of traditional furniture are scattered through the museum.

From here you can head for Od. Filellínon and Síntagma.

8 • Psirí and the ancient sites of the Kerameikós and Academy

The Kerameikós, a delightful and fascinating archaeological site with a good small museum, is 1km down Ermoú from Monastiráki, in the corner of the triangle formed by Ermoú and Piraiós, with Athinás as the third side (**Maps 3,7; 2,8 etc**). The ancient Sacred Way to Eleusis, whose modern successor bears the same name (Ierá Odhós), began here. Below it is the old gas works (Gázi), now a splendidly refurbished monument of Industrial Archaeology. The rest of the triangle, which stretches as far as Omónia, includes the interesting old quarter of Psirí, full of local colour, and the spacious Plateía Koumoundoúrou, an important bus terminal opening on to Piraiós. Beyond Piraiós (1.5km from

Kerameikós) is Plato's Academy, now an extensive archaeological park with scattered remains. The area between the two sites is rather run down but has some attractive old houses; you need to keep to the minor roads to see them, thereby following the ancient route as closely as possible.

- **Access**. The description begins at Monastiráki (pp 145, 147), but instructions for direct approaches to the individual sites are given in the relevant places. **Transport**. The whole route described is just over 2km (one way); there is no means of covering it in continuous sequence by public transport but taking a **taxi** from Kerameikós to the Academy would reduce walking to the minimum.

Psirí: between Monastiráki and Omónia

Below Monastiráki, Ermoú becomes wider, noisier and less appealing, with furniture shops and builders' merchants. To the right you can plunge into the tortuous narrow streets of Psirí, a working quarter, now being developed but still attractive. In Od. Ayías Théklas, close to Monastiráki, Byron stayed (at no. 11) on his first, ten-week, visit to Athens in 1809–10, later immortalising the 13-year-old daughter of the house, Terésa Makrís, as the 'Maid of Athens'. Od. Evripídhou, full of traditional shops, forms the further boundary of Psirí. The commercial area between there and Omónia is more regularly laid out but nonetheless busy and colourful.

As you continue down Ermoú, the 14C church of the **Ayy. Asómati** gives its name to a small square on the right, a pretty oasis by a busy junction.

Od. Ayíon Asomáton (no. 45, although a modest little house, was designed by Ziller and has two Caryatids at first-floor level; being restored) forms one boundary of the Kerameikós excavations, continuing to join Piraiós, just below the spacious **Plateía Koumoundoúrou** (Eleftherías), a meeting-place for Kurdish refugees. In Od. Kriezí just off the square is the Armenian **church of St Gregory**, with its conspicuous onion-shaped dome. On the further side, near the junction of Odd. Menándrou and Evripídhou, is **Ay. Ioánnis stin Kolóna**. The church is built round an unfluted Roman column with a Corinthian capital (probably from a gymnasium dedicated to Apollo) which projects through the roof. It is supposed to have the power of curing fevers.

Within Plateía Koumoundoúrou, although facing Piraiós (it is no. 51), is the **Art Gallery** of the city of Athens (Mon–Fri 09.00–13.00 and 17.00–21.00, Sun 09.00–13.00; closed Sat), housed in a former school (1875). There is a good collection of 19C and 20C Greek artists and the works are well displayed in an airy and attractive setting. The catalogue has excellent illustrations; posters available include works by Bouziánis and Papaloukás. There are also temporary exhibitions. At Piraiós 35 is the original home of the Polytechnic.

Opposite Ayy. Asómati, on the other side of Ermoú, Leofóros Apostólou Pávlou climbs past Thisío Metró station, to approach the Acropolis from the west. Below this junction, in Od. Melidhóni (off Ermoú to the right), is the **Synagogue** (open Mon–Fri 10.00–12.00), in brick with a classicising façade in Pentelic marble. Opposite (at nos 4–6) is the **Centre for the Study of Traditional Pottery** (Kéntro Melétis Neóteris Keramikís, Κέντρο Μελέτης Νεότερης Κεραμεικής;

Mon–Fri 09.00–15.00, Sun 10.00–14.00; closed Sat) with excellent modern displays, including reconstructions, of manufacturing techniques and regional pottery; also a library, reading room, café and good shop.

Next (in Ermoú) is the entrance to the **Kerameikós excavations and Museum**. Opposite the Kerameikós entrance, a footbridge over the electric railway (p 135) provides another means of access to the site.

Kerameikós

The Kerameikós site contains part of the ancient City Walls, the Dipylon and Sacred Gates, the Pompeion (starting point for ceremonial processions) and part of the principal ancient Cemetery of Athens, which lay outside the walls. The Eridanos brook crosses the archaeological site from east to west. Frequently waterlogged, it has trees, flowers and plenty of wildlife.

- **Opening**. Tues–Sun 08.30–15.00; closed Mon.
  Access on foot. 1km from Monastiráki via Ermoú.
  Access by public transport. **Buses** nos 025, 026, 027 from Akadhimías, Síntagma or Monastiráki to stop in Od. Leokoríou, by the church of Ayy. Asómati, then a 5-min walk; no. 049 from Omónia (Athinás) via Piraiós to stop Palaiá Agorá (by Gas Works; see p ❤❤❤), close to site. **Metró** (Line 1): Thisío station (the stop after Monastiráki), then a 600m walk.
  Guidebooks, etc. U. Knigge, *The Athenian Kerameikós*, 1994, with useful restorations of several monuments. Also available at the site is *Eridanos: the river of ancient Athens*, 2000 (Hellenic Ministry of Culture), a fascinating account of the history of the river and its wildlife.

History

Pausanias (I 3 1) says that the area got its name from the hero Keramos, son of Dionysos and Ariadne. The earliest burials date from the 12C BC and the museum has a continuous series of grave finds dating from then until the 6C AD. As it was forbidden to bury the dead within the City Walls, the line of the Archaic Wall (not yet found but said by Thucydides to have enclosed a smaller area than the Themistoklean) can be estimated by plotting the positions of 7C and 6C graves. The terms 'Inner Kerameikós', occupied by potters and metalsmiths, and 'Outer Kerameikós', the burial area, arose after the Themistoklean Wall was built and refer to the areas respectively inside and outside the Wall.

Excavations. The Greek Archaeological Society began excavations in the Kerameikós in 1863, continuing at intervals until 1913. From 1913 to 1941 excavations of the German Archaeological Institute were directed by A. Brückner and K. Kübler. In 1956 the Institute resumed responsibility for the site, and further intensive investigations, together with conservation projects, have been directed by D. Öhly and his successors. In the course of recent excavations in advance of construction of the Kerameikós metró station (subsequently postponed because of subsidence threat to the archaeological site), huge numbers of graves were found. Of two groups of mass burials, at least one is likely to be of victims of the plague which struck Athens in 430 and the years following.

The Museum was built with funds donated by Gustav Oberländer (1867–1936), a German silk-stocking manufacturer, and is named after him. Many monuments removed from the Kerameikós in the 19C are in the National Archaeological Museum.

Gates and roads

The **Sacred Way** (Ierá Odhós) to Eleusis (pp 261, 264) passes through the **Sacred Gate**. At the festival of the Eleusinian mysteries, this was the route of the procession from the Eleusinion (p 163) in Athens to the Telesterion at Eleusis. From Eleusis, roads continued north into Boeotia and west to the Megarid and Corinthia. The **Eridanos** brook runs beside the road, through the Gate. Not far outside the Sacred Gate the road forks, with the Sacred Way continuing right, and the main **road to Piraeus** left.

The part of the Piraeus road inside the area of the excavations is often called the '**Street of the Tombs**'. This is the most thoroughly excavated section of roadway. Turned into a planned cemetery area at the beginning of the 4C BC, most of its tombs were eventually covered by layers of earth and/or later burials, to a depth of 6–9m and were thus saved from destruction when Sulla carried out extensive siege works in 86 BC (pp 61, 175).

The **road to the Academy**, also the main artery to Boeotia and northwestern Greece, started from the **Dipylon Gate**. The section near the Gate was called the **Dromos** and was extra wide to accommodate various rituals. There was apparently a separate service road for the wheeled traffic. Beyond the excavated area the Academy road mostly lies beneath modern houses and cannot be completely investigated, though excavations have been made at many points and chance finds collected. Within the Gate, the Dromos (now covered with a hard surface in the excavation area), bordered by gymnasia and stoas, climbed straight to the Agora (see p 156).

The Demosion Sema (State Burial Ground)

The particular importance of the Kerameikós area, so closely associated with the formal processions of the Dionysiac, Panathenaic and Eleusinian festivals, led to the location here of the Demosion Sema. Pausanias saw its monuments on the road from the Dipylon Gate to the Academy, but only in August 1997 was firm evidence finally found for the site. This came from an excavation at Od. Salamínos 35 (p 182), roughly 400m north-northwest of the city wall in the Kerameikós, where *polyandreia* (communal tombs) were found containing the cremated bones of warrior dead of c 450–425 BC. There were also individual graves with simple stones.

In ancient Greece war dead were normally buried where they fell but, some time in the early 5C, the Athenians began the practice of bringing home their dead, honouring them with a state funeral and burying them here. Thucydides explains the practice of funerary orations and describes (II 35–46) the famous oration of Perikles on the dead of the first year of the Peloponnesian War. Certain other individuals who had not died in war but had otherwise earned recognition from the state also received formal burials. In the Demosion Sema were the graves of Perikles, Thrasyboulos, Konon, the philosopher Zeno, the tyrannicides Harmodios and Aristogeiton, and other important figures.

For about 60 years after the establishment of the Demosion Sema (until c 425 BC), there seem to have been no private grave monuments, such honours being reserved entirely for the war dead.

The archaeological site

A short way in from the site entrance (the museum is to your left; plan pp 176–177) is a grave mound (**11**) with a **view** over the whole area, and a site orientation plan. From here you can survey the double **City Walls**, then take the path down for a closer view.

Construction

The material of the main **inner wall** was of sun-dried brick on a stone base. As the ground level rose, the brick was taken down, the stone base brought higher and the brick built up again. The stone elements visible today are therefore a series of superimposed stone wall bases. In both the Kerameikós and National Archaeological Museums are numerous Archaic grave sculptures found in the foundations of the Themistoklean Wall and in the Sacred and Dipylon Gates, thus verifying Thucydides' statement that the Athenians spared no ancient monuments in their haste to erect the City Wall. The **outer wall** consisted of a rubble core faced with uniform conglomerate blocks.

The course of the **Walls** within the archaeological site runs for 183m, interrupted only by the two Gates. The best preserved section of the inner wall is immediately to your right, at the southern edge of the site; of the outer, between the Sacred and Dipylon Gates. The inner line, built by Themistokles in 479 BC and reconstructed by Konon in 394, is 2–2.4m thick and now survives here in one course of poros blocks (Themistoklean) and two of well-jointed polygonal blocks in blue limestone (Konon), interspersed with hastily re-used marbles. Above, in creamy limestone, are two courses from a rebuilding of the walls in 307/6 BC, attested by a lengthy inscription with specifications. Further alterations were made in later Roman times, perhaps in the 3C and 6C AD. An upper section of headers and stretchers (extreme right) is probably from the time of Justinian. The outer wall (4.3m thick) and moat (no longer obvious) are later, perhaps contemporary with the Dipylon (late 4C).

Plutarch mentions that Sulla in 86 BC razed the whole line of the walls between the Sacred Gate and the Piraeic Gate, 300m to the southwest.

The first gate you come to is the **Sacred Gate**, which spanned both the Sacred Way and the Eridanos brook, the latter carried through it in a vaulted channel. The bed of the brook was given a paved surface in the early 5C. The gate chamber (Themistoklean), with inner and outer passages, is 18m deep, with a wall on the side opposite the channel, and corner towers (the one to the east added in the 4C).

South of the Gate, in the angle with the wall, the 4C BC Building Y, with a court and two rooms whose shape suggests they accommodated dining couches, may have been for ritual dining associated with a nearby shrine, or else simply a tavern in a busy location.

Between the Sacred and Dipylon Gates is a section of the Wall of Konon, on the Themistoklean line, in rusticated (rough-surfaced) polygonal masonry: much of it is only one course high. The outer wall is well preserved at this point.

Just before you reach the northwest tower of the Dipylon is one of several **boundary stones** (**1**) found on the site, and inscribed vertically ΟΡΟΣ ΚΕΡΑΜΕΙΚΟΥ (limit of the Kerameikós).

Also between the two Gates, but inside the main wall, is the **Pompeion**, a place

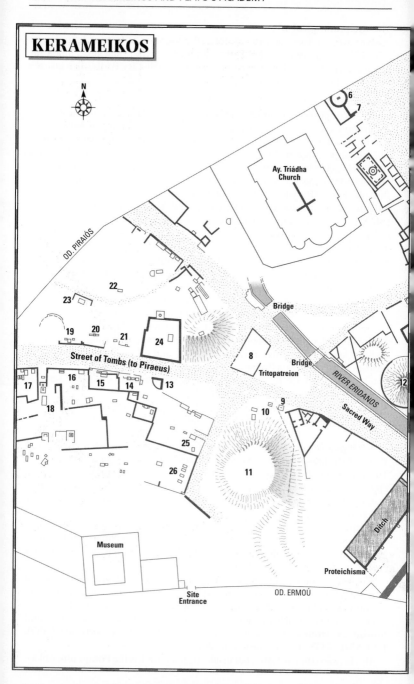

KERAMEIKOS

N

OD. PIRAIÓS

Ay. Triádha
Church

6
7

Bridge

22

23

19 20 21 24

Street of Tombs (to Piraeus)

8

Tritopatreion

Bridge

RIVER ERIDANOS

12

17 16 15 14 13

18

9

10

25

26

11

Sacred Way

Ditch

Proteichisma

Museum

Site
Entrance

OD. ERMOÚ

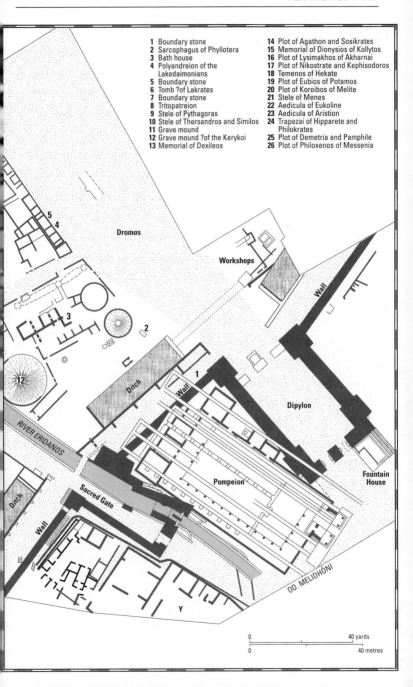

1 Boundary stone
2 Sarcophagus of Phyllotera
3 Bath house
4 Polyandreion of the
  Lakedaimonians
5 Boundary stone
6 Tomb ?of Lakrates
7 Boundary stone
8 Tritopatreion
9 Stele of Pythagoras
10 Stele of Thersandros and Similos
11 Grave mound
12 Grave mound ?of the Kerykoi
13 Memorial of Dexileos

14 Plot of Agathon and Sosikrates
15 Memorial of Dionysios of Kollytos
16 Plot of Lysimakhos of Akharnai
17 Plot of Nikostrate and Kephisodoros
18 Temenos of Hekate
19 Plot of Eubios of Potamos
20 Plot of Koroibos of Melite
21 Stele of Menes
22 Aedicula of Eukoline
23 Aedicula of Aristion
24 Trapezai of Hipparete and
   Philokrates
25 Plot of Demetria and Pamphile
26 Plot of Philoxenos of Messenia

Dromos

Workshops

Wall

3

2

12

Ditch

Wall

1

Dipylon

RIVER ERIDANOS

Fountain
House

Ditch

Sacred Gate

Pompeion

Wall

OD. MELIDHÓNI

Y

| 0 | | 40 yards |
| 0 | | 40 metres |

for preparation of processions (*pompai*), and a storehouse for ritual vehicles and equipment. The Panathenaic procession began from here. The 4C structure, bits of which survive, consisted of a colonnaded court, with a small propylon at the east (look for the wheel ruts), and a series of ritual dining-rooms on the north and west. It is known to have been decorated with painted portraits of comic poets and a statue of Sokrates by Lysippos. In emergency it was a distribution centre for corn.

The Classical building was destroyed in Sulla's siege (stone catapult balls can be seen). A successor was built on massive concrete foundations in the time of Antoninus Pius. This had a basilican form, divided into aisles by two rows of 11 pillars. The buttresses of the south wall are still prominent. This was destroyed in turn in the Herulian raid of AD 267, and again replaced in the 4C AD. The layout of both main phases is best seen from an artificial terrace in the southeast corner of the excavated area.

The **Dipylon** (the word means 'double gateway') was the main gate of the city, the largest and most used. Built at the end of the 4C BC, on the exact plan of its predecessor (the Thriasian Gate of the time of Themistokles (479), so-called because it led to the deme of Thria, near Eleusis), it was also known as the Keramic gate. In 200 BC Philip V of Macedon, who was attacking Athens for siding with Pergamon and Rome against him, penetrated the court of the Dipylon Gate and extricated himself only with difficulty (Livy XXXI 24).

The **Gate** was at the inner end of a deep court (c 13.5m x 7m), open on the west and protected by towers and thick ramparts. A good part of the southwest tower, nearly 7.5m square, is preserved. The double gates are separated by a central pier, behind which a square base supported a round marble altar dedicated to Zeus Herkeios, Hermes and Akamas (eponymous hero of the Athenian tribe Akamantis). In Classical times, a **fountain house** abutted the inner side of the southeast tower; beyond it survive some of the steps up to the tower.

An outer gate was added in the 1C BC. It was set 8m back from the line of the city wall and its two segments (the openings c 3.5m wide) were separated by a stone pier c 4m wide. Against the outer face of the pier is the base of a monument. Beyond is the excavation headquarters (no admission).

The Kerameikós **Cemetery** lay along the roadsides outside the Dipylon and Sacred Gates. Through the Dipylon Gate are (left) a late sarcophagus (of Phyllotera; **2**) and (also left) remains of a 5C bath house (**3**), of which one element is circular. Further on (left) are the remains of the Tomb of the Lakedaimonians (**4**), a polyandreion in which 13 Spartan officers who fought in the civil war of 403 BC were buried. Two of the bodies in the central chamber were named in an inscription as Khairon and Thribrakhos (mentioned by Xenophon); the third may have been the Olympic victor Lakrates (but see below). In front is a **boundary stone** (**5**).

At the point where the Academy road from the Dipylon disappears under modern Od. Piraiós, is an elaborate **built tomb** (c 400 BC; **6**) erected over 5C potters' kilns. Lakrates the Spartan (see above) is suggested as a possible occupant. There is a **boundary stone** (**7**) on the east side.

Our knowledge of the original character of this road can be augmented by literary evidence and limited excavations further north. After the great sacrifice at the Panathenaic festival, the citizens feasted on the meat in the Kerameikós. Just outside the Dipylon Gate a huge heap of cattle bones has been found. Post-holes found here are thought to have belonged to tents which accommodated the diners and/or to stalls set up by traders at festival times. Inscriptions come from polyandreia of the dead of battles at Potidaia, the Hellespont and Corinth.

About 185m north of the Dipylon was the peribolos of Artemis Kalliste (walls and a votive relief discovered at Od. Plataíon 11). The Academy (p 183) is c 1.5km northwest of the Dipylon.

Retracing your steps and keeping the prominent church (Ay. Triádha) to the right, you cross first the excavations where some 8000 inscribed ostraka, discarded from the Agora in antiquity, were found in 1966. After crossing the Eridanos you reach the **Tritopatreion (8)** in the angle of the Sacred Way and the Street of the Tombs. Three boundary stones define this triangular precinct of the Tritopatreis, figures who may have been connected with ancestor worship (an inscribed boundary stone is built into the south wall of the Tritopatreion).

Opposite this, to the south, is the **Stele of Pythagoras (9)**: the inscription tells that he was Athenian *proxenos* (unofficial consul) at Selymbria in Thrace in the early 5C BC and was given a state burial at Athenian expense. The grave itself, which has not been excavated, is inside a very high stepped base. Another stele (**10**) belongs to the Corcyraean envoys Thersandros and Similos who came to Athens at the outbreak of the Peloponnesian War (Thuc. I XXII): the tomb finds in the museum are consistent with a 5C date but the monument was refurbished in the 4C and the lettering on the stele is contemporary.

Behind these rises an enormous **grave mound (11)** erected for two foreign dignitaries 550–525 BC; on top is the orientation plan where you started. Opposite, on the north side of the Sacred Way and beyond the Eridanos, is another large mound (**12**) of the 7C. This may have belonged to the old Attic clan of the *Kerykoi*, since it was the burial place of the herald Anthemokritos, a member of that clan who was murdered in Megara shortly before the beginning of the Peloponnesian War and whose grave is mentioned by several ancient writers, including Pausanias (I 36 3). It was partly surrounded by a wall in the 4C. Close by to the west are several tumuli.

The **Street of the Tombs**, the initial section of the road to Piraeus, in which you are now standing, is a planned funerary avenue begun c 394 BC. It is about 8m wide and has been excavated for over 90m. The cemetery, on terraces to either side of the road, was divided up into plots reserved for wealthy Athenians and metics (aliens with citizenship rights). About 20 plots have been discovered.

Grave plots (*Periboloi*) and monuments

Plots were usually defined by a monumental boundary wall, within which the graves were inserted and on which memorials were set. In the Kerameikós all types of 4C funerary monument are represented. Stelai may be plain with a finial in the form of a palmette anthemion, or more elaborate with figured scenes in relief. These scenes are usually framed by architectural elements. The depth of relief gradually increases, culminating in the naïskos or aedicula, in effect a little temple in which the figures stand in the round, or nearly so. Columns may be topped by a device or animal. Large marble vases (one-handled lekythoi and two handled loutrophoroi, the latter for unmarried people) were particularly popular

Kerameikós: grave plot with stelai, etc

in this period. In 317 BC Demetrios of Phaleron decreed restraint in funerary monuments and limited them to a plain trapeza (stone table) or a kioniskos (cippus, or small undecorated column). Wells provided water needed for the ceremonies.

Left is the important **Memorial of Dexileos** (**13**; cast in situ, original in museum), the 20-year-old son of Lysanias of Thorikos who was one of five knights killed at Corinth in 394 BC. The relief was set on top of a crescent-shaped poros base with two sirens, the whole on a massive conglomerate foundation. Its text is unique among Attic grave inscriptions for recording the dates both of the birth and of the death of Dexileos—414 and 394 BC. The scene shows Dexileos as a cavalryman in the act of killing an adversary. The lance and horse trappings were bronze. A tall stele crowned with palmette commemorates Lysanias; another smaller one behind is to Lysias and Melitta, brother and sister of Dexileos. On a trapeza are the names of Lysanias, another brother, and his family.

The adjacent plot (**14**), of the brothers Agathon and Sosikrates of Herakleia, contains the **Aedicula-stele of Korallion**, wife of Agathon, as well as a tall stele of Agathon and Sosikrates. A monument to **Dionysios of Kollytos** (**15**) has an aedicula (no relief) backed by a pillar-stele topped by a fine bull in Pentelic marble. In the plot (**16**) of **Lysimakhos of Akharnai**, which has retaining walls in fine polygonal masonry, are a Molossian dog (Molossia in Epirus was famous for its dogs) in Hymettian marble and a unique grave relief of the 4C BC, showing a funeral feast with, in the foreground, an old man in a rowing-boat.

The old man may be Charon and the setting the banks of the Styx. The plot of **Nikostrate and Kephisodoros** (**17**) is in the angle of a side road which climbs to the **Temenos of Hekate** (**18**). An inscription suggests that there was also a shrine of Artemis Soteira somewhere near.

Returning to the north side of the main street, you find the plot of **Eubios of Potamos** (**19**), with a stele of Euphrosyne (c 386), the wife of Eubios, and the monument of Bion, his nephew, in the form of a Doric column, formerly topped by a loutrophoros. Next comes the compound of **Koroibos of Melite** (**20**) with Koroibos' own stele, the loutrophoros (in relief) of his grandson Kleidimos and a cast of the well-known **Aedicula of Hegeso** (original in National Archaeological Museum, room 18). The monument was originally set up elsewhere but was removed to this site in antiquity. Beyond are stelai of Samakion and Menes (on horseback; **21**). Further back are the aedicula of Eukoline (**22**), showing the little girl with her dog, and another of Aristion (**23**), the boy portrayed with a pet bird and a slave holding a *strigil* (skin-scraper) while, below, a mourning siren is supported by kneeling figures. Next to Samakion and Menes, on the side of the mound where the church of Ayía Triádha originally stood, are (**24**) **small trapezai**—of Hipparete, grand-daughter of Alkibiades, and wife of Phanokles of Leukenoe—and of Philokrates of Kydathenaion.

In the side-road to the right are graves of two actors, Makareus and Hieronymos. The plot (**25**) of the sisters Demetria and Pamphile contains a fine **aedicula**, with Pamphile seated and her sister standing. Beyond is the plot of Philoxenos of Messenia (**26**), with a statue of his wife and three trapezai, one for himself and two for his sons; also tombstones of slaves.

The Oberländer Museum

Room I has important **sculpture**, much of it Archaic in style and recovered from the Themistoklean wall where it had been used as building material and sometimes reshaped for the purpose. To the right is the original **Dexileos Monument** (P 1130; see above). Because of its precise date, the piece is a sound indication of the style of Athenian sculpture at the beginning of the 4C BC. A bronze **cauldron** (5C), which contained ashes wrapped in red patterned silk, may have held the remains of Alkibiades since it was found in the mound which was crowned by his grand-daughter's gravestone. The 5C **stele of Ampharete** (P 1221) holding her infant grandchild has excellent drapery: the inscription identifies those portrayed and indicates that both are dead. To the left is the main part of the room, with the 5C **stele of Eupheros** (P 797) showing the youth with his *strigil*. On a grave stele (P 1132) of 570–560 BC is a warrior with staff and sword; a sphinx forms the finial (P 105) of another stele, c 550 BC. A base (P 1001; c 560 BC), with four horsemen in relief, found in the south tower of the Dipylon, may belong to the Discobolos relief in the National Museum (**38**, p 200). A horse and rider (P 1051) is c 520 BC. A seated man (P 1052) comes from a grave monument of c 530 BC. The base of a grave monument (I 190; c 515 BC) for the Carian Tymnes, son of Skylax, has an inscription with three lines in Greek and three in Carian (Caria was a region of southwest Anatolia). Skylax may be the famous Carian sea captain who first explored the Indus region, the coasts of the Indian Ocean and the Red Sea (Hdt. IV 44). In the doorway, a stele fragment (P 1054; c 550 BC) shows a **boxer** with a cauliflower ear, and the thongs of a glove tied round his wrist.

Room II To see the remainder of the collection in chronological order, you should return to the entrance and room II, which has terracotta **figurines** and an extensive and important collection of **vases** of the Sub-Mycenaean, Proto-Geometric, Geometric and Proto-Attic phases (11C–7C), crucial to the study of the development of Greek, and especially Attic, pottery. Among them are the earliest Post-Mycenaean pictorial **representation of a horse** (10C; Case 6, no. 560), a terracotta **stag rhyton** (10C, Case 43) with wheelmade body and a Phoenician bronze bowl (late 9C, Case 9). There are also some bronze (including a spiked boss from a shield of perishable material) and iron weapons and jewellery, and occasional gold objects.

Rooms III (to c 460 BC) and IV Grave groups of the Archaic, Classical, Hellenistic and Roman periods. The **black- and red-figure pottery** includes some by well-known painters (the Lysippides Painter, the Amasis Painter, the Kleophrades Painter). The **terracottas** include a group of four mourners attached to a base. There are **ostraka**, from a total find of about 18,000, with the names of Themistokles and other famous citizens. Room IV includes **white-ground lekythoi** with funerary scenes, fragments of **Panathenaic amphorae** and a hydria by the Meidias Painter.

Outside the museum are various funerary sculptures and (on the wall) part of the mosaic decoration of a dining-room (room 6) in the Pompeion.

Two hundred metres below the site entrance is the junction with Piraiós and, opposite, the former gas works, which have been restored to form an imaginatively designed **Museum of Industrial Archaeology**, and a venue for temporary exhibitions and concerts (☎ 210 346 7322). The complex is known as Tekhnópolis. The area beyond is Rouf. Its odd name comes from the Bavarian owner of a villa here in the 19C. It is now rather run-down and largely occupied by Pomaks from Thrace.

Plato's Academy (Akadhimía Plátonos)

• **Access on foot**. From Kerameikós, about 1.5km via Odd. Salamínos/ Plátonos. To get into Salamínos, turn right out of the site, right again at the junction with busy Piraiós, then left into Salamínos, the third street opposite. **Access by bus**. No. 051 (Akadhimía Plátonos, ΑΚΑΔΗΜΙΑ ΠΛΑΤΩΝΟΣ) from Od. Menándrou (beside the church of Ay. Konstandínos, below Omónia): note that the bus's actual destination is the major bus station at Kavállas and Kifissoú. For the site, alight in Od. Kratílou (see plan, p 183).

On the Omónia side of Salamínos is the area of **Metaxouryío**, which takes its name from a mid-19C silk factory, (*metáxi* means 'silk') at the junction of Keramikoú and Millérou. Part of the building is being restored. At Salamínos 35/Leonídhou is the Demosion Sema site (p 174). Beyond Plateía Metaxouryíou is Od. Lenormán, named after the French archaeologist Charles Lenormant. In 1985 the excavation of an underpass to carry Lenormán under Od. Konstandinoupóleos led to important archaeological discoveries (no longer visible) close to the ancient road from the Erian gate to the hill of Hippios Kolonos. These consisted of a large cemetery, mainly Archaic and Classical in

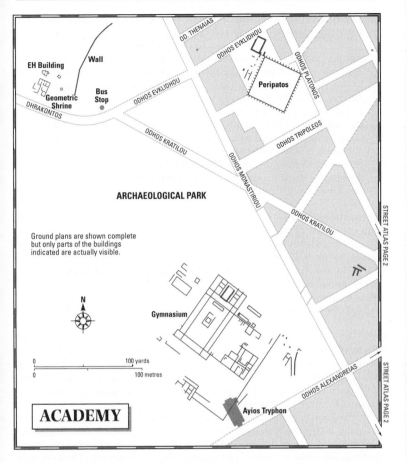

ACADEMY

date, and the debris of pottery factories which made vases and votives, some of them for the cemeteries.

Known particularly as the seat of Plato's school of philosophy, the **Academy** was one of the three major Athenian gymnasia. These were centres of athletic and intellectual activity and, in the case of the Lyceum, of military training. The Academy lay six ancient stades (1104m) from the Dipylon gate, by a direct road (p 174). The modern church of Ay. Trífon, at the corner of Odd. Marathonomákhon and Alexandreías, marks the south corner of the Academy. Its position was confirmed in 1966 by a boundary stone discovered in situ.

History

According to tradition the Academy, correctly the Hekademeia, was founded by Hekademos, who told the Dioscuri (the Lakedaimonian Kastor and Polydeuces) where their sister Helen was hidden (at Aphidna—she had been abducted by Theseus, king of Athens). In gratitude to Hekademos, the Lakedaimonians always spared it when they invaded Attica (Plutarch, *Theseus* 32). Twelve sacred olive trees grew here, supposedly offshoots of Athena's tree on the Acropolis. In the 6C BC Hipparkhos built a wall round the Academy (see below) and the River Kifissos was diverted about this time. Kimon converted the place 'from a bare, dry and dusty spot into a well-watered grove with shady walks and running tracks' (Plutarch, *Kimon* 13). It was a gymnasium in the time of Aristophanes (*Clouds* 1002). Plato taught in the Academy c 388 BC, at which time he lived between there and the hill of Kolonos; he was buried on his estate. In 86 BC Sulla had the Academy trees cut down to make siege engines. A few years later Cicero set one of his philosophical dialogues, the *De finibus*, there. Funeral games in honour of the dead buried in the Kerameikós were held in the Academy and there was also an altar of Prometheus, the goal of torch races from Athens.

Excavations (1929–40) were begun in by the Greek architect P. Aristophron and continued by members of the Greek Archaeological Society. The area, roughly bounded by the streets of Monastiríou, Alexandreías and Antigónis, and divided in two by Kratílou/Dhrákontos, is over 300m from one end to the other. This has now been converted into a huge **archaeological park**, with the Peripatos (see below) just outside its limits. Although parts are scruffy, and the often insubstantial remains have to be traced among the trees, this effort to recreate the rural atmosphere of the Academy has had pleasing results.

In a pretty square (with a taverna) north of Od. Tripóleos are parts of the **Square Peristyle** (re-excavated 1979–80) which is sometimes thought to be the Peripatos (covered walk) frequented by Plato and Aristotle. The building itself belongs to the late 4C, but there is evidence of earlier structures on the site, in the Late Geometric and Archaic periods. Some Roman buildings have been excavated nearby. The entrance to the main park is opposite.

At the opposite end of Tripóleos from the park and now enveloped by the city, is the hill of **Hippios Kolonos** (56m). It was the refuge of Oedipus in Sophokles' *Oedipus at Colonus*, its flowers celebrated by the chorus (lines 688–719). On its bare top, above the trees, are tombstones of Charles Lenormant (1802–59) and Karl Ottfried Müller (1797–1840), both archaeologists who died in Athens.

In the northern part of the park, a few courses of the western part of a **Peribolos Wall** (perhaps that of Hipparkhos) has been exposed for nearly 140m (a stretch of the eastern circuit is also preserved in the basement of Od. Plátonos 105). During the clearance of debris inside the wall, many schoolboys' slates of the late 5C or early 4C BC were found: inscriptions included the names of Sophokles and Demosthenes. Outside the wall to the south, under a roof, is a large **heroön** of the Geometric period (8C–7C). Its mud-brick construction is well preserved and it has seven rooms and an eschara, 1.5m in diameter, for the hero's cult. Between this and the wall is a house of the Early Bronze Age (3rd millennium BC), which may later have been regarded as the **House of Hekademos** and thus the stimulus for the building of the heroön. Many vases have been found in this area which is honeycombed with pre-Mycenaean graves and later cremation burials. A large stone well, with an inscription on its mouth, has been reconstructed.

In the southern sector, towards the church of Ay. Trífon, are the extensive but scrappy remains of a building of the late Hellenistic or Early Roman period belonging to the gymnasium, probably a **palaistra**. The stone bases in the side rooms were for book chests.

9 • The Olympieion, the Ilissós and the Stadium

The temple of Olympian Zeus is massively impressive and the Olympieion site spacious and attractive. The area of pleasant parkland between the temple and the bed of the Ilissós river gives a hint of the idyllic setting of the area in antiquity, even if the ancient buildings are badly preserved and mainly of antiquarian interest. The First Cemetery of Athens has good modern funerary sculpture. The restored Stadium, an antiquity only in name, is nonetheless an imposing monument, nestling below the tree-clad Ardhittós. A short walk beyond brings you to the National Art Gallery and landmark Hilton Hotel.

- **Distance on foot**. Map 8,3–4. From the Olympieion to the Stadium is about 1km; from there to the Hilton Hotel, a further 1.2km.
  Access by public transport. **Trolley buses** nos 2, 4, 11 and 15 stop in Stadhíou and Síntagma, then go along Filellínon and cross Amalías into Leofóros Olgas. There is a stop (Agalma Víronos) for the Olympieion at the beginning of Olgas, then one at the Stadium. From the Stadium you can continue to the Hilton by **buses nos** 450 or 550 (Dhélta Falírou to Khalándri/Kifissiá) along Leofóros Vasiléos Konstandínou. **Metró**. Akrópolis station (Line 2) is about 700m walk from the Olympieion entrance; Evangelismós (Line 3) is 200m from the National Gallery.

On foot you set off from Síntagma by Leofóros Amalías, as described on pp 91–93, turning left into Leofóros Vasilíssis Olgas along the south side of the Záppion Gardens.

The Olympieion (Sanctuary of Olympian Zeus)

Along Olgas, on the opposite side of the road, is the entrance to the site (08.30–15.00; closed Mon). Its main feature is the imposing columns of the massive Temple of Olympian Zeus, formerly known as *Kolónnes* and still sometimes referred to as *Stíles* (the columns).

Past the ticket office are (left) traces of a small propylon in the peribolos wall (p 187). Other remains between the boundary and the road are not directly connected with the sanctuary:

A section of the **Themistoklean Wall** (479 BC) and the **Hippades Gate** (both sides of the sanctuary boundary) include re-used drums from columns of the Peisistratid Olympieion. Also visible is a defensive ditch, added in the 4C, and a stretch of ancient roadway. The 3C AD Valerian Wall (p 188) diverged from the Themistoklean circuit near this point, to take in the City of Hadrian. Only fragments remain of the important 5C AD basilica at the Olympieion (otherwise known as St Nicholas of the Columns) which was also here.

Up to the right are interesting **Roman baths**. Built c AD 124–31 and used until the 7C, these had four public halls with mosaic floors and three bath

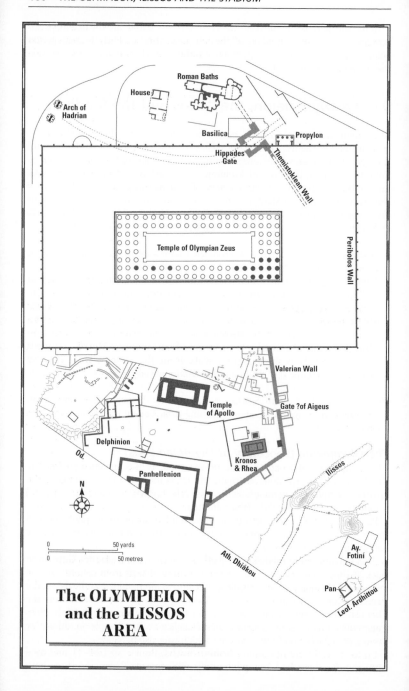

Roman Baths

House

Arch of Hadrian

Basilica

Propylon

Hippades Gate

Themistoklean Wall

Temple of Olympian Zeus

Peribolos Wall

Valerian Wall

Temple of Apollo

Gate ?of Aigeus

Delphinion

Kronos & Rhea

Ilissos

Od.

Panhellenion

N

Ay. Fotiní

0   50 yards
0   50 metres

Ath. Dhiákou

Pan

Leof. Ardhittoú

The OLYMPIEION and the ILISSÓS AREA

chambers along the south side. To the right of the entrance was an apsidal nymphaion with fine *opus sectile* floor and niches for statues. The baths partly overlie a house of the 4C BC. A second house has a pebble mosaic. Beyond, outside the site boundary, is the Arch of Hadrian (p 93).

The Sanctuary of Olympian Zeus is set on an artificial terrace surrounded by a huge **Peribolos Wall**, in squared blocks of Piraeus stone and with regular buttresses. The rectangular precinct measures 205 x 129m, the combined length of its sides equivalent, as Pausanias observed, to four ancient stades. Near the main entrance, between the site entrance and the **Doric propylon**, the buttresses and vaulted drains are Hadrianic in date; otherwise the wall is mostly restored.

In the centre are the massive remains of the **Temple of Olympian Zeus**, the largest temple in Greece, although not in the Greek world. It took 700 years to complete.

History

According to legend Deukalion founded a temple here over the chasm through which the waters receded after the primeval flood. Pausanias says that this was commemorated annually by an offering of flour mixed with honey thrown into the cleft. The tradition may have arisen because the earliest shrine was linked by a subterranean passage to the River Ilissós.

The first large-scale temple was apparently begun by the tyrant **Peisistratos** in the 6C BC. Aristotle (*Politics*) suggests this was to keep the people too busy to conspire against him. But the stylobate was never completed and much of the material was re-used in the Themistoklean Wall. Recent research suggests that the crepis and sekos were constructed in the Classical period, not later than the 4C. In 174 BC **Antiochus Epiphanes**, king of Syria, restarted work on the building, employing the Roman architect Cossutius, who substituted the Corinthian order for the (probably) original Doric. When construction had reached the entablature, it was again interrupted, and was put back further in 86 BC when Sulla removed some of the shafts and capitals to Rome for the Capitoline temple. The temple was finally completed by **Hadrian**, who dedicated it on his second visit to Athens c AD 130. For the cella he commissioned a chryselephantine statue of the god (a copy of that by Pheidias at Olympia), along with a colossal statue of himself. About 1450 Cyriac of Ancona recorded 21 columns standing with architraves. In 1760 one was converted into lime by the Turkish governor for the construction of a new mosque. Another fell in the great storm of 26 October 1852.

The **stylobate** measures 107.4 x 41m. The lower two steps, in poros, are original; the upper, in marble, was partly restored in 1960–61. The **plan** is dipteral and octastyle (20 x 8), with an extra row of **columns** at front and back. Of the 104 columns, in Pentelic marble, 13 survive in a group at the southeast with part of the architrave, and two others further west. The structure shows in the fallen column: base, 16 drums and capital in two sections. The base diameter is 1.7m and the height 17m. The original height of the front was c 27.4m. The blocks of the architrave weigh up to 23 tons. In the Middle Ages a stylite lived on the architrave covering the two western columns of the group. The form of the cella is uncertain, although Vitruvius, the 1C BC architect, says that it was unroofed.

The Ilissós area

To omit the Ilissós area and Leofóros Ardhittoú, turn right out of the Olympieion entrance down Leofóros Olgas and make straight for the Stadium; otherwise, leaving the site gate and turning sharp right, you follow a narrow path between the huge boundary wall of the Olympieion and the modern sports complex (p 190). This takes you into an appealing wooded area, especially attractive in spring and pleasantly reminiscent of the countryside outside the walls of ancient Athens as lyrically described by Plato at the beginning of the *Phaedrus*. This parkland covers the so-called Ilissós area, excavated by Threpsiádhis in 1956–57 prior to construction of the Ardhittós highway, which involved covering over the River Ilissós. Most of the buildings in this part of ancient Athens are not very well preserved and have been identified on the basis of Pausanias' description of his visit. In antiquity, the district along the bank of the Ilissós, outside the city wall, was known as *Kepoi* (the gardens). Beyond the river was the area known as *Diomeia*.

On the far side of the park, Ardhittoú (from left) joins Kallirróïs (right) at a major junction. Opposite is Vouliagménis, an inland route to Glifádha, etc. The Kallirróïs bridge carries Ath. Dhiákou, the continuation of Amalías, over the Ilissós bed to this junction.

Along the path you come to the further corner of the Olympieion precinct wall. Beyond are remains of several buildings. To the right (40m) of the path runs a section of the **Valerian Wall**, built of material quarried from most of the ancient structures in the vicinity. A **gate** in the wall may be that called after Aigeus (a mythical king of Athens, the father of Theseus, who also gave his name to the Aegean Sea; Plutarch, *Theseus* xii).

Next are foundations of a large Doric temple (6 x 13 columns) of the 5C BC, probably the **Temple of Apollo Delphinios**. Beside it, the rock was cut back to accommodate a structure in Archaic polygonal masonry, probably the Law Court of the Delphinion.

We know that, in antiquity, a **Pythion** (Sanctuary of Apollo Pythios) 'on the wall' lay to the southwest of the Olympieion. Two fragments of an altar of this god have been identified from their inscription (now in the National Museum). This records a dedication of Peisistratos the Younger, quoted in full by Thucydides (VI 54). Some other finds (1965–68) below Od. Iosíf ton Rógon (on the other side of Ath. Dhiákou; no visible remains) may locate the actual site of the sanctuary.

Returning east you see (partly under the road) remains of the **Panhellenion**, a sanctuary of Hera and Zeus Panhellenios, built under Hadrian in AD 131/32. It had a small Corinthian temple in a peristyle court. Nearer the Valerian Wall is the **Precinct of Kronos and Rhea**, with substantial foundations of a Doric temple of the 2C AD.

At this point, you must cross the bed of the Ilissós towards the modern church of Ay. Fotiní. Just beyond the church, a rectangular rock-cut chamber (two sides survive) may have been a stone quarry or a shrine, since a **figure of Pan**, now so eroded as to be almost invisible, was carved in the face at right-angles to the church and parallel with the main road. The goat haunches of the god are about 120cm along from the corner of the chamber and 40cm up from the lower edge of the rock.

The **River Ilissós** rises at two sources on Mt Imittós—one at Kaisarianí, the other at Ay. Ioánnis Theológos. The single river was important in Classical times. Its bed, now almost always dry, has been covered (by Odd. Mikhalakopoúlou, Vas. Konstandínou, Kallirróïs) or canalised, much of it in the late 1950s. From Ay. Fotiní it disappears beneath the modern bridge (an older predecessor is below) and road. Its further course runs south of the Mouseion Hill into Fáliro Bay.

   Above the bridge, at or near the point you crossed the bed, is a shallow fall where the water once flowed over a ridge of rock. The topography of this part of the river is immediately recognisable in an 1805 painting by E. Dodwell (shown in Travlos, *Pictorial dictionary*—see Select bibliography). The ancient Kallirrhoë Spring may have been here on the north bank where there was a flow of water until the early 1960s.

About 275m downstream below the Kallirróïs bridge is the probable site of one of the three famous gymnasia of ancient Athens, that of **Kynosarges**. An inscription naming it was found near the church of Ay. Pandeleímon on Od. Kallirróïs and, in June 2000, part of the inner propylon in the excavation of a plot at Od. Diamandopoúlou 1: the latter can be seen.

Beyond the Ilissós

Across Ardhittóu, between Odd. Thomopoúlou and D. Koutoúla, which run parallel to Anapáfseos, are some scanty remains of the terrace wall of the small so-called Temple on the Ilissós, probably the **Temple of Artemis Agrotera**, which was discovered and drawn by Stuart and Revett in 1751–55 (p 63) and destroyed by the Turks in 1778. Its design is so close to that of the Temple of Athena Nike on the Acropolis that it must be the work of the same architect (perhaps Kallikrates). Later it became an Orthodox church but was abandoned after a Roman mass had been said there in 1674. The visible graves are Christian.

   Up the hill and best approached via Od. Anapáfseos is the newly fashionable quarter of **Mets**, called after the first Athenian beer-house there, itself named from the site of a German victory in the Franco-Prussian War. It extends up the hillside to the **Próto Nekrotafío Athinón** (First Cemetery of Athens; Mon–Fri 07.30–12.30, 15.00–17.30; Sat 07.30–15.00; Sun 08.00–13.00) (Map 8,5) where, in sumptuous tombs,

The tomb of Heinrich Schliemann in the Próto Nekrotafío Athinón (First Cemetery)

often in Classical styles and decorated by leading sculptors of the day, lie many famous Greek citizens—and some foreigners—of the 19C and 20C. Heroes of the War of Independence include Kolokotrónis (1770–1843), Makriyiánnis (1797–1864), Androútsos (c 1790–1825) and the generalissimo Sir Richard Church (1784–1873). Writers include Rangavás (1810–92), Soútsos (1800–68), and the statesman-historian Kharílaos Trikoúpis (1833–96). **Kharílaos Trikoúpis** was one of the most important Greek liberal politicians of the 19C. He served as a diplomat in London, as Greek foreign minister, then prime minister (1881). He followed an independent foreign policy and was responsible for the radical reorganisation of state machinery and numerous practical projects, including the cutting of the Corinth canal.

Also buried in the cemetery are the benefactors George Avéroff (1818–99), Andréas Singrós (1828–99) and Andónis Benáki (1873–1954). The mausoleum of the German archaeologist Heinrich Schliemann (1822–90) is decorated with reliefs of the Trojan story, while that of Adolf Furtwängler (1853–1907) has a marble copy of a sphinx which he found on the island of Aíyina. One of the best known sculptures in the Cemetery is the *Sleeping Maiden* (1878) by Yannoúlis Khalepás (p 232), a memorial to Sofía Afendáki.

Ardhittós hill and the Stadium

Ardhittoú runs back to a major junction with Leofóros Olgas (left). In the angle, next to the Olympieion, are the tennis club, the Olympic swimming-pool and the Ethnikós Athletic Club. Near the Kolimvitírio bus stop and athletics track, once an island in the river, are remains (accessible only by special permission) of the Basilica by the Ilissós (mosaics in the Byzantine Museum).

Opposite the junction (right) is the hill of **Ardhittós** (ancient *Ardettos*). The continuation of Ardhittoú is Leofóros Vasiléos Konstandínou. The hill (no access), also known as *Helikon*, was where in antiquity the Heliasts (members of the Heliaia Law court; p 163) took their oath. On it are traces of a Temple of Fortune erected by Herodes Atticus (p 278), who may also have built the bridge over the Ilissós immediately opposite the stadium, which stood until 1778. On the opposite height (no access), beyond the stadium, are remains, identified on the basis of an archaistic inscription in situ referring to the 'Marathonian hero', as the **Tomb of Herodes**, who died at Marathon but was given a public funeral at Athens.

The **Stadium** lies in a natural valley between the two hills, closed with an artificial embankment to form the sphendone. Faithfully restored in 1896–1906 by Anastásios Metaxás, it fits well with the description of Pausanias who saw the gleaming Pentelic marble of the first restoration as you now see the pristine whiteness of the second. The plateía in front (café) has a statue of George Avéroff who financed the work.

History

The original Stadium may have been constructed under Lykourgos in 330 BC. Under Hadrian's presidency of the games, 1000 wild beasts were baited in the arena. For the games of AD 144, the Stadium was re-seated in marble by Herodes Atticus. From later antiquity the place was used as a quarry and most of the marble was carried away. In 1869–70 Ernst Ziller cleared the site, initially at his own expense and later with the support of King George I of the Hellenes. In 1895 Avéroff (p 192) financed restoration of the marble for the revival of the Olympic Games there in 1896. At the same time the sphendone was provided with seats. The restoration work was completed in time for the extra games, held as a tenth anniversary celebration in 1906 and attended by King Edward VII of Great Britain and Ireland.

In antiquity, the course was a straight track, one stade (600 Greek ft) long, hence the name Stadium (from *stadion*). The length of the Greek foot varied slightly from place to place, but the Athenian track measured about 185m. Down the centre was a row of pillars. Four of these, in the form of double herms, have been found. The finishing point was in front of the sphendone, crowned by a Doric stoa, which sheltered the top corridor. A Corinthian propylon, no longer visible, formed a ceremonial entrance at the open end.

The oval arena is 204 x 33m, in its restored form incorporating a modern running track with space in the centre for field sports. There is a training track at the level of the top of the seating. At the east end a tunnel leads to the changing rooms and offices behind.

The course is bounded by a low marble parapet, behind which is a paved promenade with drains. On the far side of the promenade, the tiers of seating rest on a substructure 1.6m high and thus get an uninterrupted view. The side tiers are slightly curved for better visibility. The seats are reached from the promenade by 29 narrow flights of steps, 12 on each long side and five in the sphendone. There are 47 tiers, divided into two blocks by a horizontal diazoma above the 24th row. The capacity is 60,000. Superior seating for important guests is provided in a block on the west side and in the front row of the sphendone.

Across the main road from the Stadium is the southeast entrance to the Záppion Gardens, with two bronze statues—a discus thrower (1927) and a huge figure of Karaïskákis, a hero of the War of Independence, by Michael Tómbros (1966).

At the beginning of Fokianoú, which runs from the forecourt of the Stadium to Od. Eratosthénous, is (right) the **Philatelic Museum** (Mon–Fri 08.00–14.00; closed Sat, Sun).

Pankráti and Leofóros Vasiléos Konstandínou

Along Konstandínou (**Maps 8,2; 7,7**), just beyond the Stadium, Od. Eratosthénous leads (right) up to Plateía Plastíra at the heart of Pankráti, a former working-class suburb named after one of the Olympic contests (*pankration*). Nearby Plateía Varnáva has one or two pleasant unpretentious restaurants and cafés.

Further along Konstandínou (left) is a statue of the US president Harry Truman. After the crossing with Leofóros Vasiléos Yeoryíou II comes (left) the long marble-faced **Odheíon** (College of Music; I. Despotópoulos, 1970-76), which was constructed over part of the site of the ancient Lyceum (p 225). Opposite, another building in a similar style is the **National Research Institute** (Ethnikó Idhrima Erevnón). Past Od. Rizári, an attractive park (left) lies in the angle with Vasilíssis Sofías. At the junction you come to the National Gallery and the Hilton (pp 228–229).

10 • Omónia to Ambelókipi

The most interesting features of this area are the Polytechnic and National Museum buildings in Patisíon and the large Pedhíon Areos park to the north of Alexándras. Patisíon is a lively and interesting street but Alexándras is long, noisy and tiring, although important as a main route out of Athens.

- **Distance on foot**. Maps 3,3–6; 2; etc. From Omónia to the Pedhíon Areos is just under 1km; from there to Ambelókipi a further 3km.
  Access by trolley bus. No. 7 (circular; stops at the top and bottom of Panepistimíou, at the Polytechnic, etc) covers the route in the direction described; no. 8 in the opposite direction. There may be an extended wait, or a change of vehicles, at the Ambelókipi stop.
  Metró. Omónia to Ambelókipi (Line 2, change at Síntagma to Line 3).

Leofóros Patisíon, officially 28 Oktomvríou (the date of the Greek rejection of the Italian ultimatum in 1940), runs from just above Omónia to the northern suburbs.

About 200m along on the right (bus/trolley bus stop) is the **Politekhnío** (Polytechnic; formally Ethnikó Metsóvio Politekhnío), which teaches Fine Art, Architecture, Civil Engineering and other scientific and mechanical subjects not offered by the university. The 'Metsóvio' element in its title comes from the home town (Métsovo) of several of its main benefactors (see below), who are also commemorated in the names of adjacent streets (Avéroff, Tosítsa, Stournára). The institution, founded in 1836, was transferred to this site in 1872. Modern buildings were added to the rear in 1946. The School of Fine Arts (where Giorgio De Chirico studied) still has its administrative offices here; the teaching departments have moved to Piraiós 258.

Public benefactors

George Avéroff (1818–99) left Greece for Alexandria as a young man and made a fortune there from trade. He put much of his money towards public works in Greece and Alexandria. Projects included refurbishment of the Panathenaic Stadium and construction of the battleship named after him (p 247). **Michael Tosítsas** (1787–1856) was an earlier emigrant to Alexandria where he gained considerable influence and wealth through his association with the Egyptian regent Mohamed Ali. He was the first president of the Greek community in Alexandria. Towards the end of his life he came to Athens and financed several major projects. **Nikólaos Stournáras** (1806–53), nephew of Tosítsas and brother-in-law of Avéroff, was another wealthy Alexandrian and public benefactor.

Two side pavilions in Doric style face inwards on to a court which fronts the main façade, whose entrance is an Ionic portico at first-floor level approached by a double stair. The elegant inner court has Doric columns in the lower storey, Ionic porticoes in the upper. The complex was designed by Kaftanzóglou and built, in Pentelic marble, in 1862–80, with considerable changes to the original plans.

The recent history of the Polytechnic has been a chequered one. In 1973, student occupation of the buildings was brutally ended by the police and became the focus of opposition to the military regime, which fell the following year.

Next to the Politekhnío, and fronted by attractive gardens (expensive café under the trees), is the National Archaeological Museum (p 194). Opposite the museum is the imposing former Akropole Palace Hotel, now being restored.

Further on (c 1km from Omónia), Plateía Aiyíptou opens on the right at the foot of Leofóros Alexándras. This is crossed by Od. Mavrommatéon (parallel to Patisíon), with bus terminals (for rural Attica; also Thessaloníki) in and to either side of the square.

On the far side is the **Pedhíon tou Areos** (Field of Ares—Ares is the Greek equivalent of Mars), a large and pleasant park, with a café, laid out in 1934. Originally a training ground for cavalry regiments, it now regularly accommodates book fairs and horticultural and other exhibitions, with stalls along the avenues. In front of the main entrance is a **Statue of King Constantine** (1868–1922). An avenue behind is flanked by busts of heroes and martyrs of the revolution of 1821. On the side facing Alexándras is a **War Memorial** (1952), in Pentelic marble: it commemorates soldiers of the UK, Australia and New Zealand 'who fought for the liberty of Greece' in the Second World War. Three cenotaphs, each with a bowl for a sacred flame, carry the arms of the three countries. On a stepped plinth is a seated lion with, behind, a tall stele topped by a statue of Athena, with spear and shield.

In the park, near a chapel of Ay. Kharálambos, is a **Monument to the Ierós Lókhos** (Sacred Battalion), an irregular brigade of students formed to fight for Greek independence, commanded by A. Ipsilánti. It was unnecessarily sacrificed in 1821 at Dragashan in Romania.

At the far (northeast) corner of the park, which is divided by a subway, is the **Skholí Evelpídhon**, formerly the Military Academy, now law courts. Its function changed following the restoration of democracy in 1974, when the Academy was moved to Vári in Attica. The fine building, erected in 1889–94, was designed byZiller and paid for by Avéroff. Employing an ornate mixture of the ancient orders, the façade of the main building has Corinthian columns and pilasters at first-floor level above a plainer triple doorway. In front is a bronze **Statue of a Youth** (Ath. Apártis, 1940). This was cast in Paris and later damaged by rifle fire. In Od. Boúsgou are several pleasant restaurants and ouzerís.

The broad and noisy **Leofóros Alexándras** continues along the south

Skholí Evelpídhon: the former military academy

side of the park. It is named after the Greek princess (1870–91), wife of Tsar Alexander III, who died in childbirth in Moscow. The buildings are largely undistinguished and it has never developed a distinctive character. Halfway up on the left, on the site of the former Avéroff Prison (Filakés Avéroff—the name is still used as a bus terminal), is a massive building with a marble façade. This contains the **Areios Págos** (Supreme Court, the name taken from its ancient predecessor). Just beyond (left) at no. 173, the headquarters of the security police includes the **Aliens' Bureau**. Opposite is the stadium of the **Panathinaïkós Football Club** (PAO), although the first team now plays elsewhere; behind it rises Likavittós. To the left Od. Panórmou offers a direct bypass to Leofóros Kifissías. Alexándras continues to the major junction at Ambelókipi (p 232) where it meets Vasilíssis Sofías (right), Leofóros Kifissías (left) and (ahead, then left) Od. Mesoyíon.

11 • National Archaeological Museum

The museum is a 'must' for visitors to Athens. If at all possible, try to make time for more than one visit. The museum—itself an impressive structure—houses a spectacular collection of finds from all over Greece (although new finds are now mostly retained in local museums), and some from further afield, including Troy. The glories of the National Museum are its Prehistoric finds, especially those from the Shaft Graves at Mycenae, ancient sculpture (occupying all the rooms round the circumference of the ground floor), vases (upstairs) and bronzes. There is a good Egyptian section and a rich display of material from the excavations at the remarkable site of Akrotiri on Thira, preserved beneath volcanic debris.

• **Access on foot**. Map 3,2. 700m north of Omónia, in Od. Patisíon.
  Access by public transport. **Trolley bus** nos. 2, 3, 4, 5, 11, 13, from Síntagma (Vasilíssis Sofías, or Leofóros Amalías on Olympieion side of Parliament building) to Politekhnío stop, a few metres from the museum. This is the first stop in Patisíon, although some way along. **Metró**. To Omónia (Lines 1, 2) or Viktória (Line 1) stations, the latter slightly nearer.
  Opening. Summer (1 Apr–15 Oct) Tues–Sun 08.00–19.00; Mon 12.30–19.00. Winter (16 Oct–31 Mar) Tues–Fri 08.00–15.00; Mon 11.00–15.00; Sat, Sun, holidays 08.30–15.00. There may be some variation in closing times.
  Cafés. In basement off central atrium: access from entrance hall. Also in gardens outside museum. Both relatively expensive.
  Shop. Next to café. Sells plaster casts of ancient sculptures, other reproductions, limited selection of books, guidebooks to sites, videos, cards. Postcards, slides and guidebooks to the museum are sold in the entrance hall.
  Guidebooks, etc. A leaflet showing the layout of the collections is given free with tickets. Several general and usually rather superficial guidebooks are available. A more detailed catalogue of the *Collection of sculpture* (1968) by S. Karoúzou is in English; a volume on the prehistoric collections is in French and German only. A good and well-illustrated account of the Roman material is K. Rhomaiopoúlou, *Collection of Roman sculpture* (c 1997). There is a leaflet on the Stathátou collection.

The National Archaeological Museum (Ethnikó Arkhaiologikó Mouseío) is housed in a fine **neoclassical building** (1866–89, extended 1925–39) fronted by pleasant gardens, with a café under the trees. The design by L. Lange was modified, after his death, by Th. Hansen. Steps lead up to the entrance, a spacious portico with four Ionic columns. To either side are open galleries with pilasters. The wings at each end have plain pediments.

> **Note** Before seeing the collections, you may find it useful to read the earlier sections of the chapter 'Art and architecture' in this book (pp 71–79).

The displays are described in the following order.

Ground floor Prehistoric collections, rooms 3–6; sculpture, rooms 7–35 , also basement court; bronzes, rooms 36–39 (part of 37 and 38–39 closed at present); Egyptian collection, rooms 40–41; Stathátou collection, room 42. Rooms 43–45 have temporary exhibitions. **Note** that changes are being made to the displays of sculpture and the labelling improved: consequently some rooms may be closed.

Upper floor (closed at time of writing due to damage from the 1999 earthquake). Finds from Akrotiri on the island of Thira, room 48; pottery and other small finds, rooms 49–56.

Prehistoric collections

Immediately opposite the entrance (room 1), across the hall (room 2), are the Prehistoric rooms (3–6). If you can restrain yourself long enough from the dazzling Mycenaean collection in the large central room to take the material in chronological order, begin with the narrow **room 5** to the left. This contains **Neolithic, Early** and **Middle Bronze Age** (c 6000–c 1600 BC) finds from the **Greek mainland** (Dhimíni and Sésklo in Thessaly, Orkhomenós in Boeotia, Askitarió, Ayios Kosmás, Néa Mákri and Rafína in Attica), also from Early Bronze Age graves on the island of Léfkas, from **Troy** (presented by Sophie Schliemann) and from **Poliókhni** on the island of Límnos, the latter showing connections with Troy. Much of the material is pottery, the Dhimíni and Sésklo wares being particularly sophisticated and attractive. A wall case illustrates the Neolithic pottery sequence with sherds. Also on display are terracotta and stone figurines, stone and bone tools and ornaments, and obsidian cores and objects.

   Room 6, on the other side of the Mycenaean hall, has objects from the **Cycladic islands**, many of them excavated by the great Greek archaeologist Khrístos Tsoúntas in the late 19C. Most of the material is Early Bronze Age but it also includes material from the British excavations at Phylakopí on Mílos (Early–Late Bronze Age) in 1896–99.

   Virtually all categories of Cycladic Bronze Age **pottery** are represented here: EC (Early Cycladic) I burnished and incised; ECII painted, also burnished and stamped/incised—note particularly the curious 'frying-pan' shape whose function is unknown; ECIIIA highly burnished Anatolian shapes; ECIIIB painted with Geometric patterns. More immediately appealing are the **marble figures**, characteristic of the first two phases of the period. A wall case shows the sequence of types. The earliest are in simple 'violin' shapes, but the most common are female with arms folded across the chest. 3978 is an exceptionally large figure (1. 52m), from Amorgós. Similar but more complex pieces (from Kéros) play a lyre and a flute. Such figures are usually found in graves. The **marble vases** are attractive, in simple forms often related to those of the pottery. There are also objects (mainly blades) of obsidian, a kind of volcanic glass (in Greece found almost exclusively on the island of Mílos) widely used in prehistoric times for tools and weapons, and **silver** and **bronze** tools, ornaments and weapons.

The finds from **Phylakopí** include Middle and Late Bronze Age pottery (some imported). Among the former are distinctive 'beaked' jugs, some with odd patterns of imps; the latter include many shapes and motifs based on Cretan prototypes. Also influenced by Crete are Late Bronze Age fresco fragments including one with flying fish. A decorated stand shows fishermen with their catch.

The Mycenaean displays

Now for the central **room 4**. This is dominated by the spectacular contents of the Shaft Graves in **Grave Circle A at Mycenae** (*Blue Guide Greece*, 6th edn, pp 221–32), all but one of which were excavated by Heinrich Schliemann (p 141) in 1874–76. These graves, covering a period of about 150 years at the beginning of the Late Bronze Age, contain objects of unbelievable richness and variety and suggest the sudden and spectacular enrichment of the rulers of this important centre. The slightly earlier **Grave Circle B** (discovered over 70 years later) is smaller and less wealthy, but nonetheless has some fine objects.

Apart from the shaft grave finds, there is other material from Mycenae (from chamber and tholos tombs, and from the citadel), and from other Mycenaean sites in the Peloponnese (Midéa, Prósimna, Pylos, Tiryns, Váfio) and Attica (Peratí, Spáta).

The cases are not numbered in sequence. The numbers assigned to the objects correspond to those in the *catalogue raisonnée* of G. Karo, *Die Schachtgräber von Mykenai*, Munich, 1930.

No summary description can do justice to these objects which deserve detailed study. Some of the most important are noted below with comments on the categories of material and trends which they represent.

To either side of the entrance are fascinating stone grave **stelai** from Grave Circle A. Stone carving was relatively rare in Mycenaean Greece and the designs, which include warriors and horse-drawn chariots, are crude and in shallow relief. Some large bronze vessels were probably imported from Crete.

The first central case (**27**) has key objects: fine **gold masks** placed over the faces of the dead; **gold cups**, including the famous '**cup of Nestor**' sometimes thought to be related to that described by King Nestor in the *Iliad*; exquisite **daggers** of bronze inlaid with scenes in gold, silver and niello (a black compound), one with a hunting scene.

Case 4 (left) has **gold-leaf dress ornaments**, large **bronze swords** and the **gold panels** decorated with stylised motifs which covered a small wooden box. The panels provide a good example of the stylisation characteristic of Mycenaean rather than Minoan art. Other objects show a more naturalistic Minoan

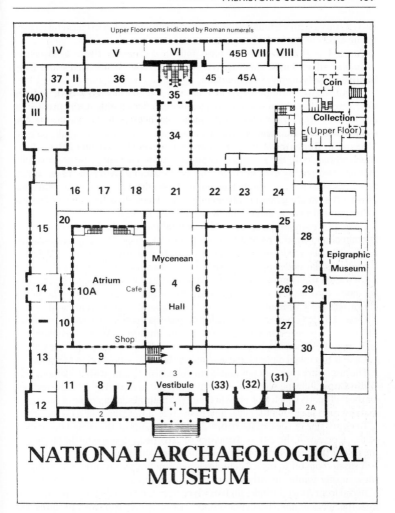

Upper Floor rooms indicated by Roman numerals

NATIONAL ARCHAEOLOGICAL MUSEUM

approach. Distinction between the two has preoccupied scholars of the Shaft Grave finds. Many of the objects are clearly Cretan in origin or inspiration and this connection formed the basis for subsequent developments in Mycenaean art.

Case 18 (right) has silver and gold **rhyta** (vessels for pouring liquids in rituals) in the form of animals' heads, another manufactured from an ostrich egg, and bronze swords with gold fittings.

In **Cases 5 & 6** (left) are finds from Grave Circle B, including (Case 5) a small but exquisite bowl, possibly Cretan, of rock-crystal with a handle in the form of a duck's neck and head.

Case 23 (centre) has a large **diadem of gold leaf** and **17** (beyond) a selection of engraved **sealstones** of various materials, and some fine gold signet rings, also engraved with various scenes. Seal carving was another art form taken over by the Mycenaeans from Crete.

Cases 1 (right) and **26** (left) have finds from chamber tombs at Mycenae, including **silver cups**, small carved **ivories**, Cretan **stone vases** and large **bronze vessels**, again of Cretan types.

A central case (unnumbered) includes the plates of a **boar's-tusk helmet** which would have been sewn on to a leather cap. This highly distinctive item is described by Homer and provides the most convincing evidence for Bronze Age elements in the Homeric poems. Also here are characteristic small, painted Mycenaean **figurines** in the phi, psi and taf shapes (named after letters of the Greek alphabet: Φ, Ψ, Τ). In a separate case (left) is a unique head of painted plaster. Also (right) in a separate case is the famous **Warrior Vase**, a 12C representative of the relatively uncommon Mycenaean pictorial style, with a file of warriors (wearing, among other equipment, boars'-tusk helmets). Beside it is a rare painted stele, which originally had incised decoration.

Case 31 (centre) has ivories and **Linear B tablets** from Mycenae. These tablets contain administrative records in an early form of Greek. The script was adapted from a Cretan predecessor (Linear A), which was used to write a different language, so far undeciphered. **Case 9** (right) has more tablets, from Pylos.

On the left wall, impressive even though heavily reconstructed, are Mycenaean **frescoes** (procession, boar hunt, warriors, a bull-leaping scene—the latter, characteristic of Minoan Crete, rare for the mainland) from Mycenae and Tiryns.

Case 15 (left) has more examples of pictorial pottery (chariots, etc from Tiryns), also bronzes. In **Case 33** (centre) are finds from Midéa, including fine gold cups of Minoan inspiration, bronze swords with gold fittings, bronze vessels.

Case 8 has inlaid daggers and gold objects from Mirsinokhóri in Messinía.

The last centre case contains finds from Váfio, near Sparta, with the famous gold '**Vafio Cups**' showing scenes of the netting of bulls in a country setting—perhaps for the bull-sports which took place in Crete. The naturalistic rendering of the scenes makes it most likely that the cups came from Crete or were made by a Cretan artist.

To either side of the exit (to **room 21**) are elements of the carved decoration of the doorway of the 14C BC **Treasury of Atreus** (a tholos tomb at Mycenae); the rest of the surviving material is in the British Museum.

A small room off to the left contains important finds from various Mycenaean sites, mostly tombs, in Athens and Attica, Salamis and elsewhere in Greece. Material from Attica includes an **ivory lyre** from the Menídhi tomb (p 251), and from the Spáta tombs a particularly fine series of Mycenaean **ivory plaques** and other objects with relief decoration of sphinxes, etc in typically stylised Mycenaean manner.

Sculpture
To visit the Sculpture Collections, return to the entrance hall and turn right into **room 7**.

Archaic
Rooms 7–13 contain Archaic Greek sculpture of the 7C–5C BC. You can trace the forms used, the technical and stylistic developments and appreciate the scale of works of the period.

Monumental stone sculpture

Monumental stone sculpture developed, initially under the influence of Egypt and the Near East, in the mid-7C BC. The most characteristic freestanding types are the **kouros** (male) and **kore** (female), with seated variants. These figures also appear, with modifications, in relief sculpture. The kore series and the architectural sculpture of the period is better studied in the Acropolis Museum. The size of some of the kouroi, almost all made for sanctuaries or cemeteries, is astonishing. A general trend, which was probably much less uniform than it seems in retrospect, towards greater naturalism (especially in the use of modelled rather than incised linear forms) can be easily appreciated by comparing the earlier with later examples. Some regional features can be distinguished.

The two main classes of non-architectural **relief sculpture** were grave and votive **stelai**. The former adorned tombs or burial plots, the latter were offered as dedications in sanctuaries. Distinctions lie in subject matter rather than style.

Room 7 has several important early sculptures. 1: Statue of **Artemis**, dedicated at Delos by Nikandre of Naxos (inscription on left side), c 640 BC. The form is rigid, the face in the Daedalic style, derived from the Near East, with triangular face, low forehead, wig-like hair. 57: Seated figure, possibly of a goddess, from Ayioryítika in Arcadia, c 630 BC. 2869: Part of small limestone metope with head in Daedalic style, from Mycenae, perhaps the temple of Athena, c 630 BC.

In the same room, 770–9: Pottery and ivory **statuettes** from a Geometric grave. The naked female figure and 'polos' cap (a cylindrical head-dress worn by goddesses), as well as the material, show Near Eastern influence (Greek female figures were always clothed at this period). 804: Huge **'Dipylon' amphora** (grave marker), of the Geometric period from the Kerameikos, with scenes of the laying-out (*prothesis*) of the dead and of mourning, c 760 BC.

Room 8 (Kouroi, Korai). 2720: Colossal (3.05m tall; restored) **kouros** from the sanctuary of Poseidon at Sounion, c 590 BC. The style is linear; the scale shows that these figures made an architectural contribution to their setting. 3645: Torso of a second kouros. 3372, 3965: The 'Dipylon' head, from a kouros, c 590 BC. 56: Grave monument of Dermys and Kitylos from Tanagra, c 580 BC.

Three smaller galleries open off room 8.

Rooms 9, 10 and 10A contains Archaic freestanding and relief sculpture, mostly fragmentary. The most interesting pieces are in **Room 9** (from right). 81: Base (inscribed) of a statue by the famous sculptor Phaidimos, from Voúrva, Attica, c 550 BC. 22: Kore from Delos, end 6C BC. 15: Head of Boeotian kouros, c 580 BC. 9: Kouros in distinctive Boeotian style (awkward anatomy), from Orkhomenos, 580-70 BC. In **room 10A** is 1673: Part of the pedimental sculpture of a small building near the Olympieion, with a typical Archaic theme of two lions attacking a bull, c 500 BC.

Return to **room 11** (follows 8), with Grave Stelai, funerary and votive Kouroi. 1558: Melos kouros, slim with little anatomical detail (island style), c 550 BC. 21: *Winged Nike* (Victory) from Delos, c 550 BC. The half-kneeling pose is conventional for running in Archaic art. 10: Naxian kouros from Ptoön, c 550 BC. 4889: Exquisite **kore**, discovered in 1972 in a cemetery at Merenda (ancient *Myrrinhous*), near Markópoulo, Attica, together with 4890: the Merenda **kouros**. The inscription shows that the kore was the grave marker of Phrasikleia, and the sculptor was Aristion of Paros, though the style is Attic, c 550 BC. 2687: Tall grave stele from the Kerameikos, cut back for use as building material in the Themistoklean city wall, and crowning sphinx. The tall, narrow form and single figure are typical of earlier Archaic stelai. 1906: Volomandra (Attica) kouros, c 550 BC. 38: Fragment of grave stele with head of discobolos (discus-thrower), attributed to the Rampin Master (pp 126, 181), c 550 BC.

On entering room 13, you can immediately turn left into **room 12**, with 14: Unfinished kouros from Naxos, with tool marks, c 540 BC. 13, 4545: Part of colossal kouros from Megara, c 540 BC. 3728: Good example of a herm from Sífnos, c 520 BC.

The large **room 13** has a kouros from the island of Keos (3686), c 530 BC. 3851: the **Anávissos** (Attica) **kouros**, whose fully modelled anatomy and short hair mark it as a later work, c 530 BC. The base is inscribed 'Stop and mourn at the tomb of dead Kroisos, whom furious Ares slew, as he fought in the front rank'. 12 and 2005: Kouros from the sanctuary of Apollo at Ptoön in Boeotia. 1959: Relief of a running hoplite (foot soldier), c 500 BC. 3711: Seated figure of Dionysos, from Athens, c 520 BC. 3072–4, 3897 are fragments of a seated Dionysos from Dhiónissos (ancient *Ikaria*), Attica, probably a cult statue, c 520 BC. 30, 31: Interesting examples of painted stelai. 3938: the **Aristodikos kouros** of c 510 BC, from Keratéa in Attica (name inscribed on base). Two decorated **statue bases**, recovered from the Themistoklean wall—3477: Nude youths playing 'hockey'; chariots, 3476: Similar youths wrestling, jumping, throwing the javelin, playing a ball game, and encouraging a fight between a dog and cat. The figures have the characteristics of Late Archaic sculpture, c 510 BC. In a wall case are a pair (1926) of stone *halteres* (jumping weights), swung by long-jumpers to give them added impetus. 25: Fine **stele of the warrior Aristion**, by the sculptor Aristokles, from Velanidhéza (Attica), c 510 BC. Some traces of the original colours remain. 3687: Rare example of a draped kouros (typical rather of East Greece) from Athens.

Transitional

Room 14 has various **warriors' heads** (1933–8, 1940, 3459; 500–470 BC) from the sanctuary of Aphaia on Aíyina, some from dedications in the sanctuary, some possibly belonging to figures in the pediments. Other pieces include 4506: The arm of a colossal acrolithic statue of Athena. 39: Grave **stele** signed by Alxenor of Naxos, from Orkhomenós in Boeotia, showing a bent elderly man with a staff, accompanied by his dog, early 5C. 11761: Bronze figure of Poseidon from the sea off Livádhostro (Boeotia), c 480. Also Ionic columns— (4478–9) from the temple of Poseidon at Sounion, two (85, 4797) from columns supporting votive offerings.

Classical

Room 15 takes you into the Classical period.

Classical anatomy is more subtly and realistically modelled. Decline of the Archaic love for patterned detail shows in the more generalised treatment of the hair and drapery. Faces take on a bland serene look. The term 'Severe Style' is used for the first phase of Classical sculpture.

The centrepiece (X 11036) is a remarkable **bronze statue of Poseidon** wielding his trident (missing), c 460 BC, found in the sea off Cape Artemision (Euboea) in 1928. Facing you at the entrance are two excellent reliefs: (3990) part (with male head) of an elegant **votive medallion** in Parian marble, found on Milos, c 460 BC, and (3344) a **votive slab** from Sounion showing an athlete crowning himself. Votive reliefs in the room (several interesting pieces) are all from outside Athens (see room 16). Other sculptures include (left; 127) the marble **'Finlay' crater**, with figures copied from the famous Athena and Marsyas group by Myron; (left; 1664, 1664a) Roman copies of statues of Theseus and the Minotaur; and (right; 107) a herm (figure of Hermes) in the familiar form of a head set on a tall pillar, with genitalia. Towards the far end is the **Omphalos Apollo**, called after the base (46) found with, though not belonging to it, in the Theatre of Dionysos in Athens. The figure is a copy (2C AD) of a 5C bronze. Against the far wall is the famous **Eleusis relief** (126; p 265), c 440 BC, showing figures central to the sanctuary's cult: Demeter hands the ears of corn to Triptolemos, who is to distribute them to mankind, while her daughter (Persephone, or Kore) crowns him with a garland. To the right of this is displayed the remarkable terracotta **Niinnion pinax** (11036) from Eleusis (mid-4C BC) with a scratched inscription at the bottom explaining its dedication by N. to 'the Goddesses' (i.e. Demeter and Persephone). The subject matter is thought to be a unique depiction of Demeter and Kore, with Iakkhos, receiving participants in the mysteries at the sanctuary.

Funerary monuments

Some funerary monuments are in the form of large stone vases of the lekythos (p 212) shape with scenes in relief. The relief stelai (more common) are much lower than in the Archaic period and are often capped with finials either in the form of a palmette or of the pediment of a building. As time goes on the architectural type becomes the most common and takes the form of a full architectural frame, with pillars to either side and a pediment above. The depth both of the frame and of the relief of the figures gradually increases until (in the Hellenistic period) the figures, virtually in the round, are contained within a naïskos. In style the figures become more expressive. In the Late Classical period (4C BC) the emotion shown is rather generalised and often sentimental; later it is more specific. Some subjects are standard, such as family groups—including servants and sometimes animals—bidding farewell to the departed often with a handshake, or warriors in their hour of glory.

Room 16 has Classical grave monuments from c 440 BC, when Athenian production restarted after a gap in the earlier 5C, probably due to a decree forbidding excessive expenditure, and many of the following rooms (17–28, 34) are largely devoted to votive and funerary stelai.

Prominent pieces include (4485) the fine **marble lekythos of Myrrhine** (c 420 BC), found in Síntagma Square. The scene shows Hermes Psychopompos (the conductor of departed souls) leading Myrrhine to the River Akheron, while her relatives look on. Among many reliefs a fine **stele** (715) of Pentelic marble, c 430 BC, probably from Sálamis, shows a beautifully sculpted youth, with his grieving slave leaning against a pillar. A cat sits on the pillar; above is a birdcage. Many of the stelai of the later 5C are of very high quality, possibly because the large body of expert sculptors who had been engaged on the decoration of the Parthenon were now free to undertake such work.

The sculpture in **room 17** is mostly votive. 1783, from Néo Fáliro, is decorated on both sides: on one the local hero Echelos carries off his bride, Basile, in a chariot, with Hermes as *nymphagogos* (escort of the bride); on the other is Artemis, with gods and nymphs. 1500, from Piraeus, shows **Dionysos**, reclining on a couch, approached by actors holding their masks. 2756 (from the samesite as 1783), c 400 BC, was dedicated by Xenokrateia. She is shown leading her child Xeniades to the river-god Kephissos with, left and right, Apollo and Acheloös. The room also contains some architectural sculpture, an acroterion (1112) and a seated figure (3410) of c 450 BC from the Temple of Poseidon at Sounion, and metopes and part of a cornice with lion-head waterspouts from the Argive Heraion, late 5C BC.

Rooms 19 and 20 are entered from room 17 (19 is the section immediately to the left; 20, to the right, is L-shaped). In **room 20**, various reliefs are followed by copies of major works, by Pheidias and others. The Cassel and Medici Apollo types are represented, the names deriving from the collections in which the main examples are held. The former is thought to be the **Athena Parnopios** (Averter of Locusts) of Pheidias, a work which is mentioned in literary sources. 200–202: Statuettes from Eleusis (2C AD), copying figures from the west pediment of the Parthenon (*Kekrops and Daughter*, etc). Most interesting are **copies of the Athena Parthenos**. The **Varvákeion Athena** (129) was discovered in 1880 near the school of that name in Od. Athinás. One-twelfth the original size and made in the 2C or 3C AD, it seems to reproduce all the original features. Only the pillar, on which the goddess's right hand rests, may reflect a later repair. 128: The **Lenormant Athena** is an unfinished miniature copy of the Roman period.

Room 19 includes (3949) a Roman copy, found in Athens, of the cult statue of Nemesis at Rhamnous.

From rooms 19/20, a door and stairways lead outside to the pleasant **inner court** (access to café), with grave stelai and Roman sarcophagi, also eroded marble sculpture from a 1C BC wreck near Antikíthira (see below, room 28): the figures here are Roman copies of earlier works (Odysseus, Diomedes, etc).

Room 18 has late 5C and 4C funerary monuments (stone lekythoi, stelai and three white-ground pottery lekythoi). 3624 is the famous **stele of Hegeso** (c 400 BC; see Kerameikos, p 181): Hegeso sits examining a necklace, originally painted, from a jewel-box held by her maid. 2744 and 754 are parts of the war memorial, found northeast of the Dipylon, erected by the city of Athens in honour of hoplites and cavalry who fell at Koroneia and near Corinth in 394 BC. The names inscribed on the cornice include that of Dexileos whose personal stele is in the Kerameikos Museum (p 181).

Room 21 is on the central axis of the museum. It connects directly with the Mycenaean gallery (room 4) and gives access to the remaining sculpture rooms (22–33) as well as rooms 34 onwards and the upper floors.

Room 21 itself has freestanding and relief sculpture from the Classical to Hellenistic periods; some pieces are Roman copies. The centrepiece is the latest, a striking Hellenistic (2C BC) group of **Horse and diminutive jockey**, straining for victory. The realistic features and expression of the boy-jockey are typical of the Hellenistic period and make a striking contrast with the idealistic representations of Classical sculpture, here exemplified by (1826) a copy (c 100 BC) of the **Diadoumenos** (athlete binding on his victory wreath), a noted bronze by Polykleitos of the mid-5C BC. Late Classical artists are represented by the Matron of Herculaneum, a copy of a Greek statue by either Praxiteles or Lysippos; the best known of a series of copies was found in Italy, at Herculaneum. 218, the Hermes of Andros, was found on the Cycladic island of Andros. It is a Roman copy of an original of the school of Praxiteles.

Room 34 is arranged to suggest an **open-air sanctuary**, in which there are various votive reliefs, statues and an altar. The altar (1495) is that dedicated by the Athenian Boule (Council, pp 66, 154) in the Agora to Aphrodite Hegemone and the Graces. Although quite small, it is fairly typical in form, with a stepped base. A narrow moulding with small Ionic volutes surrounds the upper 'business' surface which is itself left roughly dressed. Nearby is a statue (303: Roman, from Epidauros) of Hekate, goddess of the crossroads, shown in typical threefold form. 4466 is a striking relief, on an inscribed base, from the Cave of the Nymphs on Mt Pentelikon, 4C BC. The surface is roughly hollowed to suggest a cave, in which are three nymphs, Hermes, Pan and two figures making a libation. On 4465, from the same site, three nymphs, Hermes and Pan are approached by three worshippers, the latter smaller in scale. Also in the room are objects from an open-air Sanctuary of Aphrodite, near Dhafní, by the Sacred Way to Eleusis (p 264). Other reliefs, associated with the cult of Herakles, show the hero in various of his labours.

Returning to the main series of sculpture rooms, **room 22** has fascinating works from the **Sanctuary of Asklepios at Epidaurus**. The softer features and delicate, clinging drapery style are typical of the end of the 5C and earlier 4C BC. The pedimental sculptures of the temple of Asklepios (c 380 BC) are reconstructed against the left (west) and right (east) walls. The west pediment had a battle of Greeks and Amazons: the central Amazon is well preserved. The acroteria (possibly representing Breezes), to the side, are flying female figures with clinging drapery. The east pediment shows incidents from the capture of Troy, although the figures are fragmentary and hard to identify. The styles of the two pediments are in sharp contrast. As opposed to the softer style of the west, sharp drapery lines contrast with flat planes in the eastern figures but most striking is the way that limbs are outlined with deeply channelled drapery. This distinctive characteristic appears also in one of the acroteria, on a separate pedestal at the right-hand end of the right wall. Although fragmentary the figure was clearly winged and may be Eros. This drapery feature appears clearly also in another, freestanding, sculpture (299) from the site, displayed in the centre of the room, a stooping figure of Hygiaea (Health). Inscriptions recording the temple accounts show that several sculptors were involved, one of them the famous 4C artist Timotheos. A good case can be made out (see M. Robertson, *A history of Greek art*, Cambridge, 1975, pp 397ff.) for attributing the Eros, east pedimental group and related figures to him. Also in the room are part of the cornice of the Epidauros Tholos, acroteria from the Temple of Artemis and a relief showing Asklepios, in characteristic seated pose, and members of his family.

Rooms 23–24 house more funerary monuments (4C). The increased depth of relief and multiplicity of figures is noticeable. In **room 23** is the outstanding **Ilissos stele** (869, c 340 BC). The deceased, a fine figure sometimes attributed to Skopas, leans against a pillar. A diminutive slave squats at his feet, while his aged father stands to the right.

Rooms 25–27 (off 23–24) are often neglected, but undeservedly so. They contain mostly **votive and record reliefs**.

> ### Votive and record reliefs
> **Votive reliefs** generally show the deity to whom they were offered, with his or her family, performing typical acts (e.g. Asklepios healing) or being approached by worshippers, sometimes with offerings or sacrificial animals. The deities can be recognised by particular attributes (Hermes' wand, Cybele's lions, Artemis' bow) or features of style (Asklepios is bearded, avuncular, often seated and half-draped) or associations (family groups). **Record reliefs** commemorate, with an inscription and associated scene, important formal public or private agreements or honours (e.g. a treaty between two states, illustrated by figures personifying both).

In the L-shaped **room 25** are several **dedications to the Nymphs**, the form suggesting (like those in room 34) the caves in which they were worshipped. There is an increasingly pictorial tendency in later reliefs (late 4C onwards). 1469 is a record of the transmission of the sacred funds of Athena by her treasurers of 398/97 BC. 1341 shows a **Carter leading his waggon** to Asklepios, in supplication. 1467 records a **Treaty between Athens and Corcyra** (Corfú) in 375 BC, with personifications of the two states. At the corner of the room are (693–6) votive figures of children holding various offerings, from the sanctuary of Eileithuia (goddess of childbirth) at Agrai, near the River Ilissos. There follow numerous reliefs (mostly 4C) dedicated to **Asklepios**. His sacred healing snakes are often in evidence as are other members of his family. Some of the scenes show him attending to patients reclining on couches and presumably refer to the ritual of incubation, where the sick slept overnight in his sanctuary and were visited by the God. Others show him approached by votaries. 258, the **Asklepios of Mounychia** (3C–2C BC), is expressive. 1377: An Asklepios relief in unusual form where the god is shown in a shrine, separate from and at right-angles to the panel with worshippers.

In **room 26** is a scene in which an elderly man carries a huge votive leg, presumably in thanks for a cure.

Room 27 has several examples of **funeral feasts** where heroes (who were mortal and therefore belonged to the earth, as opposed to gods who were immortal and of the heavens) feast on couches. Men of high status and achievement were also sometimes 'heroised' in this way. A group of reliefs show the goddess **Cybele** with several of her common attributes—throne, lions, polos hat, drum, *phiale* (offering plate).

Room 28 has sculpture of the Late Classical period (4C BC), though the major 4C sculptors (Lysippos, Praxiteles, Skopas) are disappointingly represented. The display begins with the last of the Attic funerary monuments (a decree of 307 BC banned their further production). That of **Aristonautes** (738) shows the armed soldier fully in the round within a naïskos. There are some fine bronzes which well illustrate the softer 4C style and the smaller heads of the period, which give the figures a more human feel. One such, the **Marathon boy** (from the sea off Marathon), is late 4C and reflects the style of Praxiteles. The **Antikythera youth** (13396; c 340 BC), with inlaid eyes and carefully made lashes, was found with other bronze and marble (p 202) sculpture in a wreck off the island of that name (near Kíthira, off the south coast of the Peloponnese). Between the two, stone sculptures include (3614) an interesting **relief panel of an Amazonomachy** which closely reflects the style of a famous mid-4C monument, the Mausoleum at Halikarnassos (modern Bodrum, Turkey), on which several famous sculptors are supposed to have worked. Distinctive are the knobbly male anatomy, the 'calligraphic' drapery and the tendency to diagonal stances. 1773 is a base signed by Bryaxis (one of the Mausoleum sculptors), though the modest horses and tripods depicted look more like the work of an assistant. 1762 is the head of a Roman copy of a Praxiteles Aphrodite.

6439, from Olympia, is the bronze **head of a boxer**, whose tousled beard and battered face show the increasing interest in realism and portraiture of the period. 3602 is a delicate **head of Hygiaea** from Tegea; it represents the contrasting slightly sentimental yet Classicising strain in 4C sculpture. By the exit are a boar and two heads from the pediments of the Temple of Athena Alea at Tegea (near Tripolis, in Arkadia), c 340. Although battered, these are probably the work of Skopas; the deep eye-sockets suggest powerful feeling.

Hellenistic and Roman
Room 29 is the first of two devoted to **Hellenistic sculpture**, that is from the death of Alexander the Great in 323 BC.

Realism and portraiture
The trends towards realism and portraiture, first evident in the 4C, are greatly intensified in Hellenistic work, though a traditional Classical strain is still prominent. There is more interest in children, also in trivial subjects and more superficial treatments of deities or themes (see 3335). In general there is much more variety of both subject and style in Hellenistic sculpture, not all of it immediately appealing but of considerable historical interest.

No. 247 in **room 29** is a fighting Gaul from Delos (c 100 BC) which exemplifies the new approach. The **cult statue of Themis** from Rhamnous (231) by Khairestratos, c 300 BC, is more traditional in style. Three slabs of a fine **base from Mantineia** (215–21) have scenes of Apollo and Marsyas (who unsuccessfully challenged Apollo to a contest of flute-playing in which the loser was to be flayed alive), and six of the nine Muses. It probably supported a group of figures by Praxiteles, seen by Pausanias. 1734–7 (with restored drawing on wall) are impressive **heads by** the 2C BC sculptor **Damophon**, whose career has been illuminated recently by finds from Messene (*Blue Guide Greece*, 6th edn p 296). They come from a group showing Despoina and Kore (Demeter and Persephone), with giants, from the Sanctuary of Despoina at Lykósoura in Arkadia. A piece of the robe of Despoina is also shown. The head of the giant **Anytos** is particularly impressive, with splendid plastic treatment of the beard, powerful and exuberant; but the debt to the Classical tradition is still evident.

Room 30 continues the Hellenistic sequence. In a style not dissimilar to Damophon's is the massive **head of Zeus** by Eukleides, from Aigeira, 2C BC. 13400, etc: **Bronze head** of a philosopher from the Antikíthera wreck (see above, room 28), also other parts of the figure. 235: Statue of Poseidon from Melos, c 140 BC. 14612: Bronze head from Delos, c 100 BC—a careworn portrait. 1156, etc: Votive and funerary reliefs. Of two portraits (362–3; c 100 BC), the male is much more realistic. 3335: **Pan accosting Aphrodite** who defends herself with a sandal while an Eros attends; from Delos, c 100 BC. Against the left wall is an attractive frieze with a marine *thiasos* (company of figures). From Melos is a huge equestrian statue of c 100 BC.

The excellent display of **Roman sculpture** begins in room 31, opened in 1995.

Greek influence on Roman sculpture

Although Greece came under the political control of Rome, her artistic tradition, initially at least, dominated that of her conqueror and many of the leading artists were Greeks. Thus numerous features of Greek style, form and subject continue but there are very distinctive elements, notably an obsession with portraiture, some highly realistic, some idealised as in the 'cuirassed' statues of Roman emperors.

In the centre of the room is 23322: Part of a fine bronze **equestrian statue of Augustus**, c 10 BC. Nos 259–60 (left on entering): 'Neo-Attic' relief slabs show an interest in copying earlier styles. 320, etc are **'veristic' portraits** of the 1C BC; the term signifies a harsh realism. 241, a Hermes from Aíyio, is more traditional. The **Delos figure** (1828) combines a portrait head with an idealised torso, c 100 BC. 547, etc show members of the first, Julio-Claudian, dynasty of Roman emperors. The heads are genuine portraits but lack the harshness of Republican verism. A colossal (1759) headless statue from Megara shows the **Emperor Claudius** with the attributes of Zeus. 348, etc: Portraits of the Flavian emperors. 1233: Grave stelai, in the Greek tradition but with a greater tendency to frontality and disproportion.

The side **room 31A** (The Diogeneion Gymnasium) contains heads from hermaic stelai and some complete examples, also one or two inscriptions with lists of officials. Found built into the Late Roman Wall, they are all thought to have come from the Diogeneion, an Athenian gymnasium of the 2C–3C AD whose actual location is uncertain (p 170). They were set up to commemorate the holders of the post of *kosmetes* (senior official of the Gymnasium), and other officers. They portray Athenian citizens in styles which mix the traditional with newer features of Roman taste. Two of the inscriptions, with representations of boats, commemorate victories in *naumachiae*.

Room 32 begins (left) with portraits of the period AD 96–138, including the emperors Nerva, Trajan and **Hadrian**, whose philhellenism shows in the style of his portraits (249, etc; he was the first emperor to sport a full beard) and in those of his favourite, **Antinoüs** (417). 1644 is a typically Roman cuirassed statue with rich decoration on the armour. 263 is a rather cold and lifeless Roman Asklepios, unsuccessfully copying an earlier original.

The display continues with material of the Antonine period (AD 138–92). 572 is a head of Marcus Aurelius, 3740 an interesting representation of **Lucius Verus**, with a typically Roman contrast between rich and tousled hair and unnaturally smooth skin. Portraits (4810) and reliefs associated with **Herodes Atticus** (p 278) and his favourite, Polydeukion, were found at his villas at Kifissiá and Loúkou (in Arkadia). Recent excavations at the latter (*Blue Guide Greece* 6th edn, p 251) have produced splendid finds of sculpture. 1186 is a typical Roman sarcophagus (2C AD) decorated with scenes of the mythological hunt of the Kalydonian boar, perhaps symbolising the sporting pleasures to await the deceased in the next world. Grave stones include 1192, with a striking depiction of a landscape backing an image of the dead man hunting a boar with his dog. 261 (centre; 2C AD) is a maenad sleeping on an animal skin.

Room 33 takes you into the later Roman empire—the Severan dynasty (193–235 AD), the Tetrarchs and Constantine, the first Christian emperor (284–363 AD). An elaborate table support (170) from a workshop in Asia Minor (c 170 AD) has figures of Dionysos, Pan, a satyr, etc.

Portrait styles changed frequently in this period—some (3563) harking back to idealising Greek prototypes, others (1764) harshly realistic, occasionally employing a technique called 'negative modelling' (e.g. 635) where the hair does not appear to be positively modelled, but is chipped into the surface of the stone. There are strong contrasts between light surfaces and dark hollows, achieved by extensive use of the drill. The effects produced are often impressionistic rather than naturalistic. Tetrarchic portraiture is more abstract; that of Constantine and philosophers of the period, other-worldly. The grave stelai are more crudely carved and the figures less well proportioned. Frontality and abstraction are common. These characteristics anticipate Byzantine work and indeed the story of ancient sculpture has now to be followed in the Byzantine Museum (p 225).

You should now return to room 34 (above). Through this are the remaining ground floor displays.

Bronzes; the Egyptian and the Stathatos collections

The display of **bronzes** begins in **room 36** (left) with the K. Karapános collection, the fruits of excavations at the sanctuary of Zeus at Dodona and elsewhere, donated to the state in 1902.

Bronze was a popular material in antiquity, both for practical implements and for works of art and decoration. It was often the preferred material for large-scale statues, though few of these have survived to the present day. Bronze objects of all kinds were dedicated in large numbers in sanctuaries, and the finds in this room reflect the variety. Some are inscribed with the name of the donor and/or the deity to whom the offering was made. The word 'ANEΘHKEN' (s/he dedicated) can sometimes be made out. Figurines reflect the style of their period. Some portray the deity to whom they were offered: a fine piece (16546) on a separate stand shows Zeus hurling his thunderbolt. Anonymous figures have lost the attributes by which they could be identified, or may have represented the donor, or servants intended to do the will of the god. The room also contains Archaic terracottas of Artemis from Corfu, Hellenistic and Roman heads, grave stelai and a reconstructed Roman chariot with some of its original bronze fittings.

In **room 37** the most important ancient method of **bronze casting** is illustrated by the *cire-perdue* or lost-wax system—a fine skin of wax, modelled over a core of other material, was replaced in firing by molten bronze. Thus hollow-cast objects were produced which were both lighter than solids and saved an enormous amount of valuable metal.

The rest of the room contains a fine range of **bronze votives** from various sites, including Boeotia (the Ptoön sanctuary and the Kabeirion), Macedonia, Thessaly and the north, and Crete (Idaean cave).

From this room you can reach the **Egyptian Collection** (rooms 40, 41). Opened in 1995, the galleries are attractively set out, with good panels of background information in Greek and English. The wide range of objects covers all periods from Pre-Dynastic to Roman. Minor objects include ceramic, alabaster and faïence vessels, and small-scale sculpture. Among the larger sculptures are some striking pieces in wood, and others of types which may have provided protoypes for Archaic Greek monumental sculpture, specifically the kouros and seated figure forms. **Room 40** has more sculpture, including pieces of the Hellenistic period, painted anthropoid coffins, a mummy and three fine 'Fayum' mummy portraits.

The **Helen Stathatos Collection** (**room 42**) was presented to the museum in 1957. It consists of a great variety of objects of all periods from prehistoric to Byzantine, from Thessaly, Khalkidhikí and Macedonia—and a particularly rich selection of ancient jewellery and goldwork.

The upper-floor galleries

Note Although these are closed at the time of writing (see above), the description has been retained in the hope of early reopening.

The first-floor galleries are mainly occupied by the collection of post-prehistoric **ancient pottery**, displayed in chronological sequence. Room 52 also contains **votives** from major sanctuaries at Argos, Perakhóra and Sparta and the unique **terracotta metopes** from the Temple of Apollo at Thermon in Aetolia. Opening off the landing is an important display of pottery, bronzes and frescoes from the spectacular prehistoric settlement at **Akrotiri on Thira**, preserved beneath volcanic debris.

Akrotiri

The first room contains numerous examples of **pottery** dating to the site's main period of occupation (beginning of the Late Bronze Age, 16C BC). Much of it is local, though often imitating Minoan prototypes. Especially attractive are some of the pictorial scenes with vegetation, dolphins and birds. Among the finds are many Minoan and some Mycenaean imports. There are stone vessels, also bronze objects including sickles and scale balances. Impressive **bronze vessels** resemble finds from the palace at Knossos, and probably came from Crete. A striking exhibit is a wooden bed, reconstructed by pouring plaster into the holes in the pumice left after the decay of the wood. The form of a wicker basket was similarly recovered.

In the second room are the splendid **frescoes**. These include swallows and lilies in a rocky landscape; and antelopes and boxing children (perhaps juxtaposed to compare rites of passage in the human and animal kingdoms).

The state of preservation of these paintings is unique for the Aegean Bronze Age. They are clearly based on Cretan models in technique, style and subject, but there are also local Cycladic, and possibly Mycenaean features.

Leaving the Akrotiri exhibition, you turn left into the **Vase Rooms**. (For an outline history of Greek vase-painting see p 72.)

Vases

Vases fulfilled many different functions. Accordingly they were made in a wide range of shapes which often varied in detail from period to period (and whose names are forbidding to the uninitiated). The **amphora**, normally for storing or transporting liquids although sometimes used in the Geometric period for marking graves, is one of the commonest of the larger shapes in its numerous variations. In black- and red-figure a series of cups (the **kylix**; pl. kylikes) bore different decorative schemes, both inside and out; the circular interior field (tondo) provided a special challenge to painters.

Geometric pottery

Room 49 begins with the earliest Iron Age pottery in the **Proto-Geometric style** (11C–10C). In contrast to the latest Mycenaean pottery, after the fall of the palaces, Proto-Geometric vessels are finely formed and have neat, if limited decoration. Characteristic is the use of the compass and multiple brush to form precise groups of concentric circles and semicircles.

The following **Geometric style** (Early—early 9C; Middle—later 9C/earlier 8C; Late—later 8C) sees first a move to predominantly dark-ground vases. Then comes a progressive increase in the extent of decoration, the introduction of the characteristic meander motif and the appearance of figured scenes, often illustrating funerary ritual or fighting. The former include the *prothesis* (laying out of the dead on a bier and mourning) and *ekphora* (funeral procession). The very largest vases were used as grave markers. In the final stage, the figures take over most of the vase's surface, and both they and the decoration are less carefully drawn. Curvilinear motifs begin to intrude. Regional Geometric styles are closely related to those of Athens but have their own idiosyncracies—the stepped meander of Argos, the precise linear banding of Corinth.

The continuous rhythm of the best Geometric decoration emphasises the structure and volume of the vases and represents great achievement in harmonising decoration and shape. In later periods, the emphasis on figured scenes made this balance difficult or impossible to achieve.

As you move into **room 50** the transition from Geometric to **Orientalising style** (7C) becomes apparent—larger figures partly drawn in outline, disappearance of pure Geometric ornament, introduction of curvilinear and vegetable motifs (e.g. 313 the **Análatos hydria**). Most of the pottery of this period on display is from Attica (Proto-Attic), although there is a small wall case with typical Corinthian aryballoi (miniature vases for perfumed oil) of the time (Proto-Corinthian). Corinthian miniaturism, and the early introduction of the black-figure technique (see below) contrast with Attic monumentality and silhouette-and-outline drawing. Mythological scenes become more common. Cases at the end of the room include regional Orientalising styles. An interesting example is the Wild Goat style from Rhodes with its characteristic shape, the trefoil-mouthed jug (*oenochoe*). Also typical, this time of the island of Melos, are a series (911, etc) of 'Melian amphorae' with Orientalising motifs and figured mythological scenes.

Painters and potters

Signatures on pottery come either in the form ΕΓΡΑΨΕΝ ('he painted') or ΕΠΟΙΗΣΕΝ ('he made'), occasionally both together. Potter and painter were sometimes different people, sometimes the same. The names of painters which you see on the labels only occasionally come from direct signatures on the individual vases. Sometimes, on an unsigned vase, the style of an individual is identifiable from other work of his which is signed. When a group of vases can be identified on stylistic grounds as the work of one person but none of them carries his signature, the painter is given a name which may be based on the subject matter of a particularly striking vase (the Pan Painter); on the name of a place, collection or museum in which some of his main work is found (the Painter of Boston [i.e. Museum] 7560; the Edinburgh Painter); or on that of a potter who made and signed some of his vases (the Amasis Painter).

Black-figure pottery

With **room 51** you find the adoption by Attic artists of the black-figure technique, invented in Corinth but used there mainly on much smaller-scale vases.

A special firing process was used to create black figures against the natural clay ground, with details incised. Some of the early scenes, dominated by friezes of animals with rosettes in the field, are closely based on Corinthian motifs, but the Attic preference for figured scenes, often from mythology, comes to dominate the subsequent history of Greek vase painting.

An early example (1002; c 600 BC), with the large and rather ungainly figures characteristic of this experimental phase, is the **Nessos amphora**, with scenes of Herakles and the centaur Nessos (on the neck) and the Gorgons (on the body). Subjects have to be identified either by the nature of the action (Theseus and the Minotaur can hardly be mistaken) or the attributes of the participants (for instance, Herakles wears a lionskin and carries a club, and Hermes has winged sandals, a distinctive cap and figure-of-eight wand).

Room 52 is remarkable not only for pottery, although there is plenty, but for the **votive deposits** from important sanctuaries and for the unique metopes from Thermon.

On the far side of the room a case (39) of black-figure pottery includes an important early (c 580 BC) fragment by the painter **Sophilos** showing the funeral games of Achilles, with spectators perched on a grandstand. The scene and some of the participants are titled, and Sophilos has signed the vase (in retrograde script), as he did another fragment in the case.

To your right when you enter room 52 are finds from the **Temple of Hera at Argos**, in the Peloponnese (*Blue Guide Greece*, 6th edn, p 241), with a reconstructed scene of the site. They include a fine house or temple model. Also displayed are numerous votives from another sanctuary of Hera, that at **Perakhora**, opposite Corinth on the north side of the Gulf of Corinth. There are ceramic, bronze and terracotta dedications, as well as numerous ivories, the majority of the Archaic period. There is another building model, often thought to represent the earliest (8C) temple on the site which, like the model, had an apsidal end. The other sanctuaries represented are both Spartan, of **Athena Khalkioikos** and **Artemis Orthia**, the latter with numerous exotic ivories and some tiny lead figures. There is a fine painted sphinx, an Archaic acroterion from the Temple of Artemis at Kalydon. A case of Corinthian pottery shows the local 6C **Animal Style**. In a centre case are some interesting **painted wooden plaques** (c 525 BC) from a sanctuary of the Nymphs at Pitsa, near Corinth. The best preserved shows a group of worshippers approaching an altar with gifts, including an animal for sacrifice.

The most spectacular finds in the room are at the far end—painted **terracotta metope panels** and antefixes from the Doric temple of Apollo at Thermon. These belong to a period (c 630 BC) before temples and their sculptures were made of monumental stonework. The scenes, painted by Corinthian artists, use the same conventions as black-figure vases and show mythological figures, including Perseus and Orion the hunter.

Room 53 contains mature black-figure pottery. Case 56 has high-quality fragments found in excavations on the Acropolis, with the work of various important painters—Lydos, Nearkhos, the Amasis Painter. A majestic fragment by Nearkhos shows Achilles, his squire and horses. Some Etruscan pottery is displayed, as well as 6C island pottery and examples of sarcophagi decorated in the black-figure technique, whose production centred on the Greek city of Klazomenai in Asia Minor. Funerary plaques (some by **Exekias**, the most important painter in this style) for attachment to tombs were also worked in black figure.

Room 54 starts with numerous jugs of the lekythos form, much used in funerary ritual. Some are on a white ground (for white-ground lekythoi decorated in the standard technique, see p 212). To the left is the first example of a **Panathenaic amphora**, a type filled with sacred oil and given as a prize in the Panathenaic Games: the decoration always shows the goddess Athena on one side, and the event (here a chariot race) on the other. **Case 69** again has high-quality fragments, of both vases and plaques, from the Athenian acropolis. Some are red-figure, allowing a close comparison in technique with black-figure. A calyx-crater by Syriskos (Acropolis 735; c 480 BC), showing Theseus and the Minotaur, exemplifies the new technique in a large-scale mythological scene.

Red-figure pottery
Rooms 55 and 56 illustrate the development of the red-figure style which gradually superseded black-figure after its invention c 530 BC. The latter, however, never entirely died out for some traditional forms (e.g. Panathenaic amphorae)

Black- and red-figure
In both techniques, the black/red contrast was produced by the firing process, not by coloured paint. In **black-figure**, the figures appeared black against the natural clay colour of the vessel, and any details were incised; in **red-figure pottery**, the background was black and the figures were 'reserved' in the natural colour of the clay. Details were painted in using either raised 'relief lines' or flat 'dilute lines'.

The red-figure technique offered a figure colour closer to that of human flesh, and thus less remote, and a method of depicting detail which allowed subtler definition of anatomy, drapery, etc. Although at first red figures are often awkward and formal (comparisons with Archaic sculpture can easily be seen), they later become much freer as artists exploit the new possibilities, especially in variety of pose. It is arguable, however, that such ambitious efforts are not really suitable to vase decoration for which the more formal and patterned surface treatment of black figure was ideal. Red figure died out during the 4C BC, perhaps because artists were overreaching themselves as they employed the techniques and strove for the effects of panel painting in an inappropriate format.

To your left on entry to **room 55** is a well-known vase by the **Pan Painter** (9683; c 470 BC) showing Herakles, with characteristic club and lionskin, setting about the attendants of the Egyptian king Busiris. Busiris sacrificed all foreigners who set foot in his country but Herakles turned the tables on him. In the first case to the right, a group of three hydrias illustrate the decreasing sensitivity of red-figure artists to the relationship of decoration to shape: in spite of the fact that the shoulder is at a sharp angle to the main body of the vase, the whole surface is treated as a single field.

White-ground lekythoi were mainly produced in the 5C BC (some other shapes were occasionally decorated in the same technique). The method used was different from both black- and red-figure, involving polychrome decoration with painted detail, on an applied white ground. The lekythoi were mainly used in funerary rituals (taking offerings of perfumed oil to the tomb, where they were then left) which are often depicted on the vases themselves. Other scenes related to death include personifications of Sleep and Death (both winged) carrying off a youth (e.g. 12783 by the Quadrate Painter; c 420 BC) and Charon ferrying the departed across the River Styx (e.g. 17916 by the Sabouroff Painter; c 450 BC).

Another good example of red-figure is a vase, perhaps by Polygnotos (18063; c 430–420 BC) showing the abduction of Helen. At the end of the gallery, before you double back down the further side, cases illustrate the uses of some special vase types: the *chous*, employed in the festival of the Anthesteria, and the *lebes gamikos*, used in marriage ceremonies. Another case contains undecorated **black-glaze pottery**, an important class of Classical pottery, with elegant shapes and a fine surface finish.

The display continues with later **red-figure work** in which three characteristics are particularly evident: a preoccupation with less elevated themes; a more finicky style with extensive linear detail and sometimes added colour and gilding; and the positioning of figures on different levels, a feature adopted from larger-scale wall-painting and unsuitable to vase decoration. The first two characteristics can be seen in 1629, a work of the **Eretria Painter**, c 430 BC. This unusual shape, the *epinetron*, was placed over the knee and the roughened part of its surface used in the carding of wool. Varying levels can be seen on a *pelike* of the late 5C BC (1333) with a Gigantomachy.

Case 119 has some Boeotian black-figure Kabiric vases with comical figures, often padded and sometimes ithyphallic, used in ritual at the Sanctuary of the Kabiri near Thebes.

Numerous examples of 4C red-figure include regional styles.

The Epigraphic Museum
Opening. 08.30–15.00. Closed Mon.

Although in the same building as the Archaeological Museum, this has a separate entrance in Od. Tosítsa. Some of the material is housed in two external courts; the rest in the entrance hall and four rooms (1 and 11 to the left of the hall; 2 and 9 to the right). The first of each pair is more in the nature of a store, with relatively little labelling; the second attractively arranged and fully labelled in Greek and English.

The museum is well worth visiting since it forcefully brings home the importance of inscriptions to an ancient Greek community, and their striking physical presence in both towns and sanctuaries.

The collection contains some of the most important inscribed documents found on ancient sites—decrees, laws, tribute lists, building records, inventories, treaties, casualty lists, dedications with artists' signatures, etc. Major events in Greek history are highlighted.

Among the texts are: **Room 1**: Athenian tribute lists (tax payments of Athens' subject allies); accounts for the Athena Parthenos of Pheidias. **Room 11**: inscribed votive columns from the Athenian Acropolis; statue bases from the same site; the earliest (8C) known inscription. **Room 9** altar dedicated by Peisistratos the Younger; 5C copy of Draco's law code; specifications for the arsenal of Philo at Piraeus; building accounts from Eleusis and Rhamnous; the Troizen stele, with a text of Themistokles' decree of 480 BC, ordering the evacuation of Athens and the naval preparations in advance of the Battle of Salamis.

12 • Plateía Kánningos, Leofóros Akadhimías and Kolonáki

The central part of Akadhimías is open and attractive, with the Cultural Centre fronted by lawns and fountains. Kolonáki Square is lively rather than appealing but Plateía Dhexamení is pleasant. Patriárkhou Ioakím has expensive shops. The far end of the walk, beyond the Maráslio, is quieter and has one or two interesting buildings.

- **Distance on foot**. Maps 3,4; 6,5–6; 7,5. 1.5km from Plateía Kánningos to Kolonáki square; 2.3km (total) to Moní Petráki.
  Access by bus. Nos. 022 or 060 (minibus), from Kánningos (the 022 stop is just off the square in Od. Khalkokondíli) or the Academy, cover the whole route.

Among trees in **Plateía Kánningos** is a statue, by Sir John Chantrey, of the British foreign minister George Canning (1770–1827), erected in 1931 to honour his services to the cause of Greek independence. On the plinth, which has shrapnel marks, an additional inscription commemorates Canning's great-grandson who died in Greece in 1941.

The crowded square, which has one or two good buildings, is dominated by the massive Ministry of Commerce (Ipouryío Emboríou, ΥΠΟΥΡΓΕΙΟΝ ΕΜΠΟΡΙΟΥ) on the north. Streets on this side of the square lead to the south side of the National Museum.

Akadhimías, named after the Academy which it backs, runs parallel with Stadhíou and Panepistimíou but begins in Plateía Kánningos, the other side of Patisíon from Omónia. It is a main route for vehicles making for the eastern and northeastern suburbs.

Much of Akadhimías is occupied by tall and rather plain 1930s' blocks of offices and flats. At the Kánningos end (corners with Emmanouíl Benáki), good neoclassical buildings are being restored. To the right, dominating a small square, is the large **church of Zoödhókhos Piyí** (D. Zézos, 1845). At no. 59 is the **Theatre Olympía**, which is the headquarters of the **National Opera and Ballet Companies** (Lirikí Skiní).

The street opens out behind the Library/University/Academy complex (pp 142–143) and there are numerous bus terminals. On the left side of Akadhimías, a former hospital (1837; the wings are later additions) stands behind lawns and gardens and has been beautifully restored as a **Cultural Centre** (Pnevmatikó Kéntro; open 09.00–13.00; 17.00–21.00, closed Sun evening and all day Mon) for the city of Athens. It hosts good exhibitions (listed in *Now in Athens*, p 20), though these are mainly geared to a Greek audience, and has some interesting publications. In the basement is a **Theatre Museum** (Mon–Fri 09.00–14.00) and Centre for Theatrical Research. The displays illustrate the history of the Greek stage, ancient and modern, and include various sets. The dressing-room of Katína Paxinoú has been reconstructed. Beyond is the Kostís Palamás Building (1857–59), popularly known as the Rose Building (Roz Ktírio), originally a boys' high school, then university laboratories. Now a cultural centre for the University, it contains the library of the Theatre

Museum. Outside, a modern sculpture commemorates students, teachers and ancillary staff of the University who died in resistance to the German occupation of 1941–44.

The view up Od. Massalías (left) reaches to the walls of the compound of the **École Française d'Athènes**, in Od. Dhidhótou (which continues to Kolonáki Square as Od. Anagnostopoúlou). The oldest (1846) archaeological institute in Greece, it has occupied this building since 1874. The writer Edmond About was a student in 1851–53. The school's main centres of activity in Greece have been Delphi, Delos and Mallia (Crete). It publishes monographs and the important periodical *Bulletin de Correspondance Hellénique*.

Further up Akadhimías (no. 40, left) is the marble-fronted Tamíon Parakatathíkon kai Dhaníon (Deposit and Loan Fund). Od. Omírou (left) climbs to the jagged rock of the Skhistí Pétra, above pretty Plateía Likavittoú, not far from the École Française. At Akadhimías 36 is the **YMCA** (or XAN; Khristianikí Adhelfótita Néon). English lessons for foreigners are offered in June and July (☎ 210 362 6970). Off to the left in Od. Dhimokrítou (at no. 7) is a small **Museum of Costume** (Mouseío Istorías Ellinikís Endimasías, ΜΟΥΣΕΙΟ ΙΣΤΟΡΙΑΣ ΕΛΛΗΝΙΚΗΣ ΕΝΔΥΜΑΣΙΑΣ; open Mon, Wed, Fri 10.00–13.00), with a regularly changed display from its large collection of Greek regional dress, and some publications.

As the street bends to approach Vasilíssis Sofías, you take Od. Kanári (left) which climbs towards Kolonáki. On its corner with Akadhimías is the **Film Archive of Greece** (Tainiothíki tis Elládhos) and **Cinema Museum** (open Mon–Fri 09.00–13.30) with material relating to the history of the Greek cinema; films are also shown.

Kanári climbs to **Kolonáki Square**, centre of the most fashionable quarter of Athens, on the lower slopes of Likavittós. It contains the British Council and various nondescript buildings. The upper side is has many cafés, mostly indifferent, very expensive and permanently crowded, although the old-fashioned *Likóvrisi* is good. The square is officially called Filikís Etairías (Friendly Society) after a secret organisation established in 1814 with the objective of freeing Greece from Ottoman domination. Neighbouring streets (Tsakáloff, Skoufá, Anagnostopoúlou) and sculptures in the square recall founding members. Its colloquial name ('Little column') comes from a piece of ancient column still to be seen in the southwest segment of the central garden.

From the top corner of the square, you can climb up to the pleasant **Plateía Dhexamení**. There is a quiet café here and an open-air cinema in summer. The name refers to the **reservoir** underlying the square, begun by the Roman emperor Hadrian and completed by Antoninus Pius. For the related inscription see p 92. Its supply was brought in by an aqueduct from Tatóï in the foothills of Mt Párnitha. The reservoir was recommissioned in 1840, refurbished in 1869 and again, together with the aqueduct, in 1929. Although still in use it is now of much less importance. There is a ceremonial Blessing of the Waters here at Epiphany.

From the same point of Kolonáki Square, the pleasant tree-lined Patriárkhou Ioakím runs along the side of Likavittós, parallel to but four streets above Vasilíssis Sofías. It is lined with expensive shops and flats and has *Mondial*, an excellent *zakharoplasteíon*, at no. 31. At the far end is the neoclassical **Maráslion** (original building by D. Kállias, 1906; girls' college addition by N. Mitsákis and others, c 1930), which operates both as a secondary school and a teachers' training college. It was a donation of G. Maraslí (1831–1907), a wealthy Greek from Edessa in the Ukraine.

The other side of the Maráslion, a large and attractive garden contains the British School at Athens (normally, but incorrectly, known as the British School of Archaeology) and the American School of Classical Studies. Above the American School is the elegant **Gennádhion Library** (1926; Mon, Tues, Fri 09.00–17.00; Wed, Thur 09.00–20.00; Sat 09.00–14.00; shorter hours in midsummer) with wings devoted to Byzantine and Modern Greek studies. It was donated to the School by a former Greek minister in London, and erected by the Carnegie Foundation.

The **British School at Athens**, opened in 1886, is a research centre (hostel, library, archaeological laboratory, etc) for British scholars studying any aspect of Greek life or culture, ancient or modern. Studies are published in the *Annual of the British School at Athens, Archaeological Reports* (see Select bibliography, p 88) and other series. It is known for excavations at Knossos, Mycenae, Perakhora and elsewhere. The **American School of Classical Studies** (1881) performs a similar function for American scholars. Journals in which members' work appear include *Hesperia* and the *American Journal of Archaeology*. Among major excavations are Corinth, Isthmia and the Athenian Agora.

Past the American School is the large and pleasant court of the **Moní Petráki**, a monastery in the 17C and now a theological seminary. The buildings have been much restored but the main church (14C) has antique columns and capitals, and frescoes (18C) by the prolific painter G. Márkou of Argos.

Below the schools is the Evangelismós Hospital, which looks on to Vasilíssis Sofías (see p 228).

13 • Likavittós

From the top of Mt Likavittós (ancient *Lykabettos*)—a prominent conical hill just east of the city centre—there are spectacular panoramic views taking in Athens' striking setting as well as the layout of the city. On a clear day you can experience the magical purity of the renowned Attic light, which shows up crystal clear the lines of buildings in the far distance.

The view contains an intriguing mixture of sea, bare mountainsides and tiers of houses, greenery and concrete, crooked old tiled buildings and tall modern blocks—the elegant and the ramshackle.

In spite of the encroachment of buildings the higher slopes are pleasantly wooded and you can climb to the bare summit by paths among the trees (see below). All approaches are steep. Off the formal path from Loukianoú is a small 16C church of Ayios Isídhoros and on the summit another, dedicated to Ayios Yeóryios.

- **Access on foot**. Map 6,4. From Síntagma, via Kolonáki Square, Odd. Patriárkhou Ioakím and Loukianoú, then a stepped path (3 mins west of the funicular station) to the summit—c 45 mins. Or informal paths from Od. Sarandapíkhou, or Kleoménous (east end)—20 mins from road.

  Access by public transport. **Bus** no. 060 (minibus; for Likavittós, ΛΥΚΑΒΗΤΤΟΣ) from Od. Vas. Iraklíou (far side of National Archaeological Museum; also stops in Akadhimías, behind Academy), to the stop (Likavittós 4th) at the corner of Kleoménous and Ploutárkhou; thence **funicular railway** (most days 09.15–23.45, Thursday 11.15–23.45; €1.47 single, €2.93 return, children €0.73/€1.47; ☎ 210 722 7065) to the summit. About 20–30 mins from the centre, depending on traffic and timetables.

  Access by car/taxi. Via Od. Sarandapíkhou (the Likavittós ring road) and the access road to Likavittós theatre; from here a stepped path leads to the summit. A 10-min drive from central Athens, then 10 min climb.

  Cafés/restaurants. Halfway up the stepped path (good view of the Acropolis) from the top of Loukianoú; an expensive one (09.00–01.00) also on the summit.

Apart from the fine views, the Likavittós summit is the best place to get your bearings. Take a map and street plan. A pair of binoculars is useful, although coin-operated telescopes are provided.

History and legend

Mentioned occasionally in ancient literature, the hill has a legendary origin. The rock of Lykabettos was being carried by Athena for use in the construction of her citadel on the Acropolis. Shocked by the news that Aglauros and Herse (daughters of Kekrops, the first king of Athens) had defied her instructions and looked into a chest in which Erichthonios (a later king of Athens) was concealed, she dropped it in its present position.

In 1941 Likavittós was the operations centre of the Greek Air Force and last mainland HQ of King George until he retreated to Crete before the German advance. Cannon for ceremonial salutes are located here.

The setting

The seaward view is irresistible. In the middle ground is the **Acropolis**, which seems quite modest from this angle, rising above the Agora and the heart of the ancient city. Beyond, the sweep of **Fáliro** (*Phaleron*) **Bay** curls (right) to the hill of Kastélla, the acropolis of ancient **Piraeus**, whose main port is out of sight behind it. Off Piraeus, the island of **Salamína** (*Salamis*) closes the bay of Elefsína (*Eleusis*).

In the other direction (left) you can follow the coast to the point where Mt Imittós runs down to the sea near Vouliagméni. Cape Soúnio (*Sounion*) is further down the coast, unseen. Out at sea is the island of **Aíyina** (*Aegina*) with the sharply conical Mt Oros, sometimes clearly visible, sometimes hidden in the haze.

Athens has expanded to fill most of the plain, which is closed on one side by the sea and on the other three by mountains. **Imittós** (*Hymettos*), to the southeast, is famous for a rosy glow in the light of the setting sun. On its further side lies rural Attica (mod. Attikí), reached either via the coast or inland by a road through the foothills between Imittós and **Pendéli** (*Pentelicon*), the latter heavily scarred by marble quarries. On Pendéli's lower slopes is the lush suburb of Kifissiá. Follow the mass of Imittós (moving behind the church to do so) till it declines to the gap before Pendéli. Further round, through the larger gap between Mt Pendéli and the mass of **Mt Párnitha** (*Parnes*) to the north, run the national highway and railway line to central and northern Greece.

Párnitha blocks the northeastern side of the plain, dividing Attica from Viotía (*Boeotia*). Wild and uninhabited above its lower slopes, the mountain is a world away from the humming city below. The final piece of the frame is the slighter **Mt Aigáleos**, diverging southwest from Párnitha towards the sea beyond Piraeus. Through a gap in Aigáleos, at Dhafní, runs the main road west for Corinth and the Pelopónnisos (*Peloponnese*).

The modern city

The essential structure of modern Athens can be worked out from the seaward end of the terrace.

In the centre are the two main squares, Síntagma and Omónia, linked by Stadhíou and Panepistimíou. The mass of the back of the **parliament building** in the foreground (half-left), locates **Síntagma**.

Looking right from Síntagma, halfway down Panepistimíou you can make out the major triad of public buildings—the **Academy, University** and **National Library**—seeming low among the tall modern blocks; before them, down a side street, you can glimpse a corner of Plateía Kolokotróni, the other side of Stadhíou.

Omónia itself is hidden, but you can see **Od. Ayíou Konstandínou** descending from its lower side.

To the right of Omónia, the **Politekhnío** and **National Archaeological Museum** stand next to each other in Patisíon, mixing old tiled roofs and newer concrete in their construction. Further out are the massive telecommunications dishes on the **OTE building**. Beyond it but further right, in the middle distance, you can see the traffic moving on the national road to the north not far from its junction with the route (west) to the Peloponnese.

In the foreground of the same vista are the low wooded hill of **Stréfi** and beyond it the extensive gardens of the **Pedhíon Areos** in the angle of Patisíon with Leofóros Alexándras; the line of the latter is clear. In the park are the formal buildings of the Skholí Evelpídhon and, partly hidden behind the rock of the Likavittós theatre, the white marble façade of the new law courts. **Mt Tourkovoúni** rises at the back, blocking the view of the gap between Pendéli and Párnitha.

South (left) of Omónia, Athinás, the broad street which joins it to Monastiráki Square at the foot of the Acropolis hill, is largely invisible, though you can catch a glimpse of the busy traffic in a gap between buildings. The **Temple of Hephaistos** at Thisío, about 500m to the west of Monastiráki, stands out prominently on the far side of the ancient Agora.

Ermoú, which links Monastiráki with Síntagma, is narrow and out of sight, but the dome and twin campanili of the **Cathedral** stand out in the parallel Od. Mitropóleos, likewise ascending to Síntagma.

Focussing again on Síntagma, to the left is the **National Garden** and Záppion Hall with its circular core, and beyond is the **Stadium** below the hill of Ardhittós (ancient *Ardettos*). Right of the garden the tall columns of the **Temple of Olympian Zeus** are prominent, and the broad line of **Singroú** which carries traffic to the coast.

From the nearer side of the Parliament building, you can pick up **Vasilíssis Sofías** and follow it round left, past the National Garden and the neoclassical **Saróglio** (Officers' Club), to locate the V-shaped junction with Vasiléos Konstandínou. Here the tall modern **Hilton Hotel** stands opposite the **National Gallery**; beyond them, a wide highway climbs towards Kaisarianí. Higher up and to the left are the massive buildings of the new **University** campus among trees below **Kaisarianí**. Behind the Saróglio, in Vasiléos Konstandínou, is the long, low, marble **Odhío** (College of Music), apparently constructed over part of the recently identified Lyceum (p 225). Beyond it on the other side of the road is the **National Research Centre** (Kéntron Erevnón).

As you look in this direction, half-left and immediately below Likavittós are the huge buildings of the **Evangelismós Hospital** with, nearer you, the more elegant **British and American Archaeological Schools** in a large garden.

Along Vasilíssis Sofías past the Hilton junction is (left) the new marble **Mégaro Mousikís** (Concert Hall), then the United States Embassy. The first of the tall blocks is the **Athens Tower** where Od. Mesoyíon diverges right to pass the muddy-coloured **Pentágono** (Defence Ministry) and swing right towards the declining foothills of Imittós.

Not far on from the Athens Tower is the junction with Alexándras, at Ambelókipi. Beyond the crossing, the road continues as Leofóros Kifissías, another main highway out of Athens, roughly parallel to the national road but serving the northern suburbs.

The hills of Athens and the ancient city

Although the plain in which modern Athens stands is in parts quite flat, several hills not only give it a particular character but are a help in orientation. They have exercised a positive influence on the layout of both the modern city and its ancient, much smaller, predecessor.

Some of these hills are remnants of the Tourkovoúni (ancient *Anchesmos*) range. The most prominent of these are long, bare-topped **Tourkovoúni** itself, which rises inland, and Likavittós, with the smaller wooded peak of **Stréfi** (p 218) and the tiny **Skhistí Pétra** above Plateía Likavittoú.

In the seaward direction is the **Acropolis**. Behind it, the **Hill of the Muses** (*Mouseion*) is crowned by the prominent monument and tomb of Philópappos. Circling round to the right from the Acropolis and hardly distinguishable from each other are the **Areópagos**, the **Pnyx** and the **Hill of the Nymphs**. The last named is topped by the dome of the old Observatory. The open area below them is the **ancient Agora**, with the Temple of Hephaistos at Thisío prominent on the further side.

From the bottom right-hand corner of the Agora a strand of green leads your eye to the site of the **Kerameikós**, identifiable by a large church and the buildings of the former Athens Gas Works (Gázi; p 182) close by.

From the Kerameikós ran the Sacred Way to Eleusis. Its modern successor the **Ierá Odhós** (inland, or right, of the Kerameikós) follows the long green patch of the **Votanikós** (Botanic Gardens). In this direction was the ancient Academy. Beyond and to the left the broad tracks of the state railway are clearly visible. Od.

Piraiós can be made out as a line halfway between the railway and the sea, heading for Piraeus. The electric railway (Metró Line 1; and see below) is invisible but runs parallel to Od. Piraiós, then loops away to Néo Fáliro, before heading for Piraeus.

The Acropolis and the Agora lay at the heart of the domestic quarters of the ancient city, but some important places, such as the Academy and the Stadium, were outside the walls.

The fortifications of Athens

Likavittós is a good viewpoint from which to plot the fortifications of Athens throughout her history.

Mycenaean Only the Acropolis was fortified (p 102, etc).

Archaic No Archaic fortifications are known.

Classical The walled circuit, originally constructed under **Themistokles**, which defended Athens from the early 5C BC, can be roughly located by reference to a few key points close to its course. Starting at the Dipylon gate in the Kerameikós, it ran towards present-day Omónia, then parallel to and on the far side of Stadhíou and, below Síntagma, to the Temple of Olympian Zeus. From there it headed for the Mouseion hill.

The **Long Walls**, also 5C, were the Northern Wall, the Phaleric Wall and the Southern Wall. The last was slightly later in date and subsequently superseded the Phaleric Wall. From a point on the seaward side of the city circuit, at the Hill of the Nymphs, the Northern Long Wall followed the line of modern Od. Piraiós. The course of the Phaleric Wall is not entirely certain (see R.L. Scranton in *AJA* 1938) but it may have run from below the Mouseion Hill just to the west of Leofóros Singroú, following a line of low hills now obscured by building, through the suburb of Néa Smírni, to the coast at Palaió Fáliro, not far east of the point at which Singroú reaches the coast.

The Southern Long Wall started near the later monument of Philópappos on Mouseion Hill and followed the line of the electric railway to Piraeus.

Thus the first system protected the whole of Phaleron Bay, while the second provided a fortified connection between the defences of Athens and those of Piraeus.

Roman The **Valerian Wall** (mid-3C AD) was mostly built on the remains of its predecessor but the circuit was extended at the east to take in a roughly triangular shaped area which included (in modern terms) the Parliament building and had its apex near the Presidential Palace, on Iródhou Attikoú. Sections of the wall have been found in the National Garden.

The **Late Roman** (or Post-Herulian) **Wall** enclosed a very much smaller area on the north slope of the Acropolis. Its walls reached inland from the east and west extremities of the Acropolis, with the northern part incorporating the south wall of the Library of Hadrian, close to Monastiráki. The cathedral (see p 146) in Mitropoleos is not far outside its northern line.

Medieval In the 11C(?) the wall called **Rizókastro** ran round the lower slopes of the Acropolis at the level of the Theatre of Dionysos.

Early Ottoman (after 1456) These fortifications made use of the Late Roman Wall with the propylon of Hadrian's Library as a gate, also relying on the outer walls of houses on the perimeter to form a circuit.

Later Ottoman The fortification of **Serpentzés** was on the west and south slopes of the Acropolis (p 129), and thus invisible from Likavittós; the **Wall of**

Ipapandís (p 129) ran from the west entrance to about halfway along the north slope. The Ottoman **Wall of Hasekí** (1778) followed the line of the Themistoklean wall but with gates in different positions.

14 • Síntagma to Ambelókipi via Vasilíssis Sofías

A broad, busy and important avenue, Vasilíssis Sofías has several embassies and official buildings, as well as excellent museums and galleries: the Benáki Museum, the Goulandrís Museum of Cycladic and Ancient Greek Art, the Byzantine Museum, the War Museum and the National Gallery. For sightseeing, the route is best taken in sections, or at least broken by an early lunch (perhaps at the outstandingly good *Fátsio*—p 35).

- **Distance on foot**. Maps 6,7–8; 7,5–4. 2. 3km (1.3km to the Hilton/National Gallery).
  Access by public transport. **Trolley buses** nos. 3, 8 from Patisíon, Kánningos or Akadhimías. The Síntagma stop is in Vas. Sofías. For the return, substitute no. 7 for no. 8. Several suburban **buses** cover this route, or the first part of it.

At the top of Panepistimíou turn left into Leofóros Vasilíssis Sofías (Queen Sofia St), with embassies and ministries to the left, some in fine old mansions. The first major junction is with Akadhimías, opposite the side of the Parliament building next to the National Gardens.

Benáki Museum
At the junction with Od. Koubári, is the Benáki Museum (Mon, Wed, Fri, Sat 09.00–17.00; Thur 09.00–24.00; Sun 09.00–15.00; closed Tues; café/restaurant; shops. Note: Meals in the restaurant on Thurs evening must be booked in advance (☎ 210 367 1000. Entry free on Thurs).

Perhaps the most eclectic and intriguing museum in Athens, it represents the fruits of a lifetime's collecting by Andónis Benáki (1873–1954), born into the Greek community in Egypt. He donated them to the Greek state, together with his house, in 1931. The museum has since been extended several times and was reopened in July 2000, after further extension and complete reorganisation of the exhibitions and technical facilities. The fine collection of Islamic pottery, bronzes, etc are to be located in another building at Kerameikós.

The displays succeed both in bringing out the visual appeal of the individual objects and in demonstrating their contribution to the character and continuity of Hellenic culture from antiquity to the present day. Although they are presented in roughly chronological order, thematic considerations take precedence.

No summary description can do justice to the extraordinary range and richness of the contents which are perhaps most interesting to the majority of visitors for the picture they provide of **post-Classical** Greek history and culture.

Ground floor The entrance hall and front rooms recall the building's period as a private residence. Paintings include two preliminary studies by Ghízis and a seascape by Volonákis.

Galleries I–VIII Prehistoric and Classical antiquity to the end of the Roman period: **I** Neolithic pottery and **figurines**; obsidian; Early Bronze Age pottery. **II** Early Cycladic marble figures and vases; Minoan, Mycenaean and Cypriot Bronze Age objects; Early Helladic and Mycenaean **gold**- and silver-work; Geometric vases and metal objects; Daedalic figurines; some Orientalising and Archaic pottery, including pieces with **relief decoration**. **III** Orientalising and Archaic pottery, including Corinthian and Attic (some with interesting mythological scenes) and figurines; bronze and gold objects; stone sculpture; a Corinthian terracotta revetment. **IV** Classical red-figure and white-ground pottery; terracotta and bronze figurines (note the small bronze **Herakles**); helmets and weaponry; architecture and sculpture (Roman copy of the Hermes of Alkamenes). **V** Sculpture, including copies of heads of Athena by Alkamenes and of the Apollo Sauroktonos (Lizard-slayer) by Praxiteles. **VI** Vases with scenes in relief; grave relief; decorated bronze mirrors; gold wreaths and jewellery; votive terracotta figures. **VII** Attic black-glaze, Attic and Apulian red-figure, and Cypriot pottery; Hadra ware, Megarian bowls, Alexandrian pottery with relief scenes; jewellery and bronze and silver vessels; faience, marble and terracotta figures and heads; sculpture; part of Boeotian grave stele; Hellenistic/Roman gold and silver, including the **Thessaly Treasure**; Roman pottery, figurines, gold amulets and jewellery, glass and bronze vessels. **VIII** Roman funerary and other sculpture; architectural fragments; gold jewellery; gold and ivory figurines; ivory plaques; sculptures from Gandhara, Palmyra and Phrygia (**grave relief**) in Late Antique style.

Galleries IX–XII Early Christian, Byzantine and early Post-Byzantine. **IX** Early Christian domestic vessels of glass, bronze and terracotta; jewellery; bronzes; decorated silver vessels (both mythological and Christian subjects); coins; Egyptian **funerary portraits** (3C AD), encaustic icons and fragments of 7–8C **paintings**; decorated textiles, architectural pieces. **X** Replica of apse mosaic from Ay. Sophia, Constantinople; 13C double-sided icon of the Virgin and Child (Brephokratousa); part of **mosaic** of the Virgin from the Studios monastery, Constantinople; illuminated books; jewellery; bronzes; coins; silver icon; fragments of wall-painting; part of marble templon; stone **relief** with military saints; sgraffito pottery (10–15C). **XI–XII** Outstanding **icons** of 13–16C, many of Cretan schools; gold-embroidered veil with Christ and the Communion of the Apostles; in XII, note **St Ann and the Virgin** (attrib. to Angelos Akontatos); silver bull of Demetrios Palaiologos, 1456; composite carved and gilded wooden iconostasis; icon (military saints) of the important 16C painter **Michael Damaskinos** (16C), showing Renaissance influences; two icons signed by **El Greco** (*St. Luke*; *Adoration of the Magi*); manuscripts and maps.

First floor

Galleries XIII–XXVIII Greek culture during the years of Ottoman occupation (17C-early 19C): secular and ecclesiastical objects, including clothes, textiles, furniture, pictures and memorabilia. **XIII** The Dodecanese, Cyclades and Cyprus: map of Crete, c 1700; many splendid **embroideries** (including a *sperveri* (bed-tent) from Rhodes); costume; rugs; furniture and carved and/or **painted** wooden objects; Iznik and Kütahya pottery; marble **door frames** and fanlights, also relief sculptures, from Ios, Tínos and ?Sífnos; gold jewellery. **XIV** Similar fine material from the northern Greek islands and Asia Minor. Note especially the furniture, embroidery and pottery from **Skíros** and the partial reconstruction of a Skirian sitting room; decorated plates from Turkey (Cannakale), Italy and France; jewellery. **XV** Northern Greece and Asia Minor, Thrace and Macedonia. **XVI** Paintings, copper engravings with panoramas of Constantinople, embroideries, jewellery, metalwork, etc from Asia Minor. **XVII–XX** Objects from Macedonia and Epirus include (**XVII**) the entire carved and painted wooden panelling of the reception room of a house in Kozáni c 1750, with European and Ottoman, as well as traditional Byzantine, elements; the other (Stathátos) room (**XIX**) is similar in style and date; ceiling paintings from a house in Kastoriá, c 1800; gold- and silver-work (**XX**) for which Epirus and Macedonia were particularly known; inlaid chests and casket. **XXI** Thessaly, west and northwest Greece, the Ionian islands. Similar material, including embroidery and costume, jewellery, pottery, lead and tin vessels; paintings by 18C & 19C visitors (Dodwell, Cartwright, etc); sedan chair. **XXII** Paintings (Lear, Williams, etc) showing sites in the Peloponnese; costume, embroidery and carved furniture; some sculpture, including coat of arms from the Benáki family mansion in Kalamáta. **XXIII** Numerous watercolours, etc (especially of Athens), with a drawing of Khalkís (1844) and an eyewitness scene of the bombardment and explosion of the Parthenon in 1687; views of ancient monuments, rural life and scenery; Sir William Gell's sketchbook; material relating to Byron; view of Marathon (oil) by Edward Lear (1854); tombstone (1916) from Marathon; Attic and other costume. **XXIV** Saronic Gulf islands. Carved and painted interior of a house on Idhra (1800); paintings, costume etc. **XXV–VI** Ecclesiastical art. Vestments, church plate, carved and gilded furniture, embroideries—many intricately worked and decorated pieces; icons; silver-covered gospels. **XXVII** 17 and 18C ecclesiastical painting etc. Parts of carved wooden iconostases; numerous icons, including a monumental Transfiguration, c 1600, and a 17C Macedonian Virgin Odegetria, with elements in relief (stucco); ritual equipment. **XXVIII** Elaborate items of church plate and three icons.

Second floor

This is mainly occupied by the café/restaurant, temporary exhibition gallery and lecture room. The small **rooms XXIX–XXXII** illustrate aspects of daily life: music and dancing, publications of the Greek Enlightenment, sea travel (including ex-votos), agricultural production, home-made artefacts, especially wooden and ceramic.

Third floor (not thoroughly labelled)
Vestibule, Galleries XXXIII–XXXVI. Greek culture from the revolution in 1821 to the present day: **XXXIII** Pictures, weapons, memorabilia, etc illustrate the lives of figures associated with the revolution—the national poet Dionysios Solomós, Lord Byron, Rígas Feraíos, Ali Pashá of Ioannina, Ipsilántis, Patriarch Gregory V, the Souliot women, Archbishop Germanós of Patras, Kolokotrónis (his **flag** bearing the legend 'Freedom or Death'), Karaïskákis, Bouboulína, Miaoúlis, Kanáris, and other figures and incidents. **XXXIV** Setbacks in the Greek campaign; the election and arrival of Kapodístria, first president of Greece, at Náfplio (painting); further paintings and memorabilia; paintings to accompany the memoirs of General Makryiánnis (1797–1864) by the **Zográfos** family.

XXXV The Liberation of Greece and the court of Otho, its first monarch. 32 lithographs by P. von Hess of scenes related to the Liberation; royal memorabilia; contemporary costume. **XXXVI** The Cretan uprising of 1866–69; Greek monarchs and politicians (especially Elefthérios Venizélos); wars in the 19C and 20C; the Asia Minor defeat in 1922; court costume. Modern Greek artistic life and achievement are represented by a substantial number of 19C and 20C paintings by major artists (Bouziánis, Diamandópoulos, Ghíka, Kóntoglou, Móralis, Pantazís, Papaloukás, Parthénis, Tsaroúkhis, Volonákis), and manuscripts and mementoes of poets such as Kaváfis, Sikelianós, Rítsos, Seféris and Elítis—the last two being Nobel prize winners.

By the side of the Benáki Museum, Od. Koubári leads quickly into Kolonáki Square (p 215). Opposite Koubári, Od. Iródhou Attikoú runs beside the National Gardens to the Stadium (p 190). On the corner are the **Barracks of the Evzónes** who provide the ceremonial guard (p 141) for the Tomb of the Unknown Soldier. Further down Iródhou Attikoú (left) is the modest **Presidential Palace** (Ziller, 1890), residence of the king after the restoration of 1935, and of the president since Greece became a republic in 1974.

Two streets beyond the Benáki Musem is Od. Neofítou Dhoúka, with the N.P. Goulandrís Foundation and **Goulandrís Museum of Cycladic and Ancient Greek Art**, opened in 1986 (Mon, Wed–Fri 10.00–16.00; Sat 10.00–15.00; closed Sun and Tues; half-price on Sat; shop; pleasant café). The exhibition space available in the original museum has been extended by the acquisition of the **Stathátos mansion**, on Vasilíssis Sofías, a fine town house designed by Ziller (1885). The two are connected by a passage.

The museum has a good collection of ancient art from Prehistoric to Roman times, with some outstanding individual objects; it is particularly rich in **marble figurines** and other material of the Cycladic Early Bronze Age. These figures, most often of the female folded-arm type, vary considerably in scale. The majority have been found in graves (about 10 per cent of graves contain figures), though some come from settlements. Their function is much debated, but they must have had religious significance.

On the ground floor are explanatory panels (temporarily removed to the fourth floor in favour of another exhibition). The first floor has Cycladic (mostly Early Bronze Age) pottery, marble vases and figures (most of modest size but one c 1.4m, possibly a cult statue), metal weapons and vessels, some obsidian. The second floor displays objects of the Prehistoric (non-Cycladic) to Hellenistic periods—pottery, terracottas, jewellery and other metalwork, glass. Temporary exhibitions are housed on the third floor, and the fourth floor has the C and R Polítis collection of Prehistoric and Classical art.

Access to the new wing (Stathátos mansion) is via the entrance hall. The house, with neoclassical details (note the rooftop terracotta sculptures above the Vas. Sofías entrance), has been beautifully restored. Off the lovely circular hall are rooms with the antiquities collection of the Athens Academy and modern art. On the first floor temporary exhibitions are displayed, often of exceptional interest. As the main road bends left, an imposing building on the opposite side (corner of Riyílis) is the Saróglio or **Officers' Club** (1924) of the Greek armed forces.

Behind it (at present you need to walk a few yards down Riyíllis and peer through holes in the fence), in 1997, were identified remains of the Lyceum (Líkio), one of the three great Athenian gymnasia of antiquity and long sought by archaeologists.

A large building with a courtyard and stoas must be the palaistra of the **Lyceum Gymnasium**. The southern part of the palaistra lies beneath the Athens Odhío (Odeion College of Music). Extensive watercourses found in the excavations harmonise with ancient reports that the area was well irrigated from the source of the Eridanos on nearby Mt Likavittós.

> ### The Lyceum
> According to ancient writers the Lyceum (named after a shrine of Apollo Lykeios) was beyond the Diokharous gate, on the slopes of Lykabettos. In addition to more normal functions, it provided a parade ground for youths in military training and at one time also housed the office of the polemarch (the third archon, who was in charge of military matters). In 335 BC Aristotle set up his philosophical school in the Lyceum: his disciples acquired their name 'peripatetics' from their custom of walking in a *peripatos* (colonnade) as they conversed. Some 250 years later the Roman general Sulla cut down the trees of the Lyceum to make siege engines.

Excavation evidence for original building in the 4C BC, its destruction in the 1C BC, then subsequent rebuilding, and further destruction in the 3C AD, all fit ancient references to the first monumental construction under Lykourgos and the damage by Sulla followed, much later, by the Herulians.

The Byzantine Museum
The Byzantine Museum (strictly the Byzantine and Christian Museum), next to the site of the Lyceum, occupies the fine Villa Ilíssia built in 1848 in a Florentine style by the architect Kleánthis for the Duchesse de Plaisance (see overleaf). The museum was installed in 1930 and has been recently extended.

> Born in the USA of French and American parents, Sophie de Marbois (1785–1854) married one of Napoleon's generals, from whom she got her title **Duchesse de Plaisance** ('Plakentía' in Greek). They were later divorced. Cultured but eccentric, a strong supporter of the Greek revolution, and initially a friend of Kapodhístria, she came to Greece in 1830. The circle she received here included the sculptor David d'Angers, and the writers Edmond About and Théophile Gautier.

The museum (Tues–Sun 08.30–15.00; closed Mon) provides an excellent introduction to Early Christian and Byzantine art and architecture. Particularly helpful is the layout of Rooms II–IV as church interiors of successive periods, with characteristic architectural features, furnishings and decoration. The austere clarity of Early Christian sculpture, rarely surviving in situ, is well illustrated. The icons and wall paintings are fine, but less didactically presented. (For more background information see under Art and architecture, pp 79–83).

From the ticket office, you cross a large court in the centre of which is a copy of a fountain shown in one of the mosaics in the church at Dhafní. In front of it is a 4C mosaic and the quatrefoil font from the church of Ayy. Apóstoli in the Agora. Sculptural fragments to the right of the court are from basilicas of the 5C–7C; those to the left from churches of the 9C–15C. In the surrounding arcades are mosaics and architectural members.

To the right is the entrance to the new galleries, mostly below court level, at present used for temporary exhibitions. From the exit you get a good view of the other side of the original building, then walk round to enter it from the court.

Ground floor

In the entrance portico are sculpted architectural members, and a *simantron* (a wooden board struck to call the faithful to church). The vestibule has examples of Early Christian sculpture of the 4C–6C. A doorway comes from **Ay. Dhimítrios** in Thessaloníki; there are inscribed fragments of a cornice from the Acropolis, as well as other columns, capitals, etc and heads from the decoration of a sarcophagus.

You turn right into **room II**, set out and furnished as a 5C–6C **three-aisled basilica**. The *naos* is divided from the *hieron/iero* by transennae and a central free standing arch. In the apse is a semicircular *synthronon* and a *cathedra* in the centre. The *iera trapeza* is a square table with a circular central depression, set on four columns. Below is a reliquary in the form of a miniature sarcophagus, sunk into a cruciform slot. In the prothesis and diaconicon are reliefs and inscriptions. On the right side of the nave is a copy of an *ambo* from Thessaloníki, and a 4C marble prothesis table, decorated with animals in the Hellenistic tradition.

Round the walls a wide variety of **sculpture** illustrates the Christian interest in symbolic motifs, in plant and animal decoration, and in heraldic schemes; other motifs, such as the *Good Shepherd*, *Sirens* and *Sphinxes*, were inherited from pagan antiquity. In the right aisle is a charming relief of the nativity (95); in the left, a funerary relief showing *Orpheus and animals*; on the back wall are various thorakia. To either side of the altar are inscriptions, one on a wooden cross.

To the left is **room III** with **sculpture**, mainly of the 11C–12C, including some Frankish. On the lower walls are several thorakia, with relief decoration using typical Byzantine motifs, both symbols and figures. On the **left (west) wall** are two marble icons of the Virgin (*Brephokratousa* and *Hodegetria*, two iconographic types; the terms mean 'holding the child' and 'showing the way'). Marble arches from Franco-Byzantine tombs have representations of the *Descent into Hell*. A thorakion (161) is decorated with a tree of life flanked by lions and surrounded by a Cufic inscription. On the upper north wall are reliefs with pagan mythological subjects (176, *Herakles and the Erymanthian Boar*; 178, *Centaur playing a lyre*), probably from secular buildings. 175 is a 4C BC grave relief adapted to Byzantine ideas. On the **east wall** is (150) a fine marble plaque with a carving, painted in encaustic (a form of inlay using hot wax), of three apostles, from the Moní Vlatádhon, Thessaloníki. An arch (155) from the entrance to a Franco-Byzantine church has reliefs of the nativity. A capital (217) has a monogram of Irene, empress of Constantinople (AD 797–802). On the **south wall** are reliefs of the Frankish period, including heads (246, etc) of Venetian doges, from Corfú.

Room IV reproduces a **domed-inscribed-cross church** (p 80) of the 11C. The sanctuary is separated from the nave by a marble templon. This has a sculptured architrave (a copy of that from the Byzantine phase of the Erechtheion) above pillars with capitals; the lower part has thorakia. In the floor under the dome is a rectangular central slab with a sculptured eagle, symbol of the Byzantine emperors. The floor of the sanctuary is in *opus alexandrinum*. The carvings are from Athenian churches.

Room V is a **Post-Byzantine church** type, a simplified basilican form, square and plain (though the flat ceiling is inaccurate). The decoration, mostly 18C, shows some Ottoman influence. The ornate wooden iconostasis, reconstructed out of fragments from Ithaka and Kefallinía, has elaborate carved decoration and the usual icons. The bishop's throne was brought from Asia Minor in 1923. The painted *epitaphios* from Kímolos was used in procession at the feast of the Koímisis. A *choros* hangs from the ceiling with wooden icons suspended from it. On the walls are good fragments of frescoes from Athens (Ay. Filothéi), Atalándi and Delphi.

First floor

This is reached via the outside portico. Room numbering continues from the Ground Floor. The vestibule, **room VI** has icons and two examples of 'Royal Doors', the doors which lead into the sanctuary from the nave. **Room VII** has the main display of **icons**, some of them very fine. They vary (see p 82) in type (some are double-sided) and belong mostly to the 14C–15C; several come from Asia Minor. It is invidious to make a selection. Unusual are (89) a 13C relief panel with *St George* from Kastoriá and (145) a mosaic icon of the *Virgin Episkepsis (Glykophilousa)* from Trilia on the Sea of Marmara. A double-sided icon (177) of the 14C combines the *Virgin Hodegetria* surrounded by panels illustrating the *Dodekaorto* with, on the other side, the *Preparation of the Throne*. New accessions include a 12C *Raising of Lazarus*, and some good icons of the *Virgin*.

Room VIII contains interesting, mainly 13C, **frescoes** from churches at Merénda and Oropós (Attica), Tánagra, Lakonía, Náxos and Antíkira among other places. Examples of Byzantine **minor arts** include pottery flasks and lamps, bread stamps, glass, metal vessels, ivories, jewellery and crucifixes.

The Villa Ilíssia, now the Byzantine Museum

Room IX also has minor arts—objects in wood, metal (much of it decorated) and ivory; and a good collection of Byzantine and Post-Byzantine pottery. **Room X** has **vestments** in chronological sequence including Coptic pieces of the 5C–7C; also croziers and icons sheathed in silver.

Opposite the Byzantine Museum, in Od. Ploutárkhou is the architecturally unappealing **British Embassy**. The ambassador's residence in the parallel Od. Loukianoú is an attractive older building.

Next door to the Byzantine Museum, with its entrance at the far side, in Od. Rizári, is the **War Museum** (Polemikó Mouseío, ΠΟΛΕΜΙΚΟ ΜΟΥΣΕΙΟ: Tues–Sat 09.00–14.00, Sun and holidays 09.30–14.00, closed Mon; café in basement), an unusually successful modern building constructed under the military dictatorship (1967–74) to demonstrate the prowess of Greek arms through the ages.

Outside are several aircraft, with access ladders, and a range of missiles and heavy artillery, the latter dating from the 19C Wars of Independence onwards. In the centre is a pleasant courtyard.

On the ground floor is the outstanding **Pétros Saróglou collection** of armour and weapons of various periods, especially the 19C.

At the **mezzanine** level are displays mainly relating to the Second World War—the Middle East, including El Alamein; Rimini; the Ierós Lókhos brigade formed out of Greek officers in exile; the German occupation; the Liberation. Also illustrated is the Greek participation in the Korean War. A final gallery is devoted to Cyprus from antiquity to the present day.

The most extensive displays are on the **first floor**. There is a paucity of original material but the many photographs, maps, plans, models, paintings and prints are comprehensive and well chosen to illustrate sites, artefacts and personalities. Room A covers Neolithic to Classical periods, including part of the Váos collection of Melian obsidian. Room B deals with the campaigns of Alexander the Great; Room Γ, the Byzantine wars; Room Δ, the Turkish occupation (good prints). Room ΣΤ, the Greek Wars of Independence of 1821–28; Room Z, the period 1828–1908; Room H, the Balkan wars; Room Θ, the Balkan Wars/First World War, 1912–18. Room I (subdivided) covers the Asia Minor campaign, 1919–22; the Italian War of 1940; the German invasion and occupation of 1941; the Battle of Crete; regimental flags and roll of honour. In the **basement** is a chronological display of uniforms and more material from the Saróglou collection; also an auditorium and the café.

A little further on (left), a small public garden fronts the huge **Evangelismós Hospital**, founded in 1881. A new wing with 483 beds was opened in 1983, the gift of John Diamandís Patéras, after whom the section of Od. Alopekís behind the hospital has been renamed.

Opposite the Evangelismós, Vasilíssis Sofías meets Leofóros Vasiléos Konstandínou in a major V-junction by the towering Hilton Hotel. Opposite the hotel stands the huge *Droméas* (Runner; 1988), a figure made out of slabs of glass by Kóstas Varótsos. Leofóros Vasiléos Alexándrou drops past the Hilton, then climbs towards the suburb of Kaisarianí on the lower slopes of Imittós. In the V formed by the junction of V. Sofías and V. Konstandínou is an attractive park.

National Art Gallery

On the corner of Vas. Konstandínou and Vas. Alexándrou, opposite the Hilton, stands the National Art Gallery (Ethnikí Pinakothíki, ΕΘΝΙΚΗ ΠΙΝΑΚΟΘΗΚΗ; Mon–Sat 09.00–15.00, also Mon and Wed only 18.00–21.00, Sun 10.00–14.00; closed Tues). Strictly named the 'National Gallery and Aléxandros Soútzos Museum', the institution was established in 1954 with the consolidation of the former National Gallery (founded 1900) and the Aléxandros Soútzos legacy, left to the nation in 1886 for the foundation of a museum of painting. According to the donor's wish, the formal title incorporates his father's name. The endowment was unexploited until 1954; construction began in 1964 and the gallery was opened in 1976. The collection also includes works belonging to the E. Koutlídhis Foundation. The front hall and lower galleries are often occupied by temporary exhibitions. There are occasional concerts, recitals, dance performances, etc.

The excellent **Permanent Collection**, on two floors, is reached by a passageway opposite the entrance. Reopened in Dec 2000, it is the only comprehensive collection of 19C and early 20C Greek art and should certainly be seen, both for the quality of some of the work—virtually unknown in western Europe—and for the light it sheds on Greek cultural history. Note that contemporary art is better represented in the Vorrés Museum in Paianía (☎ 210 664 2639 but not described in this Guide), the Pierídhis Museum in Glifádha (p 247) and the Frisíras Museum in Pláka (p 171). See also the Museum of Contemporary Art, p 234.

On the ground floor (left) are a selection of the Gallery's Western European paintings and (right) Greek work of the 19C. Upstairs is the 20C material (including artists born up till 1940). Some sculpture is in the main exhibition; other works are displayed in the garden but this is not always accessible and the pieces there are badly labelled. The galleries have clear and helpful wall-panels, which add considerably to the following short summary; the basic handbook, *Four centuries of Greek painting*, 2000, has good illustrations and an informative text.

Western European paintings

Many are by minor artists or of uncertain attribution. Interesting works include two 14C Crucifixions, one from the workshop of Paolo Veneziano, the other attributed to the Master of the Pesaro Crucifixion. An Episode from Genesis (?) is attributed to Mariotto Albertinelli (1474–1515).

Note also *St Margaret* (c 1550), from the workshop of Jacopo Tintoretto. Flemish painting includes several works by the Brueghel family (Jan Brueghel II, *The rest during the flight into Egypt*). *Elizer and Rebecca*, c 1730, is attributed to Giovanni Tiepolo. Later paintings include a *Still Life* (1866) by Fantin Latour. A prime place is given to **Delacroix**'s exquisite *Greek Warrior* (1856). Also here is Rodin's fine bronze, *The Prodigal Son* (1889).

The reserve collections contain a substantial number of prints by Dürer, Goya and Manet; also paintings by 20C French masters, including Picasso, Albert Marquet, Utrillo and Picabia, which were presented to the Greek people to commemorate their country's liberation from German occupation.

The Greek paintings

The display begins with works by **El Greco** (*Concert of Angels*—detail, *St Francis of Assisi, Crucifixion*) and Post-Byzantine icons of the Cretan-Italian and Ionian schools.

Late 18C portraits by **Nikólaos Koutoúzis** (1741–1813) and **Nikólaos Kantoúnis** (1767–1834), both from the Ionian island of Zákinthos, show the influence of western (chiefly Italian) attitudes to both style and the function of painting which were new to Greece. The Ionian islands were never under Turkish control and thus more accessible to foreign influence though, until the late 18C, this was negligible in comparison with that of the Byzantine tradition.

The nineteenth century

The 19C material can be roughly divided into two groups: the Greek Mainstream and Genre painting.

Mainstream. The most important painters are **Nikifóros Lítras** (1832–1904), **Nikólaos Ghízis** (1842–1901) and **Yióryios Iakovídhis** (1853–1932). The first two, educated in Germany, were strongly influenced directly by the Munich School. Ghízis in particular emulates the German Romantic movement in choice of subject, sober palette and often turbulent brushstrokes (*Destruction at Psará*, 1878). Lítras excelled in scenes and characters from the café, the street and the family circle. His work is lighter and less anguished than that of Ghízis. Iakovídhis paints in the tradition of Lítras, but with more impressionistic results in both colour and execution (*Children's concert*, 1900).

Genre. This group consists mainly of historical, seascape and portrait painting. **Theódhoros Vrizákis** (1814–78) is the main interpreter of the epic **historical** style, depicting scenes from the Greek War of Independence (*Lord Byron at Mesolongi*; 1861). Chief exponents of **seascapes** in the latter part of the 19C were **Konstandínos Volonákis** (1837–1907), **Ioánnis Altamoúras** (1852–78) and **Vasílis Khatzís** (1870–1915). These artists are represented by many interesting, and often lovely, seascapes and admirably executed naval battles.

The 19C and 20C groups are bridged by the work of **Konstandínos Parthénis** (1878–1967; many examples). This Alexandria-born artist has had a considerable influence on the course of Greek painting, since he established the Impressionist style and introduced Art Nouveau elements. His many themes included religious, mythological and landscape subjects. His later work, influenced by Byzantine art, has a spiritual and idealistic character (*Musicians*, 1930–35).

The twentieth century

From c 1900 to 1950 Greek painting was characterised by pluralism of expression. In contrast to the 19C, when most Greek artists culled inspiration from the Munich School, the 20C had three main sources: the Byzantine and Classical heritage, the Folk and popular tradition, and the contemporary European mainstream. Among the more significant artists of the period are the following.

Fótis Kóntoglou (?1898–1965), who came to Greece from Asia Minor in 1922 and was one of the first artists in Greece to draw directly on the Byzantine heritage. Much of his early painting of secular themes was in a Byzantine manner (wall paintings at his home in Kipriádhi, Athens, 1927). In later work he concentrated mainly on ecclesiastical decoration and hagiography.

Konstandínos Maléas (1879–1928) and **Spíros Papaloukás** (1892–1957) reflect the initial influences of Parisian art in Greece, particularly in their treatment of light and of the flat surfaces of colour as, for instance, in Maléas' *Monemvasia* (1918–28). **Yióryios Bouziánis** (1885–1959), the leading Greek exponent of Expressionism, studied in Paris and subsequently in Munich. Curiously, his palette differs from that of the German Expressionists, being dark and sombre. **Yánnis Tsaroúkhis** (1910–89; see also the Tsaroúkhis Museum, p 249) was influenced both by the popular tradition and by modern trends which he combined to create original paintings with a vital local character (*Kafeneion To Neon*, 1935). In his early work **Yánnis Móralis** (1916–; see also p 171) drew on Classical prototypes for the human figure (*Mourning*, n. d.). His later, more abstract, paintings again show Classical derivation in the innate balance and equilibrium of composition. **Níkos Engonópoulos** (1910–86), also a poet, was the most important representative of Surrealism in Greece but his bold bright colours produce a more exuberant version of the style.

Alékos Kontópoulos (1905–75) is important as the painter who introduced Abstract art to Greece after 1950. However, his later paintings usually included some recognisable form or image. **Yánnis Spirópoulos** (1912–90), Greece's foremost abstract artist, won international acclaim after being awarded the Unesco prize at the 1960 Venice Biennale. His predominantly dark and heavily textured paintings are flat, without spatial depth, and have well-structured and tectonic compositions.

A leading Greek painter of the 20C, extensively represented in the gallery, is **Nikos Khatzikiriákos-Ghíkas** (1906–94; see also p 141), the main Greek exponent of Cubism. *Open door* (1927) is the earliest work. *Barracks* (1927) represents a Surrealist stage which preceded his Cubism. The 1950s were the most fertile and significant stage in his career, as can be seen in *Athenian balcony* (1955) and *Sunflower and trellis* (1956).

Other significant artists whose work reflects various currents in later 20C Greek painting include Panayiótis Tétsis (1925–), Níkos Kessanlís (1930–), Kóstas Tsóklis (1930–; see also p 261), and Dhimítris Mitarás (1934–).

The gallery has a small collection of works of the self-taught primitive painter **Theófilos Khatzimikhaïl** (1878–1934; see also Museum of Folk Art p 171 and *Blue Guide Greece*, 6th edn, p 425), now much admired. His interpretations of religious, popular and mythological themes are striking; the naive and detailed style full of narrative.

Sculpture

Among the most important 19C sculptors is **Pávlos Prosaléntis** the elder (1784–1837), who worked chiefly in marble and was largely responsible for reviving the art in Greece (*Plato*, 1815). **Dhimítrios Philippótis** (1834–1920) and **Yióryios Vroútos** (1843–1909) also worked in marble. While Prosaléntis preferred realistic themes taken from daily life, Philippótis and Vroútos drew on subjects from mythology (*Echo*, 1887). Vroútos' work is executed in the tradition of Classical sculpture, except when he indulged in sculptural acrobatics and produced precariously balanced works like *The Spirit of Copernicus* (1877). Leonídhas Dhrósis (1834–1882; *Penelope*, 1873), one of many sculptors from the island of Tinos, still known for its artists and marble-workers, was responsible for much of the neoclassical decoration of the Academy (p 142).

Yiannoúlis Khalepás (1851–1937) is one of Greece's most important and creative sculptors. Among his commissions were several tombstones (p 190). In the gallery a collection of small clay works, such as *Secret* (1925) and *Aphrodite* (1931), in which the subject consists of a head or bust combined with a small figurine, reveal a strange—in effect schizophrenic—coexistence of clumsiness and vitality. In fact Khalepás suffered bouts of serious mental illness. His small clay works have an inner tension which imbues them with a forceful presence.

Among the 20C sculptors, several of whom are represented by public works in the streets and squares of Athens, the most remarkable are **Mikhaílis Tómbros** (1889–1974; see also p 191), whose simplified forms, in marble and bronze, are often loosely based on ancient prototypes; Mikhaílis Lekákis (1907–87), whose interesting wooden abstract forms are labyrinthine and free (*Rhythm*, 1959–74); Khrístos Kaprálos (1909–93; *Horse's head*); Thanássis Apártis (1889–1972; *Woman washing*, 1943); Akhilléas Apergís (1909–86); and Konstandínos Andréou (1917–) who makes abstract-constructivist sculptures from welded metal sheets. Similarly orientated is the work of Tloupás Filólaos (1923–) and Konstandínos Koulentianós (1918–95), both of whom have lived and worked in Paris.

Other interesting works include *Zalonga* by Yióryios Zongolópoulos (1903–; see also pp 140, 261) and *Acrocorinth* (1965) by Kléarkhos Loukópoulos (1908–95).

Continuing (c 1km) along Vasilíssis Sofías you will pass several hospitals to the right. Left is the **Párko Eleftherías** with a statue of the statesman Elefthérios Venizélos (pp 64, 139), and a **museum** to him (Tues–Sat 10.00–13.00, 18.00–20.00; Sun 10.00–13.00; closed Mon) containing personal effects, photographs, documents and books. The **Arts Centre** (Κέντρο Τεχνών) has exhibitions and a pleasant café. Beyond is the imposing marble **Mégaro Mousikís** (Concert Hall; for booking, p 52), usually known just as 'tó Mégaro' (begun 1976; opened 1994). Its programmes are varied and of high quality. Beyond is the United States Embassy (Walter Gropius and H. Morse Payne Jnr, 1960–61), whose architectural interest is largely hidden behind a forbidding perimeter fence. Of the many hospitals in the vicinity, architecturally the most interesting is the neoclassical **Ippokrátio** (*Hippocrateion*), to the right.

By the **Athens Tower** (Pírgos Athinón; right), Od. Mesoyíon diverges for central and southern Attica (the Mesóyia), Marathon, etc.

A little further on, at Ambelókipi, Vasilíssis Sofías meets Leofóros Alexándras (from Patisíon and the Pédhion Areos), then continues, as Leofóros Kifissías, for Kifissiá and the northern suburbs.

15 • Piraeus via Néo Fáliro

Piraeus (Piraiás) is a thriving commercial, passenger and naval port with a cheerful, bustling atmosphere, less claustrophobic than central Athens. Two smaller harbours (Zéa and Tourkolímano) cater for yachts and other craft. There is plenty to enjoy, whether you prefer the liveliness of the main front and back streets (often still with an old-fashioned bazaar-like atmosphere), interesting food, the relative calm of the Aktí peninsula and the summit of Kastélla, or reminders of Classical antiquity. The Archaeological Museum has outstanding bronze statues and good stone sculpture, and the Naval Museum is unique in Greece. There are excellent views of Athens, Imittós and the Saronic gulf from the coast.

Boats for the Cyclades leave from quays close to the station, others (see below) are further away.

Practical information

 Getting there from Athens
By metró

Line 1 20 mins from Omónia; trains every few minutes to Piraiás station.

By bus

No. 040 from Od. Filellínon (Síntagma) via Leofóros Singroú, Kallithéa and Tzitzifiés, entering Piraeus by Sint. Pezikoú; 049 from Omónia (Od. Athinás) via Od. Piraiós, entering Piraeus by Gr. Lamvráki. Bus times (c 30 mins) vary according to traffic, but are always longer than the train journey. Note that bus stops are in the centre of Piraeus, not by the passenger quays, and the terminus of the Athens buses is at the very far end of the port, below the Khatzikiriákio Orphanage. From there you need to take another bus to the quays if you are carrying luggage.

 Where to stay and eat
See pp 23–4, 34–6.

 Getting around
By bus

Useful buses, from the square outside the Metró station, are no. 904 for Khatzikiriákio and Freattídha, via the Naval College and Aktí peninsula (p 242), Naval Museum and Zéa harbour; 915 to Profítis Ilías (summit of Kastélla) and Veákio Theatre. From outside the Metró station, 859 Piraeus–Dhrapetsóna stops along the waterfront, traverses Eëtioneia and passes the best-preserved ancient tower (p 241); 843 for Pérama (Sálamis ferries).

By trolley bus

No. 20, from opposite the Metró station for Zéa, Kastélla (ring road), Tourkolímano and Néo Fáliro (the terminus is about 200m from Néo Fáliro Metró station); 20 (outside station; opposite direction) for Dhrapetsóna, via Ay. Dhionísios, far side of harbour and ancient Eëtioneia.

Hydrofoils

From Zéa (Pasalimáni) to Kéa, Kíthnos; Póros, Idhra, Spétses, Leonídhi, Monemvasía, etc.

Main shipping quays

Aktí Posidhónos for Aíyina (**Note:** including hydrofoils), Póros, Idhra and Spétses; opposite Metró and Plateía Karaïskákis for the Cyclades; Aktí Miaoúlis (east end) for the Dodecanese and north Aegean, (west end) for foreign ports; Aktí Kondíli for Crete.

Post office
Odhós Fílonos/Tsamadhoú.

Police
Ay Konstandínou 11, ☎ 210 412 2501.

 Festival
Blessing of the Waters at Epiphany (6 January), a colourful religious ceremony by the harbour.

From Athens to Piraeus, via Singroú

From the Temple of Olympian Zeus the broad, fast and rather featureless **Leofóros Singroú** (named after Andréas Singrós, 1828–99, a successful businessman of Chiot descent, who made most of his money in Constantinople and endowed numerous philanthropic institutions in Athens and elsewhere) heads for 6km straight to the coast. To the left, between Singroú and Kallirróïs, is the former **Fix Brewery**, remembered as a scene of fierce fighting in 1941. Part of the original building now houses the **National Museum of Contemporary Art** (Ethnikó Mouseío Síngkhronis Tékhnis; Tues–Sat 11.00–19.00, excluding Thurs 12.00–22.00; free 17.00–22.00; closed Mon). From central Athens the easiest access is by Metró (Line 2) to the Singroú-Fix station (100m). There is not yet a permanent collection but the initial exhibitions have been of a high standard. The church of **Ay. Sóstis** (2.5km, left) was built by Queen Olga after an attempt on the life of King George I failed in 1897.

To the right of the road is the suburb **Kallithéa**, to the left **Néa Smírni** (New Smyrna); the latter's name indicates its origin as a refugee settlement (p 64). You pass (left) a series of luxury hotels and, at no. 387, the **Planetarium** of the Evyenídhis Foundation (sessions on Sun only, hourly 11.00–16.00, except 14.00). To the left is **Palaió Fáliro** (Old Fáliron). Keep right where the road divides at the **racecourse** (soon to be transferred to a new site near Markópoulo). Much of the land between the road and sea, with parks, paths and marinas, has been reclaimed over the last 30 years. Tsitsifiés (7km) used to be noted for *rebétika*, the urban folk music of Greece. From here, you are following the course of Fáliro Bay.

Fáliro (Phaleron) Bay

Fáliro Bay, shallow and exposed, stretches from the headland of Palió Fáliro (ancient *Phaleron*) on the east to the Kastélla (the acropolis of ancient *Munychia*) promontory on the west. From here Theseus was supposed to have departed for Crete to deal with the minotaur, and the Athenian contingent for Troy. Until the beginning of the 5C BC the Athenians beached their warships here. Today visiting ships of foreign navies can sometimes be seen in the bay.

There was a station for flying boats opposite the racecourse until the Second World War, with a Brindisi–Istanbul service from 1926 and Imperial Airways routes to India and Australia from 1939.

Next is **Néo Fáliro** (New Fáliron; 8km). In antiquity the area was called *Halipedon*, a marshy district either side of the mouth of the River Kifissós, the latter now a squalid canal debouching into the bay just before the Peace and Friendship stadium. In 1875 Néo Fáliro was developed as a holiday resort. Its Metró station is between the Karaïskákis Stadium (inland), home of the

Olimpiakós football team, and the vast boat-shaped Stadium of Peace and Friendship (towards the sea). In the square outside the station is a memorial to Karaïskákis, who was killed in Piraeus in 1827 (p 245), set up in Otho's reign.

Sections of both northern and southern Long Walls (see Ancient defences, p 239; also p 220) have been located at various sites in this area. Some parts of the latter are visible at the northeast corner of the junction of Odd. Emmanouilídhis and Soultáni, towards Od Piraiós.

Looking along Piraiós towards Athens, the Parthenon and the Acropolis are stunning, prompting one to reflect how awe-inspiring they and the great bronze statue of Athena Promakhos would have seemed in antiquity.

The **Stadium of Peace and Friendship** complex is set in 3.25 hectares of land, with tennis courts, a marina and other facilities. The indoor stadium has a seating capacity of 16,000, concert and recreation halls, and facilities for many indoor sports. The grounds are connected with the station by a subway and provide a convenient short cut to the Kastélla promontory.

Beyond the station (200m) is the terminus of trolley bus no. 20 (Néo Fáliro–Dhrapetsóna, via Kastélla). The main road, here called Skilítsi, is joined on the right by Piraiós, direct from Omónia.

The 040 bus turns left from Skiltsi into Sint. Pezikoú where (Kalamáki stop, at corner with Pílis; or c 250m walk from Metró station via Od Alipédhou), to the left and right of the road in Odd. Pílis, Zanní, Dhistómou, Kódhrou, Kolokotróni etc, are remains of the **Asty Gate** and the ancient fortifications. This was where the *Hamaxitos* or carriage-road entered the city. Its round towers of the Themistoklean period were later rebuilt square. Much masonry from the ancient wall is built into houses around.

The bus continues into the centre of Piraeus, which can be just as easily reached from the waterfront. The best car route to the main port from Piraiós and Leof. Athinón is via Leofóros Athinon-Piraiós (the continuation of Piraiós), turning left into Od. Retsína for Plateía Ippodhamías, across which you continue by Od. Goúnari to (11km) the central harbour.

Introducing Piraeus

The port of Greece since antiquity, Piraeus (ΠΕΙΡΑΙΕΥΣ; modern Piraiás, often in accusative Piraiá) now has a population of 476,304, making it the third-largest centre in the country. Piraeus took a new lease of life with the development of Athens as the capital of Greece from 1834. It is the seat of a bishop, as well as a major naval and commercial shipping centre.

Layout

A glance at the map (see overleaf) shows that the town lies along a peninsula, called Aktí (*Akte*), since antiquity. The modern street plan reflects the ancient layout, with two grids on different alignments. Od. Sakhtoúri, running from one side of the peninsula to the other, just west of the point where the harbour of Zéa (also the ancient name) makes a deep indentation from the south, marks the dividing line between the two parts. The eastern sector includes, also on the south, the smaller harbour of Tourkolímano (ancient *Munychia*), or Mikró Limáni, which lies below the Munychia acropolis, now Kastélla.

On the far side of the main port (*Kantharos*) were the peninsula of *Eëtioneia* and inlet of *Krommydaron*, on the way to modern Dhrapetsóna which, together with adjacent Níkaia (formerly Kokkiniá), is an important manufacturing centre.

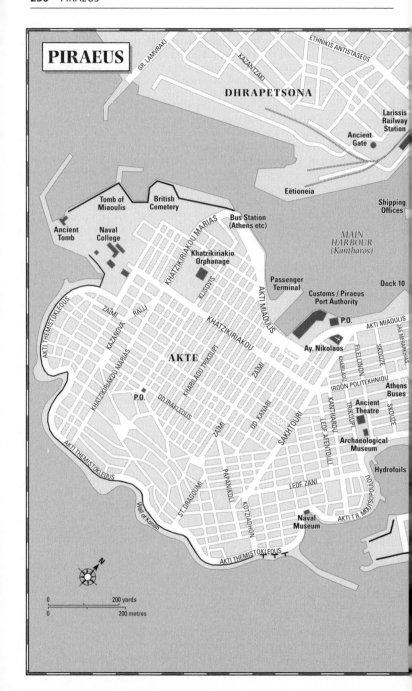

PIRAEUS

DHRAPETSONA

ETHNIKIS ANTISTASEOS

GR. LAMVRAKI

KAZANTZAKI

Larissis Railway Station

Ancient Gate

Eëtioneia

Shipping Offices

Tomb of Miaoulis

British Cemetery

Bus Station (Athens etc)

MAIN HARBOUR (Kantharos)

Ancient Tomb

Naval College

KHATZIKIRIAKOU MARIAS

Khatzikiriakio Orphanage

KLISOVIS

AKTI MIAOULIS

Passenger Terminal

Dock 10

Customs / Piraeus Port Authority

P.O.

AKTI MIAOULIS

2AS MERARKHIAS

AKTI THEMISTOKLEOUS

ZAÏMI

RALLI

KAZANOVA

KHATZIKIRIAKOU

KHATZIKIRIAKOU MARIAS

AKTE

KHARILAOU TRIKOUPI

ZAÏMI

ZAÏMI

Ay. Nikolaos

FILELLINON

KHARILAOU

SKOUZE

IROON POLITEKHNIOU

Athens Buses

P.O.

OD. IRAKLEDUS

DD. KANARI

SAKHTOURI

KANTHAROU

LEOF. AFENTOULI

TRIKOUPI

Ancient Theatre

SKOUZE

AKTI THEMISTOKLEOUS

Wall of Konon

ZAÏMI

Archaeological Museum

Hydrofoils

ST. DRAGOUMI

PAPANIKOLI

KOTZIADHON

LEOF. ZANI

NOTARA

MOUTSOPOULOU

AKTI T.R.

Naval Museum

AKTI THEMISTOKLEOUS

```
0        200 yards
0        200 metres
```

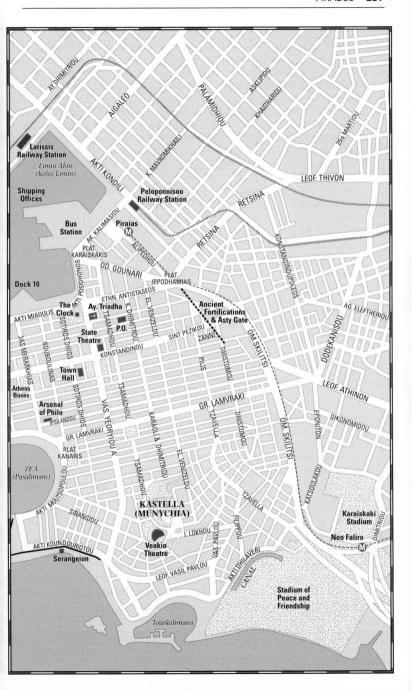

Larissis
Railway Station
*Limin Alon
(Kofos Limin)*

Shipping
Offices

Bus
Station

Dock 10

AKTI MIAOULIS

2AS MERARKHIAS

BOUBOULINAS

Athens
Buses

*ZEA
(Pasalimani)*

Serangeion

AV DHIMITRIOU

AIGALEO

AKTI KONDILI

PALAMIDHIOU

ASKLIPIOU

KHADDHARIOU

25is MARTIOU

LEOF. THIVON

K. MAVROMIKHALI

RETSINA

RETSINA

KONSTANDINOUPOLEOS

Peloponnisou
Railway Station

AK. KALIMASIOU

Piraias
Ⓜ

ALIPEDHIOU

PLAT.
KARAISKAKIS

SONOHOISIO

OD. GOUNARI

PLAT.
IPPODHAMIAS

ETHN. ANTISTASEOS

The Clock

AKTI POSEI

SOTIROS DHIOS

Ay. Triadha

K.DHMITROU

TSAMADHOU

EL.VENIZELOU

State
Theatre

P.O.

KONSTANDINOU

SINT PEZIKOU

ZANNI

Ancient
Fortifications
& Asty Gate

DHISTOMOU

AG. ELEFTHERIOU

DODEKANISOU

Town
Hall

SOTIROS DHIOS

TSAMADHOU

VAS. YEORYIOU A.

KARAOLI & DHIMITRIOU

PILS

GR. LAMVRAKI

DHISTOMOU

TZAVELA

OM. SKILITSI

LEOF. ATHINON

EPONITON

OIKONOMIDOU

Arsenal
of Philo

IPSILANDOU

GR. LAMVRAKI

TSAMADHOU

EL.VENIZELOU

PLAT.
KANARIS

TSAMADHOU

KATSOULAROU

Karaiskaki
Stadium

AKTI MOUTSOPOULOU

SIRANGIOU

KASTELLA
(MUNYCHIA)

I. LOKHOU

VAS. PAVLOU

TZAVELA

FILIPPOU

OM. SKILITSI

Neo Faliro
Ⓜ

DHIMITRIOU

AKTI KOUNDOURIOTOU

Veakio
Theatre

LEOF. VASIL PAVLOU

AKTI DHILAVERI

CANAL

Stadium of
Peace and
Friendship

Tourkolimano

History

Originally an island, Piraeus continued to be geographically isolated in Archaic times by the marshes of Halipedon (p 234, Néo Fáliro). While Corinth and Aegina remained the strongest maritime powers, the Athenians kept their triremes on the beach of Phaleron Bay which, unlike Piraeus, was in full view of the city. About 510 BC Hippias, feeling insecure in Athens, began to fortify Munychia. Themistokles created an Athenian fleet of 200 ships and chose Piraeus as its base. In 493 BC he began an ambitious scheme of fortification. By the beginning of the Peloponnesian War in 431 BC, the three Long Walls (p 239) were complete. By the end of the war the Phaleric Wall had decayed, and the conditions of peace offered by Lysander, after the defeat of the Athenians at Aigospotami in 405 BC, included the destruction of the remaining Long Walls as well as the fortifications of both Athens and Piraeus.

At the height of Athenian power, the population of Piraeus consisted largely of metics (resident aliens). They controlled much of its manufacture and trade and gave the city a cosmopolitan and radical character, partly through the introduction of exotic cults. A good example of such a cult was that of the Thracian Bendis, who became identified with Artemis.

The opening scene of Plato's *Republic* is set in Piraeus, at the house of the aged Kephalos.

In 404 BC Thrasyboulos sought the help of the people of Piraeus, launching from Munychia his *coup d'état* against the Thirty Tyrants. Later, Munychia became the main seat of the Macedonian garrison which controlled Athens for most of the period from 322 to 229.

By 200 BC, when Philip V of Macedon attacked Athens, the Long Walls had been abandoned, although Piraeus (its walls repaired by Eukleides and Mikion c 306–298) was flourishing as a commercial centre. The Roman garrison used it as a base. In 86 BC Sulla ravaged the city, destroying the Arsenal and the docks.

Strabo speaks of Piraeus as an unimportant village but it seems to have revived early in the Roman imperial period and was a base for Constantine's fleet as late as AD 322. After Alaric's raid in AD 396 it lost importance.

In 1040 Harold Hardrada the Viking, in the service of the Byzantine emperor, disembarked at Piraeus to suppress an Athenian revolt. In medieval times Piraeus was known as Porto Leone, from a huge marble lion which stood on the shore (p 242); then by the Turks as Aslanliman.

When Athens became the capital of Greece in 1834, hardly a house was standing in Piraeus. Resettled by islanders with trading instincts similar to those of the ancient metics, it grew rapidly through the 19C and played a large part in the revival of Athens. The population rose from c 4000 in 1840 to 11,000 in 1870 and 75,000 in 1907. It was swollen to three times the previous number by refugees from the Asia Minor catastrophe of 1922.

In 1854–59 Piraeus was occupied by an Anglo-French fleet to prevent Greek nationalists embarrassing Turkey, an allied power in the Crimean War. In the Second World War the port was put out of action and 11 ships sunk on the first night of the German air attack (6 April 1941) when the moored *Clan Fraser*, carrying 200 tons of TNT, blew up along with two other ammunition ships.

It is now a port of call for East Mediterranean lines as well as being the focus of services to the Greek islands.

The ancient defences

The **Long Walls**, sometimes called the 'legs' (σκέλη) were part of the original system of Themistokles. The first (Northern) long wall ran from Athens to Piraeus; the second (Phaleric) from Athens to the far (east) end of Phaleron Bay. These were completed c 456 BC (Thuc. I 108). A third (Southern) long wall parallel to the northern was built by Kallikrates, under the direction of Perikles, against the possibility of surprise landings in Phaleron Bay.

The northern and southern walls started from points in the city wall of Piraeus, converged to 183m of each other and then ran parallel towards Athens, to the vicinity of the Pnyx. Much of the northern long wall follows the line of Od. Piraiós and has been buried beneath the road; the southern is largely on the route of the electric railway. Sections can be seen in Néo Fáliro (p 235), also on the seaward side of the Metró line between Kallithéa and Moskháto stations, just on the Athens side of Moskháto. The walls' course can be best viewed from the summit of Likavittós (p 220).

Between the walls was a **roadway**. Another, probably the carriage-road (αμαξιτός; Hamaxitos) mentioned by Xenophon (*Hellenica*, II 4 10), ran outside the northern wall. For the Asty Gate, by which it entered the city, see p 235.

The 5C **Themistoklean City Wall** protected all three harbours (*Kantharos*, *Zea* and *Munychia*). Each had a fortified entrance, probably closed by chains. The west half of *Akte* was excluded from the defensive line, which crossed the peninsula from northwest to southeast. On the landward side it followed the solid land behind the *Halai* marsh (p 241), and in the direction of Athens, the contour of the ground. The total circuit was 60 stadia (Thuc. II 13), the equivalent of over 11km.

The **reconstructed circuit** (4C) has been attributed to **Konon** (Xenophon, *Hellenica* IV 8), but an inscription shows that it must have been started before his victory at Knidos and was probably finished only after 346 (Demosthenes XIX 125). Changes included shortening the north side by running the line across the *Choma* (p 240) to Eëtioneia but extending it round the whole shore of the Akte peninsula.

The ancient city

Ancient Piraeus was laid out in the time of Perikles by Hippodamos of Miletos, the most famous town planner of antiquity. It had a grid plan with the different zones of activity (commercial, religious, domestic) defined by boundary stones (see Piraeus Museum; another in the Athens Epigraphical Museum, Room XI), and represents the clearest example of Hippodamos' approach to planning.

The needs of the fleet were given special consideration, and 1000 talents were spent on Ship-sheds and dry docks. Demosthenes mentions the ship-sheds of Piraeus in the same breath as the Parthenon and the Propylaia. In 330–322 BC there were 372 of them (196 in Zea, 82 in Munychia and 94 in Kantharos). This level of provision corresponds roughly with the size of the Athenian navy (about 400 ships) in the time of Lykourgos, who completed the facilities with the construction in 346–329 BC of a naval Arsenal (*Skeuotheke*) at the harbour of Zea, designed by the architect Philo and rediscovered in 1988 (p 244).

The ancient harbour and its facilities

The Great Harbour was also called *Kantharos* (goblet, presumably from its shape, although the relationship is now difficult to understand). Apart from the new outer harbour (see below) the form of the ancient port is quite closely reflected in the modern. The naval and commercial sectors were kept separate, as they still are. The naval area was the shore of Eëtioneia and the north shore of Akte, beyond the present Attica Customs HQ (ΔΙΕΥΘΥΝΣΗ ΤΕΛΩΝΕΙΟΝ ΑΤΤΙΚΗΣ)/Piraeus Port Authority (ΚΕΝΤΡΙΚΟΝ ΛΙΜΕΝΑΡΧΕΙΟΝ ΠΕΙΡΑΙΩΣ) building, which was then a temple site, and the passenger terminal. The Commercial Quay (*Emporion*) was on the site of the modern berths along Aktí Miaoúlis and off Plateía Karaïskákis. It was divided in two by a jetty called the *Diazeugma*, roughly where Gate E (and offices and a cafeteria of the Port Authority, ΟΛΠ) now is. This quay was lined by five stoas, one of which was located (not visible) c 140m from the quay southeast of Gate E. Other fragments of the Emporion are built into the foundations of the cathedral church of Ay. Triádha. The short south mole which projects from Plateía Karaïskákis corresponds to the ancient *Choma*. This was the point of assembly where, the night preceding naval expeditions, the trierarchs had to report to the Council of 500; the first three to arrive were rewarded.

For the *Kophos Limen* and *Eëtioneia*, see below.

The office of the **Trierarchy**, established by Themistokles, was a form of taxation under which the state provided the bare hulls of new warships, while the duty of fitting them out, launching the vessels and training the crews fell in rotation to the richest citizens. A trierarch sailed with his ship and was responsible for its repair during his term of office.

After 337 BC the entrance to the harbour, 50m wide, was protected by two moles with towers or lighthouses. These projected from the south end of Eëtioneia (part still survives) and the north shore of Akte. Today an outer harbour, formed by the construction of two breakwaters in 1902, contains naval stores and yards, commercial wharves and a dry dock.

A useful study of the ancient city is R. Garland, *The Piraeus*, Duckworth, London, 1987.

Tour of Piraeus

The sights of Piraeus are described in continuous sequence, but instructions are provided for leapfrogging sectors which may not interest you.

• **Walking**. The total distance of the main route described, from Od. Goúnari (near the Piraeus Metró station) to Néo Fáliro station, is nearly 10km. However, several points on the way can be reached by **bus** (p 233), allowing segments of the route to be walked in isolation. If you make straight for Zéa, you will find many of the most interesting sights within easy reach. The walk round the Aktí peninsula from the shore near the Naval College to the harbour of Zéa is 3.5km: from there, via Tourkolímano, to the Néo Fáliro station, just over 3km.

On reaching the port by Od. Goúnari (p 235), you will see opposite the berths for boats and hydrofoils to Aíyina and the islands in the Saronic Gulf. Beyond them to the right, on the far side of the road, is the important local bus terminal in Plateía Karaïskákis, beyond which again are ticket agencies and quays with boats for the Cyclades.

If you follow the road round to the right, you soon come to the Metró station, an impressive building (which may also be your point of arrival).

Eëtioneia

Continue past the station (p 233 for transport), round the further side of the harbour, for the more distant passenger quays, ancient *Eëtioneia* and *Krommydaron* and modern Dhrapetsóna.

At the station of the Peloponnese railway (right), you turn left along the dreary Aktí Kondíli which bounds the far side of the square inner harbour. In antiquity this was a miry lagoon called *Halai* (or *Kophos Limen*; κωφός λιμήν, silent harbour), a relic of the marshes which once surrounded Piraeus.

At the far end is the Lárissa station of the state railway and, stretching left along the side of the station, the peninsula of Eëtioneia, which Thucydides called 'the mole of Piraeus'. This peninsula and the inlet of Krommydaron on its far side were both included in the ancient fortified circuit. In 411 BC Theramenes provided Eëtioneia with separate fortifications but these were demolished on a change of policy (Thuc. VIII 92). The 4C walls enclosed only the peninsula.

Between the waterfront and the railway, sidings cross the road at a point where there are traces (3–3.6m thick) of the **Wall of Konon**, and then enter the modern quays which have obliterated the ancient shipbuilding yards (νεώρια) and slipways (νεώσοικοι). Over the rails is the entrance to the inlet of Krommydaron, now the Dry Docks (Monímes Dhexamenés, Μονίμες Δεξαμενές). In 1866 five marble altars were found here, one with a Phoenician inscription. On the west side are some traces of the **Themistoklean Wall**, slighter than that of Konon.

Opposite the entrance to the Monímes Dhexamenés, about 600m from the station and stretching back towards it, a low hill (16m) was ringed by Konon's wall. The impressive **Eëtioneia** (or Aphrodision) **Gate**, excavated by the French School in 1887 and recently cleaned and restored, can be seen to the northwest by walking up Od. Kanári (or descending it by bus no. 859, see above): the semicircular towers are more than 9m in diameter. The Gate takes its alternative name from a sanctuary dedicated to Aphrodite Euploia, goddess of navigation; this is known from inscriptions and was probably around here. Od. Kanári will then take you back to Aktí Kondíli.

Central Piraeus

After—or instead of—visiting Eëtioneia, you can leave Od. Goúnari in the opposite direction. After 200m you come to **To Rolóï** (The Clock), an important landmark. Here you have a choice. (1) You can continue along the waterfront past berths and Gate E, and join the later part of the route by ascending Od. Filellínon (just before the Limenarkhíon offices) or—considerably longer—carry on right to the end of the waterfront (Athens, etc bus terminal) and climb Od. Khatzikiriákou Marías past the Orphanage to reach the Aktí peninsula road. At the point where you leave the waterfront a copy of the **Lion of Piraeus** (p 242) was set up on a tall plinth in 1997. (2) The route described below goes straight up the hill from The Clock to the public buildings of central Piraeus.

Climbing Leofóros Yeoryíou tou Prótou (George I), you pass (left) the cathedral church of **Ay. Triádha** (Ziller, 1915–16; destroyed 1944, rebuilt 1958–62; ancient building remains in crypt, easiest to visit Sundays) and, opposite, the Plateía Themistokléous. Formerly the Tináneion, this formal garden was laid out in 1854 by Barbier de Tinan, the French vice-admiral in command of the allied occupation force of Piraeus during the Crimean War. Just beyond, on the corner of Od. Fílonos, were found in 1959 the *Piraeus kouros* and other magnificent ancient bronze statues (see Archaeological Museum, p 244). On the corner (left) of a major crossroads is the imposing **Dhimotikó Théatro** (A. Lazarímou, 1885; pleasant, quiet cafés at side), diagonally opposite Plateía Koraï with the Dhimarkhíon. Turning right here into Od. Iróön Politekhníou, you are walking along the spine of the Aktí peninsula with the main harbour to your right. On the same side, in the north angle of Odd. Skouzé and Filellínon, an **archaeological park** has remains of Roman houses and shops of the 2C–6C AD, overlying earlier buildings.

From this point you can either take a longer route along Iróön Politekhníou, which bends (interesting **Art Gallery** at 91; ☎ 210 419 4585 for opening), becomes Khatzikiriákou and continues to the orphanage and the Aktí coast, or cross the road into the lower part of Kharíláou Trikoúpi and make straight for the Archaeological Museum and Zéa.

The Aktí (*Akte*) peninsula

The rocky and often deserted coast provides a pleasant walk, especially in the late afternoon when Salamis and the islands of the Saronic Gulf are thrown into relief by the setting sun, which falls full on Imittós and the coast to the east. The coast road from the Naval School to Zéa is followed by the no. 904 bus. Along much of the route are restaurants and cafés, the most informal and pleasant towards the tip of the promontory.

At the end of Khatzikiriákou (at the junction with Khatzikiriákou Marías which comes up from the harbour), you can continue straight ahead to the restricted area or turn left and then right for the coast.

This western end of the peninsula (see map) was once a royal park. Now a restricted military area with a **Naval College**, some points of interest are visible only from the sea. On the northern edge—the ancient promontory of *Alkimos*— once stood the great marble lion (there is a modern copy at the bottom of Khatzikiriákou Marías). About 275m west of Alkimos are some graves of English soldiers and a monument to Admiral Andréas Miaoúlis (1769–1835). Behind it was quarried the blueish-grey Piraeic stone; further on, seaward of the light-house, are a rock-cut grave traditionally known as the Tomb of Themistokles and a poros **column**, re-erected in 1952, which marked the south entrance to the harbour.

When you reach the sea south of the Naval College, Aktí Themistokléous follows the indented shore of the peninsula. Lower courses of the **Wall of Konon** (4C) are visible for most of the way—impressive not least for their extent.

The lion of Piraeus

The statue, which probably came from Delos, was inscribed in runes by Harald Hardrada in 1040 (p 238). It was carried off to Venice by Morosini in 1687. From the lion Piraeus got its alternative names of Porto Leone and Porto Draco, the latter because of the creature's fearsome aspect.

The road follows the wall closely and is sometimes supported by it. The wall runs close to the sea and is built mainly of blocks cut from the rocks on which it stands. The curtain, 3–3.5m thick, is reinforced at intervals of 46–55m by square towers. A short section of the wall of Themistokles survives south-east of the signal station on the highest point of the peninsula. Beyond the Metaxás Cancer Institute, on the site of the former Institute of Hydrology in the Villa Skouloúdhis, polygonal masonry at the base of Konon's wall shows where the earlier wall was at first carried some way to the southwest of the point at which it turned across the peninsula.

The lion of Piraeus

On a patch of reclaimed land between the road (Aktí Themistokléous) and the sea, 500m beyond the Institute, is the **Naval Museum of Greece** (Naftikó Mouseío Elládhos, ΝΑΥΤΙΚΟ ΜΟΥΣΕΙΟ ΕΛΛΑΔΟΣ; Mon–Sat 0900–1400, closed Sun, Mon, and all August; ☎ 210 451 6264). In front, a formal garden has guns, conning towers, torpedo tubes and the like. Opposite you, inside the main entrance, the building incorporates part of the Themistoklean Wall. To the right are carvings and models of ancient ships, including a fine trireme, and representations of the Battle of Salamis. In the rooms to the left of the entrance, the order is chronological with Byzantine battles and Battle of Lepanto explained with the help of drawings and plans. Among interesting documents is a letter from Admiral Nelson, dated 1792, from New York. Displays relating to the War of Independence highlight the careers of admirals like Miaoúlis and Kanáris, and the Battle of Navaríno. Later Greek naval exploits are celebrated, and the course of Greek naval warfare to the present day illustrated by relics salvaged from the sea, pictures, uniforms, flags and ship models. There is a floating branch of the Naval Museum at Palaió Fáliro (p 247).

Zéa

Below the road as you round the promontory beyond the Naval Museum are substantial sections of the Themistoklean Wall, at the western entrance to Zéa (also accessible direct from the town centre, as described above). Once the ancient military harbour (*Stratiotike Limen*), it is now a crowded marina and a base for hydrofoil services. The harbour is a landlocked basin, connected to the sea by a channel c 100m broad and 200m long, lined on either side with ancient walls, terminating at the inner end of the channel in two short moles. Construction of the new yacht basin, incorporating a bay to the west, has modified the shoreline here and narrowed the entrance to Zéa.

In antiquity the port contained 196 **Ship-sheds** (model in the Naval

Museum). Many of these have been excavated and remains can be seen (through grilles) preserved in the basements of buildings on the waterfront, including Od. Sirángou 1, and some near the Naval Museum. The flat beach round the harbour basin was enclosed by a wall c 15m from the water's edge. This formed the back of the sheds, with average width 6.4m and separated from each other by plain columns of Piraeic limestone. The columns which supported the roofs were probably of wood. Within each shed the rock was hollowed out to form a slipway.

Above Zéa, at Khariláou Trikoúpi 38, is the excellent **Archaeological Museum** (08.30–15.00; closed Mon), newly rearranged. It contains finds from Piraeus, western Attica, the Saronic Gulf islands, and the island of Kíthira. The sequence starts on the upper floor. In the **Foyer** is a plan of sites and one of the **boundary stones of Piraeus** (p 239). **Room 1** (top of stairs) has finds from **shrines** (of Artemis Munychia, Zeus on Mt Parnes, also from a deme sanctuary of Halai Aixonides) and the newly excavated Minoan peak sanctuary on Kíthira; also material connected with the life of the **Agora** (relief with measure-standards from Salamis) and the **navy** (bronze ram and stone anchors). **Room 2** has fine **pottery** of all periods (from Méthana, Salamis, Trákhones and Troizen); some illustrates the lives of children, women and the Athenian citizen, respectively. Also Mycenaean chariot figurines, and a bronze harp. **Rooms 3 and 4** have the magnificent **bronzes** found in 1959 (p 242). They may be part of Sulla's loot in 86 BC, subsequently overlooked. The superb **Piraeus Kouros** (530–20 BC) is the oldest known large-scale hollow-cast bronze, with clay filling and iron supports preserved. It was a cult statue of Apollo, holding a bow and *phiale* (bowl for offering), perhaps from a northeast Peloponnesian workshop (?Kanakhos of Sikyon). The other figures are: **Athena** (griffins and owls on her helmet), c 350–340 BC; **Artemis**, a quiver on her shoulder, attributed to Euphranor, c 340–330 BC; another Artemis, perhaps a copy of an original from c 325 BC. There are also a cylindrical East Greek Archaic kore (c 580 BC) and a kouros from Aíyina. **Room 5** has a seated cult statue of **Cybele**, with remains (feet) of a lion beside her, set within the restored outline of the temple in which they were found (excavated in Moskháto c 1975). Other votives include a famous scene of **Asklepios** treating a patient, hero banqueting reliefs (5C) and two herms (1C BC). In **room 6** are Classical **grave stelai**. The display continues downstairs with Late Classical and Hellenistic stelai and funerary sculpture (**rooms 7 and 8**). **Room 8** is dominated by the massive **Funerary monument** from Kallithéa (figures in an aedicula on a high base, with reliefs of an Amazonomachy and Zoömachy, or animal conflict), c 400 BC, restored by the late S. Triándi. **Room 9** contains Hellenistic sculpture and **room 10** an interesting Roman display. Prominent are fine **neoclassical reliefs** of Amazonomachies, c AD 200, some copied from the shield of the Athena Parthenos. Portraits include heads of the emperors Claudius (1163) and Trajan (276) and full-size statues of Hadrian.

Next to the museum are the scanty remains of the **Theatre of Zéa**, a Hellenistic structure of the 2C BC which—unusually—was not altered in the Roman period. The rock-cut cavea was divided by 14 flights of stairs. The orchestra is surrounded by a covered channel.

On the far (northeast) side of Zéa, near the junction of Bouboulínas (the third street inland parallel to Filellínon) with Ipsilándou, preserved in a building at Ipsilándou 170, are exciting remains of the Skeuotheke or **Arsenal of Philo**, discovered in 1988. These can be seen from the road, with an explanatory panel. The architect's complete specification for the building (model in Naval Museum) was found in 1892 and the remains so far found correspond with this. Built by the 4C architect Philo of Eleusis to contain equipment of the fleet, it measured about 131 x 18m. The interior was subdivided by two rows of piers. The exterior had a Doric frieze (not in the specifications). The roof was pitched with a pediment at each end, below which were two doors. The northern entrance falls within the main excavation area.

On the other (northeast) side of Zéa is the shady **Plateía Kanáris** with a good restaurant, the **9 Adhélfia** (Nine Brothers), at Od. Sotíros 48 and a good zakharoplastíon, the **Karaván**, opposite; also here is the landing-stage for liberty boats of visiting fleets, a feature which carries on the ancient military use.

Follow the road round the harbour up to the promontory which closes its east side. Here, in a salient of the fortification, were a number of wells (φρέατοι), suggesting that this may have been the site of ancient *Phreattys*, where a criminal court tried those charged with homicide committed abroad. The judges sat on shore while the accused pleaded from a boat so as not to pollute the land. At the neck of the promontory was the site of the Asklepieion where reliefs were found in 1886 (Museum, p 244).

About 200m beyond the promontory (on no. 20 trolley bus route), you can descend steps opposite the end of Od. Ouílsonos (unmarked) to caves by an open-air shadow-puppet theatre. The caves are thought to be the site of the **Serangeion** (σήραγξ, hollow in the rock), a bathhouse dedicated to the hero Serangos. An older name To Spílaio tou Paraskevá (the Cave of Paraskevás), after a restaurateur who set up shop there, survives (just) in the faded name (ΠΑΡΑΣΚΕΥΑ) of a trolley stop a little higher up on the other side of the road.

The entrance to the complex is railed off but accessible. Immediately to the right, off the present entrance, is a remarkable circular cloakroom with 26 compartments for the bathers' clothes. In the doorway to the cloakroom and in the hall outside are fine mosaics (covered), one of Skylla, the other a figure (possibly Serangos) in a four-horse chariot. The main bath, further in (inaccessible), has apsidal recesses and is connected to the sea by another rock-cut passage (11.8m long) a little to the west.

You can now choose either to climb Kastélla or continue round the coast, above or below Tourkolímano.

Kastélla (acropolis of *Munychia*)

The main road swings inland above Tourkolímano through the terraced houses of Kastélla. Up to the left you can climb—most directly by Od. Irakléous—past the Veákios theatre and up the **Hill of Munychia**, the acropolis of ancient Piraeus. It commands all three harbours and has views of Fáliro Bay and the Saronic Gulf. For direct access by bus from Metró station, see p 233.

There are some pleasant restaurants including *I Oraía Míkonos* and *To Stéki tou Zísi*.

In 403 BC Thrasyboulos made Munychia the base of his operations against the Thirty Tyrants who were then in control of Athens. In 1827 Karaïskákis was killed here during an abortive attempt led by Sir Richard Church to relieve the Greek garrison of the Athenian acropolis. General Thomas Gordon held the hill from February until May, but the defeat of an attempt on Athens from Fáliro Bay put an end to the expedition and the siege.

Above the Veákio, the modern chapel of Ay. Ilías, near the summit, may mark the site of a celebrated sanctuary of Bendis (p 238). However, other sites have been suggested for Bendis, while the Sanctuary of Artemis Munychia is sometimes located here instead of on the Yacht Club promontory (see below).

On the west slope of the hill, discovered in 1888 but now covered, was the ancient Theatre of Dionysos referred to by Thucydides (VIII 93). The entrance to the so-called Cave of Arethusa, 65m deep and containing an elaborate water-supply system (ancient but of uncertain date) reached by 165 rock-cut steps, has been closed by a building of the modern water authority (ΕΥΔΑΠ) on the west side of the hill above the junction of Odd. Tsamadhoú and Ríga Feraíou.

Tourkolímano (Mikrolímano)

Instead of—or after—climbing Kastélla you can keep to the main road, which runs above a beach, then drop down past the luxurious **Yacht Club of Greece** (Naftikós Omilos Elládhos) on a promontory. During its construction in 1935 remains were found (including an inscription), often thought to be of the Temple of Artemis Munychia.

Below, you come to the picturesque yacht basin of **Tourkolímano** (now mostly signed as 'Mikrolímano' or Mikró Limáni'), gay with coloured sails and lined with restaurants, unfortunately notorious for scandalous overcharging.

The harbour retains the form of the ancient port of Munychia, which was protected by two long moles, each ending in a lighthouse tower, and had an entrance only 36.5m wide. The north mole is a good example of ancient marine fortification and bears lower courses of a massive structure of unknown purpose. The harbour had slips for 82 triremes. Some foundations of these can be seen beneath the water to the north and south. Nothing of the buildings (probably wooden) survives but there are some traces of the surrounding wall.

From Tourkolímano you can continue (1.4km, there is a short cut through the grounds of the Stadium of Peace and Friendship) to Néo Fáliro Metró station. Alternatively, from the street above you can catch a bus or trolley bus to the station or back to Piraeus.

DAYS OUT OF THE CITY

Brief descriptions of some places of interest in the city outskirts and nearer suburbs are followed by a series of excursions to places of interest in the countryside around Athens. All are accessible by public transport. Travelling times by bus are given and some idea of how long you might need at the destination for a careful but not exhaustive visit. City and suburban bus services are frequent (mostly every 15–20 minutes on weekdays from early morning to about 20.00; fewer in the evening and at weekends).

The suburbs of Athens

On the coast road towards Soúnio

Flísvos Marina

At Palaió Fáliro (7km from central Athens) is a marine branch of the Naval Museum of Greece (p 243). Sights include the **battleship Avéroff** (open to visitors Mon, Wed, Fri 09.00–13.00; Sat, Sun 11.00–15.00; closed Tues, Thur; ☎ 210 983 6539), *Olympias*, the modern version of an ancient trireme, and other vessels. The *Avéroff*, launched at Leghorn (Livorno) in Italy in 1910, was flagship of the Greek fleet until 1951.

- **Bus**. B2 from Panepistimíou (in front of Academy) for West Airport (old) via the coast, as far as the Flísvos Marina (Μαρίνα Φλοίσβου; stops Trokadéro or Oulén).
  Timing. 2 hrs 30 mins travel each way, including a short walk, and 1 hr at site.

Pierídhis Gallery of Modern Art

On the nearer outskirts of Glifádha (10km further on), left of the dual carriageway and between the Oasis and Miranda hotels, is the Pierídhis Gallery of Modern Art (Leofóros Posidhónos, previously Vasiléos Yeoryíou, 29; check times by telephone, ☎ 210 898 0166/210 894 8287. The gallery shows either temporary exhibitions or a selection of the Pierídhis Collection, which contains many excellent works (including Mitarás, Fasianós, etc).

- **Bus**. A1, A2 for Voúla and Vouliagméni from Panepistimíou (in front of the Academy) to Glifádha (stop: Glifádha 4).
  Timing. 3 hrs (45 mins travel each way and 1 hr at the gallery).

East of the city, on the slopes of Mount Imittós

Monasteries

Ay. Ioánnis Karéas

The monastery of Ay. Ioánnis Karéas (11.00–12.30, 18.00–19.30 daily, ☎ 210 765 2746), with a restored 11C church, is high on the mountainside, surrounded by cypresses and a variety of other trees in a lovely garden court. From the carpark below the monastery you can set off for walks.

- **Bus**. 203 from Akadhimías (behind National Library) to Karéa; then a 500m climb.
  Timing. 2 hrs (30 mins travel each way and 1 hr at the monastery).

Kaisarianí

The 11C monastery of Kaisarianí (08.30–15.00; closed Mon), dedicated to the Presentation of the Virgin (Eisódhia tis Theotókou), is an attractive complex in a lovely setting (picnic area). The frescoes are 17C–18C. About 15 mins walk to the southwest, on a hill with views over the city, are remains of an Early Christian basilica and two other churches.

- **Bus**. 224 (stops in Patisíon, Kánningos and Akadhimías), 20 mins to the suburb of Kaisarianí; the monastery is 30 mins further on foot, or take a taxi.
  Timing. 2.5 hrs (1.5 hrs travelling, 1 hr at the site—although you may well want to linger).

Ay. Ioánnis Theológos

The walled monastery of Ay. Ioánnis Theológos (09.00–12.00, 16.30–18.30 daily, ☎ 210 652 8774) is pleasantly situated among trees, in the lower foothills of Imittós, beyond the suburb of Papágos. The church is 13C; the narthex was added in the 15C; the frescoes are 16C. The circuit wall (17C) includes a circular tower. Some parts of other buildings remain.

- **Bus**. 408 from Akadhimías (behind University) to Papágos (6km) and 1.5km walk; or get off on the main road (near junction with Od. Anastáseos opposite the far end of the Defence Ministry—Pentágono—building) and take a **taxi**. The Pentágono can also be reached by **Metró** (Line 3) to Ethnikí Amina.
  Timing. 2.5 hrs (1.5 hrs travel and 1 hr at the site).

Ay. Ioánnis Kinigós

The monastery of Ay. Ioánnis Kinigós (St John the Hunter; opening variable, check with Tourist Police or EOT) is set among pines, high on the slopes of Imittós above the suburb of Ay. Paraskeví, with panoramic views of the city.

The original church was 12C; the narthex, campanile and west chapel were added in the 17C, the arcade on the south in the 18C. The frescoes are Post-Byzantine, with some traces of earlier work. The cloister is charming.

- **Bus**. A5 from Akadhimías (behind Academy) to Ay. Paraskeví stops ERT (in Greek EPT—the Greek Radio and Television headquarters) or 'Parádhissos; then 2km steep climb. Or get off in the large square in Ay. Paraskeví and take a taxi.
  Timing. 2.5–3 hrs (30 mins bus, 30–45 mins walk, 1 hr at the monastery).

Northeast of Athens in the direction of Kifissiá

The Olympic Stadium

The Olympic Stadium is home to the Panathinaïkós football team and will be the major venue of the 2004 Olympic games. Completed in 1992 (for the 1996 Olympic Games, which were not awarded to Greece) and set in 100 hectares, it seats 80,000 spectators. There is a wide range of facilities and accommodation.

- **Bus**. A7 from Plateía Kánningos every few minutes for **Kifissiá**, some continuing to Ekáli and Néa Erithraía; B7 for Kifissiá via Maroússi. Both pass about 500m east of the Olympic Stadium.

Metró. Line 1 to station Iríni (EIPHNH), by the Olympic Stadium.
Timing. If you go by road this is very much dependent on the traffic (approximately 25 mins). By rail, the stadium is about 20 mins from central Athens.

Tsaroúkhis Museum

The Tsaroúkhis Museum (Wed–Sun 09.00–14.00; closed Mon, Tues; ☎ 210 806 2636/7) occupies the former house of the painter (p 231) on the outskirts of Maroússi (Od. Ploutárkhou 28, close to the corner with Od. Knossoú). The attractive. small, neoclassical house, among trees, was built in the 1930s and Tsaroúkhis lived here till his death. Space is limited but a selection of the excellent collection of his work is always on view. The staff are helpful, and there are good posters, postcards and books.

• **Metró** (Line 1) to the KAT Metró station (the last stop before Kifissiá), c 500m from the museum. From the arrival platform, cross the line and turn left out of the station along Od. Irodhótou for c 250m. The fourth street on the right is Knossoú which you ascend for another 250m.
Timing. 2.5–3 hrs (30 mins by train, 15 mins' walk, 1 hr at the museum).

Pendéli Monastery, Palace of Rodhodháfnis and Observatory

The monastery of Moní Pendéli is close to the ancient quarries that were the source of the celebrated Pentelic marble, and several other things of interest, including a palace of the Duchesse de Plaisance (p 225) and the Athens **Observatory** (open days roughly two per month on Fri evenings, essential to telephone, ☎ 210 613 1247/210 804 0619).

The wealthy and pleasantly situated monastery (open 09.00–22.00 daily) was founded in 1578. The buildings are mainly modern, but the chapel has 17C paintings. The katholikon has important modern frescoes (by Rállis Kopsídhis) in the narthex. The foundation played a leading role in Greek education (exhibition in crypt) under Turkish rule.

At Palaiá Pendéli beyond, the **Palace of Rodhodháfnis** was built in a Gothic style for the Duchesse de Plaisance by Kleanthis (p 225). She died (1854) and is buried here. The tomb is close to the war memorial. The locations of these and other buildings associated with the Duchesse are given by Korrés (p 250).

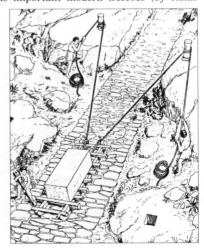

Marble quarries

On **Pendéli** (*Pentelikon*), the mountainous range which borders the Attic plain on the northeast, lay the famous marble quarries of antiquity. These are about 1.5km northeast of the monastery. Because of the complexity of the modern

Illustration showing the way Pentelic marble was brought down the mountain in antiquity

quarry road system the approach is obscure and you are advised to take a guide or consult plans in the excellent *From Pendeli to the Parthenon* by M. Korrés (Greek edn, Athens, 1993, also in an English translation). One approach is through Néa Pendéli (see below), turning right c 500m from the main road into Od. Perikléous, which gives access to the mountainside. This point can also be reached from the monastery or from Palaiá Pendéli.

The **quarry of Spiliá** (700m), about 750m east of the end of Od. Perikléous in a direct line, is close by one of the special roads (illustration, p 249) built for transport of the marble. In its northwest corner is a large stalactite grotto containing twin chapels, one of which has some 13C frescoes.

- **Buses**. A6, B6 to Khalándri from Od. Vasiléos Iraklíou (north side of National Archaeological Museum); then local buses 426 (Palaiá Pendéli; best for monastery and Rhodhodháfnis—for the latter and the tomb, get off at the roundabout beyond the monastery) and 423 (Néa Pendéli). The monastery is 1.5km beyond the turn for Néa Pendéli.
  Timing. 30–45 mins to the monastery, depending on buses; to see this and Palaiá Pendéli would need a morning or an afternoon. The marble quarries are an expedition in themselves.

North and northwest of the city

The Railway Museum
The Railway Museum (ΣΙΔΗΡΟΔΡΟΜΙΚΟ ΜΟΥΣΕΙΟ; open Tues–Fri 09.00–13.00; Wed also 17.00–20.00; Sat, Sun 10.00–13.00; closed Mon; ☎ 210 512 6295), at Skiókou 4, across the railway line and almost opposite the entrance to the long-distance bus terminal at Od. Liossíon 260, is an unusual and fascinating surprise. The contents illustrate the history of the Greek railways. Various locomotives and carriages include an elaborate smoking car from the train of the sultan of Turkey which was captured in 1913.

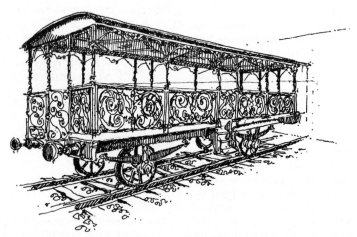

The smoking carriage of Sultan Abdul-Aziz, now in the Railway Museum

- **Bus**. 024 (stops in Síntagma, Panepistimíou (in front of National Library). Tríti Septemvríou) for Tris Yéfires (ΤΡΕΙΣ ΓΕΦΥΡΕΣ) as far as Liossíon 260—stop Praktoría (ΠΡΑΚΤΟΡΕΙΑ), for long-distance bus terminal.
  Timing. 1.5 hrs (30 mins' travel and 1 hr at museum).

Omorfi Ekklisía

The church called Omorfi Ekklisía deserves its name, 'Beautiful Church' (the dedication is to Ay. Yeóryios). Although normally closed and on a busy road, its surroundings have been landscaped and the elegance of the structure and its elevated situation make a visit worthwhile. The church is probably 12C, the important frescoes are by a Thessalonikan artist of the 13C/14C. The south chapel and narthex, originally thought to be more recent, are now regarded as contemporary. The use of rib vaulting (a western feature) in the chapel is extremely rare.

- **Bus**. 608 for Galátsi (ΓΑΛΑΤΣΙ), from Panepistimíou (in front of National Library) or Patisíon, then a 15-min walk beyond terminus.
  Timing. 1.5 hrs (30 mins each way and 30 mins at the church).

Roman aqueduct

About 1km northwest of the Omorfi Ekklisía as the crow flies (considerably more on foot; take a street plan if you are walking), near the junction of the broad Od. Antisintagmatárkhou Kirkídhi and Emmanouíl Pappá, is a splendid section of the aqueduct built by the Roman emperor Hadrian to carry water from Parnes to Likavittós.

- **Metró** (Line 1) to Néa Ionía station, then c 500m walk. Leave the station from right-hand platform, turn left and continue alongside railway until fourth right turn into Od. Filellínon which takes you to the junction mentioned above.
  Timing. 1.5 hours (15 mins each way by train, 15 mins' walk each way, 30 mins at site).

Menídhi tholos tomb

The Menídhi tholos tomb is an important and interesting monument but the excursion is really one for enthusiasts as the site is closed, although the dromos (approach passage to the tomb entrance) is visible from outside the boundary fence.

The tomb (13C BC) has a large (8.35m diameter) chamber and a very long (26.5m) dromos. Excavated by the German School in 1879, the finds (including items of gold, silver and ivory, as well as pottery) are in the National Archaeological Museum. Instead of the usual relieving triangle (empty triangular space above the door to relieve pressure on the lintel block of the doorway), there was a series of stone slabs set horizontally.

- **Bus**. Γ9 from Od Khalkondíli (below Plateía Kánningos) to **Kókkinos Mílos,** a few metres past the site fence (stop: Kókkinos Mílos 5).
  Timing. 1.5 hrs (30 mins each way and 30 mins at site).

Mount Párnitha

Mount Párnitha (*Parnes*) looms over the plain to the northwest. The lower slopes of Párnitha offer greenery and welcome respite from the summer heat; higher up you get spectacular views, cool air, snow and skiing in winter, and the opportunity for walks either over the bare, forbidding mountainside, or through gentler glens.

Ay. Triádha, a little mountain resort amid pine woods, 33km from the centre of Athens, is 2.5km from the Grand Hotel Mont Parnes (left fork on further side of village; télépherique) with a superb panorama. It is 7km (right fork) to the radar station (no admission) that crowns **Karábola** (1413m), the summit of Párnitha, where in antiquity there were two altars of Zeus mentioned by Pausanias.

● **Bus**. 714 (twice daily, Mon–Fri), to télépherique (for hotel) from Akharnón 16 (Plateía Váthis, below Archaeological Museum). On Saturday (twice a day) and Sunday (four times a day), buses climb the mountain to Ayía Triádha and the Hotel.

The Temple of Poseidon at *Sounion* (Soúnio)

In a dramatic cliff-top situation, overlooking the Saronic Gulf, the Temple of Poseidon is a compelling focus for this excursion, although Byron's experience of 'Sunium's marbled steep, Where nothing save the waves and I may hear our mutual murmurs sweep' can only be shared out of season and in the morning, since the site is a popular day trip, especially to view the sunset.

The route takes you out of Athens by Leofóros Singroú and along the busy coast. After Vouliagméni (25km), things become calmer, and the coast is ruggedly attractive, with fine views of the Saronic Gulf and its islands and of the southern part of the Attic peninsula. The towns and villages, however, are largely featureless, and the resorts, often newly-developed seaside suburbs of centres further inland, deserted out of season.

● **Bus** (no number) to Soúnio (70km in c 1hr 50 mins), hourly, from Od. Mavrommatéon (east side of Alexándras; stops also in Stadhíou, at Plateía Klafthmónos, and Od. Filellínon). After reaching Soúnio the bus continues to Lávrio, then makes for Athens by the inland road, allowing you an alternative return route, via Lávrio, Keratéa, Markópoulo, Koropí and Paianía, re-entering the city through the suburb of Ay. Paraskeví. Half-day coach-trips to Soúnio are available from CHAT, Key Tours, etc, p 30.
Timing. By public transport you need at least 6 hrs for the complete trip, allowing 2 hrs at the site.

Cape Soúnio is a precipitous rocky headland 60m above the sea. The low isthmus which joins it to the mainland separates the sandy and exposed bay of Soúnion on the west from a rocky but more sheltered inlet to the east. On the highest point of the headland rise the bright and elegant columns of the temple of Poseidon.

History of Sounion

In Classical times the deme of *Sounion* (Latin *Sunium*) was proverbial for its wealth, probably deriving from the valuable mines and quarries within its territory. Regattas were held near the sanctuary in honour of Poseidon. After the Battle of Salamis the Athenians dedicated here a captured Phoenician ship (one of three; Hdt. VIII 121). Some years before, the Aeginetans had seized the sacred Athenian *Theoris*, the ship that conveyed the envoys

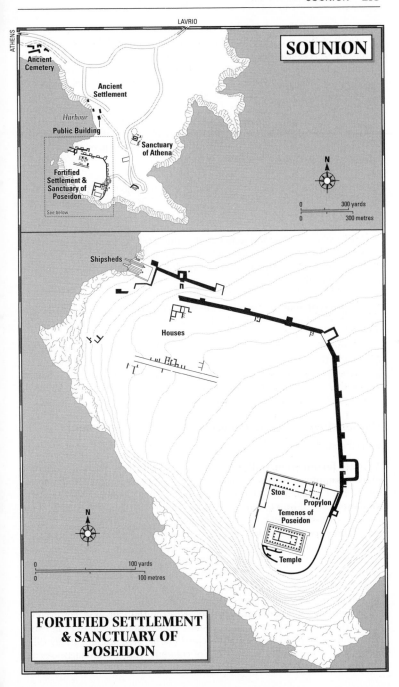

SOUNION

LAVRIO

ATHENS

Ancient Cemetery

Ancient Settlement

Harbour

Public Building

Fortified Settlement & Sanctuary of Poseidon

Sanctuary of Athena

See below

N

0   300 yards
0   300 metres

Shipsheds

Houses

N

0   100 yards
0   100 metres

Stoa

Propylon

Temenos of Poseidon

Temple

FORTIFIED SETTLEMENT & SANCTUARY OF POSEIDON

(Θεωροί) to Delos, while it lay at Sounion (Hdt. VI 87). The town was a port of call of the corn ships from Euboea to Piraeus. The Athenians fortified it during the Peloponnesian War and in 413 BC (Thuc. VIII 14).

The inhabitants were known for harbouring, and readily enfranchising, runaway slaves. On one occasion a strong gang of slaves seized the fortress and devastated the neighbourhood. The Roman author Terence mentions Sunium as a haunt of pirates. Later it was a favourite resort of the corsairs, one of whom, Jaffer Bey, is supposed to have destroyed some of the columns of the temple. One of three of the crew who escaped the foundering of a Levantine trader here was the second mate, the poet William Falconer, who immortalised the incident in *The Shipwreck* (1762).

Excavations The Temple of Poseidon was measured by Revett (p 63) in 1765 and by the Society of Dilettanti in 1812. Byron's name is carved on a pillar. The site was excavated by Dörpfeld (p 104) in 1884 and by the Greek Archaeological Society in 1899–1915. In 1906 two colossal kouroi (National Archaeological Museum) were found in the debris to the east of the temple. Since 1958 some columns have been re-erected. In recent years there have been further excavations by the Greek Archaeological Service and the German Institute.

The **ancient deme of Sounion** was scattered over a large area. It is not clear where the main settlement was located (this site, a centre in the Agriléza valley and Pasalimáni, on the coast towards Lávrio, are candidates). A large columned public building was discovered (1923; no remains visible) at the head of the bay to the north of the sanctuary, and pottery and tombs on the hill beyond suggest an ancient settlement there (Papahadzis). It is debatable whether the houses contained within the area later fortified would have held the whole population or were mainly for military personnel.

The sanctuary of Poseidon and the fortified settlement

• Open daily, 10.00 to sunset.

A double **fortification wall**, c 500m long, with square towers, enclosed the whole **acropolis**, forming a semicircle from the bay of Sounion on the northwest, where part is well preserved, to the cliff edge on the south. Parts of a substantial area of **houses and streets** have been excavated in the middle of the site, also **ship-sheds** down by the sea at the northwest corner.

The **Temenos of Poseidon** occupies the southeast angle of the fortified area, its precinct supported by terrace walls on the north and west. The entrance was on the north, by Doric propylaia, built in poros and marble in the 5C. On the west side, a square room separated the gate from a stoa, which ran along the peribolos wall. Five bases remain of the six interior columns that divided it lengthwise. At right-angles to this on the west is a second stoa.

The **Temple of Poseidon**, near the edge of the cliff, is a conspicuous landmark from the sea. Its dazzling distant whiteness proves illusory at closer hand, since the columns are of grey-veined marble quarried at Agriléza (5km north by an ancient road), where bases of columns of the same dimensions can still be seen. The attribution of the temple to Poseidon was confirmed by an inscription. The design of the temple has been ascribed (W.B. Dinsmoor) on stylistic grounds to the architect of the Hephaisteion at Athens (the Theseum Architect), and dated c 444 BC. It stands over the foundations of an earlier structure in poros stone, founded shortly before 490 BC and unfinished at the time of the Persian invasion.

The Doric peristyle had 34 columns (6 x 13), resting on a stylobate of 31.1 x 13.4m. Nine columns remain on the south side and six (four re-erected in 1958–59) on the north side, together with their architraves. The columns have fewer flutes than usual (16 instead of 20).

The position of the Ionic frieze (see below) which lined all four sides of the interior space in front of the pronaos is also unusual (compare with the Hephaisteion, p 149).

The frieze blocks (the scenes are badly eroded) are in the Lávrio Museum. Parts of seven (of the original nine) slabs from the section over the entrance to the pronaos are preserved. On them are shown the Battle of Lapiths and Centaurs, apparently too a Gigantomachy and exploits of Theseus, the latter also recalling the Hephaisteion.

The external metopes were left blank (possibly because the site is so exposed). The pediments, which contained sculpture (an acroterion, and a seated figure probably from this part of the building are in Athens), had a raking cornice with a pitch of 12.5 degrees instead of the more usual 15 degrees.

Colossal kouros from the sanctuary of Poseidon at Sounion, now in the National Archaeological Museum

The **interior** had the usual tripartite plan. Both pronaos and opisthodomos were distyle in antis. The only surviving elements are the north anta of the pronaos, with its adjacent column, and the south anta, which was reconstructed in 1908.

The **seaward view** from the temple over the sea is striking, and particularly romantic at sunset or dawn. To the east lies Makrónisos; about 11km south is the rocky Ay. Yióryios (ancient *Belbina*). The nearest islands to the southeast are Kéa, Kíthnos and Sérifos. Further south, even Mílos can be made out on a clear day. To the west is Aíyina, in the centre of the Saronic Gulf, with the east coast of the Peloponnese behind.

Inland of the tourist pavilion, visible from the sanctuary on a low hill in a bend of the approach road, are sketchy remains of a small **Sanctuary of Athena Sounias** of c 450 BC. Vitruvius remarked on the irregularity of the temple's plan, with an Ionic colonnade along the east and south sides of the structure. The cella was 5.9 x 3.8m, with four columns in the middle in the form of a square. The cult statue stood at the back. Immediately to the north are remains of a small Doric temple (distyle, prostyle) probably dedicated to the hero Phrontis, whose tomb may have been in a roughly oval precinct at the northwest corner of this site.

Reconstruction of the Sanctuary of Athena at Sounion

The Sanctuary of Artemis at *Brauron* (Vravróna), and Pórto Ráfti

The Sanctuary of Artemis at *Brauron* has intriguing mythological connections, a fine reconstructed stoa and an excellent museum. The setting of the east-coast harbour at Pórto Ráfti is delightful and a good objective for a summer day's excursion.

- **Buses**. From Od. Mavrommatéon to **Markópoulo** (30km in 1 hr), half-hourly; also to **Pórto Ráfti** (36.5km in 1 hr), hourly. **Brauron** (Vravróna; 36km) can then be reached by the Markópoulo–Vravróna bus (twice daily, early morning and early afternoon). Alternatively, the half-hourly 304 service from the Ethnikí Amina Metró station (Line 3) to **Artemis** (Néa Loútsa) terminates at the Hotel Mare Nostrum, c 30 mins' walk from the Sanctuary of Artemis (less if the intervening valley is dry).
  Timing. 5–6 hrs are needed to accomplish the Brauron excursion in comfort, allowing time to see the site and museum. Using public transport Pórto Ráfti is best visited separately, although you can get there from Brauron by returning to Markópoulo and changing buses.

Passing beyond the mountain chain which encircles Athens, you enter the Mesóyia (the inland) to find, beyond the busy main roads which are the least attractive feature of rural Attica, fields, olive groves, extensive vineyards and a cluster of rather ungainly small towns, most of which have grown from village size in the last 30 years.

The attractive **Sanctuary of Artemis Brauronia** Thur, Fri, Sat, Sun 08.30–15.00; check days with EOT) lies just beyond the Artemis/Loútsa fork at the foot of a low hill, immediately below the little Late Byzantine chapel of **Ay. Yeóryios**.

History of Brauron

The name Vráona (Βράωνα) is a medieval corruption of Βραύρων but the ancient name has been readopted in the accusative Βραυρώνα (Vravróna/Vráona).

Brauron, one of the 12 ancient communities antedating the Attic synoikism, is situated in the broad and marshy valley of the subterranean Erasinos river, c 1.5km from the sea. The district apparently comprised the townships of *Halai Araphenides* (now Artemis, formerly Loútsa), a little to the north, and *Philiadai*. Peisistratos had estates in the neighbourhood.

In legend Iphigeneia brought to Brauron the image of Artemis which she and Orestes stole from Tauris (Euripides, *Iphigeneia in Tauris*, 1446–67). In one version she is virtually identified with the goddess and performs the ritual sacrifice of her brother; in another she herself dies at Brauron. A wooden image was taken by the Persians from Brauron to Susa. In Classical times the savage rites had been moderated, and Artemis was worshipped in her function as protectress of childbirth. The *Brauronia* was a ceremony held every four years, in which Attic girls between the ages of five and ten, clad in saffron robes, performed rites which included a dance where they were dressed as bears (see Aristophanes, *Lysistrata*, 645). The connection between bears, childbirth and Artemis recalls the legend of Callisto, an Arkadian princess who bore a child to Zeus and was changed into a bear—according to one version by Artemis. However, the purpose of the ritual remains mysterious.

In the late 4C BC the site suffered from flooding, and by the time of Claudius it was deserted; the early 1C AD writer Pomponius Mela, in his geographical survey of the inhabited world, *De situ Orbis* (II 3), claims that Thorikos and Brauron, formerly cities, were by then only names.

Excavations (1946–52, 1956–63), carried out with difficulty in the waterlogged valley by J. Papadhimitríou for the Greek Archaeological Society, show occupation since Middle Helladic times (earliest on the hill above).

The site

Beyond the chapel (above), a small shrine marked the entrance to a cavern whose roof collapsed in the 5C BC. The cave seems to have been venerated in Archaic times as the **tomb of Iphigeneia**. Other tombs probably belong to priestesses of Artemis.

On the lower ground are the remains of a **Doric Temple** of the 5C BC, measuring c 20 x 10m; its foundations stand on rock-hewn steps (possibly the 'holy stairs' mentioned by Euripides). Here were discovered dedicatory reliefs in coloured terracotta, bronze mirrors and votive jewellery. Many of these had been deposited in a **sacred pool** (now dry) below the temple.

Adjoining the temple is a huge Π-shaped **Stoa**, built before 416 BC. Inscriptions found within describe it as the 'Parthenon' of the *arktoi*, or 'bears'. It had nine dining-rooms (remains of tables and dining couches). Part of the colonnade (note the tall pillars which would have supported votive reliefs) and entablature were re-erected in 1962.

Just to the west is a remarkable stone **bridge** of the same period.

Inscriptions list other buildings (gymnasium, palaistra, stables, etc.) which have not so far been found.

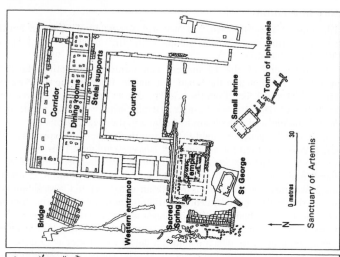

Sanctuary of Artemis

Corridor · Dining rooms · Stelai supports · Courtyard · Western entrance · Bridge · Sacred Spring · Temple · St George · Small shrine · Tomb of Iphigeneia

0 metres 30

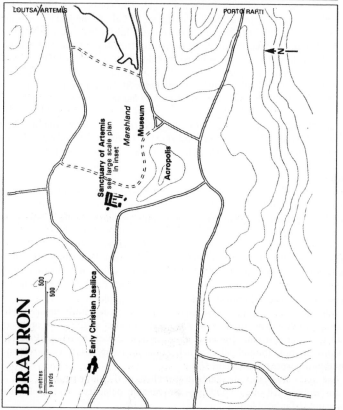

BRAURON

LOUTSA/ARTEMIS · PORTO RAFTI

Early Christian basilica

Sanctuary of Artemis
see large scale plan
in inset

Marshland · Museum · Acropolis

0 metres 500
0 yards 500

The interesting **Museum** (round the next bend in the road. Tues–Sun 08.30–15.00; closed Mon) has five rooms and a sculpture court. In the foyer, models reconstruct the appearance of the site. **Room 1** has a wide variety of objects offered in the sanctuary (vases, figurines, mirrors, jewellery, etc), some inscribed to Artemis; the sculpture in **rooms 2 and 3** includes marble statues and heads of the little girls and boys who served in the sanctuary. Some very fine 4C marble reliefs show worshippers approaching Artemis, and the goddess and her family. **Room 4** has a long series of vases and other objects from tombs at Merenda (ancient *Myrrhinous*). In **room 5** are Geometric finds from Anávissos; also Late Helladic IIIC (the final phase of the Mycenaean civilisation, c 1200–1075 BC) material from the important cemetery at Peratí (see below). Here too is important Middle Helladic and Mycenaean pottery from the acropolis of Brauron and tombs in the locality. The **court** has funerary monuments, mostly from Merenda.

Two kilometres beyond the museum is a right fork to **Pórto Ráfti** (7km from Brauron; no bus), while the left branch terminates at **Khamólia** (3km; camping, swimming).

Pórto Ráfti lies on a beautiful bay, tree-backed on the north and with sandy beaches to the south, also one of the best natural harbours in Greece, though not much used. The beach was the last in Attica to remain in Allied hands in April 1941, when 6000 New Zealand troops were evacuated. Now a busy resort, with private holiday homes and flats and a few hotels, it has acquired some less attractive suburbs. Nevertheless the development is largely confined to the coastal strip and the fine setting is dominant.

The bay is divided by a narrow rocky spit (Ay. Nikólaos, with tavernas, especially *To Dhíkhti*), off which is the islet of Prasonísi. It is protected from the sea by the islets of Ráfti and Raftopoúla. On Ráfti is a colossal Roman seated marble statue, popularly known as the 'tailor' (ráftis, ράφτης). This is the source of the modern name of the town.

Lávrio and *Thorikós*

Lávrio (pop. 8846) is a lively town, about 9km from ancient Soúnio, with marinas and an expanding port. There are one modest hotel, plenty of cafés and restaurants, and a large and colourful street market on Thursdays. Some attractive 19C buildings include a small market. The description is orientated to an approach from the north (Markópoulo, Thorikós).

The main ancient settlement was *Thorikos*, 2.5km north of the town.

• **Bus** to Lávrio (55km from Athens in 1.5 hrs; taking passengers for Keratéa and beyond only), runs hourly, or more frequently on Sundays and holidays, from Od. Mavrommatéon. These buses usually continue, after an interval, to Soúnio and thence to Athens by the coastal route (p 252). After Keratéa most buses now follow the new main road to Lávrio, dull but with some remains of mining establishments visible to either side. (The more interesting but tortuous old road passes near the little mining hamlet of **Pláka**, with a view down towards the bay of Thorikos. The site of ancient *Thorikos* is a short distance from the main road.) **Timing**. c 6 hrs.

Thorikos

The archaeological area is reached by turning left at a prominent sign (PPC: Public Power Corporation) and again at a smaller sign to 'Ancient Theatre of Thorikos'. The site, on the lower slopes of its acropolis—the conical hill of Velatoúri (prehistoric tombs)—is being restored.

The chief remains are an early elliptical **theatre**, close to which are a small temple of Dionysos and remains of an Archaic and Classical cemetery; a restored ore washery; a block of houses incorporating round towers (possibly for storing grain), later converted into workshops; a double temple (of Hygiaea?) with adjacent stoa. There is a tower 200m west of the theatre by the old Athens road, standing to a height of c 3.5m.

About 500m west and slightly south of the theatre—but best reached from a turning (Od. Dhervenakíon) 50m south of the junction of the old and new roads from Markópoulo—are remains of a peripteral **Doric building** (32 x 14.7m, with doorways in each of the long sides) of the later 5C BC. It has an unusual plan, with seven columns at the ends and 14 at the sides. The problem of its identity is not yet solved but it has been thought to be a Temple of Demeter. Much of its materials were transported to Athens in Augustan times and re-erected in the southeast corner of the Agora.

Towards the sea the promontory of **Ay. Nikólaos** divides the bay of Portomándri from Frankolimáni, a smaller bay to the north, now occupied by the power station. It provided a deep refuge, halfway between Piraeus and Rhamnous. At the neck of the promontory there are slight remains of a fortress of c 412 BC.

On the northern outskirts of Lávrio former mining buildings are being converted into a **technological park**. In Leofóros Andréa Kordhelá, off to the right as you come in, are two museums (signed).

The delightful new **Archaeological Museum** (Wed–Mon 10.00–15.00; closed Tues) has a good map of metallurgical and other ancient sites, explanations of the mining and silver working processes, also mining inscriptions; slabs of the frieze from the Temple of Poseidon at Sounion; finds of pottery, sculpture, etc from Thorikos, Sounion, Pasalimáni and elsewhere in the area; Final Neolithic, also earlier and later material, from the Kítsos cave; and a fine Early Christian mosaic from the town of Lávrio (Ay. Paraskeví). The small **mineral museum** (Wed, Sat, Sun 10.00–12.00, ☎ 229 202 6270), 200m further up the road, occupies a 19C building originally belonging to the French company that developed the mines.

Both the ancient and more recent (19C–20C) importance of the area derived from its mineral wealth, which contributed greatly to the power and prosperity of ancient Athens. There are many interesting sites connected with mining and ore processing in the area (see map and descriptions in archaeological museum; no access by public transport).

Reverse of silver tetradrachm (c 480–460 BC) showing the owl, symbol of Athens.

Dhafní and *Eleusis* (Elefsína)

Anyone hoping to recapture the atmosphere of antiquity by following the Sacred Way from Athens to Eleusis on foot will be sadly disappointed, since a good deal of the route is now urban and horribly industrialised. Nevertheless, the compensations are substantial. The mosaics at Dhafní monastery are exceptional. The Sanctuary of Demeter at Eleusis is fascinating, and well complemented by its museum. The Ierá Odhós (passing the Museum of Ancient Cypriot Art) is a much more pleasant route than the main Leofóros Athinón, which carries most of the long-distance traffic for Corinth and beyond.

Note that the **Dhafní monastery is closed** at the time of writing because of damage in the 1999 earthquake.

- **Buses.** A16 for **Elefsína** (22km; 45 mins), via the Ierá Odhós, passes Dhafní (11km; 20 mins); B16 goes via Leofóros Athinón. Both leave frequently from Plateía Koumoundoúrou (Eleftherías). From the city centre, local bus 026 for Votanikós, from Akadhimías, Síntagma (lower side), etc will take you to Plateía Koumoundoúrou (also the Museum of Cypriot art).
  Asprópirgos buses (from Plateía Koumoundoúrou) will also do for Dhafní via the Ierá Odhós. From Piraeus to Elefsína, the 845 goes from Plateía Karaïskáki.
  Trains (for Pátras and other places in the Peloponnese) go to Elefsína, every 1–2 hrs from Stathmós Peloponnísou (27km in 40–60 mins).
  Timing (by bus). Dhafní 2 hrs; Eleusis 4 hrs; both sites 5 hrs. To see both places in one day and allow time for diversions, it is a good idea to be at the first point of call early in the day, bearing in mind that the sites close at 15.00. Train travel would require considerably longer. Detailed exploration of the site at Eleusis requires several hours.

Opposite the Kerameikós you turn right from Od Piraiós into the Ierá Odhós which preserves both the name and, very largely, the original course of the ancient **Sacred Way** followed by initiates from Athens to Eleusis. Although there are now few signs of the tombs and shrines described at length by Pausanias, sections of the roadway itself and numerous examples of the tombs which lay beside it have been regularly uncovered in excavations.

At Kastoriás 34–36, about 800m along the Ierá Odhós (right; best bus access from other end by 025/026 from Akadhimías/Síntagma to Sp. Pátsi (stop in Leofóros Athinón) is the Athinaïs complex, housed in a former silk factory (1925) and its modern extension. Apart from cafés, restaurants and cinemas, this houses the **Pierídhis Museum of ancient Cypriot Art** (Mon–Sat 09.30–15.00, 17.00–23.00, Sun 10.00–15.00; closed Tues). Opened in 2001, it has four galleries (Prehistoric; Geometric-Archaic; Classical, Hellenistic and Roman; Byzantine and Medieval) with some impressive objects, interestingly displayed. Notable are the Prehistoric figurines and pottery, Archaic and Classical terracotta sculpture, Roman glass and Byzantine/Medieval pottery, some of the latter showing scenes of knightly activities (falconry). On the first floor is an **Art Gallery**, its contents drawn from the Pieridhis collection (p 247). Among the works at present on display are K. Tsóklis, *Dhéndro* (Tree; 1983) and G. Zongolópoulos, *To paikhnídhi ton fakón* (The game of the lenses; 1979). Both these artists have contributed impressive works to the decoration of new Metró stations (Ethnikí Amina and Síntagma respectively).

Dhafní

The **Monastery of Dhafní** (08.30–15.00; closed Mon; closed at time of writing, p 261) is surrounded by a high battlemented wall. Both church and walls incorporate ancient materials from a sanctuary of Apollo, on the same site, mentioned by Pausanias but destroyed c AD 395. The convent owes its name to the bay trees (*daphnai*) sacred to Apollo, which once flourished in the neighbourhood.

The monastery, founded in the 5C or 6C, was dedicated to the Virgin Mary. It was rebuilt at the end of the 11C, but sacked by Crusaders in 1205. In 1211 Otho de la Roche gave it to the Cistercians, who held it until 1458. Two dukes of Athens, Otho himself and Walter de Brienne, were buried here. Reoccupied in the 16C by Orthodox monks, it was subsequently abandoned in the War of Independence. Restorations were made in 1893 after the building had been used in turn as barracks and a lunatic asylum. The structure was strength-ened in 1920, and more radical restoration undertaken after the Second World War.

The fortified enceinte and a few foundations inside near the northeast corner survive from the site's earliest Christian phase. Of the 11C monastic buildings only some foundations of the great refectory can be seen on the north side. The pretty cloister

Christ Pantokrator: dome mosaic from Dhafní monastery

(restored), south of the church, dates from the Cistercian period, with the addition of 16C cells. Sculptural fragments, Classical and Byzantine, are displayed round it. The two sarcophagi, ornamented with fleurs-de-lys and Latin crosses, are sometimes supposed to be of the Frankish dukes.

The church

The church (plan, p 263) is a fine example of Byzantine architecture of c 1080, with an added exo-narthex, which was restored in 1961 to the later form given to it by the Cistercians. The pointed arches and crenellations provide an interesting contrast with the re-used Classical pillars. The truncated west tower on the north side had a Gothic belfry. The three-light windows of the church are separated by mullions and surrounded by three orders of brickwork. The lights are closed by perforated alabaster slabs. The drum of the dome has round engaged buttresses between each of its 16 windows.

You enter from the cloister by the south door. The most exciting feature of the interior is the marvellous **mosaics** (binoculars are useful for detailed

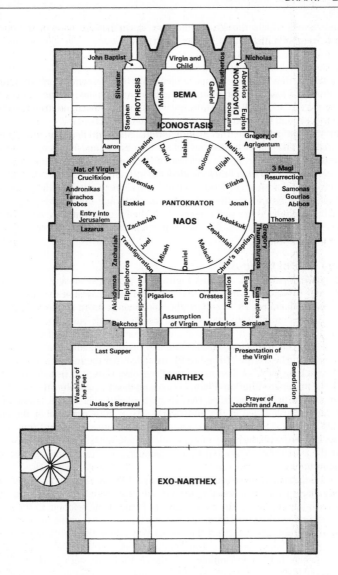

Washing of the Feet

John Baptist
Virgin and Child
Nicholas
Silvester
PROTHESIS
Michael
BEMA
Gabriel
Eleutherios
Aberkios
Euplos
DIACONICON
Laurence
Stephen
ICONOSTASIS
Aaron
Gregory of Agrigentum

Annunciation
David
Isaiah
Solomon
Nativity
Moses
Elijah
Nat. of Virgin
Crucifixion
Jeremiah
Elisha
3 Magi
Resurrection
Andronikas
Tarachos
Probos
Ezekiel
PANTOKRATOR
Jonah
Samonas
Gourias
Abibos
Entry into Jerusalem
Zachariah
NAOS
Habakkuk
Thomas
Lazarus
Joel
Zephaniah
Micah
Daniel
Malachi
Gregory Thaumaturgos
Transfiguration
Christ's Baptism
Akindymos
Zachariah
Elpidiphoros
Anempodismos
Pigasios
Orestes
Auxentios
Eugenios
Eustratios
Bakchos
Assumption of Virgin
Mardarios
Sergios

Last Supper
Presentation of the Virgin
NARTHEX
Benediction
Judas's Betrayal
Prayer of Joachim and Anna

EXO-NARTHEX

DAPHNI
0   3 metres

examination) which, though fragmentary in comparison with their original extent, are of outstanding quality, with some scenes fully preserved. The naturalism, subtlety of colouring, and delicacy and charm of detail all contribute to the striking overall effect.

In the narthex the most complete scenes are the *Presentation of the Virgin*, the *Prayer of Joachim and Anna* and the *Betrayal by Judas*. On the vault of the dome is a remarkable *Pantokrator*, uncompromisingly stern, on a gold ground. The frieze round the drum below has saints and prophets.

In the squinches are the *Annunciation*, *Nativity*, *Baptism* and *Transfiguration*. The *Nativity* has fine details of animals and landscape, and the *Baptism* is remarkable for the depiction of the River Jordan. On the west side of the north arm, the *Entry into Jerusalem* has interesting perspective effects (note the little boy's foreshortened feet); a child sits in a tree to watch. In the sanctuary, though the Virgin above the apse is fragmentary and the vault is empty, the flanking Archangels are well preserved. Of the frescoes that once adorned the lower walls of the church, four are still comparatively clear. There is a crypt beneath the church.

From Dhafní to Eleusis

Beyond Dhafní the broad and busy highway drops, past an ancient Sanctuary of Aphrodite (right, niches in rock), to the bay of Elefsína. Most of the Sacred Way has been obliterated. At the shore the road swings north to pass (right) the Límnes Koumoundoúrou, now salt marshes and ponds but, in antiquity, two small lakes (the *Rheitoi*) whose fish were a special privilege of the Eleusinian priesthood. The *Rheitoi* marked the boundary between Athens and Eleusis.

Inland from here is the **Thriasian Plain**, called after the ancient deme of *Thria* and stretching for c 14.5km along the Eleusinian Gulf. It is usually identified with the Rarian (or Rharian) Plain, in Greek myth supposedly the first area to be sown and the first to bear crops. Here Demeter made the ground lie fallow while her daughter remained in the underworld. The plain is now one of the most highly industrialised areas in the country; its oil tanks, chimneys and cargo quays combine with the heavy motor traffic to make the last 6.5km of the Sacred Way the least romantic road in Greece. Salamis is often obscured by dust and sulphur fumes.

At 21km from Athens you turn right (sign ΕΙΣΟΔΟΣ ΕΛΕΥΣΙΝΑΣ) just before a large garage to follow the old road, still called 'Ierá Odhós'. Very soon you approach a bridge under the main highway. Immediately before it, to the left of the road and opposite the Léfkes bus stop, are four complete arches of a splendid **Roman bridge**, which carried the Sacred Way across the Eleusinian Kifissos. The bridge, 5.5m wide and c 46m long, built of poros, probably dates from AD 124 when Hadrian was initiated into the Eleusinian mysteries. About 30m of the Sacred Way have been found to the west. Between the Roman bridge and the road is a well (*pigádhi*), with a marble surround, which has given its name to the vicinity (Kaló Pigádhi).

You continue under the bridge and along the Ierá Odhós into **Elefsína** (22km from Athens), an expanding industrial town (22,793 inhabitants). The chapel of **Ay. Zakharías**, on the right at the entrance to the main square, has an attractively restored exterior but little of interest inside. The church, however, stands among the substantial remains (columns, foundations, fragments of walling) of an **Early**

Christian basilica. On this site was found the famous relief of Demeter and Kore (p 201). You approach the main archaeological site along a pedestrian precinct. Building remains found in excavations here and in the open space in front of the site entrance are thought to be of a pompeion belonging to the sanctuary.

Ancient Eleusis

The ancient city of *Eleusis*, birthplace of the dramatist Aeschylus (525–456 BC) and home of the Sanctuary of Demeter and the Eleusinian Mysteries, was situated on a low rocky hill (63m) which runs parallel with and close to the shore. The Sanctuary is at the east end, the much less investigated town to the west. The **Sacred Way** (large sections, paved and with kerbs, have been traced here) from Athens led direct to the Sanctuary. The site lies left of the modern road at the entrance to the town, but the approach is signposted from the centre.

The Sanctuary had a continuous history from Mycenaean to Roman times, and extensive excavations have resulted in an archaeological site of considerable complexity. Its great interest lies partly in the unique ceremonies which the physical remains reflect and partly in the chance to compare material (the fortifications, for example) of different periods of antiquity.

History of Eleusis

Legends of the foundation of a city at *Eleusis* by Eleusis, a son of Ogygos of Thebes, before the 15C seem substantiated by remains of Middle Helladic (18C–17C BC) houses. Tradition tells of wars between the Athenians and Eleusinians in heroic times, resulting in the deaths of Erechtheus, king of Athens, and of Immarados, son of the Eleusinian Eumolpos. Eumolpos was reputed to be the first celebrant of the mysteries of Eleusis.

The introduction of the cult of Demeter is ascribed by the Parian Chronicle (an inscribed marble slab from the Cycladic island of Paros giving miscellaneous dates in Greek history) to the reign of Erechtheus (c 1409 BC) and by Apollodoros to that of Pandion, son of Erichthonios (c 1462–1423 BC). The first shrine (?) on the sanctuary site is dated by pottery to the Late Helladic II period (15C BC), though there is nothing concrete to connect it with Demeter. The 'Homeric' *Hymn to Demeter* (late 7C BC) gives the orthodox version of the institution of the mysteries by Demeter herself (see Mysteries, overleaf).

Eleusis seems to have been a rival of Athens until coming under Athenian control about the time of Solon. From then on the cult grew and the sanctuary was constantly enlarged. Its reputation became panhellenic and initiation was opened to non-Athenian Greeks. Rebuilding was carried out by Peisistratos, who doubled the size of the area and enclosed it with a strong wall; but his work fell victim to the Persian invasion. Kimon initiated the reconstruction which was completed under Perikles. His Telesterion (Hall of the Mysteries) was to survive, with modifications, to the end. Eleusis suffered under the Thirty Tyrants (p 60), who established here a fortified base against Thrasyboulos, massacring those who opposed them. The sanctuary was extended again in the 4C BC. The town remained a stronghold throughout the Macedonian period.

Under the Pax Romana the sanctuary was adorned with a new gate. The imperial transformation of Eleusis probably began under Hadrian. In AD 170 the sanctuary was sacked by the Sarmatians, but was immediately restored at the expense of Marcus Aurelius. At his initiation in 176 the Emperor was allowed to enter the *anaktoron*, the holy of holies, the only lay person so honoured in the whole history of Eleusis. Emperor Julian was initiated, completing his sanctification (according to Gibbon) in Gaul; Valerian (253–60) reorganised the defences of the site in the face of threats from barbarian tribes (Goths and Herulians); Valentinian allowed the Mysteries to continue, but Theodosius' decrees and Alaric's sack were jointly responsible (c 395) for their end. The town was abandoned after the Byzantine period and not reoccupied till the 18C.

The Mysteries

The 'Homeric' *Hymn to Demeter* recounts the anciently accepted mystique of the cult's divine foundation. While gathering flowers, Persephone (or Kore, the Maiden), Demeter's daughter, was carried off by Hades (Pluto) to the Underworld. During her quest for Persephone, Demeter came to Eleusis, where she was found resting on a rock (the 'Mirthless Stone'), disguised as an old woman, by Metaneira, consort of the ruler of Eleusis, King Keleos. The goddess's attempt to reward the king's hospitality by making his infant son Demophon immortal through fire was interrupted by Metaneira, whereupon Demeter revealed her identity and commanded Keleos to build a megaron in her honour. To this she retired, vowing that she would neither return to Mount Olympos, home of the gods, nor allow crops to grow on earth until Persephone was delivered up. Finally Zeus commanded Hades to return the girl but, because she had eaten pomegranate seeds (a symbol of marriage) while in the Underworld, she was bound to return there for part of every year. Before leaving Eleusis, Demeter broke the famine and gave to Triptolemos, second son of Keleos, seeds of wheat and a winged chariot, in which he rode over the earth, teaching mankind the use of the plough and the blessings of agriculture.

Candidates for initiation into the mysteries were first admitted to the Lesser Eleusinia which were held in the month of Anthesterion (February/March) at Agrai, in Athens, on the banks of the Ilissos. Once accepted as *mystai* (initiates), they were allowed to attend the Greater Eleusinia, which took place in Boëdromion (September) and lasted nine days, beginning and ending in Athens, during which time a truce was declared throughout Hellas. On the seventh night the qualified mystai became *epoptai* (initiates of the highest grade).

These annual celebrations (*teletai*) consisted of a public secular display and a secret religious rite. The former, the responsibility of the Athenian Archon Basileus and his staff, took the form mainly of a procession (*pompe*) from Athens to Eleusis. The religious rite was entirely in the hands of the hierophant (initiating priest) and priesthood of Eleusis, hereditary offices of the Eumolpids and the Kerykes, important Eleusinian families. The senior officials included the *dadouchos* (torchbearer) and the *hierokeryx* (herald). The procession took place on the fifth day. It was headed by a statue of Iakkhos, a god associated with the cult, and the *hiera* (sacred objects), which were carried in baskets (*kistai*).

During the Peloponnesian War, when no truce was declared, the procession was reduced; for some years after the Spartan occupation of Dekelia it went by sea. In 336 BC, the news of the destruction of Thebes by Alexander the Great caused the only recorded instance of the procession's cancellation after it had set out.

The fundamental substance of the Mysteries, the character of the sacred objects displayed and the nature of the revelation experienced were never divulged. Alkibiades was condemned to death *in absentia* (though later reprieved) for parodying part of the Mysteries; Aeschylus was almost lynched on suspicion of revealing their substance on the stage. It is thought probable that a pageant (*dromena*, things done) was performed representing the action of the Hymn of Demeter. Initiation carried with it no further obligation, but seems to have been spiritually uplifting. Cicero derived great comfort from the experience.

Eleusis attracted the attention of western travellers from Wheler (p 116) in 1676 onwards. E.D. Clarke carried off a statue to Cambridge in 1801. The propylaia were uncovered in 1812 by the Society of Dilettanti. Systematic excavations, started by the Greek Archaeological Society in 1882, were greatly extended by K. Kourouniotis in 1917–45, especially after the Rockefeller Institution had provided a grant in 1930. Both the earlier work and that done since the war by G.E. Mylonas, A.K. Orlandos and J. Travlos are well presented in Mylonas, *Eleusis and the Eleusinian Mysteries*, 1962. There has been much recent work by the Greek Archaeological Service.

Eleusis and the cinema

The excellent film *Ayélastos Pétra* (Mourning Rock, 2000), directed by Phílipps Koutsaftís, shot over a period of ten years and depicting the history both of excavation and of industrial Eleusis itself, enjoyed great success in Greece and is occasionally shown abroad. Note that *Ayélastos Pétra* is usually translated 'Mirthless stone', as in the text below.

The museum (p 273) contains two good **models** of the sanctuary, at different stages of its development. In view of the complexity of the remains, you may wish to look at these before studying the site. You can also get a good idea of the layout of the excavations from the terrace in front of the prominent 19C chapel overlying the Faustina temple (p 275).

From here you can go on to see the forecourt, the two propylaia, the telesterion, the southeast walls and the museum in a relatively short visit. For a detailed exploration of the remains you would need several hours. The acropolis is unrewarding and care is needed there since there are unfenced cisterns.

The Sanctuary of Demeter and Kore

The archaeological site lies at the foot and on the east slopes of the acropolis and includes the greater part of the Sanctuary of Demeter and Kore and its dependencies. The sanctuary was protected on three sides by the main city wall and separated from the settlement, on the fourth side, by a dividing wall. As you pass through the site entrance gate, the **Sacred Way** changes from a modern to an ancient paved road, ending in a spacious square before the city walls.

This **Great Forecourt** was part of the new monumental entrance planned probably in the reign of Antoninus Pius, and thus belonging to a late stage of the sanctuary's development. Here the mystai gathered to perform the necessary acts of purification before entering the sanctuary. A summer festival of music and drama now takes place here, using part of the forecourt as an auditorium and the Great Propylaia as a stage.

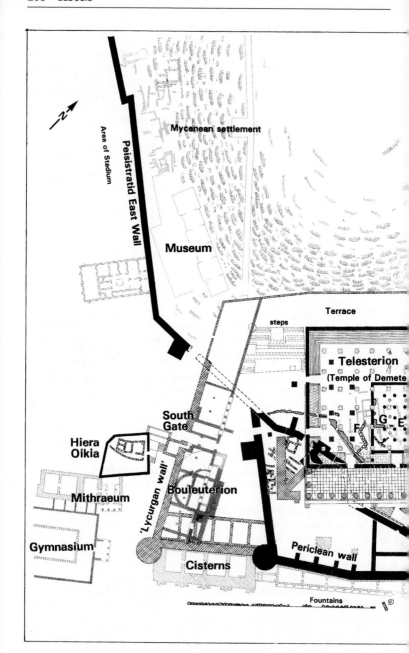

Mycenean settlement

Peisistratid East Wall

Area of Stadium

Museum

Terrace

steps

Telesterion

(Temple of Demeter)

G E

F

South
Gate

Hiera
Oikia

'Lycurgan wall'

Bouleuterion

Mithraeum

Gymnasium

Cisterns

Periclean wall

Fountains

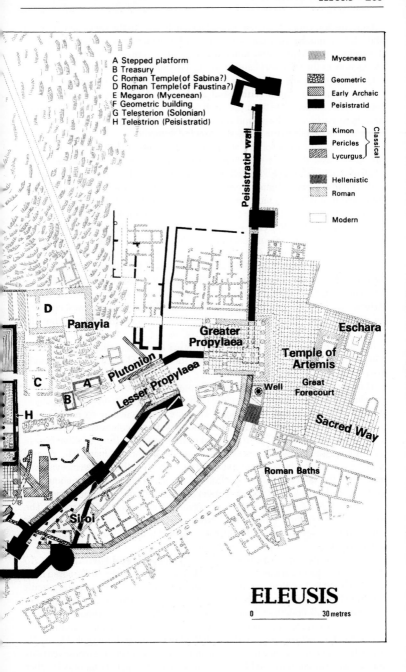

A Stepped platform
B Treasury
C Roman Temple (of Sabina?)
D Roman Temple (of Faustina?)
E Megaron (Mycenean)
F Geometric building
G Telesterion (Solonian)
H Telestrion (Peisistratid)

Mycenean

Geometric

Early Archaic

Peisistratid

Kimon
Pericles } Classical
Lycurgus

Hellenistic

Roman

Modern

Peisistratid wall

D

Panayia

Greater Propylaea

Eschara

Temple of Artemis

Plutonion

Lesser Propylaea

Well

Great Forecourt

C

A

B

H

Sacred Way

Roman Baths

Siroi

ELEUSIS

0   30 metres

From the forecourt, the Great Propylaia led directly to the sanctuary; to right and left triumphal arches gave access towards the main gate of the town and to the visitors' quarter of baths, hotels and recreation centres. Many of the marble blocks now in the forecourt came from the buildings that defined its limits.

On the left side are, in succession, the remains of a stoa, a fountain (with a columned façade), and a **triumphal arch**, one of two (see above) faithfully copied on a smaller scale from the Arch of Hadrian at Athens. The foundations have been partially restored and the gable reassembled in front. An inscription reads 'All the Greeks to the Goddesses and the Emperor'.

Next, between a tower of the 5C circuit and the side of the Great Propylaia, is the sacred well that passed throughout Classical times for the **Kallikhoron** (Well of the Fair Dances). The well-head, beautifully made of polygonal masonry with clamps, probably dates from the time of Peisistratos (6C). Mylonas has suggested that this is, in fact, the Parthenion (Well of the Maidens), mentioned in the Hymn as the place where Demeter rested. The name Kallikhoron may have been transferred to it from the well near the Telesterion after the significance of the Parthenion had become attached to the 'Mirthless Stone' on which the goddess actually sat (pp 266–267).

In the centre of the court are the scanty remains of the marble, amphiprostyle **Temple of Artemis Propylaia and Poseidon**. It must have been quite new when described by Pausanias. The **altar** to the east was presumably dedicated to Artemis, that to the north probably to Poseidon, while at the northwest corner is an **eschara**, constructed in Roman tiles over remains which show that the sacred nature of the spot goes back to the 6C BC.

On the right side of the forecourt are another stoa and remains of the second triumphal arch. The part of the site beyond these can be looked at after the main area.

The **Great Propylaia**, built in Pentelic marble on a concrete core by Marcus Aurelius or his predecessor, are a close copy of the Propylaia on the Acropolis in Athens, both in plan and dimensions. They are approached by six marble steps and face northeast. The façade contained six Doric columns. Parts of the entablature (Doric frieze) are to the right of the steps, as is the medallion bust of (?) Marcus Aurelius which occupied the middle of the pediment. The central passage was flanked by six Ionic columns (bases in situ). The transverse wall was pierced by five doorways; the threshold of the small one to the left shows the greatest wear. At some time of danger (possibly under Valerian) the Doric colonnade was closed by a thick wall, turning it into a fortified entrance. The single door that then formed the entrance has left a roller groove in the pavement. Crosses scored on the pavement probably derive from Christian fears of pagan spirits.

Beneath the gateway is a corner tower of the **Peisistratid Fortifications**. To the west this enceinte remained the city's defence in later times; to the east a later wall enclosed a Classical extension to the city, when the Peisistratid circuit continued to serve as the peribolos of the sanctuary. Between the two walls are numerous small buildings dating mainly from the time of Kimon. The area between the two propylaia seems to have been a level forecourt in Roman times.

Turning half left you proceed through the **Lesser Propylaia**, probably on the site of the original entrance to the inner sanctuary. The structure whose remains you see was vowed to the goddesses by Cicero's friend Appius Claudius Pulcher (inscription) in his consulship (54 BC) and completed after his death by two nephews. It consisted of two parallel walls, each 15m long with Ionic attached columns, enclosing a passage 10m wide. The passage is divided into three at its inner end by two short parastadia (secondary walls) parallel to the exterior walls. Forward of the doors, whose supporting rollers have left prominent grooves, were antae; the bases in front of them carried two Corinthian columns. The inside façade had Caryatids instead of columns. Parts of the inscribed architrave and frieze are recomposed at the side. The frieze consists of triglyphs and metopes, both carved with emblems of the cult: ears of corn, *bucrania* (bulls' heads), sacred baskets, etc.

The inner **Precinct of Demeter** was, for 2000 years, an area forbidden to the uninitiated on penalty of death. To the right is the **Plutonion**, a triangular precinct of the 4C BC, enclosing a cavern sacred to Pluto (Hades). A shrine was built at its mouth in the Peisistratid period; the surviving foundations are of a temple completed in 328 BC (a dated inscription has been found referring to the purchase of its wooden doors).

Following the processional road, you come next to a rock-cut stepped **platform** (Plan A) which adjoined a small building, perhaps a **treasury** (Plan B). The platform may have served as a stand for spectators of the sacred pageant. Mylonas suggests that the '**Mirthless Stone**' can be identified with the worked piece of rock that projects here above the pavement of the Roman Sacred Way. Also by the wayside, a **thesauros** (offertory box), made from a boulder, has a slot for contributions.

The levelled terrace beyond the treasury supported a **temple** (Plan C), possibly dedicated to Sabina, wife of Hadrian, on whom the Greeks had conferred the title of New Demeter.

From here you ascend to the large square platform on which the Telesterion stood.

The Telesterion

The first shrine decreed by Demeter 'beneath the citadel and its sheer wall upon a rising hillock above the Kallikhoron' occupied a restricted site on steeply sloping ground. Each time the sanctuary was enlarged, the artificial terrace on which it stood had to be extended. As a result, each shrine escaped complete destruction by being buried under the next. The result is an archaeological palimpsest of rare completeness but considerable complexity.

The Telesterion, where candidates were initiated into the Mysteries, is an almost square chamber (53 x 52m) partly cut into the rock of the acropolis and partly built on a terrace. The existing remains are mainly of the Periklean rebuilding (with the addition of the 4C Portico of Philo), as finally remodelled by Marcus Aurelius.

History of the building

Excavations have revealed traces of at least six earlier structures on the same site. The Mycenaean megaron (remains of two walls in the northeast half of the hall—Plan E) was a chamber c 17m square. This was replaced by a Geometric structure (Plan F), a Solonian telesterion (Plan G) and again by the telesterion of Peisistratos (Plan H), which occupied the northeast corner of the final structure. This hall had five rows of five columns each, with a portico on the northeast front, and was destroyed by the Persians. Kimon incorporated the ruins into a rectangular hall, designed round the old *anaktoron* (see below), and with seven rows of three columns each. It was apparently not finished. Perikles probably instigated a grander design in which the building again became square, doubling that of Kimon. This was first entrusted to Iktinos, whose plan to support the roof on only 20 columns (foundations visible) had to be abandoned for technical reasons. The design was replaced by another by Koroibos, which was completed after his death by Metagenes and Xenokles. Lykourgos may have ordered the Portico of Philo. The L-shaped foundations that extend beyond the east and south corners show that earlier plans for building a peristyle were started. After the sanctuary was sacked by Sarmatian invaders, the Romans restored the interior with somewhat makeshift columns and extended the northwest side another 6 ft into the rock.

The **Periklean telesterion** (Plan H) had, on each of the four sides, eight tiers of seats, partly built and partly rock-cut. These were interrupted at six points, for two doors on each of the disengaged sides. The hall accommodated 3000 people. Six rows of seven columns each supported the (? wooden) roof; they were in two tiers separated by an epistyle (possibly with a frieze). The bases of most of the columns remain; one of them has as its top course a re-used block of the 1C AD, showing the extent of the Roman restoration.

In the centre of the building, on the site it had occupied from the beginning, was the **anaktoron** ('holy of holies', literally 'palace') a small rectangular room roofed somehow by Xenokles with an *opaion*, or lantern, of which no trace has survived. By the side of the anaktoron stood the throne of the hierophant.

The location of the anaktoron can be seen from the excavation trench left open in the floor of the main chamber. It contains remains of four architectural phases (Mycenaean, Solonian, Peisistratid and Kimonian), of which the most obvious are parts of a corner of the Solonian telesterion (Plan G) in grey polygonal masonry and some column bases belonging to the Kimonian phase.

The solid walls of the exterior of the telesterion, broken only by doorways, must have enhanced the air of mystery. In the 4C the southeast front was adorned by the **Portico of Philo** whose pavement and massive supporting wall (18 courses of masonry) form one of the most prominent features of the site. This was completed, according to Vitruvius, in the reign of Demetrios of Phaleron. The huge prostoön (columned porch) had a colonnade of 12 x 2 unfluted Doric columns.

In front of the Portico of Philo was a **court**. This stood on an artificial terrace, enlarged with each successive reconstruction, in which the fortification wall of the previous sanctuary was often used as a retaining wall for the new. The greater part of the Late Classical fill has been removed to show the successive stages, making clear the steepness of the natural contour, but obscuring the form of the court.

Walking forward from the portico you can inspect its impressive foundations, parts of the walls and other structures.

Sections of the **Wall of Peisistratos** are roofed with corrugated iron to preserve the upper part, which was made of unbaked bricks. A stretch immediately below the centre of the Portico of Philo shows where Kimon filled the Persian breach in the mud-brick wall with limestone masonry in alternately large and narrow courses (pseudo-isodomic), based directly on the Peisistratean socle. The inner face is rough and evidently retained a fill of earth. Within this wall parts of an Archaic polygonal terrace wall can be seen. Beyond the Peisistratid corner-tower are the remains of a Kimonian **gate**. This was later blocked by the Periklean **siroi** (pits for keeping corn), where the first-fruit offerings were stored; several of their rectangular piers are prominent.

You now return past the portico. In the 5C the south side of the court was bounded by the **Periklean Wall**. In the following century this became largely redundant when the sanctuary was extended to the new **South Wall of Lykourgos**. Against the inside face of the Lykourgan wall (at a high level) are some remains attributed to successive Hellenistic and Late Roman rebuildings of a **bouleuterion** (council chamber): the apse of its main room can be picked out against the Wall, near the Lykourgan **South Gate**.

Down below, outside this gate, is a trapezoidal precinct wall of polygonal masonry. Within are the foundations of a sacred house, the **Hiera Oikia**, a Geometric building dedicated to the memory of a hero: it was destroyed early in the 7C BC, but remained a scene of religious rites into the Archaic period. Beyond are some traces of a **Mithraeum** (temple of Mithras). Further again a Roman **gymnasium** is easily located by the remains of its entrance portico (column bases). What may be a terrace wall of the dolicho (3C–2C BC racecourse) has been found in the built-up area beyond the site fence.

The first three of these buildings can be seen from above, but you can descend to the corner of the site enclosure past the Gymnasium (this point is also accessible by a path from the Great Forecourt along the outside of the fortifications), to get an instructive panorama of contrasting types of ancient wall construction. Looking from there towards the museum you see the perfectly fitted polygonal masonry (6C) of the peribolos of the Sacred House. To the right is the Lykourgan Wall (?370–360 BC), one of the best preserved examples of ancient fortification, with both a square and a round tower. On four slightly receding courses in pecked Eleusinian stone are set tooled courses in yellow poros, probably a conscious matching of the Periklean style. In the direction of the site entrance the Lykourgan Wall is masked by ruined Hadrianic cisterns beyond which, still against the outer face of the (here Periklean) Wall, is a row of Roman fountains. Here the **Periklean east wall**, like the Lykourgan, has a separate socle, which is rusticated, while the upper courses are bevelled. Further on, the higher courses, in haphazardly re-used masonry, belong to the Valerian reconstruction.

On either side of the Telesterion a flight of steps was cut in Roman times to give access to a wide terrace, 6m above the hall floor on the west side.

The museum

You climb the southern steps to the site museum. Outside are a **Roman sarcophagus** (c AD 190) in marble with a well-carved scene of the Kalydonian boar-hunt (the lid does not belong); two representations in white marble of torches (c 2.5m high), an emblem frequently associated with Demeter and Kore and the Mysteries; a capital from the Lesser Propylaia; a fine **head of a horse**; and marble lekythoi.

Room I (to the right). Copy of the Niinnion Tablet, a red-figured votive *pinax* now in the National Archaeological Museum (p 201); the figures are believed to be performing rites from the Mysteries—if so, it is the only known representation. A votive Roman **marble piglet** represents an animal particularly associated with Demeter. There is a reconstruction of one corner of the geison of the Peisistratid telesterion; an Archaic kouros (c 540 BC); a fine **Running girl** (c 485 BC) from the pediment of the Hiera Oikia, an early example of the use of drapery to create a feeling of movement. In the centre is a famous **Proto-Attic amphora** (7C BC), depicting Odysseus blinding Polyphemos and Perseus slaying Medusa. **Votive reliefs**: marble stele depicting Demeter seated, holding ears of corn, with (probably) Hekate, holding torches (c 475 BC); stele (411 BC) showing a fight between Athenian cavalry and Spartan hoplites, with a rare depiction of a landscape; a decree of 421 BC concerning the construction of a bridge over the *Rheitoi* (p 264); the relief shows Demeter and Persephone (left), Athena (armed) and a citizen of Eleusis (right).

In **room II** (entrance-hall) is a cast of the most famous **Eleusinian relief**, now in the National Archaeological Museum, Athens (p 201). Facing the door is a fine **statue of Demeter** (headless and armless), perhaps by Agorakritos of Paros, pupil of Pheidias (420 BC); behind is the fragmentary relief of Lakratides (1C BC), showing Triptolemos setting out in his chariot; the statue of Persephone is Roman. Relief of Demeter on the 'Mirthless Stone' approached by votaries.

Room III Heads and statues, including an Asklepios, dedicated by Epikrates (320 BC), found in the 19C some distance from the site and probably from a sanctuary of Asklepios. Archaistic kore (her partner is in London) with bowl for ritual ablutions. **Room IV** has **models of the site** at two stages of its development (Peisistratid and Roman). **Roman statuary**: Antinoös, Hadrian's favourite, represented as a youthful Dionysos standing by the Delphic omphalos; statues of Tiberius and Nero (both veiled, as pontifex maximus); small and delicate Herakles; 5C Demeter embracing Persephone.

Room V Caryatid in the form of a *kistephore* (basket-carrier) from the inner parastade of the Lesser Propylaia (its fellow is in the Fitzwilliam Museum, Cambridge). The green **stole**, in a good state of preservation, from a burial of the 5C BC is the only linen cloth surviving from the Classical period. Amphora of c 610 BC from Megara by the Chimaera painter; inhumation burials, including that of a boy in a *larnax* (terracotta coffin); decree reliefs; votive terracottas.

Room VI Vases of all periods from Prehistoric to Late Roman, including a plain Mycenaean vase with a Linear B inscription (perhaps an unidentified Cretan place name) which recurs on the Knossos tablets and *kernoi* (multiple vessels), characteristic sacred vessels of the cult. There are some good **votive plaques**, bronze votives and two stone figurines, one Neolithic and one Early Cycladic, from the island of Amorgós.

Other buildings on the site
Beyond the museum are some Prehistoric (Middle and Late Helladic) and Roman buildings. Mycenaean houses have been found on the **acropolis** but little survives. However, there is a pleasant view towards Salamis. The Frankish tower that formerly crowned a height to the west fell victim to the quarrying activities

of the cement factory, as did a Hellenistic fort on the same site. The core of the **ancient city** was here, west of the acropolis, with some elements outside the walled circuit.

At the east point of the acropolis, above the Lesser Propylaia, a **chapel** (of the Panayía) with a detached belfry occupies part of a platform on which, in Roman times, stood a **temple** (Plan D), probably dedicated to Faustina, wife of Antoninus Pius.

From the chapel you can descend again to the Lesser Propylaia, northwest of which are some ruins of a Roman house, perhaps the property of the Kerykes, (see p 266). Further off is the **Asty Gate** of the Peisistratid enceinte; its plan, uncovered by J. Travlos in 1960, is well preserved. Still further west was the Megarian Gate. The wall has not survived, but part of the ancient road from Eleusis to Megara has been found there.

The Roman quarter to the east of the Great Forecourt is interesting for its baths, with piped water and a great drain with brick vaults and manholes at regular intervals.

Pórto Yermenó (*Aigósthena*)

You take the old road between Elefsína and Thebes, slow but attractive. The bus turns into **Vília**, a green and restful hill village. At Pórto Yermenó on the coast below is the large, well-preserved **Classical** (4C BC) **fort of ancient** *Aigósthena*. Against the north wall of the fort, a small 12C church of Ay. Anna stands in the apse of the central aisle of a huge five-aisled 6C AD Early Christian basilica. Just beyond the Vília turn, a hill is crowned by *Eleutherai* (Yiftókastro), another fine 4C BC **fort**, commanding the Káza pass. Pórto Yermenó has good swimming, a hotel, rooms and restaurants; Vília several hotels (most summer only) and other facilities.

Byzantine church amid the foundations of an Early Christian basilica within the ancient fort at Aigósthena

- **Bus** for Erithres (nine daily from Thisío), changing in Vília for Pórto Yermenó (total distance 73.5km)—two connections daily (more in summer). Yiftókastro can be reached by the direct Erithres bus, or by picking up an Erithres bus in Vília.

  Timing. The bus journey takes 1.5–2 hrs in each direction; exploring the fort needs 1–2 hrs. Adding Eleutherae by public transport would require a good deal more time and careful planning.

Marathon and *Rhamnous* (Marathónas and Rhamnoúnda)

The chief and most evocative memorial of the great Battle of Marathon in 490 BC is the Sorós (the burial mound of the Athenian dead). There is also a good museum and a host of other sites. Rhamnous is an attractive and interesting place, worth visiting as much for its romantic isolation and the beauty of its setting, as for its archaeological interest, with the Sanctuary of Nemesis and an ancient town (even though the only part currently accessible is the sanctuary). Panoramic views of the plain of Marathon can be enjoyed from the road which descends from beyond Kifissiá to the coast at Néa Mákri. However, this approach is only possible by car, as the bus goes via the coast.

- **Marathónas**. 42km from Athens in c 1 hr. **Buses** run half-hourly in the morning, hourly thereafter, from Od. Mavrommatéon.

  Rhamnoúnda. **Buses** run 5–6 times daily from Od. Mavrommatéon to Ayía Marína. You get off at the Ay. Marína turn (8.5km beyond Marathónas) and continue for another 6.5km on foot to Rhámnous (58km from Athens). There are also buses seven times daily from Od. Mavrommatéon to **Káto Soúli** (47km from Athens) via Marathon. From there **Rhamnous** is 11km on foot.

  Timing. Although the **Sorós** is easily accessible from Athens—by bus and a short walk—there is no public transport linking it with the museum (c 4km away), and viewing others of the numerous archaeological sites in the area would need to be done by car or on foot. To see the Sorós, the museum and immediately accessible sites you need about 6 hrs including the trip to and from Athens (on public transport).

  The excursion to **Rhamnous** (16km beyond Marathónas, 6.5km of which would be on foot if you are using public transport) is described separately but can be combined with Marathon easily with a car, possibly even by public transport if use of the few Ay. Marína buses is carefully planned. The bus leaves Athens through the northern suburbs and Ay. Paraskeví. The road beyond is busy and commercial buildings have accumulated along it. It is not until after the Rafína turn (27km) that you feel you are in the countryside.

Marathon

The Plain of Marathon

Although best known for the famous battle, the area has produced interesting archaeological discoveries of various periods. The plain, 10km long and 2.5–5km wide, its original character radically changed by modern drainage,

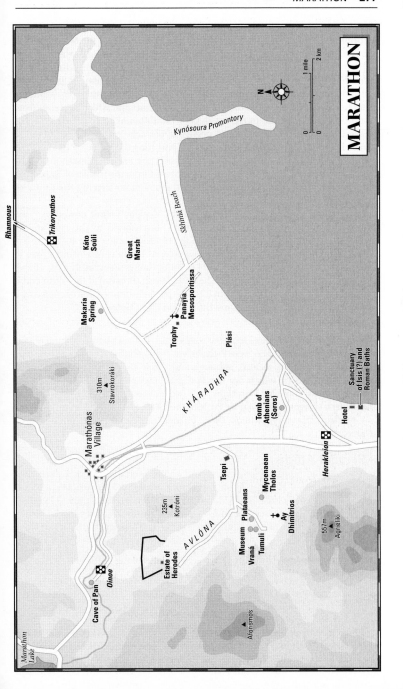

MARATHON

N

0   1 mile
0   2 km

Kynósoura Promontory

Rhamnous

Trikorynthos

Káto Soúli

Great Marsh

Skhiniá Beach

Makaria Spring

Panayía Mesosportíssa

Trophy

Plási

310m
Stavrokoráki

Marathónas Village

KHÁRADHRA

Tomb of Athenians (Soros)

Sanctuary of Isis (?) and Roman Baths

Hotel

Herakleion

Tsepi

Mycenaean Tholos

235m
Kotróni

Plataeans

Ay Dhimítrios

557m
Agrelíki

Museum
Vraná   Tumuli

AVLÓNA

Estate of Herodes

Marathon Lake

Cave of Pan

Oinoe

Aforismós

extends in a crescent shape round the Bay of Marathon, from the **Kynósoura Promontory** (with an unidentified acropolis) in the north to the promontory of Ay. Andréas (south), although the broader sweep reaches as far as Rafína (Cape Kávos). On the landward side it is shut in by the stony mountains that 'look on Marathon' (Byron, *The isles of Greece*). These are not particularly high but rise abruptly from the plain. Stavrokoráki (310m), the most northerly, is separated from Kotróni (235m) by the torrent bed of the Kháradra, which descends from Marathon Lake past the modern village of Marathónas to the sea. Geologists suggest that it would have been a negligible obstacle in the plain in Classical times. Between Kotróni and Aforismós (573m) runs the valley of Avlóna. The valley is joined at the village of Vraná (possibly the ancient Marathon) by the Rapentósa Gorge. This defile runs north-northeast from the hamlet of Rapentósa between Aforismós and Agrielíki (556m), the mountain forming the southern barrier of the plain.

In the north of the plain the Great Marsh (Megálos Váltos; nowadays criss-crossed by drainage canals) stretches from Stavrokoráki to the base of the Kynósoura Promontory, where it ends in the small salt-water lake of Drakonéra. The area includes a wetland with rare wildlife. At the time of writing a plan to build here a rowing course for the 2004 Olympic Games seems likely to go ahead, in spite of considerable opposition. The Little Marsh (Brexísa) at the south end is probably a post-Classical formation; it is now partially drained and occupied by a Greek (formerly US) naval base and the Golden Coast Hotel.

Ancient Marathon

Ancient *Marathon* was one of four townships which formed a tetrapolis (unit of four cities) in the area. The others were *Probalinthos*, *Trikorynthos* and *Oinoë*. Of these only Oinoë has been clearly located, although finds made elsewhere in the plain must belong to the others, which are mentioned in inscriptions. Suggested locations include Plási or Vraná for Marathon itself (which was definitely not on the site of the modern village); Néa Mákri for Probalinthos; Káto Soúli for Trikorynthos.

V. Petrakos, *Marathon*, Athens, 1995. Includes museum and surrounding area (Oinoë, etc).

Herodes Atticus

A name that crops up frequently, both in this area and in other parts of Greece, is that of Herodes Atticus, a famous intellectual and teacher, and a rich public benefactor. Born in Marathon in AD 103, he died there in 179. He was made a Roman senator in 143. Gibbon wittily describes the sudden wealth of Herodes' father, Julius. Discovering vast treasure buried in an old house, he decided to anticipate informers by reporting his find to the emperor. Told by Nerva to use it as he wished, he devoted large sums to public works as well as to the education of his son. After his distinguished public career Herodes retired to Athens and continued the munificence of his father. Although Marathon was his family home, he had estates in other places (e.g. at Kifissiá and at Kynouría in the Peloponnese) which were notable for their fine villas and mosaic and sculptural decoration. His public benefactions included the Odeion which bears his name, the rebuilding of the Stadium in Athens, works and monuments at Corinth, Delphi and Olympia, and numerous dedications elsewhere.

The Athenian burial mound (Sorós)

At 38km from Athens, a sign (right) directs you to the **Marathon Tomb** (open 08.30–15.00; closed Mon; there is a large car park and a café). The tomb is a mound, 10m high and c 180m round, marking the graves of the 192 Athenians who fell in the battle. The top of the mound has a view of the battlefield. At the foot is a copy of the grave stele of the warrior Aristion, found in 1839 at Velanidhéza, south of Rafína; the original (c 510 BC) is in the National Archaeological Museum. Although once thought to belong to a casualty of the battle of Marathon, the stele is in fact too early in date. The 'tombstones with the names of the fallen arranged according to tribes', which Pausanias (I 32 3) tells us were set over the Sorós, have disappeared.

Contrary to usual practice, the fallen at Marathon were buried where they fell in recognition of their outstanding valour. Excavations undertaken in 1890 confirmed the ancient tradition attaching to the Sorós: ashes and calcined bones, as well as black-figured lekythoi of the early 5C, were discovered. Obsidian arrowheads found on the surface by Schliemann six years earlier, which led him to attribute a much earlier date to the mound, may have been used by the Ethiopian archers (Hdt. VII 69). Of the other dead in the battle, no graves have been found of the slaves, who are said to have fought for the first time at Marathon. The Persian dead were probably just flung into an open trench, as Pausanias says. For the Tomb of the Plataians, see below (p 280).

The Battle of Marathon

After easily reducing Eretria in Euboea in 490 BC, the Persians crossed to Attica. Datis, their general, was probably influenced in his choice of the Bay of Marathon by Hippias, whose father Peisistratos had landed here successfully 50 years before. Meanwhile the Athenians, after despatching Pheidippides post-haste for Spartan aid, marched to Marathon and encamped in the sanctuary of Herakles (Herakleion), a strong position commanding the road from Athens. The Persian numbers, not stated by Herodotos and grossly exaggerated by later Athenian tradition, are now thought not to have exceeded two divisions of infantry (perhaps 24,000 men) and a small force of cavalry. The Athenians received unexpected aid from the state of Plataia (near Thebes), which sent its whole available force, perhaps 1000 strong, to join the 8000–9000 men of Athens. The commander was the Polemarch Kallimakhos, the archon responsible for military matters, whose staff of ten generals included Miltiades (the traditional architect of the victory), and perhaps Themistokles and Aristides.

Four days passed, with the Persians unwilling to attack the strong Athenian position, and the Athenians to leave it without the expected Spartan reinforcements. Believing he had failed to lure the Athenian army down into the plain, Datis re-embarked his cavalry to move on Athens by sea, sending a land force forward to cover the operation. Seeing them within striking distance, probably soon after dawn on 12 September 490 BC, Miltiades gave the word for action. He had left his centre weak and strongly reinforced his wings; the right wing, the place of honour, was led by Kallimakhos; on the left wing were the Plataians. The Greek hoplites advanced rapidly across the mile of no man's land before the surprised Persians could get their archers properly into action, possibly helped by tree cover (Professor A.R. Burn has pointed out the similarity of tactics used at Bannockburn). The Athenian wings were successful, while their weak centre was pierced by the Persians. The wings then enveloped the Persian centre which broke. In the ensuing rout the Persians fled to their ships. Many of them were caught in the great marsh. They lost 6400 men; the Athenian dead numbered only 192, including Kallimakhos. All were buried on the spot. A runner is said to have been sent to Athens, where he died of exhaustion after announcing the victory.

The Persian fleet, having lost only seven ships, put out to sea in an attempt to surprise Athens; but Miltiades, by a rapid march, reached Athens first, and the Persians sailed back to Asia. The battle proved that the long-dreaded Persians were vulnerable and was 'the victory of which the Athenians were proudest'. The Spartan army arrived in time to view the battlefield on the following day. Of the many legends attached to the battle, perhaps the best known are those of the ghostly assistance of Theseus, the legendary king of Attica, and of the rustic god Pan, who appeared to Pheidippides on his way to Sparta (see above)—a journey (of c 240 km) after which 'Marathon' has become a term for any lengthy trial of endurance, including the Olympic race. The impressive silence of the plain is said to resound at night to the clash of arms and the neighing of steeds—though it is almost certain that no Greek cavalry took part.

From the Sorós you can continue (c 1km) to the long, tree-backed shore (hotels, cafés; swimming).

The museum and sites at Vraná

Back on the main road, after c 1.5km a road (left) forks back to the hamlet of Vraná (4km from the Sorós site; signs to Mouseíon Marathóna). About 100m down this road (right), mostly covered by a hangar, is the archaeological site of **Tsépi**, a large Early Helladic cemetery (closed, partly visible from outside) containing carefully arranged and well-built cist graves. Both the graves and their contents are of Cycladic type.

Between this point and Vraná, the Avlóna valley stretches northwest (right). Up the valley (2.5km; follow signs to Naval Helicopter Base) a huge roughly walled enclosure (3.3km circuit), known locally as the Mándra tis Griás is identified by an inscription (see Museum) from its gateway as the boundary of the estate of **Herodes Atticus and Regilla**, his wife.

At 2.3km (right) a big tumulus (enquire at museum for access), excavated in 1969–70, is probably the **Tomb of the Plataians** who fell at Marathon, which Pausanias records as a separate memorial, although the identification is not certain. The mound, constructed entirely of stones, contains two circles of pit graves. Skeletons found were mostly of young men, and the pottery in the graves is contemporary with that in the Athenian Sorós.

Just north of the museum, under a large shelter, are Prehistoric grave circles consisting of paved slabs, each circle containing stone tombs of Middle to Late Helladic date. The skeleton of a Przewalski-type horse occupies a separate tomb but this is probably a later intrusion. There is another circle nearby.

The **Museum** (open 08.30–15.00; closed Mon) has five rooms. You turn right. **Room I** contains Neolithic pottery from the Cave of Pan at Oinoë. Finds in **room II** are from the Early Helladic cemetery at Tsépi (cases 4–5), Middle Helladic tumuli at Vraná (case 6) and Geometric graves (cases 7–8). **Room III** has vases and other finds from the Tombs of the Athenians (case 10) and Plataians (case 11); a bronze cinerary urn; boundary stones and inscribed stelai. In the centre is part of a trophy (Ionic capital, etc) erected by the Athenians (?) to celebrate the victory of Marathon. It was topped by a sculpture. Inscriptions relate to sanctuaries of Herakles and Athena. In **room IV** are Classical grave stelai and furnishings, a rare bronze mirror with wooden covers, objects from various cemeteries and Panathenaic amphorae. **Room V** contains Hellenistic and Roman finds, including an inscription concerning Herodes Atticus, and Egyptianising figures from the temple of Isis at Brexísa. In the court are lintel fragments from the Isis sanctuary and inscribed blocks from the arch of the entrance to Herodes' estate.

Rhamnous

Turning right at the lights just before Marathónas village, you follow the foot of the hills. At 46km there is a turning (right) to Skhoiniá beach, which is long and sandy. Right of the road is the projected site of the Olympic rowing course (p 278). You cross a lonely upland valley with barren hills on either side. At 51.5km, after Káto Soúli, a fork to the right would take you to the little seaside hamlet of **Ay. Marína** (ferry to Evvia).

Bearing left the road rises gradually to (58km) **Rhamnous** (commonly Rhamnoúnda), one of the least spoilt sites in Attica. The name was derived from the prickly shrub (ράμνος) which still grows in the neighbourhood. In more recent times the fortress was known as Ovriókastro, a corruption of *Evraío Kástro* (Jews' Castle).

History of *Rhamnous*

The headland was famous as early as the 6C BC for the worship of Nemesis. Its small cove provided shelter on an otherwise inhospitable coast for ships about to pass the dangerous narrows of Ay. Marína. Later a fortress was built to watch over navigation in the Euripos. This gained importance in 412 BC after the Athenian loss of Dekelia, when Rhamnous became the port of entry for food from Euboea, since it provided the only route entirely on Attic soil that did not involve passing the narrows. Rhamnous was the birthplace of the orator Antiphon (b. 480 BC), whose school of rhetoric was attended by Thucydides.

Excavation and study The **sanctuary** was first studied by the Society of Dilettanti in 1817, partially excavated by Staïs in 1890–94, and re-examined by A. Orlandos in 1922–23 (*BCH* 1924). The **fortress** was described by J. Pouilloux in *La forteresse de Rhamnonte* (1954). Since 1975 extensive reinvestigation has been directed by V. Petrakos (author of *Rhamnous*, Athens, 1991, a short archaeological guide). A site **museum** (restoration of entablature of temple of Nemesis, base of cult statue; also grave monuments) is accessible by special permission (Tuesdays only, ☎ 210 321 9792, in advance).

The site

The temples can be visited (Mon–Sat 07.00–17.00, Sun 08.00–17.00) but the **fortress** has been **closed** to the public for some years. A short description has been retained here in the hope that access can soon be restored.

Cult statue of Themis from Rhamnous, now in the National Archaeological Museum

At the head of a glen is an **artificial platform**, 45m wide, constructed in the 5C BC of large blocks of local marble laid horizontally. Nine courses are exposed at the northeast corner. The **sacred precinct** thus formed contains the remains of two temples, an altar, a stoa and a small fountain house. Although none of the visible remains are earlier than the 5C, both votive offerings and roof-tiles of the early 6C show that there was ritual activity from that time.

The smaller **temple** (possibly **of Themis**) was built on a virgin site in the early 5C. It measures 10.7 x 6.5m and consists merely of a cella in antis with a Doric portico of two columns. The walls which stand to c 1.8m are built of large polygonal blocks of white marble. Two marble seats (casts in situ) dedicated to Themis and Nemesis and three statues from the cella with inscribed pedestals (found in 1890) are in the National Archaeological Museum in Athens. The building continued in use (as a treasury/storeroom) into the 4C AD.

The first **Temple of Nemesis**, nearer the sea, was constructed at the end of the 6C BC in poros limestone as a Doric building, distyle in antis. This temple was probably destroyed by the Persians and replaced by the structure whose remains are still visible. This successor is a Doric peripteral building (6 x 12 columns), the last of four temples sometimes ascribed to the so-called Theseum architect (p 149). According to W.B. Dinsmoor, it was probably begun on the Festival Day of the Nemesieia (Boëdromion 5, i.e. 30 September) 436 BC, and is known by an inscription to have been rededicated to the empress Livia, probably by Claudius in AD 45. The interior had the usual arrangement of cella, pronaos and opisthodomos in antis. The unfinished fluting on the remaining drums of six columns (south side) suggests that the building was never completed.

Fragments have been found both of the **cult statue** of Nemesis (including a colossal head, now in the British Museum) and of its **base**. The statue (c 421 BC) was in Parian marble and the work of Agorakritos. Pausanias believed it to have been made from the very marble brought by the Persians for use as a victory monument and incorrectly attributed it to Pheidias. The base (partly reconstructed, in the site museum) has carved decoration on three sides, showing Leda introducing Helen to her real mother, Nemesis.

> ### Nemesis and Themis
> Nemesis was the compensating goddess, measuring out happiness and misery. She was especially concerned with punishing *hubris*, the presumptuous crime of considering oneself master of one's own destiny. She was known also by the surnames of 'Adrastia' (inescapable) and 'Rhamnousia', from her sanctuary at Rhamnous. Associated with the worship of Nemesis was Themis, the goddess who personified law, equity and custom.

Still within the precinct are, to the east of the temple, the foundations of an **altar** and, to the north, the scanty remains of a **stoa** of the 5C (34m long) which originally had wooden columns in its façade. In front of the stoa was a small **fountain house**, with a two-columned porch. Opposite the precinct, on the other side of the road, are the foundations of a large Hellenistic structure.

Visible beside the road below the temples are the substantial remains of some of the **funerary enclosures** (periboloi, see R. Garland in *BSA* 77, 1982, and illustration here p 180), with which it was lined. These were topped with stelai and other memorial sculptures and inscriptions commemorating the dead. The line of the road can be traced back beyond the site entrance and the remains of other enclosures, less well preserved, can be made out.

The fortress
Descending the rocky glen north towards the sea (no access at present) you reach in 10 mins an isolated hill girdled with the picturesque **enceinte** (c 1km in circuit) of the **ancient town**. The lower part of the south gateway is well preserved, as are parts of the walls (3.7m high in places), in ashlar masonry of grey limestone. Nine towers of the fortress can be made out. Recent work has been done on the east gate and four others, smaller, have also been located. There is a shrine of Aphrodite by the road leading in from the east gate to a small open square. Within the town are houses and streets (in places lined with stelai bases), remains of another temple, shrines, a gymnasium and an inner citadel. A sanctuary of Amphiaraos lies outside, to the northwest.

The *Amphiáraion*, via Kálamos

The Amphiáraion is one of the most delightful sites in the vicinity of Athens, quiet, green and wooded. The trip is strongly recommended.

- **Buses** for Kálamos (45km in 1 hour). Nine daily from Od. Mavrommatéon. From Kálamos it is 4km on foot to the site; it may be possible to find a **taxi**.
  Timing. Allow 5–6 hrs for this excursion. Travelling time is about 1 hr, plus a walk of 30 mins–1 hr in each direction (the return is uphill).

The bus follows the national highway north out of Athens then turns east (at 26km) for Kapandríti. Beyond the village a pleasant road winds over tree-clothed hills to **Kálamos** (329m), the small centre of a well-watered and wooded region above the Gulf of Evvia. From Kálamos you can get a bus (5km further) to the coastal resort of Ayy. Apóstoli (whence there is a road by the sea to Skála Oropoú).

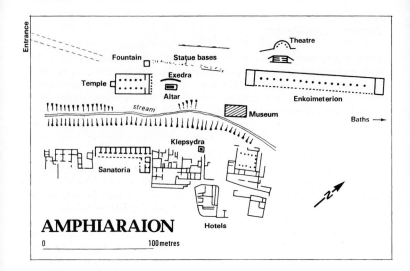

The main road from Kálamos descends in loops to the Amphiáraion (4km) in the Mavrodhilísi ravine. On foot the site can be reached by the old path (difficult not to lose), shaded by pines, which crosses the road several times. You must follow the road for the last 100m, as the entrance is beyond the bridge that crosses the stream. Walking down the road is less uncertain and not unpleasant, although the area (but not the site) has been affected by forest fires.

The Sanctuary of Amphiaraos (Amphiaraion)

The excavations (1927–30) of the Greek Archaeological Service were interrupted by the death of the excavator, Vasileios Leonardos. Illustrated guide: V. Petrakos, *The Amphiaraion of Oropos*, 1992.

Founded in honour of the healing hero Amphiaraos, the sanctuary was at once an oracle and a spa. The situation is sheltered and sunny—well suited to a resort of invalids—on the left bank of a wooded glen watered by a mountain torrent. In spring anemones carpet the site.

The Amphiaraion commemorated the elevation to divinity of the great seer and warrior of Argos, who fought as one of the Seven against Thebes. On the defeat of this expedition he fled, pursued by Periklymenos, but the earth opened and swallowed him up, together with his chariot, near Thebes. His cult was adopted by the Oropians and concentrated here near a spring famed for its healing properties. The Persian Mardonius visited the oracle before the Battle of Plataia.

Anyone wishing a consultation or cure sacrificed a ram and lay down for the night, wrapped in its skin, in the portico assigned for the purpose, and there awaited revelations to be made in dreams. The process of incubation (εγκοίμησις) was very similar to that practised in the Asklepieion (p 99). But cures did not depend entirely on these miraculous communications, since there were medical baths in the precinct. After a cure, the patient had to throw gold or silver coins into the sacred spring.

The site

● Open Tues–Sun 0800–1430, closed Mon)

From the site entrance you descend the path parallel to the stream. Right is the little **Temple of Amphiaraos**, a Doric building of the 4C, with a pronaos and a cella, the latter with internal colonnades. The foundations, partly eroded by the stream, have been restored. The base of the cult statue is still in position. The back wall was joined by a porch (marks of a door in the threshold) to the **priests' lodging**. Ten metres from the temple is the **altar**, on which the ram was sacrificed; below the altar is the **sacred spring**, into which the coins were thrown. Its waters were drunk from shells: many of these have been found.

Above the altar is a **terrace** with a line of over 30 inscribed pedestals of statues, mostly Roman. On a line with these are the remains of a long bench. In front is the **museum** (normally closed), containing numerous inscriptions, a curious early herm, torsos and, in the back court, reassembled architectural members of the temple and stoa.

Beyond are the remains of the **Enkoimeterion**, a long stoa, built c 387 BC, with 41 Doric columns on the façade and divided internally into two long galleries by 17 Ionic columns. It had a small room at either end, possibly reserved for women patients. Along the walls ran marble benches, resting on claw feet, on which the patients lay for incubation.

Behind the stoa is a small **Theatre**, with a circular orchestra and seating for 300 spectators. Five marble thrones with scroll ornaments are preserved. The proskenion (restored) has eight Doric columns surmounted by an epistyle with a dedicatory inscription.

Beyond the stoa were the **baths**. On the opposite bank of the stream are some confused remains of accommodation provided for patients, and part of a **klepsydra**, or water-clock, its bronze plug mechanism visible.

The island of Aíyina (*Aegina*)

The most accessible island from Athens, with the prominent Mount Oros intriguingly visible from so many points on the mainland, Aíyina is surprisingly unspoilt. The main town, briefly the capital of Greece in the 1820s, retains much of its original architecture and stately feeling; and there is plenty of scope for pleasant rural walks and excursions in the interior. The Temple of Aphaia, beautifully situated high on a pine-clad hillside, is an unmissable excursion, but the much less visited Medieval settlement of Palaiokhóra has equally powerful, if different, attractions. The sea approach too is exciting, with good views of Piraeus harbour, the location of Salamis and a different perspective of the city of Athens. Only the beaches are rather disappointing (small or rocky), but the nearby islets of Moní and Angístri help to compensate.

● **Boats**. Car ferries from Piraeus (quay opposite the bottom of Od. Goúnari, p 240; plan p 237—400m from the Metró station) to Aíyina town (1 hr 15 mins). In summer, several ferries per hour to Aíyina (gap between mid-morning and early afternoon). Extra services at weekends. Also to Ay. Marina (but no cars to Ay. Marína) and Souvála direct, early morning and late afternoon; and to the island of Angístri once or twice daily, plus excursions from Aíyina in summer. No direct service from Piraeus to the islet of Moní; excursions from Aíyina only.

Hydrofoils. From same quay as boats, c ten times daily to Aíyina in 35 mins. For bookings, see p 55.

Cruises. Usually from Trokadero Marína, Palaió Fáliro. Organised by CHAT, Key Tours, etc. Booking at central offices or travel agents (pp 20, 30). Trips to Aíyina incorporate an excursion by bus to the Aphaia temple. Other islands in the Saronic Gulf may be included.

Timing. You need a full day for this excursion.

Passing down the centre of the **Great Harbour** of Piraeus and heading out to sea, you see to the right the long islet of **Psitállia** (or Lipsokoutáli), now occupied by the main Athens sewage works. This is usually taken to be the ancient *Psyttaleia*, important in descriptions of the Battle of Salamis. Then, also to the right, is Salamis itself. The hill which overlooks the strait of Salamis, between Piraeus and Elefsína, was Xerxes' viewpoint of the battle.

History of Aíyina (ancient *Aegina*)

In spite of its modest size, Aegina's key position in the Saronic Gulf ensured its importance from early times. The name probably derives from an eastern divinity (Hellenised as 'Aigaios'). Neolithic finds show that the island was occupied from at least the end of the 4th millennium BC, and there was a substantial settlement at Kolónna in the Early Bronze Age. In the Middle Helladic period, when there were many links with the Cyclades, the island was an important trading centre. Thereafter it shared the Mycenaean culture of the mainland.

Legend tells of its only hero-king, Aiakos, son of Zeus and Aegina (a daughter of the River Asopos), who afterwards became one of the three judges of the Underworld. His sons Peleus and Telamon had to flee for the murder of their half-brother Phokos; Telamon afterwards became king of Salamis and father of the famous hero Ajax. The Thessalian cult of Zeus Hellanios may have been introduced by Dorians. Aphaia, to whom the island's most important temple belonged, seems to be a variant of the Mother-Goddess from Crete, perhaps imported during the early Iron Age.

Aegina may have been abandoned c 1150–950 BC, then recolonised, probably from Epidauros (Hdt. VIII 46). Lack of agricultural wealth combined with a favourable geographical location encouraged maritime enterprise. At the end of the 8C the island enjoyed parity with fellow members of the Kalaurian League, a confederation mainly of maritime states in this part of Greece (see *Blue Guide Greece*, 6th edn, p 176), and had apparently shaken off earlier subjection to Argos. By the 7C Aegina was the predominant maritime centre in the Hellenic world.

The system of coinage introduced in Argos by Pheidon (c 656 BC) was probably borrowed from Aegina (rather than the other way round); indeed it is very likely that coinage first reached Europe from the island. Its silver coins became the standard in most of the Dorian states. In the 6C Aegina was a major centre of Greek art, noted for pottery and especially for the quality of its bronze-founding. Aeginetan merchants set up a temple to Zeus at the founding of Naukratis, a Greek trading emporium on the Nile; one, Sostratos, according to Herodotos (IV 152), had also sailed to Spain, and a dedication from Gravisca in Etruria bears his name. The harbour was crowded with merchant ships (Thuc. V 53) and the Aeginetan navy grew to a formidable size, arousing the jealousy of Athens. Solon's laws prohibiting the export of corn from Attica were probably directed mainly against Aegina which, from then on, whatever its alliance, was always anti-Athenian.

Aristotle calls it 'the eyesore of Piraeus' (*Rhet*. III 10 7); Herodotos (V 82) adduces a mythical feud to explain the mutual enmity, and describes a war between Athens and Aegina (?early 6C BC) in which the Athenians were worsted.

At Salamis (480 BC) the Aeginetans atoned for their previous homage to Persia by distinguishing themselves over all other Greeks, and the battle marked the height of their power. As a member of the Spartan League, Aegina was protected from attack until the reversal of Kimon's pro-Spartan policy after his ostracism in 461, when the Aeginetans were quickly defeated by the Athenians in two naval battles. In 457 BC the city was humiliated after a siege (Thuc. I 108). At the beginning of the Peloponnesian War the Athenians expelled the inhabitants and established a cleruchy (dependent colony). The scattered remnants were allowed to return in 404 from their exile at Thyrea (in the vicinity of modern Astros in the Peloponnese) where the Spartans had accommodated them, but Aegina never recovered from this blow.

With the rest of Greece Aegina came under the control of the kingdom of Macedon in the 4C BC, and afterwards of Attalos of Pergamon, who gave the island to Rome. In Byzantine times it was for a time a joint bishopric with Keos, then independent. Paul of Aegina, celebrated for a treatise on medicine and surgery, was born here in the 7C AD. Saracen raids caused the inhabitants to shift the capital inland to Palaiokhóra (p 291) where it remained until the 19C. After 1204 the island was a personal fief of Venetian and Catalan families until, in 1451, it passed to Venice.

Captured and laid waste in 1537 by Khair-ed-Din (Barbarossa), it was repopulated with Albanians. Morosini recaptured it for Venice in 1654, and it became one of the last Venetian strongholds in the east, being ceded to Turkey in 1718.

In 1826–28 the city was the temporary capital of partly liberated Greece, and here the first modern Greek coins were minted. Many of the present inhabitants are descended from families who came at this time from the Peloponnese, or from refugees who fled here after the massacres of Greeks on Khíos and Psará.

Aíyina town

The modern town of Aíyina (6373 inhabitants), near the northwest corner of the island, occupies part of the site of the ancient city, though the latter extended much further to the north. There are cafés and restaurants on and just behind the seafront, and plenty of hotels.

The town's somewhat stately and aristocractic air derives from a series of restrained neoclassical buildings, several surviving from Aíyina's period as capital of Greece under the presidency of Kapodístrias (statue in the main square) in the early 19C.

- **Tourist information**. There are several offices on the quay. The official one is in the Dhimarkhíon (open only in season), on the waterfront at the bottom of Od. Khr. Ladhá.
  Travel agents. *Pipínis Tours*, Kanári 2, Aíyina 180 10, ☎ 22970 28780, fax 22970 28779, email pipinis@otenet.gr, www.pipinis-travel.com—and several others.
  Bus station and **taxi rank**. At north end of the quay (turn left off the boat), on the way to Kolónna, in front of Plateía Ethneyersías. Horse-drawn carriages can also be hired there.
  Restaurants. *Klimatariá*, and others round fish market.
  Other main facilities can be found on or just inland from the waterfront. There is the **Folk Museum** (Sp. Rhodhi 16; ☎ 22970 26401; open 3 days a week only— Fri 18.30–21.30, Sat and Sun 10.00–13.00 and 18.30–21.30); a **theatre** (next to the Cathedral) with occasional performances; and **cinemas** (near Markélon tower and on the coast road towards Pérdhika), mostly summer only.

> **First president of Greece**
> Count Ioánnis **Kapodístrias** (1776–1831) was born in Corfú but gained prominence as a member of the Russian diplomatic service (joint foreign minister). After 1822 he devoted his energies to the cause of Greek independence and became the first president in 1828. He was assassinated in 1831.

The harbours, waterfront and town

The **modern harbour**, oval in shape and full of various craft including some picturesque caiques, corresponds to the **ancient commercial harbour**. Its moles were rebuilt under Kapodístrias on the ancient foundations. The south mole marked the southern limit of the ancient city, forming an extension of its walls. The ancient military harbour (see below) was a little further north, protected by the Kolónna promontory.

Although inevitably somewhat commercialised, the **waterfront** (best view from the south end by the prominent Panayítsa church) is attractive, crowded with small vessels and lined with cafés, restaurants and souvenir shops, many of them in fine neoclassical buildings. The first street inland (Od. Irióti/Aiyinítou), which follows the curve of the quay, is the main shopping street and has retained much of its traditional character. There is a small fish market and, round about it, several good *mezedhopolía* (restaurants specialising in *mezédhes*, p 32).

From the Limenarkhíon (Port Authority) you can follow Od. Aiákou inland to a pretty square with the **Markélon tower** (probably 1802, although some think it late 17C and connected with Morosini's fortifications). It was the first administrative headquarters in the period when the island was the Greek capital until superseded by the more elaborate **Governor's residence** in Od. Kiverníou.

Through the square is Ay. Nikólaos, a modern church; beyond it, at the top of Od. Káprou, are some bedraggled remains of a three-aisled Early Christian basilica (Várdhia).

Not far to the south is the **Cathedral** (1806) of the metropolitan of Idhra, Spétses and Aíyina, set in a quiet and pleasant compound. Its dedication is to the Koímisis tis Theotókou. The bell-tower has a sundial commissioned by Kapodístrias. Next to it is the small **theatre** and, at right-angles, the former museum, awaiting a new destiny. The museum building was constructed for Kapodístrias in 1830 as a teacher-training institution and paid for by the French philhellene Eynard. Later it briefly housed the National Library.

The Kolónna promontory: archaeological site and museum

In the small bay on the way to the Kolónna promontory, remains of rectangular quays of the **ancient military harbour** can be seen beneath the surface of a smooth sea. The harbour was protected by the Kolónna promontory (10 mins from the quay; follow signs to Archaeological Museum), so called after the single surviving column of the Temple of Apollo. On the promontory was a citadel, fortified from Prehistoric to Christian times. In the Classical period at least, town, citadel and harbours (the line was continued into the sea by breakwaters) were all within a huge defensive enceinte. To the right, by the site entrance, is the mosaic floor of a synagogue with an inscription.

The **museum**, not overcrowded and with interesting finds, is in the same compound as the archaeological site (both open Tues–Sun 08.30–15.00, closed Mon). In the **foyer** are models of the Prehistoric White House on the Kolónna site and of a Prehistoric furnace. The **courtyard** has various funerary stelai. On the far side is a range of **three galleries**. The **left** one has Early and Middle Bronze Age pottery, much of it resembling Cycladic; some Anatolian forms. One Middle Bronze Age sherd has a rare and appealing representation of a figure riding a dolphin. Also Mycenaean pottery and figurines. The **centre** gallery has Geometric, Archaic and Classical pottery including the fine Orientalising 'Ram Jug' (Odysseus and companions escaping from the Cyclops); marble and poros architectural fragments and sculpture from the Late Archaic Temple of Apollo (Kolónna); an inscription naming the goddess Aphaia; Archaic and Classical reliefs; and a 5C sphinx. In the **right gallery** are fragments of sculpture from the Archaic Temple of Aphaia. Inscriptions include boundary stones from the Temenos of Apollo and Poseidon and from a sanctuary of Athena.

Beyond the museum is the archaeological site. The most visually striking remains are of the Prehistoric town, Archaic temple and Late Roman fortifications. Excavations of the German Institute (begun by G. Welter in 1924) were greatly extended west and south of the temple from 1969 (Austrian Institute), and continue.

On the way up is an impressive **harbour wall** belonging to the Late Roman fortification (see below).

Of the Late Archaic (c 520–500 BC) **Temple of Apollo** (formerly attributed to Aphrodite; Doric, 6 columns by 12), the only remains are part of a lone column from the opisthodomos and substantial parts of its substructure. Of its predecessors there are some scanty poros foundations of polygonal masonry. The interior of the temple was turned into a cistern in the Byzantine period, making the remains very confusing to look at. Some of the plaster of the cistern can be seen. The area in general was quarried during the rebuilding of the harbour.

The remains of the **Prehistoric Settlement** (Late Neolithic-Mycenaean) now largely dominate the centre of the site round the temple. The houses, made of thick rubble masonry and divided by narrow streets, survive to a considerable height and the **fortification wall** (several phases) was massive. The White House belongs to a type of Early Helladic building known as the Corridor House, thought to be an administrative centre.

North of the Temple, at the edge of the excavations (best seen from the road outside the enclosure fence) are the massively impressive wall and towers of the **Late Roman Fortress**, largely constructed of material taken from earlier buildings and including several blocks with inscriptions.

Close to the southeast corner of the temple are some remains of a square structure of Archaic date, possibly the Aiakeion (shrine of Aiakos, son of Zeus and Aegina). A little further on, some blocks are all that are left of a bouleuterion. West of the temple, towards the sea, remains of a circular building are thought to fit Pausanias' description of the Tomb of Phokos (son of Aiakos). Near it are the foundations of two small temples. At the end of the cape near the water, remains of a building with some Pergamene architectural features are perhaps those of an **Attaleion** (shrine to King Attalos of Pergamon). None of these monuments are very impressive. All except the Attaleion can be picked out from the temple terrace, but can be better seen (together with the Attaleion) by following the footpath round the promontory (after descending from the main site, turn right, instead of left towards the museum).

The Classical theatre and stadium are thought to have lain just beyond the boundaries of the sanctuary to the east.

Palaiokhóra, the Temple of Aphaia and Ay. Marína

Regular buses run from the port. If you are driving, from the south end of the main waterfront, at the other extremity from Kolónna, you turn left in the direction of Afaía and Ay. Marína.

On the Afaía road you soon come to the former **orphanage**, built by Kapodístrias in 1828 for children orphaned by the War of Independence and, since 1854, used successively as barracks and prison. It is now being restored for use as a historical museum of the island.

At 6km from Aíyina town is a monastery (strictly that of Ay. Triádha, but always known as Ay. Nektários) containing the embalmed body of **Ay. Nektários** (Anastásios Kefalás; 1846–1920), Metropolitan of Pentapolis and the first saint to be canonised (1961) by the Orthodox church in modern times. A hideous new church demonstrates the architectural catastrophe of modifying Byzantine forms in inappropriate materials.

Palaiokhóra

Just beyond the monastery, a signed road (ultimate destination Souvála) diverges left for (500m) the approach to Palaiokhóra—or Palaiá Khóra—capital of the island from the 9C until 1826, and twice rebuilt after destruction by Barbarossa (1537) and by the Venetians (1654). Covering the bare hillside are the ruins of more than 20 churches and monasteries, survivors from the 13C and later, some with stone iconostases and reasonably preserved frescoes. A ruined castle crowns the summit. None of the houses has survived.

Rambling on the hillside, perhaps pausing for a picnic on the terrace of either Ay. Kiriakí or Ay. Ioánnis Theológos, makes a nice excursion although it is best to try to avoid too hot a time of day, even though the distances are not great. Most of the churches are open (and, unusually, labelled with their names) but one or two of the more interesting ones are open only 09.00–14.00 daily. To contact the site guard (mornings), ask at Ay. Nektários monastery, or the restaurant by the bus stop. Most of the churches are quite accessible by good paths, but reaching the castle and more remote buildings involves a certain amount of scrambling over narrow tracks. Not all are of equal interest and, although a good deal of restoration has been done, some are in a bad state of repair. Most of the churches are single-aisled and barrel-vaulted, though a few have a more complex plan.

Sanctuary of Aphaia

The beautiful Sanctuary of Aphaia (12km from Aíyina town; open Tues–Sun 08.30–15.00, closed Mon) stands on a pine-clad hill with a splendid view over the Saronic Gulf. Erected at the end of the 6C BC or in the early years of the 5C, on the site of two earlier temples, it has been called 'the most perfectly developed of the late Archaic temples in European Hellas'.

Excavations The Late Archaic temple was explored in 1811, when its sculptures were removed to Munich (see below). Bavarian excavations undertaken

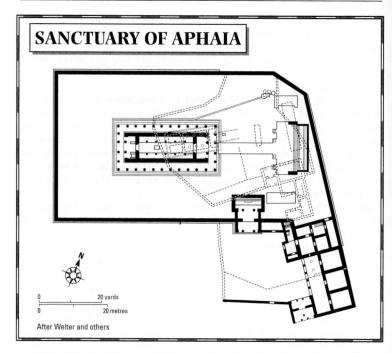

SANCTUARY OF APHAIA

0 ——————— 20 yards
0 ——————— 20 metres

After Welter and others

in 1901–03 by Adolf Furtwängler, in order to complete the sculptural groups, proved the dedication to Aphaia, the Aeginetan equivalent of the Cretan goddess Britomartis (p 287). The shrine had previously been attributed first to Zeus Panhellenios and later to Athena. Excavations by D. Öhly (from 1969) recovered numerous fragments of painted stonework from the earlier Archaic temple. Some columns and part of the entablature were re-erected in 1956–60. There was some lightning damage in 1969.

Entering the site (you may wish to visit the Museum first for orientation), you pass through the outer **peribolos wall**. To the right there are remains of ritual **dining-rooms** and the **priests' quarters**; three stucco baths served for purification rites. The artificial **terrace** on which the temple stands is approached by a **propylon** of the 5C, with an unusual arrangement of pilasters on the façade. To the east are the foundations of the latest **altar**. From its base a **ramp** rises to the stereobate of three steps on which the temple stands.

The **Temple of Aphaia** is now sealed off, partly to preserve the remaining traces of the red stucco which originally covered the floors of the pronaos and cella. It is Doric peripteral hexastyle, with 12 columns on the flanks. The local limestone used was coated with a thin layer of stucco and painted. Of the original 32 columns, 24 now stand. They are three Doric feet in diameter at the base and axially spaced at eight feet. The corner columns are thickened for optical effect. All the shafts are monolithic, except for three adjacent columns on the north flank which are built up of drums, presumably in order to leave a gap until the last moment to facilitate the erection of the interior. The architrave is well preserved and the whole entablature has been restored at the west end of the north side by the replacement of the triglyphs, metopes and cornice. The sekos has a cella, with pronaos and opisthodomos in antis. Two columns survive of the pronaos, which once housed figureheads of Samian triremes captured in their attack on the Samian colony of Kydonia in Crete. Marks can be seen on the columns where the entrance was closed off with a high grille.

The cella, the walls of which have been partly rebuilt, was divided internally by two colonnades of five columns each; above an epistyle a second row of smaller superposed columns carried a flat ceiling. Seven of the interior columns have been restored to place with three of the upper shafts. At a later date aisle floors were put in at triforium level, approached presumably by wooden stairs. The position of the cult statue is shown by marks in the floor where a railing stood round it. Only some of the figure's extremities were acrolithic (i.e. in stone), the rest being made of other materials; a fragment of the acrolithic arm is in the National Archaeological Museum in Athens. A doorway from the opisthodomos into the cella was pierced after the solid cross-wall was started and is not central.

The **pedimental sculptures** were in Parian marble. Seventeen statues found by Cockerell and von Hallerstein in 1811 were acquired by Ludwig I of Bavaria and, after 'restoration' by the Danish sculptor Thorvaldsen in Rome, sent to Munich, where they remain (in the Glyptothek). The scenes represented two combats before Troy in the presence of Athena. Parts of other figures (now in National Archaeological Museum, see p 200, and Aíyina Museum) have since come to light, some of which may have been part of earlier pedimental scenes, subsequently removed for some reason, or of a group which stood elsewhere in the sanctuary.

Figure of Herakles from the pediment of the temple of Aphaia,
now in the Glyptothek, Munich

At the northeast corner of the terrace is a cistern which caught rainwater from the roof; it connects with a 'cave' which was built as a cistern for the Archaic temple. To the west of the temple is the excavation house and an interesting and informative architectural **Museum** (Tues–Sun 09.00–15.00, closed Mon) with useful information about the site, the (painted) façade of the Archaic temple, a reconstruction of the east pediment of the later, and other finds.

Beyond the temple the road descends to **Ay. Marína** (13.5km from Aíyina town), a resort on an attractive bay, deserted in winter. The beach is crowded with hotel guests in summer. The village is commercialised but not unpleasant. Pinewoods stretch inland. Cruise ships disembark passengers for Aphaia here.

You can complete a **circuit** of the interior of the island (no bus; taxi: Aíyina–Afaía–Ay. Marína–Anítsaio–Aíyina, about €18) by continuing from Ay. Marína along a new road which climbs via Pórtes and Anítsaio to the centre of the island, crosses the shoulder of Mount Orós and descends past Pakhiá Rákhi to Aíyina town.

Glossary

See also the illustrations of Ancient Greek architecture on pp 76–77.

abaton lit: 'untrodden', inviolate (of a sacred place); an enkoimeterion

acrolithic with extremities (hands, feet etc) made of stone

acroterion sculpture set at the apex of the pediment of a building, or at a corner edge of the roof

aedicula see naïskos

aegis cuirass or shield with Gorgon's head and ring of snakes, worn by Athena

agora public square or market place

Akathist hymn 24 verses (or *oikoi*), each beginning with a different letter of the alphabet, sung in Lent. The subjects (aspects of the Incarnation, 12 of them particularly connected with the Panagia) are regularly depicted in frescoes

Amazonomachy/Gigantomachy battle between gods and Amazons/Giants

ambo (pl: ambones) pulpit in a Christian basilica; two pulpits on opposite sides of a church from which the gospel and epistle were read

amphidistyle with two columns at each end

amphiprostyle façade columns set forward of the façade of a building, at both ends (only)

andron a room for men in a Greek house; especially used as the dining-room

anta thickened end of the side wall of a building. The term 'in antis' is used to describe columns set between antae, as often in temples

anthemion floral ornament

bema raised platform (Anc.); apse of a basilica (Byz.)

breccia a composite rock (pudding-stone)

bothros pit for offerings or other ritual purpose

Caryatid statue of female figure used in place of a plain column

cathedra bishop's throne

cavea auditorium of a Greek or Roman theatre

cella main room in temple where cult statue usually stood

chiton tunic

chlamys light cloak

chryselephantine made of gold and ivory

choregos(-i) citizen(s) who bore the expense of training a chorus

choros a hanging circle in metal or wood for the display of ikons

chthonic dwelling in or under the Earth

cloisonné Byzantine building technique where stones are individually framed with bricks or tiles

conch the quarter of a sphere which forms the top part of an apse

crepidoma stepped platform on which monumental building stands

Cufic an early angular form of the Arabic alphabet used mainly for ornamental inscriptions

cuneus (-i) lit: 'wedge', wedge-shaped block of seating in the theatre

Cyclopean (of masonry) consisting of huge flat-faced but irregular blocks (Prehistoric, especially Mycenaean)

Deisis (Byz.) supplication; (in scholarship from 19C onwards) scene showing Christ with hand raised in blessing with the Virgin and John the Baptist supplicating to either side

deme township

diaconicon room to right of sanctuary in a church

diateichisma cross-wall

diazoma (pl. diazomata) horizontal passage in theatre dividing cavea

dipteral with a double colonnade

discophoros discus-carrier

distyle with two columns (as 'distyle in antis')

Dodekaorto the 12 major feasts of the Orthodox church (frequently represented in paintings): *Annunciation* (mod. Evangelismós), *Nativity* (Yénnisis), *Presentation* (Ipapandí), *Baptism* (Váptisis), *Transfiguration* (Metamórfosis), *Raising of Lazarus* (Eyersi tou Lazárou), *Entry into Jerusalem* (Vaiofóros), *Crucifixion* (Stávrosis), *Resurrection* (Anástasis), *Ascension* (Análipsis), *Pentecost* (Pentekostí), *Dormition* (Koímisis)

drafted (of masonry) stone with a chisel-dressed band round the edges as a guide for the levelling of the rest of the surface

Eisodia (tis Theotokou) Presentation (of the Virgin Mary)

encaustic technique of painting using hot wax as the medium

enkoimeterion building in a sanctuary where invalids slept to undergo ritual

ephebe/ephebos Greek youth under training (military or University)

epistyle architrave

epitaphios ceremonial pall, or cloth

Erotes figures of Eros, god of love

eschara sacred hearth or altar sunk in the ground

exedra semicircular recess in a Classical or Byzantine building; in the Classical period sometimes an independent structure

exonarthex outer forehall of a Byzantine church

gorgoneion formal image of a gorgon's head

gymnasium building complex with facilities for both athletic and intellectual education

herm pillar with phallus, topped by a bust (originally of Hermes)

heroön shrine to a demigod or heroised mortal

hexastyle with six columns in the façade

(h)iera trapeza holy table; altar

(h)iero sanctuary, in a church

himation cloak

hoplite heavily armed foot-soldier

hypaethral open to the sky

Hypapante (mod. Ipapandí) Presentation of Christ in the temple

iconostasis screen bearing icons

isodomic (of masonry) set in courses of equal height

katholikon main church in a monastery

Koímisis (tis Theotokou) lit: 'falling asleep', Dormition (of the Virgin Mary)

kore (maiden) archaic female figure

kouros (youth) archaic male figure

lesche club-house

libation drink offering, usually to deity

loutrophoros (-oi) tall vase especially associated with wedding rituals
maenad an ecstatic female follower of the god Dionysos
megaron rectangular one-room building, with the two end walls projecting to from a porch; especially the central hall of a Mycenaean palace
metope blank or sculptured panel alternating with the triglyph in a Doric frieze
Metroön Temple of the Mother of the Gods
monopteros building consisting of colonnade with no interior structure
naïskos miniature temple, often used as funerary monument
naos the body of a church (nave)
narthex forehall of a Byzantine church
naumachia mock naval combat in the flooded arena of a theatre or amphitheatre
nymphaion shrine of the Nymphs
octastyle with eight columns in the façade
odeion concert hall, usually in the shape of a theatre, but roofed
oligarch member of a small-group government
omphalos sacred stone commemorating the centre of the Earth, meeting place of the two eagles sent by Zeus
opus alexandrinum mosaic design of black and red figures on a white ground
opus sectile cut slabs of marble, of varying shapes and colours, used for floor or wall decoration
orchestra the (originally circular) area in a theatre where the chorus performed
ostrakon (-a) fragment (sherd) of pottery; especially a fragment on which name of candidate for ostracism (see p 66) was written
palaistra complex of rooms round a court, used for athletic or educational purposes; often attached to a gymnasium
Panagia (mod. Panayía) lit: 'all-holy', the Virgin Mary
Pantokrator lit: 'ruler of all', the Almighty
paraskenion (-a) side wing of skene
parecclesion (-a) chapel added to a Byzantine church
parodos (-oi) passage in theatre between paraskenion and cavea
pendentive curved triangle formed by the intersection of a dome with two adjacent arches below
peplos a one-piece mantle worn draped by women
peribolos a precinct, or the circuit wall enclosing it
peripteral surrounded by a colonnade
peristyle colonnade
pinax (pl. pinakes) flat panel or tablet, usually decorated and often votive
polyandreion communal tomb
pompeion building where equipment for processions was stored
poros soft coarse conchiferous limestone (tufa)
Prodromos lit: 'forerunner', usual epithet of St John the Baptist
pronaos porch of temple
propylon/propylaia entrance gate to a temenos; in plural form when there is more than one door
proskenion (-a) platform in front of skene
prostyle with a portico of columns in front (i.e. not peripteral)
prothesis room to the left of the sanctuary in a church
proxenos consul

quadriga four-horsed chariot

retrograde goes right to left (of writing)

scaenae frons elaborate back wall of stage in Roman theatre

sekos interior building of a temple, within the colonnade

skene lit: 'tent', the building (originally a tent) behind the acting area in a theatre, where actors changed and on which scenery was hung

sphendone the rounded end of a stadium

squinch straight or arched structure across an angle of a square building to support a dome

stele (-ai) stone slab, often with sculptural decoration and usually either marking grave or set up as offering (votive) in a sanctuary

stereobate foundations of a building below the crepidoma

stereobate foundations of a building below the crepidoma

stoa a porch or portico not attached to a larger building

stylobate top step of the crepidoma, on which a building (and its colonnade) would stand

synoikism union of separate communities in a single city-state

synthronon seat for bishop or elders in the apse of a Byzantine church

temenos sacred enclosure

templon stone screen separating bema from naos; later became the iconostasis

theme (Byz.) a province

tetrastyle with four columns

Theologos lit: 'theologian', usual epithet of St John the Evangelist

Theotokos lit: 'God-bearing', usual epithet of the Panagia

tholos a circular building

thorakion panel (to waist height), component of the lower part of the templon

transenna openwork grille at the entrance to a Byzantine chapel

triconch building plan using three hemispherical units arranged as a trefoil

triforium gallery above columns or arches

trilithon made of three monumental blocks

trireme ancient Greek galley rowed by three banks of oars

votive offering object of any kind dedicated to a deity in expectation or gratitude, and in association with a vow or prayer

Index

Select index to colour street atlas

Below is a list of the most important squares, streets and avenues shown in the colour atlas at the back of this Guide.

The references
In each case the page number is followed by that of the square or squares in which the feature is located.

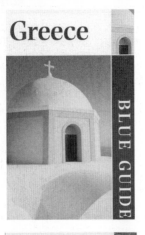

- **let Blue Guide Athens author Robin Barber also show you around Greece with this, the most comprehensive guide to ancient and modern Greece, its art, culture and history. Detailed and authoritative descriptions of major and minor Classical, Byzantine and medieval sites.**

- Robin Barber
  6th edition, revised reprint, 2001
  768pp
  ISBN 0–7136–5984–X
  £18.99

- **the cradle of European civilisation, Crete has many fascinating archaeological sites, all fully described in this completely rewritten and reorganised Blue Guide. Discover the island's beautiful, unspoilt countryside, with its astonishing variety of wild flowers and rich birdlife. Detailed practical information.**

- Pat Cameron
  7th edition, 2002
  448 pp
  ISBN 0–7136–4676–4
  £15.99

- **essential reading for anyone interested in this region. Packed with detailed practical advice, the Blue Guide provides up to date information on the improving hotel and travel facilities. There are explanations of the complex histories and societies of Albania and Kosovo from international authorities on the Balkans.**

- James Pettifer
  3rd edition, 2001
  512pp
  ISBN 0–7136–5016–8
  £17.99

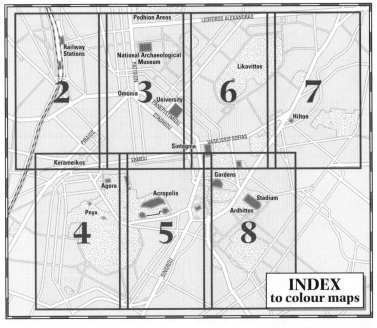

INDEX to colour maps

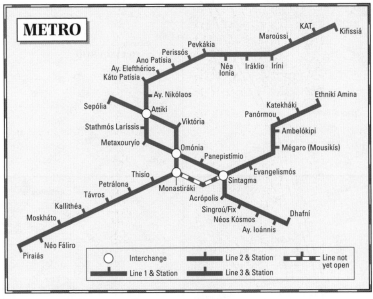

METRO

Interchange

Line 1 & Station

Line 2 & Station

Line 3 & Station

Line not yet open

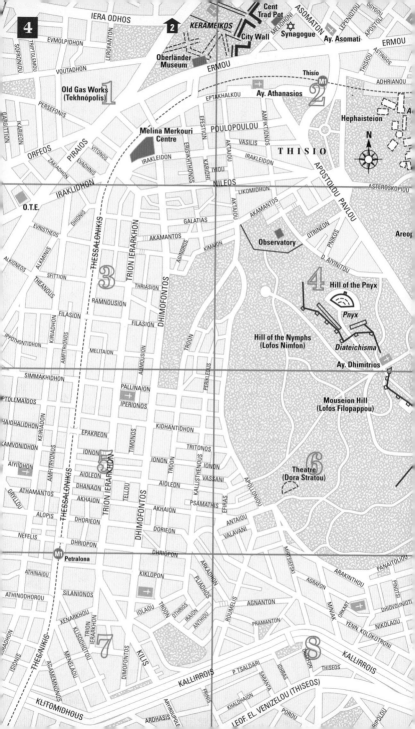

IERA ODHOS

4

EVMOLPIDHON

SOFRONIOU

TRIPTOLEMOU

VOUTADHON

LEROFANTON

KERAMEIKOS

Cent Trad Pot

City Wall

Oberländer Museum

ERMOU

Synagogue

Ay. Asomati

ERMOU

DOYGOLI

LEPENIOTOU

APOSTOLI

MELIDONI

ASOMATON

ASTINGOS

THISIOU

ADHRIANOU

Old Gas Works (Tekhnópolis) **1**

PERSEFONIS

GARGITTION

KARIENON

ORFEOS

PIRAIOS

ZAKIADHON

EVADNIS

VITONOS

EPTAKHALKOU

Ay. Athanasios

Thisio

2 M1

Hephaisteion

A

POULOPOULOU

EESTION

ENISIKTHIONOS

AMFIKTIONOS

AKTAIOU

VASILIS

IRAKLEIDON

Melina Merkouri Centre

IRAKLEIDON

IRAKLIDON

NILEOS

APOSTOLOU PAVLOU

T H I S I O

N

O.T.E.

IRAKLIDON

LIKOMIDHON

ASTEROSKOPIOU

EVRISTHEOS

DHIONIS

GALATIAS

AKTAIOU

AKAMANTOS

Observatory

OTRINEON

PNIKOS

Areo

ALKIONEOS

ALKAMINIS

SFITTION

THEANOUS

AKAMANTOS

AGINOROS

KIMAION

D. AIYINITOU

4

Hill of the Pnyx

3

TRION IERARKHON

THESSALONIKIS

THRIASION

Pnyx

IPPOTHONTIDHON

FILASION

KIRIADHON

AMFITRIONOS

RAMNOUSION

DHIMOFONTOS

FILASION

Hill of the Nymphs (Lofos Nimfon)

Diateichisma

MELITAION

AIMOUSION

TRION

Ay. Dhimitrios

SIMMAKHIDHON

PALLINAION

PERIKLEOUS

PTOLEMAÏDOS

IPERIONOS

KIDHANTIDHON

Mouseion Hill (Lofos Filopappou)

HAIDHALIDHON

KEIRIADON

EPAKREON

IONON

TIMONOS

TRITONOS

KAMVONIDHON

IONON

TRION

KALLISTHENOUS

IONON

AIYIIDHON

AMFITRYONOS

AIOLEON

AIOLEON

VASSANI

Theatre (Dora Stratou)

6

GRYLLOU

ATHAMANTOS

THESSALONIKIS

DHANAON

TELLOU

AKHAION

PSAMATHIS

APOLLONIOU

EFRAS

ALOPIS

DHORIEON

AKHAION

DHORIEON

ANTAIOU

NEFELIS

TRION IERARKHON

DHRIOPON

VALAVANI

DHIMOFONTOS

DHRIOPON

5

ATHINAIOU

M1 Petralona

KIKLOPON

ARKADHON

PLIADHOS

MIRTSIESKI

ARAKINTHOU

PANAGIOTIOU

ATHINODHOROU

SILANIONOS

AGRAFON

AGNANTON

PINOTSI

XENARKHOU

TRION IERARKHON

IOLAOU

TRION

OTHRIOS

IRAION

ANTHOU

ROUMELI

PRAMANTON

MINYAK

ORKART

DHIOVOUNIOTI

NIKOLAOU

ISIDHON

KLISODHROU

DHIMOFONTOS

KILIX

7

MENELAOU

PLOUTODHOTOU

IDIRAS

THISEOS

OREON

8

KALLIROIS

AGAMEMNONOS

THESSALONIKIS

KALLIROIS

P. TSALDARI

SARANTA

KHALDHAION

FRINIS

LEOF. EL. VENIZELOU (THISEOS)

POROU

KLITOMIDHOUS

ARDHASIS

ARGYROUPOLE

IPOLOU

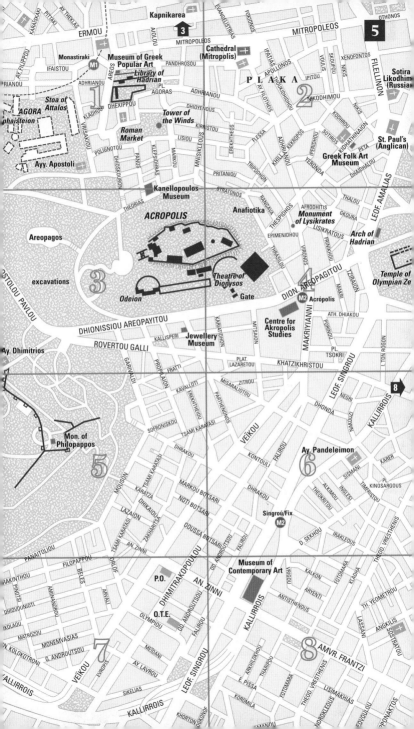

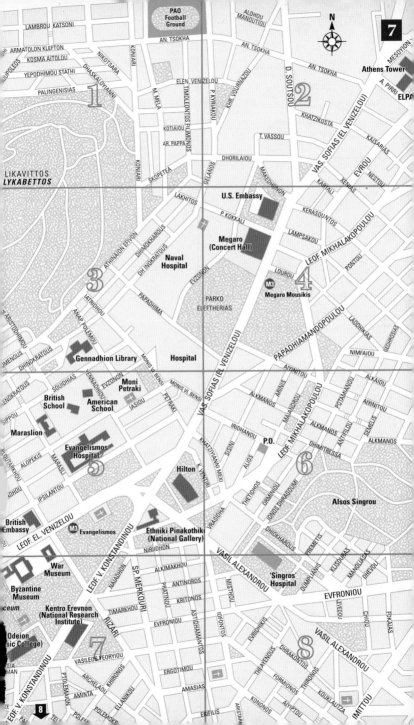

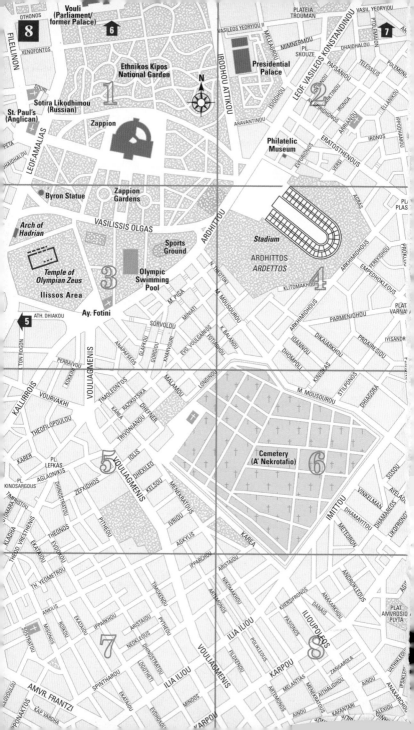